REVISE EDEXCEL GCSE (9–1)
Combined Scienc
REVISION GUIDE
Foundation

Series Consultant: Harry Smith

Authors: Pauline Lowrie, Mike O'Neill and Nigel Saunders

A note from the publisher

In order to ensure that this resource offers high-quality support for the associated Pearson qualification, it has been through a review process by the awarding body. This process confirms that this resource fully covers the teaching and learning content of the specification or part of a specification at which it is aimed. It also confirms that it demonstrates an appropriate balance between the development of subject skills, knowledge and understanding, in addition to preparation for assessment.

Endorsement does not cover any guidance on assessment activities or processes (e.g. practice questions or advice on how to answer assessment questions), included in the resource nor does it prescribe any particular approach to the teaching or delivery of a related course.

While the publishers have made every attempt to ensure that advice on the qualification and its assessment is accurate, the official specification and associated assessment guidance materials are the only authoritative source of information and should always be referred to for definitive guidance.

Pearson examiners have not contributed to any sections in this resource relevant to examination papers for which they have responsibility.

Examiners will not use endorsed resources as a source of material for any assessment set by Pearson.

Endorsement of a resource does not mean that the resource is required to achieve this Pearson qualification, nor does it mean that it is the only suitable material available to support the qualification, and any resource lists produced by the awarding body shall include this and other appropriate resources.

Question difficulty

Look at this scale next to each exam-style question. It tells you how difficult the question is.

For the full range of Pearson revision titles across KS2, KS3, GCSE, Functional Skills, AS/A Level and BTEC visit:
www.pearsonschools.co.uk/revise

Published by Pearson Education Limited, 80 Strand, London, WC2R 0RL.

www.pearsonschoolsandfecolleges.co.uk

Copies of official specifications for all Pearson qualifications may be found on the website: qualifications.pearson.com

Text and illustrations © Pearson Education Ltd 2017
Produced, typeset and illustrated by Phoenix Photosetting
Cover illustration by Miriam Sturdee

The rights of Pauline Lowrie, Mike O'Neill and Nigel Saunders to be identified as authors of this work have been asserted by them in accordance with the Copyright, Designs and Patents Act 1988.

First published 2017

25 24 23 22 21 20
15 14 13 12 11 10 9 8

British Library Cataloguing in Publication Data
A catalogue record for this book is available from the British Library

ISBN 978 1 292 13159 7

Acknowledgements
The author and publisher would like to thank the following organisations for permission to reproduce copyright material:

Photographs:
(Key: b-bottom; c-centre; l-left; r-right; t-top)

Bridgeman Art Library Ltd: Musee de Picardie, Amiens, France 30bl, Musee des Antiquities Nationales, St. Germain-en-laye, France 30bc; **Fotolia.com:** joris17 34; **Science Photo Library Ltd:** Herve Congé, ISM 6cl, Steve Gschmeissner 6br

All other images © Pearson Education

Text:
Page 61 Copyright © 2016, Re-used with the permission of the Health and Social Care Information Centre, also known as NHS Digital. All rights reserved.
Page 77 Based on data collected by the Cary Institute of Ecosystem Studies
http://www.caryinstitute.org/sites/default/files/public/images/lesson-plan/unionid_zm_graph.png

Contents

- - - - - - - - - - - - - -

A small bit of small print:
Edexcel publishes Sample Assessment Material and the Specification on its website. This is the official content and this book should be used in conjunction with it. The questions in Now try this have been written to help you practise every topic in the book. Remember: the real exam questions may not look like this.

Plant and animal cells

Animals and plants are formed from **cells**. Animal cells and plant cells have some parts in common. These parts have particular functions in a cell. Cells like these, with a nucleus and membrane-bound organelles such as mitochondria, are called eukaryotic cells.

Generalised structures

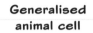

**Generalised
animal cell**

Cell membrane: controls what enters and leaves the cell, e.g. oxygen, carbon dioxide, glucose

Generalised plant cell

cell wall

Nucleus: a large structure that contains genes that control the activities of the cell

central vacuole

Cytoplasm: jelly-like substance that fills the cell – many reactions take place here

Mitochondria (single: mitochondrion): tiny structures where respiration takes place, releasing energy for cell processes

chloroplasts

Ribosomes (present in the cytoplasm but not visible at this size): where proteins are made (protein synthesis)

Worked example

Name the three structures that are found in most plant cells but not animal cells, and describe their functions. **(4 marks)**

Chloroplasts are the structures where photosynthesis takes place to make food for the plant cell.

The cell wall is made of cellulose, and is tough so that it helps support the cell and helps it keep its shape.

The large central vacuole contains cell sap, which helps to keep the plant cell rigid.

> 1 mark is for naming the three structures and there is 1 mark for each function.

> Watch out! The cell membrane and cell wall are different and separate structures.

Now try this

1 Muscle cells contain more mitochondria than skin cells. Suggest why. **(3 marks)**
2 State the names of four structures found in both plant cells and animal cells. **(4 marks)**
3 Suggest an explanation for why not all plant cells have chloroplasts. **(2 marks)**

Different kinds of cell

Some plant and animal cells are **specialised** for different functions. Bacteria have a different kind of **cell structure** from plant and animal cells.

Bacterial cells

Bacteria have a simple cell structure. Like animal and plant cells, they have a cell membrane surrounding the cytoplasm. However, they do not have a nucleus. These are called prokaryotic cells.

A single loop of **chromosomal DNA** lies free in the cytoplasm. This carries most of the bacterial genes.

cell membrane

Some bacteria have a **flagellum** to help them move.

Ribosomes are tiny structures that make proteins.

Some bacteria have extra circles of DNA called **plasmid DNA**. Plasmids contain additional genes that are not found in chromosomes.

Many bacteria have a **cell wall** for protection, but it is made of different substances to plant cell walls.

(a) Egg cells and sperm cells contain haploid nuclei. Explain how this is related to the function of these cells. **(2 marks)**

A haploid nucleus contains half the genetic information needed by an organism. When a sperm cell fuses with an egg cell, a diploid zygote is formed with all the genetic information needed for an organism.

(b) For each of the three cells shown, explain one specialisation related to its function. Do not include ideas about the nucleus. **(3 marks)**

The egg cell contains nutrients in the cytoplasm to supply the growing embryo. The sperm cell has a tail for swimming to the egg cell for fertilisation. Epithelial cells line tubes, such as the trachea. Cilia move things along the tube, such as mucus. This cell has a lot of cilia to move mucus, containing dirt and bacteria, away from the lungs.

Make sure that you can recognise an unusual feature of a cell, which may be a specialisation to allow the cell to carry out a particular function. For example, in a sperm cell the acrosome contains enzymes to digest a way through the egg cell membrane.

Egg cell

Sperm cell

Ciliated epithelial cell

1 Give **one** similarity and **one** difference between a bacterial cell and an animal cell. **(2 marks)**

2 The diagram shows a root hair cell. Explain how the shape of this cell is related to its function. **(2 marks)**

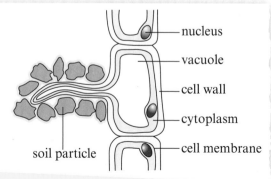

A root hair cell in a plant absorbs minerals that have been dissolved in water.

Describe how the shape of the cell is different from other cells, and then give a reason why this is an advantage.

Microscopes and magnification

As microscope technology has developed over time, we have been able to see more of the **structures of cells** and to know more about the **role** of sub-cellular structures.

Using microscopes

Before microscopes were invented about 350 years ago, people could not see the cells in organisms. Magnification enables you to see plant cells, animal cells and bacterial cells, and the structures inside them.

A **light microscope** uses light to magnify objects. The greatest possible magnification using a light microscope is about ×2000.

An **electron microscope** uses electrons to view an object. This makes it possible to magnify objects up to about ×10 million. You can see objects in cells more clearly and in far more detail with an electron microscope than with a light microscope.

 Maths skills **Calculating magnification**

$$\text{Magnification (M)} = \frac{\text{Image size (I)}}{\text{Real size (R)}}$$

☑ Measure image in millimetres (mm).

☑ Multiply by 1000 to get measurement in micrometres (μm).

☑ If the image has a scale bar, use that to find the answer.

Cover up the term you are trying to find to show the expression required to calculate it.

Worked example

| 1μm |

Calculate the magnification of this image. **(2 marks)**

scale bar (image size, I) = 20 mm
20 × 10³ = 20 000 μm
so I = 20 000 μm

real size (R) = 1 μm (from diagram)

magnification = I ÷ R = 20 000 ÷ 1

magnification = ×20 000

Worked example

Some cells were viewed by microscope using a ×4 eyepiece and a ×20 objective. Calculate the magnification of the cells seen through the microscope (see page 5 for a diagram of a microscope). **(1 mark)**

Magnification of object

$$= \frac{\text{magnification}}{\text{of eyepiece}} \times \frac{\text{magnification}}{\text{of objective}}$$

= 4 × 20 = 80

The cells will be magnified 80 times by the microscope.

Always show your working in a calculation. Even if you get the answer wrong you may be able to show that you understand the method.

Now try this

A cell is viewed under a light microscope using a ×40 objective and a ×10 eyepiece.
(a) Calculate the total magnification. **(1 mark)**
(b) The image is 1.2 mm long. Use your answer to part (a) to calculate the actual length of the cell. **(1 mark)**

Dealing with numbers

Many structures in biology are very small so you will use very small **units of measurement**.

Describing small structures

Smaller structures need smaller units:

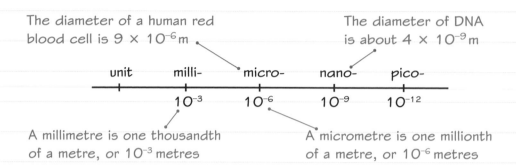

The diameter of a human red blood cell is 9×10^{-6} m

The diameter of DNA is about 4×10^{-9} m

| unit | milli- | micro- | nano- | pico- |

10^{-3} 10^{-6} 10^{-9} 10^{-12}

A millimetre is one thousandth of a metre, or 10^{-3} metres

A micrometre is one millionth of a metre, or 10^{-6} metres

There are 1000 millimetres in a metre.

There are 1 000 000 micrometres in a metre.

There are 1 000 000 000 nanometres in a metre.

There are 1 000 000 000 000 picometres in a metre.

Also, notice that there are 1000 picometres in a nanometre, or 1000 micrometres in a millimetre.

Worked example

A mitochondrion is 0.002 mm long.
Give this length in:
(a) micrometres   **(1 mark)**

2 µm

(b) nanometres   **(1 mark)**

2000 nm

> Notice that there are 1000 nanometres in 1 micrometre.

Now try this

1 Match the structure to its correct average size.

       Protein molecule   Chloroplast   Cell

       2 micrometres   10 nanometres   0.1 millimetres   **(2 marks)**

2 A human egg is 0.00013 m long. State the length of the egg in micrometres.   **(1 mark)**

3 The bacterial cell on page 3 is 2 µm long. Use this information to estimate the width of the cell.   **(1 mark)**

Using a light microscope

 Practical skills You can use a **microscope** to **observe cells**. You can then produce accurate labelled diagrams from your observations (see page 6 for how to produce a labelled diagram).

Core practical

Using a light microscope safely

- Always start with the lowest **power objective** under the eyepiece.
- Clip the **slide** securely on the stage.
- Adjust the **light source (mirror)** so that light goes up through the slide.

If you use daylight as a source of light, make sure the microscope mirror does not point directly at the Sun as this could permanently damage your eyesight.

- eyepiece
- objective
- coarse focusing wheel
- stage with clips to hold slide
- fine focusing wheel
- mirror to reflect light through slide

- Use the **coarse focusing wheel** to focus on the slide.
- Move the slide so that the cell you will draw is in the middle of the view.
- If needed, move a higher power objective into position above the slide.
- Use the **fine focusing wheel** to bring the cell back into focus.

Never use the coarse focusing wheel with a higher power objective, as it may crash into the slide.

If you cannot see the part of the slide you need with a higher power objective, go back to using the lower power objective to bring it back to centre view and to focus it before returning to the higher power objective.

Now try this

A student is given a microscope slide of a section through a leaf.
(a) Describe how the student should use a light microscope to study xylem cells in the leaf section.

(4 marks)

(b) The lens closest to the specimen is called the:
- ☐ **A** subjective
- ☐ **B** eyepiece
- ☐ **C** objective
- ☐ **D** stage

(1 mark)

5

Drawing labelled diagrams

Practical skills You can use a microscope to produce **accurate labelled diagrams** of cells and their structures (see page 5 for how to set up and use a light microscope).

Core practical

Aim

To produce a labelled diagram of a plant cell.

Apparatus

- light microscope
- unlined paper
- sharp HB pencil
- rubber
- ruler

Method

Focus the microscope on a single cell.

Carefully draw details of the parts that are important to your study. Other parts can be drawn just in outline.

Keep looking back at the specimen as you make the drawing, and only draw what you see, not what you think you ought to see.

Results

Pondweed cell ×650

chloroplast

cell walls of two neighbouring cells

cytoplasm and vacuole (not obvious)

nucleus

> If a line is in the wrong place, rub it out cleanly before drawing it in the correct position. Your drawing should be as clear as possible.

> Keep the relative sizes of structures approximately correct and label all the key parts of your drawing.
>
> Labels should be outside the drawing and label lines must not cross.
>
> Use a ruler to draw label lines to link labels to the correct parts of the drawing.
>
> Never use shading.

> Give your drawing a clear title saying what the specimen is, and always give the magnification, e.g. ×100. (See page 3 to help you calculate the magnification.)

Now try this

The photo shows some cells in a blood smear seen under a light microscope at ×1000.
Draw and label one example of each cell in the smear. **(3 marks)**

Enzymes

Enzymes are biological **catalysts** that control reactions in the body. Each enzyme is **specific** (only works with one substrate) to its substrate and the **activity** of enzymes is affected by temperature, substrate concentration and pH.

Effect of temperature and substrate concentration

At the **optimum temperature** the enzyme is working at its fastest rate.

At lower temperatures, molecules move more slowly. So substrate molecules take longer to fit into and react in the active site.

Higher temperatures cause the active site to change shape, so it can't hold the substrate as tightly and the reaction goes more slowly.

At very high temperatures the active site breaks up and the enzyme is **denatured**.

Adding more substrate at this point has little effect because the active site of every enzyme molecule is working.

At this point not every active site of each enzyme molecule is working, so adding more substrate increases the rate of reaction.

Worked example

The diagram shows an enzyme-controlled reaction.

(a) State the name of the part labelled X. **(1 mark)**

product molecule

(b) Explain the role of the active site in an enzyme-controlled reaction. **(4 marks)**

The shape of the active site matches the shape of the substrate molecules and holds them close together so bonds can form between them to make the product. The product molecule doesn't fit the active site well so it is released from the enzyme.

The **substrate** fits like a 'key' into the **active site** (the 'lock'). Enzymes are specific because only a substrate with the right shape can fit the active site.

Worked example

Draw a graph of rate of reaction against pH for an enzyme with an optimum pH of 6. Label your graph to explain what you have drawn. **(2 marks)**

Changing the pH can change the shape of the enzyme's active site, and so change its ability to bond with the substrate.

The enzyme works fastest at the optimum pH.

As you go further from the optimum pH, the rate of reaction is slower as the enzyme gradually denatures.

Now try this

1 Explain what is meant by the active site of an enzyme. **(2 marks)**

2 Enzymes in the human body have an optimum temperature of about 37 °C. Explain why our body temperature is controlled to stay at about 37 °C. **(2 marks)**

pH and enzyme activity

🧪 **Practical skills** You can **investigate the effect of pH on the rate on enzyme activity** by measuring the rate of an enzyme-controlled reaction at one pH, and comparing it with the rate at other pH values. You can revise enzymes on page 7.

Core practical

Aim

To investigate the effect of pH on amylase activity.

Methods

- Add amylase to buffered starch solution in a test tube.
- Place the tube in a water bath heated by a Bunsen burner for a constant temperature.
- Take samples of the mixture at regular intervals (e.g. every 10 s) and mix them with a fresh drop of iodine solution on a dimple tile.
- Repeat the test until the iodine solution stops changing colour when the starch/amylase mixture is added. Record the time taken for this to happen.
- Repeat the procedure at different pH values.

Starch is broken down by amylase to sugars.

Buffering the solution makes sure the pH doesn't change during the experiment.

When controlling the temperature, bear in mind the effect of temperature on enzyme action. Keeping the solution at the optimum temperature for the enzyme is best.

Iodine solution is usually yellow/orange. In the presence of starch, it turns blue/black.

Results

Record the values for each pH in a table. Then, you can draw a graph like the one given below.

Conclusion

The results show that the time taken for all the starch to be digested by the amylase decreases from pH 4 to pH 6, and then increases again. The optimum pH for this enzyme is pH 6.

🧮 **Maths skills** **Reaction rate**

You can calculate the relative rate of reaction for a particular pH, as $\frac{1}{time}$ because the mass of starch used at each pH is the same. You can then compare the rates of reaction of amylase at different pHs. For this you do not have units. For example: all starch was digested in 20 s at pH 6. The rate of reaction at pH 6 is

$$\frac{1}{20} = 0.05/s.$$

However, this is not a true rate. For a true rate of reaction you would need to have the mass of starch digested by the enzyme divided by the time taken. The units for this would be g/s.

Improvements

This method can be improved by:
- using more accurate measuring apparatus
- taking the mean of several repeats at each pH to help reduce the effect of random variation
- taking measurements over a narrower range of pH.

Now try this

1 (a) Calculate the relative rate of reaction of amylase at pH 9 in the core practical. **(1 mark)**
   (b) Explain why the graph shows that the optimum pH for this enzyme was pH 6. **(2 marks)**

2 A student repeated the experiment using solutions of pH 5.2, 5.6, 6.0, 6.4, 6.8. Explain why the results of this experiment could produce a more accurate answer for the optimum pH of the enzyme. **(2 marks)**

The importance of enzymes

Enzymes are biological **catalysts** that control reactions in the body. They catalyse reactions that **synthesise** large molecules from smaller ones and **break down** large molecules into smaller ones.

Enzymes as catalysts

Enzymes **speed up** the rate of a chemical reaction but are not used up in the reaction. This means they can be used over and over again.

Make sure you remember at least some examples of enzymes and the reactions they catalyse.

Digestion and synthesis

Some enzymes **digest** large molecules into smaller molecules. This happens in the gut where large food molecules are broken down so that they can be absorbed into the blood.

| | digestion
amylase → | | | digestion
lipase → | | | digestion
protease → | |

Carbohydrates e.g. starch for energy storage in plants → Sugars e.g. glucose for respiration (synthesis ←)

Lipids e.g. for energy storage → Fatty acids and glycerol e.g. for respiration (synthesis ←)

Proteins e.g. for muscle cells → Amino acids e.g. to make enzymes (synthesis ←)

Some enzymes **synthesise** larger molecules from smaller molecules. This is important inside cells for supporting life processes and growth.

Worked example

Complete the table.   **(3 marks)**

Large molecule	Smaller molecules it is broken down into
carbohydrates	sugars
proteins	amino acids
lipids	fatty acids and glycerol

Remember you need to mention **both** fatty acids **and** glycerol to get the mark.

Worked example

People with cystic fibrosis have thick mucus lining their gut. This stops enzymes being secreted into the gut. Explain why they need to take capsules containing enzymes before a meal.   **(3 marks)**

The thick mucus stops the body's own enzymes from entering the gut to digest the food. If people with cystic fibrosis didn't take enzyme capsules before meals, their food would not be digested into smaller, soluble molecules. As a result, they would not absorb enough nutrients.

Now try this

1 The enzyme that digests lipids will not digest proteins. Explain why.   **(2 marks)**

2 Name the part of a cell where you expect to find enzymes needed to make proteins (protein synthesis).   **(1 mark)**

Think about what you know about cell structure (see page 1 for the generalised structures of plant and animal cells).

Getting in and out of cells

Dissolved substances (**solutes**) move into and out of cells by **diffusion** and **active transport**. Water moves into and out of cells by **osmosis**.

Diffusion

high concentration of dissolved molecules (concentrated solution)

partially permeable membrane

More molecules move from the high concentration to the lower concentration than vice versa, so the net movement is **down** the concentration gradient.

low concentration of dissolved molecules (dilute solution)

Diffusion is important in the body, for example, to move oxygen into cells and to remove carbon dioxide.

Active transport

partially permeable membrane

Active transport needs energy from respiration.

low concentration of dissolved molecules (dilute solution)

high concentration of dissolved molecules (concentrated solution)

There is net movement against the concentration gradient.

Active transport makes it possible for cells to absorb ions from very dilute solutions, e.g. root cells absorb minerals from soil water, and small intestine cells absorb glucose from digested food in the gut into the body.

Worked example

The diagram shows the results of an experiment. At the start, the level of solution inside the tube and the level of water in the beaker were the same. Name the process that caused the change and explain what happened. **(3 marks)**

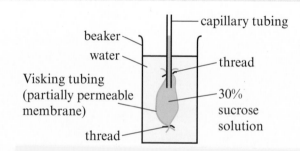

capillary tubing

beaker

water

Visking tubing (partially permeable membrane)

thread

30% sucrose solution

thread

The process is called osmosis. To start with there were more water molecules in the water than in the same volume of sucrose solution, so more water molecules crossed the membrane into the tubing than going the other way. So the level of solution in the capillary rose.

Osmosis is the name given to a special case of diffusion. Osmosis is the net movement of water molecules across a partially permeable membrane from a low solute concentration to a high solute concentration.

Now try this

 1 Define **osmosis**.   **(2 marks)**

 2 (a) Give one similarity between diffusion and osmosis. **(1 mark)**
(b) Give one difference between diffusion and active transport.   **(1 mark)**

3 A plant root is treated with a poison that prevents respiration. Explain why the root cells still absorb water from a dilute solution, but cannot absorb mineral ions.   **(4 marks)**

Remember that respiration provides the energy for active transport but there are other ways that substances can enter cells which do not require energy from respiration.

Osmosis in potatoes

Practical skills You can investigate **osmosis** by calculating the change in mass of pieces of potato that have been placed in solutions of different solute concentration.

Core practical

Aim

To investigate osmosis using potatoes.

Apparatus

potato

- pieces of potato about 3 × 1 × 1 cm
- boiling tubes
- accurate balance
- paper towels
- forceps
- solutions of different solute concentration (0, 0.2, 0.4, 0.6, 0.8, 1.0 mol dm⁻³)
- marker pen

Method

1 Mark the value of one solute concentration on one tube and repeat using a different tube for each concentration. Fill each tube two-thirds full of the appropriate solution.

2 Blot a piece of potato dry on a paper towel, then measure and record its mass. Use the forceps to place it into one of the tubes, and record the tube. Repeat for all tubes.

3 After 20 minutes, use the forceps to remove each piece of potato, blot it dry and measure its mass again. Record all final masses.

Results

The percentage change in mass of each potato slice is calculated and recorded, indicating whether mass was gained or lost.

Conclusion

The results show that when the solution concentration is very dilute, water enters the potato cells. This is due to osmosis because the solute concentration of the potato cells is greater than the surrounding solution. As the solute concentration of the solution increases above that inside the potato cells, osmosis causes water to be lost from the potato.

Remember, finding the percentage change in mass allows you to compare results from the different tubes, because the pieces of potato weren't all exactly the same mass to begin with.

Worked example

The initial mass of a potato slice was 16.52 g. After soaking in a solution the final mass was 20.15 g. Calculate the percentage change in mass.

(4 marks)

% change in mass =
$$\frac{\text{final mass} - \text{initial mass}}{\text{initial mass}} \times 100\% =$$

$$\frac{20.15 - 16.52}{16.52} \times 100 = 21.97\% \text{ gained}$$

(or +21.97%)

 The solute in the solutions must be something that is too large to diffuse across the cell membrane. Sucrose is often used.

 The change in mass may be very small. You should measure the mass in grams to 2 d.p.

Blotting removes surface water, and can help to increase the accuracy and repeatability of measurements.

Repeating the test at each solute concentration, and calculating the mean of the results, can help to reduce the effect of random variation.

Now try this

The table shows the results of an osmosis experiment using potato pieces.

(a) Calculate the percentage change in mass of potato at each concentration. **(2 marks)**

(b) Use your answers to estimate the solute concentration of the potato cells. Explain your answer. **(2 marks)**

Solution concentration (mol dm⁻³)	Initial mass (g)	Final mass (g)
0	16.52	20.15
0.2	15.90	16.70
0.4	17.06	15.69
0.6	16.88	14.36
0.8	16.23	12.32

Extended response – Key concepts

There will be one or more 6-mark questions on your exam paper. For these questions, you will need to think scientifically and structure your answer logically, showing how the points you make are related to each other. For the questions on this page, you can revise the topics on **enzyme activity** on pages 7 to 9.

Worked example

The graph shows the results of an experiment into the effect of temperature on the activity of the enzyme amylase on starch. Explain the results shown in the graph. **(6 marks)**

The graph shows that activity of the bacterial amylase increased from 30°C up to a maximum at 50°C, and then decreased as the temperature increased further to 70°C. The maximum activity is at the optimum temperature, which is about 50°C for this enzyme.

Enzyme activity increases with increasing temperature up to the optimum because particles move faster. Starch molecules fit into the active site of enzyme molecules more quickly and are broken down more quickly, releasing the active site for another starch molecule.

Beyond the optimum temperature, the shape of the active site starts to change, making it more difficult for the substrate to fit into it. So activity slows down. The active site shape changes more as temperature increases further, until the enzyme becomes denatured and stops being able to catalyse the reaction.

> Before you explain the results, describe what the graph shows. Use values on the graph to add details to your answer. Remember to include important science words that are relevant in your answer.

> Enzyme activity should be linked to how the active site of the enzyme and the substrate interact.

> Make sure you explain each part of the graph clearly, linking your knowledge and understanding to give a good explanation of what is happening.

Command word: Explain

An **explain** question requires a reason for what is happening. Use a word such as 'because' to clearly link a description with its reason.

Now try this

The graph on the right shows the effect of starch concentration on the activity of a bacterial amylase. Explain the results shown in the graph. **(6 marks)**

Mitosis

There are two types of cell division, **mitosis** and **meiosis.** Mitosis is covered here; meiosis is covered on page 20.

Mitosis is a type of **cell division** that takes place in several stages. There are two types of **cell division**. **Mitosis** is the cell division that happens in body cells. A **body cell** is any cell except those that produce **gametes** (sex cells).

The cell that is dividing is called the **parent cell** and the two new cells that are formed are called **daughter cells.** The daughter cells are identical to the parent cell, so if the parent cell is diploid then the daughter cells will be diploid too. You should be clear about the differences between meiosis and mitosis.

Three things to remember

- ✓ Mi-to-sis makes two cells.
- ✓ MiTosis makes genetically idenTical cells.
- ✓ Diploid means Double (two sets of) chromosomes.

Stages of mitosis

Each chromosome consists of two chromatids.

The chromatids separate and one chromatid from each pair is pulled to each pole of the cell. The chromatids can now be called chromosomes.

The cell splits into two. This is called **cytokinesis**.

Interphase   Prophase   Metaphase   Anaphase   Telophase

At the end of interphase, chromosomes start to become visible. The DNA has already been copied.

The nuclear membrane breaks down. Chromosomes line up along the middle of the cell.

Spindle fibres disappear and a new nuclear membrane forms round each group of chromosomes.

Remember the stages of mitosis using the mnemonic IPMAT:
Interphase
Prophase
Metaphase
Anaphase
Telophase

Worked example

(a) Body cells have two sets of chromosomes. Explain how this happens. **(2 marks)**

One set of chromosomes comes from the mother and one set comes from the father.

(b) Explain how the daughter cells are genetically identical. **(2 marks)**

Each chromosome is copied; one copy of each chromosome goes into each daughter cell.

Interphase

A cell is in interphase most of the time.

mitosis
interphase

Now try this

A cell divides by mitosis. Describe the daughter cells. **(2 marks)**

Cell growth and differentiation

Mitosis is used for growth, repair and asexual reproduction. After growth, cells can then **differentiate** into specialised cells. Growth and differentiation happen in different ways in plants and animals.

When does mitosis happen?

Normally cells only divide by mitosis when new diploid cells are needed for:
• growth
• repair (replacement of damaged cells)
• asexual reproduction.

Uncontrolled cell division

Cancer cells are abnormal cells that divide uncontrollably by mitosis to form a **tumour**.

Cells usually stop dividing when growth has finished, except when repair is needed. Sometimes the controls that tell cells when to stop dividing go wrong which leads to cancer.

Worked example

Aphids are insects that are pests of crop plants. In the summer they reproduce rapidly by asexual reproduction. Will the offspring of a single aphid be varied? Explain your answer. **(3 marks)**

The offspring will be produced by mitosis, so they will all be genetically identical to the parent aphid. They will all be diploid like the parent aphid.

Mitosis is used for asexual reproduction. This also occurs in plants, for example, when plants reproduce using bulbs or runners.

Growth in animals

In **animals**, a fertilised egg, or zygote, divides by mitosis to produce genetically identical daughter cells. These cells grow and divide by mitosis, and eventually **differentiate** into different types of cells to make up a whole organism. Differentiation creates **specialised cells** adapted to carry out a particular function. Examples of specialised animal cells include:
• red blood cells
• egg and sperm cells
• nerve cells
• bone cells
• smooth muscle cells.

Growth in plants

Plant cells divide by mitosis, just behind the tips of shoots and roots. After this the cells grow by enlarging. Young cells have small vacuoles which take in water by osmosis and enlarge, causing the cells to **elongate**. These cells can differentiate into specialised cell types. Most plant cells can **continue** to grow and differentiate throughout life.

Examples of specialised plant cells include:
• xylem   • mesophyll cells   • stoma cells.
• phloem   • root hair cells

Now try this

1 Some drugs stop mitosis. Explain why they are used to treat cancer. **(2 marks)**

2 State what is meant by a specialised cell. **(1 mark)**

3 Explain why cell differentiation is important. **(2 marks)**

Growth and percentile charts

When organisms **grow** they get bigger. Growth can be measured in different ways.

Estimating growth

increase in length

increase in mass

2.61 KG   5.36 KG

Growth is a **permanent** increase in size. For example, a balloon that is blown up a little more has not 'grown' in size.

Percentile charts

Percentile charts can help to show if a child is growing faster or slower than is normal for their age.

Babies with a mass above the 95th line or below the 5th line may not be growing properly.

A baby whose mass decreases by two or more percentile categories over their first year may not be growing normally.

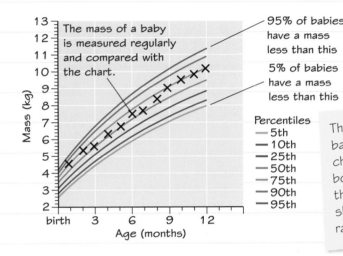

The mass of a baby is measured regularly and compared with the chart.

95% of babies have a mass less than this

5% of babies have a mass less than this

Percentiles
— 5th
— 10th
— 25th
— 50th
— 75th
— 90th
— 95th

This chart is for baby girls. The chart for baby boys is similar, but they grow at a slightly different rate to girls.

Worked example

Look at the percentile chart. The crosses mark the mass of a baby girl measured each month.

(a) State the percentile that she belonged to in her first month.   **(1 mark)**

75th percentile

(b) Do you think there was concern about this baby's mass increase in her first year? Explain your answer.   **(2 marks)**

No, because her mass varied only between the 75th and 50th percentiles, and this amount of variation is normal.

Worked example

BMI is a measure of a healthy body mass. The government has produced percentile charts for BMI in children. A child has a clinically healthy weight if their BMI is between the 2nd and 91st percentile. A parent has been told that her son is on the 70th percentile for BMI. Explain to her what this means.   **(2 marks)**

This means the child has a higher BMI than 70% of children and a lower BMI than 30% of children. Because this falls between the 2nd and 91st percentile, the child has a clinically healthy weight.

Now try this

1 Describe one way in which you could measure the growth of a plant.   **(2 marks)**

2 Describe what a percentile chart is used for.   **(2 marks)**

3 Explain why an increase in the size of a balloon is not an example of growth but an increase in the size of a child is.   **(2 marks)**

Stem cells

Stem cells have different functions in plants and animals. In humans, they have many potential uses in medicine.

What are stem cells?

Cells in an embryo are unspecialised. They divide to produce all the **specialised cells** in the body, such as neurones and muscle cells. Once the cells have differentiated they cannot divide to produce other kinds of cell.

Stem cells are cells that can divide to produce many types of cell. There are three kinds of stem cell:

- **Embryonic stem cells** are taken from embryos at a very early stage of division (e.g. 8 cells).
- **Adult stem cells** are found in differentiated tissue, such as bone or skin – they divide to replace damaged cells.
- Plants have **meristems** that are found in rapidly growing parts of the plant, e.g. tips of roots and shoots. These cells can divide to produce any kind of plant cell.

Embryonic stem cells

Embryonic stem cells have many uses, including:

- replacing or repairing brain cells to treat people with Parkinson's disease
- replacing damaged cells in the retina of the eye to treat some kinds of blindness
- growing new tissues in the lab to use for transplants or drug testing.

Adult stem cells

Adult stem cells (from bone marrow) can only form a limited number of cell types. They can be used for:

- treatment of leukaemia
- potentially growing new tissues that are genetically matched to the patient.

Using stem cells

embryonic stem cells

✓ easy to extract from embryo

✓ produce any type of cell

✗ embryo destroyed when cells removed – some people think embryos have a right to life

all stem cells

✓ replace faulty cell with healthy cell, so person is well again

! stem cells may not stop dividing, and so cause cancer

adult stem cells

✓ no embryo destroyed so not an ethical issue

✓ if taken from the person to be treated, will not cause rejection by the body

✗ produce only a few types of cell

✓ – Advantage   ✗ – Disadvantage   ! – Risk

Now try this

1 State what is meant by **a stem cell**.
   (2 marks)

2 When gardeners cut off the top of a plant, the plant usually continues to grow sideways but does not grow taller. Explain why.   **(2 marks)**

3 Explain **two** disadvantages of research into embryonic stem cells.   **(2 marks)**

4 (a) State why embryonic stem cells could be more useful than adult stem cells to replace faulty cells.   **(1 mark)**

   (b) Describe **one** practical advantage of using adult stem cells from the patient instead of embryonic stem cells to replace faulty cells.   **(2 marks)**

If an exam question asks for **two** advantages or disadvantages, make sure you give two **different** examples.

Neurones

Stimuli are detected by sensory **receptors** that send impulses along sensory **neurones** to the central nervous system. Neurones are specialised cells that carry nervous impulses.

Types of neurones

There are three main types of neurones. **Sensory neurones** carry impulses to the central nervous system. **Motor neurones** carry impulses from the central nervous system to effector organs. **Relay neurones** are found only in the central nervous system.

Sensory neurone

skin receptor cells

direction of impulse

cell body

Axon endings pass impulses to other neurones.

Dendrites collect impulses from receptor cells.

dendron

axon

fatty **myelin sheath**

carries impulses towards cell body

carries impulses away from cell body

insulates the neurone

Relay neurone

This carries impulses from one part of the central nervous system to another.

Motor neurone

The electrical impulse jumps from one gap in the myelin sheath to the next, speeding up the rate of transmission.

The electrical impulse cannot cross the fatty myelin sheath.

The axon carries the electrical impulse over long distances through the body.

myelin sheath

axon

The nerve ending transmits the impulse to an effector, such as a muscle or gland.

nerve ending

nucleus

dendrite

cytoplasm

cell membrane

Worked example

Complete the table with the name of the structure that corresponds to each function listed.   **(3 marks)**

Structure	Function
axon	carries impulses away from the cell body
dendrite	receiving impulses from receptor cells and other neurones
myelin sheath	a fatty layer that provides electrical insulation around the neurone

Now try this

1 Give the roles of sensory, motor and relay neurones in the nervous system.   **(3 marks)**

2 Explain how the structure of a sensory neurone is related to its function.   **(2 marks)**

Responding to stimuli

Sensory neurones **carry impulses** from receptors to the central nervous system.

Synapses

The point where two neurones meet is called a **synapse**. There is a small gap between the neurones. The electrical nerve impulse cannot cross this gap, and the impulse is carried by **neurotransmitters**.

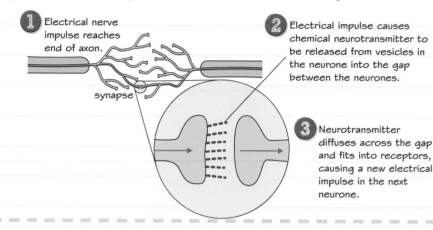

1 Electrical nerve impulse reaches end of axon.

synapse

2 Electrical impulse causes chemical neurotransmitter to be released from vesicles in the neurone into the gap between the neurones.

3 Neurotransmitter diffuses across the gap and fits into receptors, causing a new electrical impulse in the next neurone.

The reflex arc

Stimulus detected by receptor
⬇
Impulses pass along sensory neurone to spinal cord
⬇
Impulses pass to relay neurone
⬇
Impulses pass from relay neurone to motor neurone
⬇
Impulses pass along motor neurone to effector, in this case a muscle
⬇
Hand moves away from stimulus

sensory neurone — spinal cord — motor neurone — relay neurone — biceps muscle — heat receptor in the skin

If the impulses had to go to the brain to be processed, there would be many more synapses, so the response would take longer.

Reflex arcs involve only three neurones, and impulses pass to and from the spinal cord. This provides a fast response that does not involve the brain. Reflex arcs are:
• immediate (happen very fast)
• involuntary (the brain isn't needed)
• innate (not learned)
• invariable (always exactly the same).

These reflexes help protect us from immediate harm, such as the eye blink reflex which protects the eye if something comes close to it.

Worked example

Explain the role of a neurotransmitter.   **(2 marks)**

It is a chemical released from one neurone that carries the impulse across the synaptic gap to the next neurone. Without it, the electrical impulse cannot cross the synaptic gap.

Now try this

1 A person's finger gets pricked by a pin and the person removes their finger rapidly. Describe how the reflex arc causes this.   **(4 marks)**

2 Describe how impulses can pass across a synapse.   **(3 marks)**

Extended response – Cells and control

There will be one or more 6-mark questions on your exam paper. For these questions, you will need to think scientifically and structure your answer logically, showing how the points you make are related to each other. You can revise the topic for this question, which is about **neurones** and **responding to stimuli**, on pages 17 and 18.

Worked example

Motor neurones are one type of cell found in the nervous system. The diagram shows the structure of a motor neurone.

axon
cell body
myelin sheath
dendrite

Explain how the structure of a motor neurone is related to its function. **(6 marks)**

Neurones carry nervous impulses along their axons. Motor neurones carry impulses from relay neurones to effectors such as muscles or glands. They have long axons to carry impulses long distances through the body. The myelin sheath insulates the axon, making the impulses travel faster.

Motor neurones have many tiny dendrites at the end of the axon. These receive impulses from other neurones in the nervous system, connecting neurones together.

The gap between one neurone and the next is called a synapse. Chemicals released into the synapse allow the signal to pass to the next neurone.

Command word: Explain

When you are asked to **explain** something, it is not enough just to state or describe it.

Your answer **must** contain some reasoning or justification of the points you make.

 Diagrams are shown in questions to give you information that will be useful in your answers. Make sure you study them carefully.

 The question does not ask for the function of motor neurones, but the answer includes the function. This is important for explaining how the structure and function are related.

The answer mentions nervous impulses, but they could be called signals or messages instead.

This part of the answer includes a description of the synapse. It is not part of the cell itself, but an understanding of the synapse is needed to fully explain the function of a motor neurone.

 You need to show comprehensive knowledge and understanding, using relevant scientific ideas, to support your explanations. In this answer, the structure of the three main parts of the motor neurone are described and explained (the axon, myelin sheath and dendrites).

Now try this

When a bright light shines into the eye, muscles in the iris contract. The size of the pupil decreases so that less light can enter the eye. This is an example of a reflex. Describe how impulses travel through the reflex arc involved, starting with receptor cells in the eye.
(6 marks)

Think about the route, including the three types of neurones involved and the effector. Link your statements in a sensible order.

Meiosis

Meiosis is a type of cell division that produces four **daughter cells**, each with half the number of chromosomes. Meiosis only happens in gamete-producing cells, producing genetically different **haploid** gametes. The other type of cell division, **mitosis**, is covered on page 13.

Stages of meiosis

The parent cell is a diploid cell. So it has two sets of chromosomes.

The parent cell divides in two and then in two again. Four daughter cells are produced.

the other set of chromosomes

Before the parent cell divides, each chromosome is copied.

Each daughter cell gets a copy of one chromosome from each pair.

one set of chromosomes

pair of chromosomes

Each daughter cell has only one set of chromosomes. So these are **haploid** cells. The daughter cells are not all identical – meiosis results in variation.

Remember: haploid cells, produced by meiosis (me-1-osis), have 1 set of chromosomes.

The cells produced by division are always called 'daughter cells', even if they will eventually turn into sperm cells.

Worked example

Give four differences between mitosis and meiosis.
(4 marks)

Meiosis produces four daughter cells, but mitosis only produces two.

Meiosis produces genetically different daughter cells, but in mitosis the daughter cells are identical to each other and to the parent cell.

Meiosis produces haploid cells, but mitosis produces diploid cells.

Mitosis occurs in body cells, but meiosis occurs only in gamete-producing cells.

Be careful to spell mitosis and meiosis correctly. If you write something like 'meitosis' or 'miosis' it won't be clear which kind of cell division you are referring to.

Now try this

1 Describe the outcome of meiosis of a diploid parent cell. **(3 marks)**
2 Explain the importance of meiosis. **(2 marks)**

3 In terms of the number of sets of chromosomes, describe the difference between haploid and diploid. **(2 marks)**

4 The cells produced by meiosis are
  ☐ **A** diploid
  ☐ **B** genetically different
  ☐ **C** embryos
  ☐ **D** identical   **(1 mark)**

You need to say enough for 2 marks here. It may help to think about what would happen if gametes were produced by mitosis and not meiosis.

DNA

DNA is the **genetic material** found in the chromosomes in the nuclei of cells.

DNA in the cell

The nucleus contains chromosomes.

Most cells have a nucleus.

cell

chromosome

A chromosome consists of a string of genes.

DNA

A **gene** is a short piece of **DNA** that codes for a specific **protein**. You have genes for hair structure, eye colour, enzymes and every other protein in your body.

Each gene is a length of DNA. DNA is a long, coiled molecule formed from two strands. The strands are twisted in a **double helix**.

The two strands of the double helix are joined by pairs of **bases**. There are four different bases in DNA:

A = adenine   T = thymine
C = cytosine   G = guanine

G ═ C
A ═ T
C ═ G
A ═ T
T ═ A

Bases form **complementary pairs**:
A always pairs with T
C always pairs with G.

Remember: straight A with straight T; curly C with curly G.

Weak hydrogen bonds between the base pairs hold the DNA strands together.

The **genome** is all the DNA in an organism.

DNA structure

DNA is a **polymer** made of many **monomers**, called **nucleotides**, joined together.

P phosphate

base

The base can be A, C, T or G.

deoxyribose sugar

🧪 Practical skills   DNA from fruit

DNA can be extracted from fruit by:

1 grinding the fruit with sand, using a pestle and mortar, to separate the cells

2 adding a detergent to break open the membranes

3 adding ice-cold alcohol so that the DNA precipitates out.

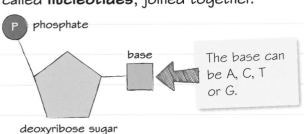

Now try this

You do not need to know the names of the bases. You just need to know their letters are A, C, T and G.

1 Write a sentence to define each of these words:
 (a) gene   (b) genome.   **(2 marks)**

2 The sequence of bases on one strand of DNA is CGAT. Write down the sequence of bases on the complementary strand, and explain how you worked out your answer.   **(2 marks)**

3 Describe the structure of DNA.   **(4 marks)**

This question has 4 marks, so the answer needs 4 different ideas.

21

Genetic terms

You need to be able to explain all of the **genetic terms** in bold on this page.

Inside a cell

When **gametes** fuse at fertilisation, they form a diploid **zygote**. Each zygote inherits different alleles (genetic variants) of their genes from their parents. This produces variation in inherited characteristics between different individuals.

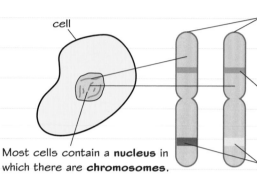

cell

Most cells contain a **nucleus** in which there are **chromosomes**.

There are two copies of each **chromosome** in body cells – each copy has the same genes in the same order along its length (except chromosomes that determine sex).

A **gene** is a short piece of DNA at a particular point on a chromosome – a gene codes for a characteristic, e.g. eye colour.

A gene may come in different forms, called **alleles**, that produce different variations of the characteristic, e.g. different eye colours.

Alleles

different alleles of the same gene – the person is **heterozygous** for this gene

Chromosomes of the same pair have the same genes in the same order.

these genes have the same allele on both chromosomes – the person is **homozygous** for these genes

Genetic definitions

The gene for coat colour in rabbits has different alleles. The allele for brown colour (B) is dominant over the allele for black colour (b). The table shows all the possible genotypes and phenotypes for these alleles.

Genotype shows the alleles (forms of the genes) in the individual. Remember that each body cell has two alleles for each characteristic – either two alleles that are the same or two that are different.

Genotype	Phenotype
BB	brown coat
Bb	brown coat
bb	black coat

Phenotype means the characteristics that are produced, including what the individual looks like.

The effect of the **dominant** allele will show when at least one copy is present in the genotype.

The effect of the **recessive** allele will only show when two copies are present in the genotype.

Now try this

Make sure you know the difference between a gene and an allele. This is a common mistake that students make.

1 Define the terms **chromosome**, **gene** and **allele**.   **(3 marks)**

2 A pea plant has a recessive allele for white flower colour and a dominant allele for purple flower colour.
   (a) Identify if the plant is homozygous or heterozygous for flower colour, and explain your answer.   **(2 marks)**
   (b) State the phenotype of the plant for flower colour. Explain your answer.   **(2 marks)**

Monohybrid inheritance

Monohybrid inheritance can be explained using **genetic diagrams** and **Punnett squares**.

Genetic diagrams

Body cells contain two alleles for each gene. In this example, both parent plants are heterozygous – they have one allele for purple flower colour and one allele for white flower colour.

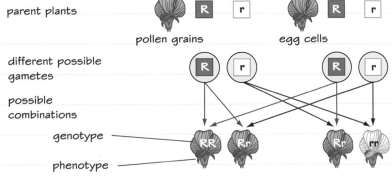

Purple colour is dominant (R). White colour is recessive (r).

Half the gametes contain one allele. The other half contain the other allele.

parent plants

pollen grains   egg cells

different possible gametes

possible combinations

genotype

phenotype

 Worked example

Green seed pod (G) is dominant to yellow seed pod (g). Complete the Punnett square to show the possible offspring for plants heterozygous for seed pod colour, and calculate the (a) ratio, (b) probability and (c) percentage of possible offspring genotypes and phenotypes. **(4 marks)**

	parent gametes	parent genotype Gg	
		G	g
parent genotype Gg	G	GG green	Gg green
	g	Gg green	gg yellow

(a) Genotype 1 GG : 2 Gg : 1gg

Phenotype 3 green : 1 yellow

(b) Genotype 1/4 (1 out of 4) GG, 2/4 (1/2) Gg, and 1/4 gg

Phenotype 3/4 green and 1/4 yellow

(c) Genotype 25% GG, 50% Gg, 25% gg

Phenotype 75% green and 25% yellow

A **Punnett square** is a different way of showing the same information about how genotype is inherited and what effect this has on the phenotype.

Genetic diagrams and Punnett squares only show **possible** offspring, not the **actual** offspring from these parents.

 Now try this

The allele for brown fur in rabbits is dominant. The allele for black fur is recessive. A heterozygous brown rabbit was bred with a homozygous black rabbit.

Use a diagram to show why half the baby rabbits should be brown.

(3 marks)

Remember to use a Punnett square when answering this question.

Family pedigrees

Cystic fibrosis (CF) is a genetic condition caused by a recessive allele. **Pedigree analysis** can be used to study the inheritance of dominant and recessive alleles.

Family pedigree showing inheritance of cystic fibrosis

You can use a **family pedigree** to show the inheritance of a genetic condition within a family, and to **predict** the chance that someone will inherit the faulty allele.

In the family pedigree below, both Ethan and Mia have CF. Ethan inherited his alleles from Arun and Beth, but they don't have the disease, so they must both be **carriers** (have one copy of the faulty allele).

Three generations are shown in this pedigree. Arun and Beth are the oldest generation.

Key
- ☐ male, runny mucus
- ▨ male, cystic fibrosis
- ○ female, runny mucus
- ◉ female, cystic fibrosis

Ethan and Mia must have two copies of the recessive allele, as they have the disease.

Worked example

The ability to taste phenylthiocarbamide (PTC) is a dominant condition. The diagram shows the inheritance of PTC tasting in one family. Describe the evidence that PTC tasting is controlled by a dominant allele.
(2 marks)

non-PTC tasters   PTC tasters

1 and 2 are both PTC tasters but they have two children who are non-tasters. Therefore PTC tasting must be dominant and non-tasting is recessive.

You are asked for **evidence** so make sure you refer to **specific individuals** in the pedigree.

🖩 Maths skills — Pedigree analysis

Look at the family pedigree above. You can calculate the **probability** of Gill and Harry having a third child with CF using a Punnett square.

Mia has the disease, so Harry and Gill must both have one copy of the faulty allele.

	Harry F	f
Gill F	FF	Ff
f	fF	ff

There is one outcome (ff) that would lead to a child having CF, and three that would not:

P(third child has CF) = $\frac{1}{4}$ or 25%

There is more about Punnett squares on page 25.

Now try this

Look at the family pedigree in the worked example above.
(a) Give the genotype of individual 2. **(1 mark)**
(b) Individuals 9 and 10 have a fifth child. Calculate the probability that the child will be a PTC taster. **(2 marks)**

Remember that the trait is **dominant** so each person only needs **one copy** of the allele in order to be a PTC taster.

Sex determination

The sex of humans is determined at fertilisation and can be expressed using **genetic diagrams** and **Punnett squares**.

Sex chromosomes

The sex of humans is controlled by one pair of **sex chromosomes**. The genotype **XX** produces the **female** phenotype. The genotype **XY** produces the **male** phenotype.

Genotype and phenotype

The genotype is all the genes of the individual. The phenotype is what the individual looks like.

Worked example

Explain the proportions of the different sex chromosomes in the gametes of men and women. **(3 marks)**

Gametes are haploid because they are produced by meiosis. As the sex chromosomes in a woman's diploid body cell are both X, all the eggs she produces will contain one X chromosome. The sex chromosomes in a man's diploid body cells are XY, so 50% of his sperm will contain one X chromosome and the other 50% will contain one Y chromosome.

Genetic diagrams and Punnett squares

We can use a **genetic diagram** or **Punnett square** to show that the sex of an individual is determined at fertilisation.

Genetic diagram

parent's phenotype	male	female
parent's genotype	XY	XX
gametes	X Y	X X
possible offspring	XX XY XX XY	

Punnett square

		possible female gametes	
		X	X
possible male gametes	X	XX female	XX female
	Y	XY male	XY male

You can usually use either a Punnett square or a genetic diagram to answer a question about inheritance. Use the one that works best for you.

Both diagrams show that, at fertilisation, there is an equal chance of producing a male or a female:
- 50% male XY: 50% female XX
- ratio of 1 : 1 male : female
- 1 out of 2 chance of either male or female.

Use a Punnett square like this.

Now try this

1 At which of the following stages is the sex of a baby determined?

   ☐ **A** when the egg is fertilised

   ☐ **B** as the foetus develops in the womb

   ☐ **C** when the baby is born   **(1 mark)**

2 A couple have two sons. The woman is pregnant with another child. Draw a genetic diagram to show the % chance of this child being a girl. **(4 marks)**

3 Explain why human eggs all contain one X chromosome. **(2 marks)**

Variation and mutation

Causes of **variation** that influence phenotype include genetic variation and environmental variation. Genetic variation happens through **mutation**.

Causes of variation

Most phenotypic features in humans, e.g. hair colour, are caused by many genes. Each of these genes may have several

differences between individuals of the same kind

Most variations are caused by a combination of genes and environment.

caused by differences in alleles they have inherited, e.g. eye colour (**genetic variation**)

combination of both causes, e.g. weight, skin colour

caused by differences in conditions in which they developed, e.g. riding a bike, scars (**environmental variation**)

alleles, so the phenotype is the result of the **combination** of different alleles for different genes. This combination of alleles that an organism inherits is the result of sexual reproduction.

Mutation

A **mutation** or **genetic variant** is created if the sequence of bases in a gene is changed. A mutation in the gene's coding DNA can affect the phenotype of an organism. If the amino acid sequence is altered, the activity of the protein produced may also be altered. However:

- most genetic mutations have no effect on the phenotype

- some mutations have a small effect on the phenotype
- a single mutation can, rarely, significantly affect the phenotype.

A mutation may cause:
- a large change in the protein produced
- a small change in the protein
- no change at all in the protein produced.

The bigger the change to the protein, the larger the effect on how the body works.

Worked example

Enzymes have a very specific shape that allows them to work effectively. Explain why a gene mutation can change the activity of an enzyme. Refer to the active site in your answer.   **(3 marks)**

A gene mutation can change the base sequence in DNA. This may produce a different protein with a differently shaped active site. The shape of the active site controls how well an enzyme works. If the shape of the active site matches the shape of the substrate better, then the enzyme will work better. But if the shape of the active site is not as good a match, then the enzyme will not work so well.

Now try this

1 Identical twins are genetically identical. Explain why they share many, but not all, of their characteristics.   **(2 marks)**

2 Explain why a mutation in a body cell will not affect a person's phenotype.   **(2 marks)**

Most mutations occur when DNA replicates before cell division. Most of them cause no change in the phenotype.

The Human Genome Project

The **Human Genome Project** is a collaboration between scientists to decode the **human genome** (the order of bases on all human chromosomes). The project was completed quickly because so many scientists worked on it at the same time. The work was published in 2003 and made freely available to scientists all over the world. The results are being used to develop new medicines and treatments for diseases.

Advantages and disadvantages of the Human Genome Project

Advantages

👍 Alerting people that they are at particular **risk** of certain diseases, e.g. types of cancer or heart disease. The person may be able to make lifestyle changes to reduce the chances of the disease developing.

👍 Distinguishing between different forms of diseases such as leukaemia or Alzheimer's disease, as some drugs are beneficial in some forms of these diseases but not in others.

👍 Allowing doctors to **tailor treatments** for some diseases to the individual, where specific alleles affect how a person will respond to treatment.

Disadvantages

👎 People who are at risk of certain diseases, e.g. cancer, may have to pay more to obtain life insurance.

👎 It may not be helpful to tell someone they are at risk of a condition for which there is currently no cure.

Worked example

Describe two possible developments as a result of decoding the human genome, and discuss the implications of these developments. **(4 marks)**

One development is the identification of genes that can cause disease. Knowing if you have a faulty gene could help a person and their family prepare for its effects, but some people would prefer not to know if they have a faulty gene because then they would worry about it.

Another development is gene therapy. This involves replacing faulty alleles in body cells with healthy ones. This would allow the affected person to live a normal life. However, people will have to decide whether the faulty alleles are replaced in gametes, so that the healthy alleles could be passed on to children.

There are many possible answers for this question, because there are many new developments. Other possibilities include: creating personalised medicines, and identifying evolutionary relationships between humans and other organisms. As well as learning about new developments you need to be able to say what the implications are.

Now try this

1 Explain **one** way in which the Human Genome Project could be useful to doctors and their patients.
      (2 marks)

2 The genome of two different humans is not exactly the same. Explain why.   **(2 marks)**

 Humans all share the same genes, but think carefully about alleles and base sequences.

Extended response – Genetics

There will be one or more 6-mark questions on your exam paper. For these questions, you will need to think scientifically and structure your answer logically, showing how the points you make are related to each other. You can revise the topics for this question, which is about **monohybrid inheritance**, on page 23.

Worked example

The ability to taste PTC is controlled by a dominant allele. A man and a woman who can both taste PTC have a daughter who can taste PTC but also a son who is unable to taste PTC. Explain these observations. **(6 marks)**

PTC is phenylthiocarbamide. It is a substance that is tasteless to some people, but tastes bitter to others.

I will use T for the dominant taster allele, and t for the recessive allele.

Suggest suitable symbols for each allele, if none are given in the question.

The son cannot taste PTC, so he must be homozygous for the recessive allele, tt. This means he must have inherited a t allele from each of his parents. The genotype of both his parents must be Tt because they can taste PTC.

This part of the answer states and explains the possible genotypes of the son and his parents.

The Punnett square shows how he inherited this genotype.

		father's gametes	
		T	t
mother's gametes	T	TT taster	Tt taster
	t	Tt taster	tt non-taster

Even in a long-answer question, a Punnett square or genetic diagram is a good way to display genetic information clearly.

The Punnett square shows that the parents have a 25% (1 in 4) chance of having a child who cannot taste PTC. They have a 75% (3 in 4) chance of having a child who can taste PTC. Their daughter will have the genotype TT or Tt because she can taste PTC.

Remember to explain the possible outcomes in terms of probability, ratio or percentage.

The answer includes logical reasoning in the explanation. The phenotype corresponding to each possible genotype is shown in the Punnett square, giving further explanation for the observations.

Now try this

In guinea pigs, rough coat is dominant over smooth coat. Two rough-coated guinea pigs were bred together. They produced seven rough-coated offspring and two smooth-coated offspring. Use a genetic diagram to explain how this occurred. **(6 marks)**

Use R for the dominant allele and r for the recessive allele.

Evolution

Charles Darwin developed a theory of evolution by means of natural selection. It is still important in modern biology.

Natural selection

Individuals of a species show variation. This can mean that some individuals will be better able to survive in their environment and produce more healthy offspring than others. This is **natural selection**, where the environment (including climate and other organisms) selects which individuals pass on their **alleles** to the next generation.

Theory of evolution in modern biology

The theory of evolution is very important in modern biology:

- ✓ It helps us understand the relationships between different species of organisms.
- ✓ It explains how new species evolve.
- ✓ It explains how different species adapt to changes in their environment.

Darwin's theory

Adults usually produce more young than the environment can support when they are adults (**overproduction**). This produces a '**struggle for existence**' by the young.

→ Some individuals have inherited **advantageous variations** in characteristics that are better adapted to the environment. These individuals will have a better chance of **survival** to adulthood.

→ Individuals with advantageous variations will pass their genes on to their young. The young may inherit the advantageous variations.

→ More individuals will have these advantageous variations in the next generation.

→ Individuals with variations that are not as well adapted to the environment will be less likely to survive.

→ These individuals will not produce young.

Worked example

African elephants are hunted illegally by poachers for their tusks. Elephants may be born tuskless due to a mutation. In 1930 in Uganda, only 1% of elephants were born without tusks. In 2010, 15% of females and 9% of male elephants were born without tusks. Explain this change using the theory of evolution. **(3 marks)**

Elephants with tusks are more likely to be poached and killed, so do not survive to pass on their alleles. Tuskless elephants are more likely to survive to pass on the allele for no tusks, so the allele for no tusks increases in frequency in the population.

One example of Darwin's theory is the development of antibiotic resistance in bacteria.

Doctors tell you to complete the full course of antibiotics, even if you feel better before the course is finished. If you do not finish taking a complete course of antibiotics, the bacteria resistant to the antibiotic can reproduce. This can result in an infection of antibiotic-resistant bacteria that is much harder to treat.

This is an example of where you may be asked to apply your understanding to a specific example that you may not be familiar with.

Now try this

Remember to use scientific terms like mutation and alleles, as well as explaining the effects on survival and passing on alleles.

Describe how Darwin's theory of evolution can explain antibiotic resistance in bacteria. **(4 marks)**

Human evolution

Some of the evidence we have for evolution leading to modern humans (*Homo sapiens*) comes from **fossils**. These include fossils of bones and teeth.

Species	**Ardi** (*Ardipithecus ramidus*)	**Lucy** (*Australopithecus afarensis*)	*Homo habilis* ('handy man')	*Homo erectus* ('upright man')	*Homo sapiens* ('wise'/modern man)
height	120 cm	107 cm	< 130 cm	179 cm	wide variety but generally taller than other species
when existed	4.4 million years ago	3.2 million years ago	2.4–1.4 million years ago	1.8–0.5 million years ago	since c. 200 000 years ago
brain size	350 cm³	400 cm³	500–600 cm³	850–1100 cm³	approximately 1200 cm³
other details	tree climber, also walked upright	walked upright, face ape-like	flat face like modern humans, used simple stone tools	long-distance walker, strongly built	user of complex tools

You do not need to remember details such as brain sizes but you do need to remember the names and the general trends.

Homo habilis and *Homo erectus* fossils were found by the archaeologists **Leakey** and his family. They wrote the first description of these early humans.

Stone tools

Stone tools also give us evidence of human evolution. The earliest stone tools are around 2.4 million years old. Over time more complex tools were made, and a greater range of tool types.

c. 2 million years old. A large stone that has had some chips flaked off it, e.g. simple hand axes

c. 40 000 years old. Made from fine flakes split from larger stones; many types of tool made this way, e.g. arrow head, spear head, scraper, knife

Worked example

Explain how stone tools can be dated from their environment. **(3 marks)**

The amount of radiation in samples of sediment just above and below the layer in which the tools are found can be used to date the sediment and so give a range of dates when the tools were left there.

The stone used to make the tools is much older than the tools, so cannot be used to date when the tool was made.

Now try this

1 Describe two ways that human-like species have evolved over the past 4.4 million years which can be seen from fossils. **(2 marks)**

2 Give two ways in which later stone tools were more complex than the earliest stone tools dating from about 2.4 million years ago. **(2 marks)**

Classification

Scientists used to classify living organisms into the following five big groups, called **kingdoms**. The kingdoms were Plants, Animals, Fungi, Protists and Prokaryotes. Scientists have now classified organisms into three **domains**.

Five-kingdom system

Carl Linnaeus originally proposed the classification of organisms into just two kingdoms, but this was later developed into five kingdoms. These are:

1 Plants
2 Animals
3 Fungi
4 Protists
5 Prokaryotes.

Three-domain system

Genetic research shows that the organisms which were grouped as prokaryotes in the kingdom system should be separated into two groups, which have been named **Eubacteria** and **Archaea**. This is because the genes of organisms in Archaea work more like those in the eukaryotes, while the genes of organisms in Eubacteria work a little differently.

prokaryotes

Eubacteria

Eukaryota includes **Plants Animals Fungi Protoctista**

Archaea mainly bacteria that live in very warm or salty conditions

This grouping forms the **three-domain** system of classification.

Worked example

The diagram shows the bones of the forelimbs of two living vertebrates. Explain how these pentadactyl limbs are evidence for evolution.

(4 marks)

humerus
radius
ulna
carpals
phalanges

human arm – for holding and working with objects

whale flipper – for swimming underwater

The limbs show the same basic pentadactyl structure. They have long bones supporting carpal bones and phalanges. This suggests that the human and the whale evolved from a shared ancestor. The differences between the limbs can be explained by evolution. The limbs have developed in different ways because they have adapted to different uses.

Many living vertebrates have the same pentadactyl (five-fingered) limb structure.

Notice that this answer explains ways in which DNA differs between different groups of organisms, and points out that closely-related organisms have more similarities in their DNA.

Worked example

Suggest how studying DNA can help scientists to work out the evolutionary relationships between different groups of organisms.   **(3 marks)**

Scientists can examine the structure of the DNA in the cells, e.g. whether it is formed into linear chromosomes or is circular. They can also find out how much non-coding DNA it contains. Then they can find the base sequence in the DNA of different organisms. The more closely related the organisms are, the more similarities there will be in their DNA base sequences.

Now try this

1 Describe the three-domain system of classification.
(3 marks)

2 Give two ways in which genetic analysis has led to the five-kingdom system being replaced by the three-domain system.   **(2 marks)**

Selective breeding

Selective breeding is when plants or animals with certain desirable characteristics are chosen to breed together, so that offspring will be produced that **inherit** these characteristics. This produces **new breeds** of animals and **new varieties** of plants. Selective breeding has taken place over thousands of years, but more recently **genetic engineering** has been developed as a way of manipulating genetics. You can learn about this on page 33.

Selective breeding in plants

| Plants with good features are crossed, e.g. plants that have good yield, are drought tolerant, or need less fertiliser. | → | Plants grown from seeds of these crosses are selected for their good features and crossed with each other. | → | Selection and crossing is repeated many times until a high-yielding variety is produced. |

Reasons for selective breeding

Plants and animals are selectively bred for:

- ✓ disease resistance
- ✓ increased yield
- ✓ better ability to cope with difficult conditions
- ✓ faster growth
- ✓ better flavour.

Worked example

The graph shows the average milk yield per cow from 1957 to 2007. The increase is mainly the result of selective breeding. Over the same period there has been an increase in cows suffering from mastitis (an inflammation of the udders), problems with their legs and reduced fertility. A farming newspaper reported this in an article entitled 'Selective breeding has improved dairy farming'. Evaluate this statement. **(4 marks)**

The graph shows that the milk yield per cow has more than doubled over these 50 years so this is useful for the farmer.

However, the cows are having more problems with their legs and udders which may be because they are producing so much milk, so this is an animal welfare issue.

It also costs the farmer more in veterinary bills.

I think that selective breeding to produce a high-yielding breed of cows is a good thing, but this should not be done at the expense of animal welfare.

Worked example

Describe how a farmer would breed cattle that have a large milk yield. **(4 marks)**

The farmer would choose a cow that produced lots of milk and cross her with a bull whose mother produced a lot of milk. The farmer would then choose the female offspring who produce lots of milk and cross them with a male whose mother had a high milk yield. The farmer would do this for many generations.

Advantage

Ethical issue

Practical issue

You can draw your own conclusion as long as it clearly relates to the information given and the benefits and risks identified.

Now try this

1 Give one advantage and one disadvantage of selective breeding.
   (2 marks)

2 Describe how a farmer could breed sheep that have thick wool.
   (3 marks)

3 Describe one problem of selective breeding in crop plants. **(2 marks)**

Genetic engineering

Genetic engineering is changing the **genome** (the DNA) of an organism, often by introducing genes from another to create **genetically modified organisms** (GMOs).

How genetic engineering works

Genes can be transferred from any kind of organism to any other kind of organism, e.g. bacteria, humans, other animals, plants.	The gene for a characteristic is 'cut out' of a chromosome using enzymes.	The gene is inserted into a chromosome inside the nucleus of a cell in a different organism.	The cell of this organism now produces the characteristic from the gene.

Worked example

Human insulin is a hormone used by many patients with diabetes. Bacteria have been genetically modified to carry the human insulin gene. The bacteria are then grown in large quantities to produce the human insulin.
Explain why bacteria had to be modified to make human insulin and describe how the GM bacteria were produced. **(3 marks)**

Bacteria don't normally produce human insulin, so they had to be modified to make it. The gene for making insulin was cut out of a human chromosome. The gene was then inserted into the bacterial chromosome, so that the bacterium made the insulin.

GM crops

GM crop plants have been genetically modified to give them new characteristics, such as:

- resistance to attack by insects
- resistance to **herbicides**, so that fields can be sprayed to kill weeds, but not the crop.

These characteristics can help the crop grow better and produce more food (an increased **yield**).

It is possible to give an advantage and then a disadvantage in the same sentence. Or you can give an advantage in one sentence and then a disadvantage in the next sentence.

Worked example

A sheep has been genetically modified to produce a protein in its milk that can be used to treat serious lung diseases in humans. Explain the advantages and disadvantages of this. **(4 marks)**

The protein is secreted in milk so the sheep is not harmed to produce the protein, although some people think it is unethical to use animals for the benefit of humans. The protein treats serious lung disease so is very beneficial to human health. However, in developing the genetically modified sheep a lot of embryos would have been made that did not successfully express the gene, so a lot of embryos are wasted to produce a GM sheep.

Now try this

1 Define **genetic engineering**. **(2 marks)**

2 Scientists have produced GM crop plants that are resistant to herbicides. The field can be sprayed with herbicide that kills weeds but not the crop.
Give **one** possible advantage of this and **one** possible disadvantage. **(2 marks)**

Extended response – Genetic modification

There will be one or more 6-mark questions on your exam paper. For these questions, you will need to think scientifically and structure your answer logically, showing how the points you make are related to each other. You can revise the topics for this question, which is about **selective breeding and genetic engineering**, on pages 32 and 33.

Worked example

Some crop plants have been modified to produce a toxin when their cells are damaged. This toxin kills caterpillars when they eat it. Evaluate the factors that should be considered before deciding to grow these crops on a large scale. **(6 marks)**

First you would need to consider whether this method of killing caterpillars is effective in increasing crop yield. Genetically modifying the crop will be expensive, so tests will need to be carried out to find out whether the increased yield brings in enough income to offset the cost of buying genetically modified seeds to plant.

You would also need to know whether the toxin is harmful to people eating the crop. Tests must be carried out to make sure the crop is safe to eat. It is also important that customers are happy to buy this crop. Some people do not like the idea of eating genetically modified food, and choose not to buy it.

Growing this crop might save time and costs for the farmer, because it has a toxin in the crop so the farmer does not need to buy a pesticide to kill the caterpillars. The toxin is always there so caterpillars should be killed as soon as they start to eat the crop. Also, there will not be any harmful pesticide residues left on the crop. If the farmer sprays his crops with a pesticide instead, this could harm useful insects as well as the caterpillars.

There is a possible ethical issue if the toxin gene transferred somehow to wild plants. This could possibly lead to wild plants containing a toxin, which could kill insects and cause problems in food chains. On balance I think it would be a good idea to grow this crop, but only after the necessary tests have been carried out.

> Do not be put off if you have not met this specific example before. You are given all the information you need. Think about identifying advantages and disadvantages, and drawing a conclusion.

> Consider what the alternative to using the GM crop might be, as this will help you to weigh up the different factors that have to be considered.

Other answers

The answer to this question could have covered other issues, such as how the development of resistance to the toxin by insects will affect the benefits of using GM crops. It could also have covered the problem that many people will not buy food from GM crops as they do not trust that it is safe. What matters in this answer is that it covers all that the question asks, and is presented in a clear and logical order.

Now try this

Selective breeding is used to produce varieties of food plants with desirable characteristics. Genetic engineering may also be used to achieve this. Compare and contrast these two methods.   **(6 marks)**

Health and disease

The World Health Organization defines **health** as 'a state of complete physical, mental and social well-being'. There are many different **diseases** with different causes.

What is health?

health — mental well-being

such as how you feel about yourself

such as eating and sleeping well, and being free from disease

physical well-being   social well-being

such as how well you get on with other people

Types of disease

Diseases may be **communicable** (they can be passed from one person to another) or **non-communicable** (not passed between people). A **pathogen** is an organism that causes an infectious disease.

Communicable	Non-communicable
rapid variation in number of cases over time	number of cases changes only gradually
cases are often localised	cases may be more widely spread
e.g. malaria, typhoid, cholera	e.g. cancer, diabetes, heart disease

Worked example

Chalara fungus sometimes kills ash trees directly, but sometimes it makes the tree more likely to be infected by other pathogens which kill the tree. Suggest how this happens.   **(2 marks)**

The fungus damages the bark and the cells of the ash tree, making it easier for other pathogens to infect the tree.

HIV is a pathogen that makes it easier for other pathogens to infect a person. In the case of HIV, this happens because of damage to the immune system.

Pathogens

Pathogens include bacteria and viruses, fungi and protists. When a few pathogens **infect** you (get inside your body) they can reproduce very rapidly. Large numbers of pathogens make you ill.

Bacteria are much smaller than human cells.

Viruses are much smaller than bacteria.

bacterium
Bacteria may release **toxins** (poisons) that make us feel ill. Some types of bacteria invade and destroy body cells.

virus
Viruses take over a body cell's DNA, causing the cell to make **toxins** or causing damage when new viruses are released from cells.

fungi
Fungi are eukaryotic organisms.

protist
Protists are eukaryotic organisms. Many are free-living but some are pathogens.

Now try this

1 Name four types of organism that can act as a pathogen.   **(4 marks)**

2 A stroke is caused when a blood clot blocks an artery in the brain. This stops oxygen reaching part of the brain and nerve cells die. State whether a stroke is a communicable or non-communicable disease. Give a reason for your answer.   **(2 marks)**

Pathogens make you feel ill when they damage cells or change how cells work.

Common infections

Different kinds of pathogens can cause different diseases with different symptoms. You need to be able to describe the **infections** given on this page.

Infection	Type of pathogen	Main symptoms
cholera	bacterium	• watery, pale-coloured **diarrhoea**, often in large amounts (watery faeces)
malaria	protist	• **fever** (high temperature) • **weakness** • chills • sweating
HIV/AIDS	virus	• mild flu-like symptoms may occur when first infected • often, no symptoms for a long time • eventually, **repeated infections** (e.g. TB) that would not be a problem if immune system was working properly
tuberculosis (TB)	bacterium	• lung damage seen in **blood speckled mucus** • **weight loss** • **fever** and chills • night sweats
Ebola	virus	• internal bleeding and fever (**haemorrhagic fever**) • severe headache • muscle pain • vomiting • diarrhoea (frequent watery faeces)
Helicobacter	bacterium	• **inflammation** in stomach causing pain • stomach ulcers leading to bleeding in stomach
ash dieback *Chalara*	fungus	• leaf loss • bark **lesions** (damage) • **dieback** of top of tree (crown)

Worked example

Describe a communicable disease caused by a bacterium and the symptoms of the disease.

(3 marks)

TB is a communicable disease. Two of its symptoms are blood speckled mucus and weight loss.

You could choose any of the other communicable diseases in the table. One mark is for naming the disease, then two marks for two symptoms.

Now try this

Give one example of a pathogen from each of the following groups, describing two signs of the infection it causes:

(a) virus   **(2 marks)**
(b) protist   **(2 marks)**
(c) fungus   **(2 marks)**

Make sure you know which group each pathogen belongs to.

How pathogens spread

Understanding how pathogens are spread can help us to find ways of **reducing** or **preventing** their spread.

Malaria

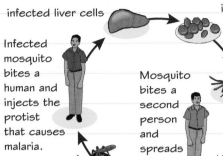

infected liver cells

infected red blood cells

Infected mosquito bites a human and injects the protist that causes malaria.

Mosquito bites a second person and spreads malaria.

Mosquito becomes infected with parasite when it takes a blood meal.

The protist that causes malaria is spread by a **vector**, the mosquito.

Watch out! Vectors are not pathogens. Vectors carry pathogens from one person to another. Vectors are one way infectious diseases are spread.

HIV

The human immunodeficiency virus, **HIV**, enters the blood and reproduces inside white blood cells, causing white blood cell destruction.

Eventually so many white blood cells are destroyed that the immune system cannot work properly. This stage is called **AIDS**. The person becomes ill with a disease, such as tuberculosis, that would not be a problem if their immune system was working properly.

Ebola virus

The **Ebola virus** causes **haemorrhagic fever**. The virus infects humans from other infected people, infected animals or objects that have been in contact with the virus. The virus infects:
* liver cells
* cells from the lining of the blood vessels
* white blood cells.

It multiplies inside these cells and destroys them. This causes fever, severe headache, muscle pain, extreme weakness, vomiting, diarrhoea, and internal and external bleeding.

Reducing the spread of pathogens

Disease (cause)	Ways to reduce or prevent its spread
cholera (bacteria)	• boil water to kill bacteria before drinking • wash hands thoroughly after using toilet to prevent spread by touch
tuberculosis (bacteria)	• ventilate buildings adequately to reduce chance of breathing in bacteria in droplets of mucus coughed out by an infected person • diagnose infected people promptly and give antibiotics to kill tuberculosis bacteria • isolate infected people so they cannot pass the infection to others
malaria (protists)	• prevent mosquito vectors biting people, by killing mosquitoes or keeping them off skin (e.g. by using a mosquito net)
stomach ulcers (bacteria)	• cook food thoroughly to kill bacteria • wash hands thoroughly before preparing food to avoid transfer
haemorrhagic fever (Ebola virus)	• keep infected people isolated because the virus is easily spread • wear fully protective clothing while working with infected people or dead bodies

Now try this

Using malaria as an example, explain the difference between a **pathogen** and a **vector**. **(2 marks)**

STIs

Chlamydia and HIV are sexually transmitted infections (**STIs**) spread by sexual activity. *Chlamydia* is a bacterium and HIV is a virus.

Spread of STIs

Chlamydia bacteria can be spread by contact with sexual fluid from an infected partner. An infected mother can pass *Chlamydia* to her baby during birth.

Common methods of **HIV transmission** are:
- unprotected sex with an infected partner
- sharing needles with an infected person
- transmission from infected mother to foetus
- infection from blood products.

Reducing or preventing STIs

The spread of many STIs can be reduced or prevented by:
- using **condoms** during sexual intercourse
- **screening people**, including pregnant women
- **screening blood** transfusions
- supplying intravenous drug abusers with **sterile needles** (HIV)
- treating infected people using **antibiotics** (for *Chlamydia* and other bacterial infections).

Worked example

All pregnant women in the UK are screened for HIV infection. Explain two advantages of this. **(4 marks)**

If a pregnant woman has HIV, this allows doctors to give her treatment to stop the infection getting worse, and also to try to stop HIV spreading to the baby. Another advantage of this is that it gives doctors a measurement of how many people have HIV. This helps them to target awareness raising and education programmes.

There are other possible answers, for example, if the woman is HIV positive, doctors may discuss with her whether to breast-feed her baby after birth or not, as breast-feeding might pass HIV on to the baby.

Worked example

About 3000 15-year-olds are diagnosed with *Chlamydia* every year. Explain how this rate of infection could be reduced. **(2 marks)**

There could be better health education in schools, so that students learn how Chlamydia is spread and what the symptoms are. This might lead to fewer young people catching Chlamydia and, if they do get it, they will realise that they need to see a doctor.

Health education can include using condoms during sexual intercourse.

Worked example

A newborn baby's eyes are infected with *Chlamydia*. Explain how this could happen. **(1 mark)**

During birth, the baby's eyes and lungs may become contaminated with vaginal fluid containing the bacteria.

Pathogens enter the body through natural openings, so the baby's eyes, nose and mouth are places where pathogens can enter the body easily.

Now try this

1 State what STIs are and how they are spread. **(2 marks)**

2 During sexual intercourse a man places a condom over his penis. Describe how this reduces his risk of being infected with an STI. **(2 marks)**

38

Human defences

The human body has both physical barriers and chemical defences to give protection against pathogens. **Physical barriers** make it hard for pathogens to enter the body. **Chemical defences** are chemicals that are produced to kill or make pathogens inactive.

Chemical and physical defences

Chemical defences

Lysozyme enzyme in tears kills bacteria by digesting their cell walls.

Lysozyme enzyme is also present in saliva and mucus.

Hydrochloric acid in stomach kills pathogens in food and drink.

Physical barriers

Unbroken **skin** forms a protective barrier because it is too thick for most pathogens to get through.

Sticky **mucus** in the breathing passages and lungs traps pathogens. **Cilia** on the cells lining the lungs move in a wave-like motion, moving mucus and trapped pathogens out of lungs towards the back of the throat where it is swallowed.

mucus traps pathogens

cilia move mucus away from lungs

cilia

epithelial cells

Remember that epithelial cells line the surface of tubes.

Worked example

Cilia move mucus away from the lungs. Describe how this protects the body from pathogens.
(3 marks)

It stops pathogens entering the lungs where they can cause disease. When the mucus gets to the throat it is swallowed and the pathogens are destroyed by the acid in the stomach.

Cilia are tiny hairs on the surfaces of cells that move together in a rhythm to move substances along, such as mucus. Their movement is a bit like a crowd of people doing a Mexican wave.

Worked example

Chemicals in cigarette smoke paralyse the cilia in the epithelium of the airways. Smokers are more likely than non-smokers to suffer from lung infections. Explain why. **(2 marks)**

When the cilia are paralysed, they cannot move the mucus containing pathogens back up to the throat. The mucus travels down into the lungs, carrying pathogens with them.

Now try this

1 Give **one** example of a physical barrier and **one** example of a chemical defence that prevents pathogens entering the body.
(2 marks)

2 Explain why someone with a skin burn can develop an infection.
(2 marks)

The immune system

The **immune system** helps to protect the body by attacking pathogens if they manage to enter the body. **Lymphocytes** are part of this immune system.

1 Each pathogen has unique **antigens** on its surface.

These lymphocytes are not activated.

2 A **lymphocyte** with an **antibody** that fits the antigen is activated.

3 The lymphocyte **divides** many times to produce clones of identical lymphocytes.

4 Some of the lymphocytes produce lots of antibodies which stick to the pathogen and destroy it. Other lymphocytes stay in the blood as **memory lymphocytes**, ready to respond immediately if the same antigen returns.

Antibodies

The antibodies produced by a lymphocyte are **specific** for one particular kind of pathogen. This means they can only destroy that kind of pathogen. They cannot destroy another kind of bacterium or virus.

This is called the **secondary response**.

Immunity

Lymphocytes respond to infection by making antibodies.

Amount of antibody in bloodstream in arbitrary units

first infection

second infection

immunity level

Time in weeks

The memory lymphocytes are made after the infection and then respond more quickly to another infection by the pathogen.

Worked example

Explain why there is a delay of a few days between a person becoming infected by a pathogen for the first time and antibodies being made.   **(2 marks)**

It takes time for lymphocytes to identify the antigens on the pathogen, and to secrete specific antibodies.

The secondary response is much faster because memory cells are already present, and can secrete specific antibodies immediately.

Worked example

Pathogens have antigens that are foreign to the body. When a pathogen enters the body, the body is exposed to these antigens. Describe two responses triggered by the antigens.   **(2 marks)**

The antigens trigger an immune response which causes the production of antibodies.
They also trigger the production of memory lymphocytes.

Now try this

Describe how the immune system of the human body defends against disease.   **(3 marks)**

Immunisation

Immunisation is when you give a person a vaccine to prevent them becoming ill from a disease.

How vaccines work

A **vaccine** contains antigens from the pathogen, often in the form of dead or weakened pathogens.

→ The person's lymphocytes produce antibodies against the pathogen and also memory lymphocytes.

→ If the person becomes infected with the real pathogen, the memory lymphocytes will give a very rapid secondary response to the pathogen. This means the person is very unlikely to become ill.

This form of the pathogen is safe. It is **inactive** and cannot cause the disease in the person receiving the vaccine.

Worked example

(a) The graph shows the number of cases of measles in the UK from 1940 to 2014. A vaccine against measles was introduced in 1968. Give evidence from the graph to support this. **(1 mark)**

The number of cases of measles drops steadily after 1968.

(b) The number of cases of measles was still quite high for some time after 1968. Suggest a reason why. **(2 marks)**

The vaccine may not have been given to all children in 1968 so there were still children who had not been vaccinated. There would also have been some adults who had not been vaccinated and caught measles.

Worked example

Describe how a vaccine can protect you for life. **(2 marks)**

Once you have received the vaccine, the immune system makes antibodies but also memory lymphocytes which stay in the body for a long time. If you ever catch the disease 'for real', these memory cells divide very quickly and produce huge numbers of antibodies.

Worked example

Explain why immunisation only protects you against one particular disease. **(2 marks)**

Each pathogen has a particular antigen. The immune system produces antibodies that are exactly the right shape to fit on to these antigens. Other pathogens have antigens of a different shape, so one kind of antibody cannot bind to a different kind of antigen.

Now try this

1 Describe the difference between a vaccine and immunisation. **(2 marks)**

2 Sometimes a person needs to receive a booster vaccination. Explain the advantage of this. **(2 marks)**

A booster injection is an extra injection given some time after the first one.

Treating infections

Antibiotics can be used to treat bacterial infections.

Antibiotics

Antibiotics are medicines that **kill bacteria** inside the body. Specific bacteria are only killed by a specific antibiotic, so the correct antibiotic must be used. Deaths from bacterial diseases have greatly decreased where antibiotics are used. **Penicillin** is an example of an antibiotic.

Some bacteria are becoming **resistant** to some antibiotics. This means that the antibiotic is no longer effective at killing or inhibiting them.

Worked example

Describe how antibiotics kill bacteria. **(2 marks)**

Antibiotics inhibit cell processes in the bacterium but not the host organism. For example, some antibiotics stop bacterial cell walls forming properly. This does not harm the host animal because animal cells do not have cell walls.

Do not confuse **antibiotics** and **antibodies**. They are very different things!

Effect of antibiotics on bacteria

The effect of antiseptics, antibiotics or plant extracts on the growth of bacteria can be studied on a **bacterial culture** in a **Petri dish**.

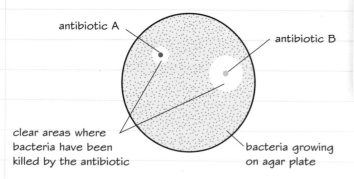

antibiotic A

antibiotic B

clear areas where bacteria have been killed by the antibiotic

bacteria growing on agar plate

Worked example

Look at the agar plate illustrated to the left. Identify which antibiotic was more effective at killing the bacteria. Explain your answer.

(2 marks)

Antibiotic B is more effective because the clear area around it is much bigger than the clear area around antibiotic A. The clear area shows where bacteria have been killed.

Now try this

1 Explain why doctors do not prescribe antibiotics if a patient has a flu virus. **(1 mark)**

2 One antibiotic works by stopping protein synthesis in bacteria but not in human cells. Explain why this antibiotic kills bacteria but is safe to use in humans. **(2 marks)**

New medicines

Medicines are chemicals that are used to treat the cause or signs of an illness. Scientists are continually developing new medicines. New medicines must be extensively tested before doctors can **prescribe** them to patients. There are several steps of testing.

Development and testing

 Discovery

New medicines are **discovered**, e.g. by screening organisms to see if they produce antibiotics that kill bacteria. They are then **developed** through a series of stages.

 Clinical trials: stage 1

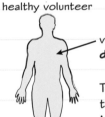

healthy volunteer

very small **dose** of drug

To check that the drug is not **toxic** (harmful).

Medical drugs are prescribed (given) by doctors to help patients who are ill.

 Preclinical testing (in the lab)

cultures of cells   cultures of tissues

animals

Antibiotics are **tested** in the lab to make sure the medicine gets into cells without harming them, and damages pathogens inside cells.

 Clinical trials: stage 2

different doses of drug

patient with the disease that the new drug is developed for

To test **efficacy** (whether it works) and to find the **optimum** dose (the dose that works best).

Worked example

Explain why a new medicine is not tested on lots of people straight away.   **(3 marks)**

This is to make sure there are no harmful side effects and also to make sure it works on people. It would be unethical to give the medicine to lots of people before it was tested for safety and to see if it works on people.

Now try this

There are several different possible answers here, but you only need to think of two of them.

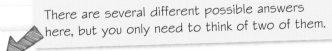

1 Two antibiotics are effective in treating a bacterial infection. When tested on a Petri dish of bacteria, antibiotic A produces a larger clear zone than antibiotic B. Suggest **two** reasons that explain why a doctor chooses to prescribe antibiotic B to a patient.   **(2 marks)**

2 Suggest **one** advantage and **one** disadvantage of using animals as models for testing new drugs rather than direct testing on humans.   **(2 marks)**

Non-communicable diseases

Many non-communicable diseases are caused by the **interaction of several factors**. Having several factors can increase the risk of developing a disease.

Factors that affect the risk of developing non-communicable diseases

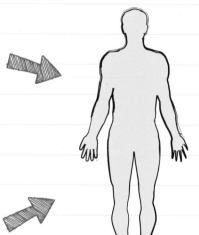

Genes (inherited factors): Different alleles of a gene may be more prone to mutation (e.g. in breast cancer) or how well you absorb nutrients (e.g. in diseases related to diet). These factors may be more common in particular ethnic groups.

Age: The older the body, the more likely that cells may develop mutations which lead to cancer.

Sex: The female hormone oestrogen has protective effects that men do not get.

Environmental: Air pollution can cause lung diseases; poisons in food and drink can damage the body.

Lifestyle factors: The way we live, including diet, alcohol, smoking and exercise, can affect our risk of developing many diseases. You can find out more about lifestyle factors on pages 45 and 46.

Some non-communicable diseases caused by these factors include cancer, cardiovascular (heart) disease, lung and liver diseases, and dietary diseases. Rates of these diseases are different between different groups of people in a country, or in different countries, according to individual exposure to these risk factors.

Worked example

The graph shows the number of deaths from heart disease in the USA for one year.

(a) Describe the effect of age on deaths from heart disease shown in the chart. **(2 marks)**

The death rate from heart disease is at least twice as high in men compared to women until the 75+ age group, when more women die from heart disease than men.

(b) Women produce the hormone oestrogen until the menopause (at about 50). Suggest whether the chart supports the idea that oestrogen can protect against heart disease. **(2 marks)**

The idea is not clearly supported, because the 65–74 category is about the same as the 45–64 group, but it does increase greatly in the 75+ group.

Now try this

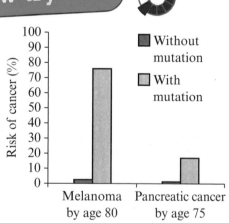

The chart shows the risk of developing some types of cancer. It compares people with a particular mutation in a specific gene with people without this mutation.

(a) Explain why the risk of cancer is shown as a percentage. **(2 marks)**

(b) Do these data support the hypothesis that this mutation increases a person's chance of developing cancer? Explain your answer. **(2 marks)**

Alcohol and smoking

Lifestyle factors including **drinking alcohol** and **smoking** increase the risk of non-communicable diseases by changing how the body works and increasing the levels of **toxins** (poisons) in your body.

Alcohol and disease

Ethanol (found in alcohol) is poisonous to cells. When absorbed from the gut, it passes first to the **liver** to be broken down. So liver cells are more likely than other cells to be damaged, leading to liver disease, e.g. cirrhosis.

This can lead to low birth weight in babies whose mothers smoke.

The damage caused by smoking

Nicotine is addictive.

Carbon monoxide reduces how much oxygen the blood can carry.

Chemicals in **tar** are **carcinogens** that cause cancers, particularly of mouth and lungs.

Substances in cigarettes can cause blood vessels to narrow, increasing blood pressure. This can lead to **cardiovascular diseases** such as heart attack or strokes.

Worked example

Incidence of liver disease per 100 000 people vs Ethanol consumed (litres per person per year)

The graph shows the incidence of liver disease and the mean ethanol consumption per person per year for different countries.

Describe and explain the relationship shown in the graph. **(2 marks)**.

As the amount of alcohol consumed increases, the incidence of liver disease also increases. This is because ethanol is poisonous, particularly to liver cells.

This is a scatter diagram. It is good for showing a link (**correlation**) between two factors. This graph shows a **positive correlation**. You might also see a graph where one factor increases while the other decreases – a **negative correlation**.

Now try this

The table shows the death rate from coronary heart disease in men who smoked different numbers of cigarettes.

Age group	Death rate			
	Non-smokers	Light smokers	Moderate smokers	Heavy smokers
35–54	0.44	0.95	1.47	1.84
55–64	5.34	6.49	6.75	6.98
65–74	10.13	10.77	10.53	14.85
75 and over	15.19	20.00	22.27	24.93

(a) Describe what these data show. **(2 marks)**

(b) Describe how smoking can lead to cardiovascular diseases, such as heart attack or strokes. **(2 marks)**

Malnutrition and obesity

Malnutrition happens when a person eats too much or too little of a nutrient. Too little of some nutrients can lead to **deficiency diseases**. If there is too much energy in the diet and not enough exercise then there will be an increase in body fat. Too much body fat leads to **obesity**.

Measuring obesity

Obesity can be measured by **BMI** or by **waist : hip** ratio.

Waist : hip ratio is calculated using this equation:

$$\text{Waist : hip ratio} = \frac{\text{waist measurement}}{\text{hip measurement}}$$

People with a high waist : hip ratio ('apples') are more at risk of some diseases than those with a lower waist : hip ratio ('pears').

Maths skills **Body mass index (BMI)**

BMI is calculated using this equation:

$$\text{BMI} = \frac{\text{weight in kilograms}}{(\text{height in metres})^2}$$

Adults who have a BMI over 30 are said to be obese.

Obesity is linked with many health problems, including Type 2 diabetes.

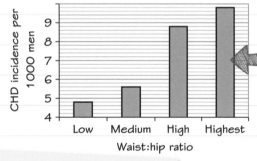

As waist : hip ratio increases, the **risk** of coronary heart disease increases.

CHD = coronary heart disease

Normal waist-to-hip ratios			
	excellent	good	average
males	<0.85	0.85–0.89	0.90–0.95
females	<0.75	0.75–0.79	0.80–0.86

You don't need to know these figures. What you must be able to do is to calculate the waist : hip ratio.

Worked example

A scientific study showed that for a 10 g increase in wholegrain fibre that a person ate each day, there was a 10% decrease in their risk of developing bowel cancer. The scientists concluded that people should eat lots of wholegrain foods every day to help them stay healthy.

Do the results of this study support this conclusion? Give a reason for your answer.

(2 marks)

The results do support this conclusion, because the more fibre the person eats the lower their risk of getting bowel cancer.

You will not be expected to know the effect of fibre in the diet, but you will be expected to answer questions like this about the effect of food on health from data that you are given. You will be given data to work with.

Now try this

1 (a) A man has a waist measurement of 109 cm and a hip measurement of 112 cm. Calculate his waist : hip ratio. **(1 mark)**
   (b) Use the table above to explain whether the man is at a higher than average risk of developing coronary heart disease. **(1 mark)**

2 A 45-year-old woman is 160 cm high and weighs 80 kg. Calculate her BMI and state whether or not she is obese. **(2 marks)**

Cardiovascular disease

Cardiovascular disease may be **treated** using medication, surgery, or by making lifestyle changes.

Lifestyle changes

Doctors will advise the patient to:
- give up smoking
- take more exercise
- eat a healthier diet (lower fat, sugar and salt)
- lose weight.

👍 no side effects

👍 may reduce chances of getting other health conditions

👍 this is the cheapest option

👎 may take time to work or may not work effectively

Medication

If lifestyle changes do not improve the patient's health, the doctor may prescribe **medication**, such as betablockers, to reduce blood pressure.

👍 start working immediately, e.g. to lower blood pressure

👍 easy to do

👍 cheaper and less risky than surgery

👎 need to be taken long term and can have side effects

👎 may not work well with other medication the person is taking

Surgery

If an artery becomes narrowed, the drop in blood flow can cause damage to tissue beyond the blockage. A wire frame, called a **stent**, is inserted into the narrowed part of the artery.

Sometimes **heart by-pass** surgery is carried out, when a new blood vessel is inserted to by-pass blocked coronary arteries.

If the blood supply to the heart muscle is reduced or stopped, the heart muscle cells cannot get enough oxygen for respiration. This means the cells die and the person has a heart attack.

👍 usually a long term solution

👎 there is a risk the person will not recover after the operation

👎 surgery is expensive

👎 more difficult to do than giving medication

👎 there is a risk the person will develop an infection after surgery

---

Worked example

Surgery is usually only carried out if the person has serious heart disease and other treatments will not work. Explain why. **(2 marks)**

When anybody has surgery, there is always a risk that they may not recover, or that the surgery will cause further damage. Therefore it is safer to try making lifestyle changes first, or give the person medication. Surgery is also more expensive. However, for serious heart disease, lifestyle changes and medication are unlikely to solve the problem, so surgery can be given straight away.

 You need to consider the risks and the expense of surgery.

Now try this

Give **three** lifestyle changes that a doctor might recommend to a person with heart disease. **(3 marks)**

Extended response – Health and disease

There will be one or more 6-mark questions on your exam paper. For these questions, you will need to think scientifically and structure your answer logically, showing how the points you make are related to each other. You may wish to revise the topic for this question, which is about **evaluating treatments for heart disease**, on page 47.

Worked example

Stanol esters are made from substances found in plants. Some scientists wanted to find out if stanol esters lower blood cholesterol. They carried out an investigation in which they added stanol esters to margarine and gave it to some people. There was also a control group. The scientists measured the blood cholesterol concentration of each person at regular intervals over several months. The graph shows their results.

Explain how the scientists should have carried out this investigation to get reliable results. **(6 marks)**

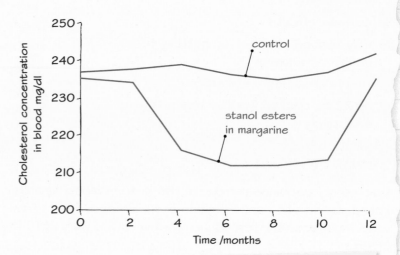

The scientists would need to carry out this investigation with a large number of people, who should be volunteers. They should be divided into two groups, matched by age and sex. One group would be given margarine containing stanol esters and the other group should be given the same margarine without stanol esters in it. The people should not know which group they are in. This is so they cannot know whether they have stanol esters in the margarine they are given. This is to avoid bias.

The scientists should measure the blood cholesterol level of each person before the investigation starts and then every month for a year. After this the scientists should assess the results from the two groups to see whether the stanol esters have reduced the blood cholesterol concentration of the people who ate that margarine compared with the people in the control group.

You might be given the results of a study like this, and be given the question 'A newspaper journalist saw these results and wrote an article entitled "Plant stanol esters in margarine reduce heart disease". Was this a correct conclusion? Give reasons for your answer.' You might be expected to note that the study only shows a reduction in blood cholesterol levels, so this does not show that there has been a reduction in heart disease. Think of other points you might make. There are other factors that should be standardised between groups, like body mass, diet and starting cholesterol level, as these also affect cholesterol levels.

Now try this

Explain how lifestyle factors might increase the chances of a person developing some kinds of cancer.

(6 marks)

Photosynthesis

Photosynthesis is the process that plants and algae use to make their own food. Plants are called **producers** because they produce their own food. Photosynthetic organisms are the main producers of food and therefore **biomass**. Biomass is the mass of living material at a particular stage in a food chain.

Photosynthesis equation

Photosynthesis can be summarised by this equation:

absorbed by **chlorophyll**

> Chlorophyll is a green substance found in the chloroplasts of some plants.

light energy

carbon dioxide + water $\xrightarrow{}$ glucose + oxygen

| from air | from soil | | a sugar | released to air as **by-product** (not needed) |

Remember that during photosynthesis there is an energy transfer from light energy to chemical energy stored in the sugars produced.

Worked example

A student set up six bottles. Each contained the same number of algal balls (gel beads containing algae), and the same volume of hydrogencarbonate indicator solution. The indicator is yellow when carbon dioxide concentration is high, orange-red when carbon dioxide concentration is the same as in normal air, and purple when carbon dioxide concentration is low. The student placed the bottles at different distances from a lamp as shown in the diagram.

After two hours, the bottles were the colours shown in the diagram. Explain the difference in colour between bottles A and B. **(3 marks)**

Bottle A has high light intensity so photosynthesis is occurring much faster than respiration. Therefore the concentration of carbon dioxide is very low. Bottle B is too far away from the light to photosynthesise very fast, but it is respiring, so the concentration of carbon dioxide is very high.

Worked example

Explain why a leaf covered in black paper makes no food.   **(2 marks)**

The black paper stops light from reaching the chlorophyll. Therefore, the leaf cannot use light energy to convert carbon dioxide and water into sugar in photosynthesis.

> Plants make food in photosynthesis, but they can only do this in the light. However, plants respire all the time, whether it is dark or light.

Now try this

1   Explain why photosynthesis is an endothermic reaction.   **(2 marks)**

2   Explain the role of plants as producers of food.   **(4 marks)**

> Remember that 'endothermic' reactions take in energy from the surroundings.

Limiting factors

Low temperature, dim light and low carbon dioxide concentration all limit the rate of photosynthesis. They are all **limiting factors** for photosynthesis.

 Practical skills **Effect of light on rate of photosynthesis**

You can measure the effect of light intensity on the rate of photosynthesis by measuring the rate at which oxygen is given off by a piece of pondweed. You can use the apparatus shown to investigate the effect of light intensity using bright and dim lights.

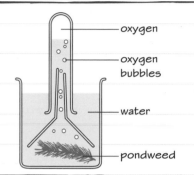

Worked example

The graph shows the rate of photosynthesis of a plant at different light intensities. Explain the shape of the graph at points A and B.   **(4 marks)**

At A, light intensity is limiting photosynthesis, because increasing the light intensity increases the rate of photosynthesis. At B, light intensity is no longer the limiting factor because increasing the light intensity does not change the rate of photosynthesis. Another factor, such as carbon dioxide concentration or temperature, is limiting the rate of photosynthesis.

Increasing only carbon dioxide concentration or temperature, while keeping other factors constant, will produce a similar graph to this.

Carbon dioxide concentration

Once CO_2 concentration is high, another factor is limiting the rate of photosynthesis.

CO_2 is a limiting factor because an increase in its concentration increases the rate of photosynthesis. There is more CO_2 to use to make sugars.

Temperature

If the temperature is too high, enzymes start to denature and the rate of photosynthesis slows down.

Temperature is a limiting factor because an increase in temperature increases the kinetic energy of molecules and increases the rate of enzyme activity making photosynthesis faster.

Now try this

 1 Define the term **limiting factor** in relation to photosynthesis.

   (2 marks)

 2 Explain why measuring the oxygen given off by a plant is a way of measuring the rate of photosynthesis.

   (2 marks)

Light intensity

Practical skills You can investigate the **effect of light intensity on the rate of photosynthesis** by measuring the change in pH of solution around algal balls. The pH changes because carbon dioxide forms an acidic solution, and photosynthesis changes the concentration of carbon dioxide in the solution.

Core practical

algal balls in indicator solution

water

Aim

To investigate how light intensity affects the rate of photosynthesis.

Apparatus

- screw-top bottles (one for each distance)
- algal balls (20 per bottle)
- universal indicator solution
- measuring cylinder
- foil or black paper
- bright lamp
- small tank of water (if lamp is hot)
- metre ruler
- pH colour chart for indicator

Change in the colour of the solution can also be measured as change in absorbance using a colorimeter.

Safety: Take care if using a lamp with a hot bulb.

Method

1. Place 20 algal balls and the same volume of indicator solution in each bottle, and replace the screw tops.
2. Check the colour of the indicator against the colour chart and record the starting pH.
3. If using a hot lamp, place the water tank between the lamp and the bottles.
4. Use the metre ruler to place the bottles at specific distances from the lamp, on the opposite side of the tank.
5. Leave the bottles for 1–2 hours.
6. Record distance and pH of each tube, using the colour chart for identifying the pH.

Using a water tank if the lamp is hot helps control for temperature, which will also vary with distance from the lamp.

Instead of distance, light intensity could be measured directly using a light meter.

Results

Draw a graph to show distance against pH.

Conclusion

As distance increases, light intensity falls and so the rate of photosynthesis decreases. This is because energy transferred by light is needed for photosynthesis to take place.

You need to be able to explain why there are the same number of algal balls in each bottle, why the volume of indicator is the same, and why the bottles are all exactly the same.

Now try this

1. Explain why rate of change in pH is a measure of the rate of photosynthesis in this experiment. **(3 marks)**
2. Explain why using a water tank is important if the lamp has a hot bulb. **(2 marks)**
3. A student covered one tube of algal balls in kitchen foil and placed it close to the tank as an addition to the method above. Explain the purpose of the tube. **(2 marks)**

Specialised plant cells

Some plant cells are **specialised** to carry out specific functions.

Phloem

Phloem contains **sieve tube elements** which have very little cytoplasm so that there is a lot of space to transport sucrose and other nutrients. It also contains **companion cells** which have lots of mitochondria. These supply energy from respiration for **active transport** of sucrose into and out of the sieve tubes.

Sucrose is **translocated** around the plant in the phloem sieve tubes (see page 54 for more on translocation).

Xylem

Xylem vessels are **dead** cells which have no cytoplasm or cell contents. This means there is more space for water containing mineral ions to move through.

They have holes called **pits** in their walls to allow water and mineral ions to move out.

The walls are strengthened with **lignin** rings, which makes them very strong and prevents them from collapsing.

They have no end walls so they form a long tube that water can flow through easily.

The wall that makes the tube is made of lignin.

 Worked example

The diagram shows two root hairs on the outside of a root. Describe how these cells are adapted to take up water and mineral ions. **(2 marks)**

Root hair cells have long extensions that stretch out into the soil. This gives them a large surface area where osmosis can take place, which means that more water molecules can cross the cell membrane into the cell at the same time. This also gives a large surface area for mineral ions to enter the root hair cell by diffusion and active transport.

 Worked example

Explain the meaning of the phrase **active transport**. Use minerals entering roots as your example. **(3 marks)**

Mineral salts cannot enter the root cells from soil water by diffusion because there is a higher concentration of mineral salts in the cells than in the soil. So the root cells have to use energy to transport mineral salts into the cells against their concentration gradient.

 Now try this

1 Explain how the presence of many mitochondria is an adaptation for active transport of mineral ions into roots. **(2 marks)**

2 Describe **three** adaptations of xylem vessels and explain how these adapt the cells for transporting water through the plant. **(6 marks)**

Transpiration

Transpiration is the loss of water by evaporation from the leaves. The movement of water from the roots to the leaves is called the **transpiration stream**.

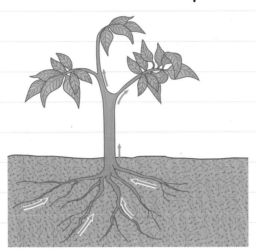

Water vapour evaporates from leaves mainly through the stomata,

↑

draws water out of the leaf cells and xylem,

↑

draws water up the stem through the xylem from the roots,

↑

and causes water to enter the roots by osmosis.

Stomata

Stomata are found mainly on the lower surface of the leaf.

The cell wall is thicker on one side of the cell than on the other.

When guard cells take in water by osmosis, they swell and this causes the stoma to open.

When guard cells lose water, they become flaccid and the stoma closes.

chloroplast — vacuole

cell wall —

stoma —

— nucleus

stoma open

stoma closed

Worked example

Four similar sized leaves were cut from the same plant. The cut end of each leaf-stalk was sealed. The leaves were then covered in petroleum jelly in the following way:

A – the upper surface only was greased
B – the lower surface only was greased
C – both surfaces were greased
D – neither surface was greased.

The mass was re-measured after 24 hours and the % loss of mass of each leaf found after a specific amount of time. The results are shown in the table.

Leaf	% loss in mass
A	40
B	4
C	2
D	43

Describe and explain these results.   **(4 marks)**

Leaves A and D lost the most mass, while B and C lost very little mass. This shows that the leaves that lost the most mass were those that did not have grease on the lower surface. Leaves lose most water through the stomata which causes a loss in mass. Leaves B and C had petroleum jelly covering the stomata so they could not lose water that way. Therefore they lost almost no water.

Do not confuse transpiration with osmosis. Water enters the roots by osmosis, but transpiration is the evaporation of water that 'pulls' water up the plant.

Now try this

1 Define **transpiration**.   **(2 marks)**

2 Describe how water moves from the soil into a plant and evaporates from the leaf.   **(4 marks)**

Stomata are mainly found on the underside of the leaf because it is cooler and shadier, so less water will be lost.

Translocation

Translocation is the transport of **sucrose** and other nutrients around a plant.

Phloem

Dissolved sugars are transported around a plant in phloem.

Plants have two separate transport systems: **xylem** and **phloem**.

dissolved sucrose needed for growth in growing regions, e.g. bud

Sucrose is produced in leaves from glucose formed during photosynthesis.

phloem in plant veins

Dissolved sucrose is carried around the plant in phloem.

storage organ (e.g. potato)

dissolved sugars converted to starch and stored in storage organs so they can be used later

---

Carbon dioxide containing radioactive carbon was supplied to a leaf of a plant as shown in the diagram.

CO₂ supplied to the plant which uses it in photosynthesis

Remember that the phloem transports sugars and organic substances in the plant. See page 52 for more information.

(a) Radioactive carbon atoms will be detected in the phloem. Explain why. **(2 marks)**

The carbon dioxide will be used in photosynthesis to make glucose. Some of the glucose will be converted to sucrose which is transported round the plant in the phloem.

(b) Describe how you could use this investigation to show that sucrose can move both up and down the plant. **(2 marks)**

This will be shown if radioactivity can be detected both above and below the leaf being supplied with radioactive CO₂.

Now try this

1 Name the **two** transport systems found in plants. **(2 marks)**

2 An aphid is an insect pest that inserts needle-like mouthparts into the veins of a plant. It feeds on sugars.
Explain which tissue in the veins the aphid feeds from. **(2 marks)**

Remember that sugars can be transported both upwards and downwards in a plant.

3 A young potato plant grows rapidly during the spring and summer. In the autumn it develops new potatoes, which are storage organs. State and explain which way sucrose moves in the phloem during the autumn, when new potatoes are developing. **(3 marks)**

Water uptake in plants

Environmental factors can change the rate of water uptake in plants.

Factors that affect transpiration

Factor	Effect on transpiration
light intensity	High light intensity causes the stomata to open. This increases the rate of evaporation of water from the leaf so more water is taken up to replace this.
air movement	Wind blows moist air away from the stomata, keeping the diffusion gradient high. So the more air movement there is, the higher the transpiration rate.
temperature	The higher the temperature, the more energy water molecules have, so they move faster which means a faster rate of transpiration.

Using a potometer

You can measure the **rate** of transpiration using a **potometer**.

1 Note the position of the air bubble on the ruler at the start of the investigation.

2 Note the position of the bubble on the ruler after a known number of minutes.

3 Divide the distance moved by the bubble by the time taken.

Rate of transpiration can be measured as

$$\frac{\text{distance moved}}{\text{time taken}}$$

reservoir for pushing air bubble to right-hand end of capillary tube

rubber stopper

capillary tube with scale

air bubble

Worked example

Three identical potted plants were watered and their mass recorded. Their pots were wrapped and sealed in plastic bags so that only the plant was in the open air. Each plant was then placed in different conditions. After 6 hours, the bags were removed and the mass of the plants was recorded again. The table shows the results.

(a) Calculate the percentage change in mass for plants B and C. **(2 marks)**

Mass in g	Plant A (cool, still air)	Plant B (warm, still air)	Plant C (warm, windy)
at start	436	452	448
at end	412	398	332
% change	−5.5	−11.9	−25.9

(b) Explain the differences in results. **(2 marks)**

The results show that evaporation of water from the plant was faster in warm air than cool air and even faster in windy air than in still air. This is because evaporation from the stomata is faster in hot and windy conditions.

Now try this

A student places a leafy shoot in a potometer. The bubble in the capillary tube moves 50 mm in 5 minutes.

(a) Calculate the rate of transpiration in mm/min. **(1 mark)**

(b) Explain why the bubble moves faster in warmer conditions. **(2 marks)**

(c) Describe how you would carry out this investigation to make sure the results in the two different conditions could be compared. **(2 marks)**

Think about what would make the comparison a fair one.

Extended response – Plant structures and functions

There will be one or more 6-mark questions on your exam paper. For these questions, you will need to think scientifically and structure your answer logically, showing how the points you make are related to each other. You can revise the topics for this question, which is about the **effect of environmental factors on transpiration rate**, on page 55.

Worked example

A student watered a pot plant and placed it on a sunny windowsill. By the early afternoon the plant had wilted. A few hours later, when the air was cooler, the plant had recovered and was fully upright again.

Explain these observations. **(6 marks)**

wilted plant   recovered plant

Plants absorb water from the soil through their roots and lose it through stomata in their leaves by evaporation in a process called transpiration.

The rate of evaporation of water from the leaf surface increases as temperature increases, because water molecules move around faster. When the temperature was high, the rate of evaporation from the leaves was faster than the rate of absorption of water from the soil. This meant there was not enough water in the plant cells to keep them strong and support the upper part of the plant, so the plant wilted.

When the plant was cooler, the rate of evaporation of water from the leaves decreased. The rate of absorption of water from the soil was then fast enough to fill all cells with water so the stems were strong enough to stand upright and support the leaves.

A good start to this answer is to identify the processes that are involved in the question.

To answer this question well, you need to explain clearly how changes in temperature affect the rate of evaporation of water from leaves. Remember to link ideas to explanations with words such as **because**, or **this means that**.

There are two situations that need to be explained in this answer: when the plant was hot, and when it was cooler. Arranging the explanations in time sequence helps to make the answer clearer.

You do not have to explain how structure is related to function when answering this question. You can revise xylem and phloem on page 52.

Now try this

Xylem and phloem are involved in transporting substances in plants.
Compare and contrast these two tissues in terms of their functions and structures. **(6 marks)**

Hormones

Hormones are 'chemical messengers' that target organs in the body.

Production and transport

Hormones are produced by **endocrine glands** and released into the blood. They travel around the body in the blood until they reach their **target organs**. Each hormone causes its target organ(s) to respond, e.g. by releasing another chemical substance.

Different hormones have different target organs and cause different responses.

Hormones and nerves

Nerves and hormones both help you to respond to changes in the environment and in your body. Hormones usually have a long-lived effect while nerves have a short-term effect. Nerve impulses work quickly while hormones take longer to work.

Release of hormones

Different endocrine glands produce different hormones.

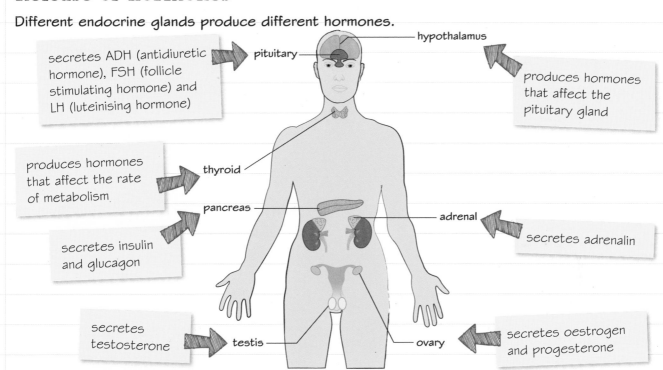

secretes ADH (antidiuretic hormone), FSH (follicle stimulating hormone) and LH (luteinising hormone) → pituitary

hypothalamus → produces hormones that affect the pituitary gland

produces hormones that affect the rate of metabolism → thyroid

secretes insulin and glucagon → pancreas

adrenal → secretes adrenalin

secretes testosterone → testis

ovary → secretes oestrogen and progesterone

Complete the table to show the target organs for each hormone.

(7 marks)

Remember: a target organ is where the hormone **acts**, not where it is produced.

Hormone	Target organ(s)
ADH	kidney
FSH and LH	ovaries
insulin and glucagon	liver, muscle and adipose tissue
adrenalin	various organs, e.g. heart, liver, skin
progesterone	uterus
oestrogen	ovaries, uterus, pituitary gland
testosterone	male reproductive organs

Now try this

1 State what a **hormone** is. **(2 marks)**

2 Give **two** differences between nervous and hormonal communication. **(2 marks)**

The menstrual cycle

Between puberty and about the age of 50, women have a **menstrual cycle** that occurs about every 28 days. During the cycle, changes take place in the ovaries and the uterus.

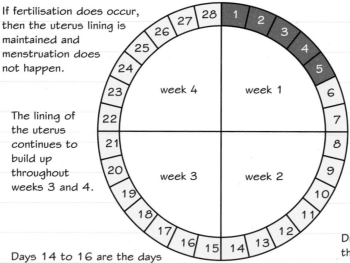

If fertilisation does occur, then the uterus lining is maintained and menstruation does not happen.

The lining of the uterus continues to build up throughout weeks 3 and 4.

Days 14 to 16 are the days when **fertilisation** is most likely to take place.

Menstruation is the breakdown of the uterus lining. It begins on day 1 of the cycle and usually lasts about 5 days.

Oestrogen and **progesterone** are two of the hormones that control the menstrual cycle.

During the second week, the lining of the **uterus** is gradually built up.

Ovulation is the release of an egg from an ovary. This usually takes place around day 14.

If fertilisation occurs, the uterus lining remains thick so that the embryo can embed in the lining and obtain the nutrients it needs.

Contraception

Contraception is the prevention of fertilisation. **Hormonal contraception** includes hormone pills, implants or injections, and works by releasing hormones to prevent ovulation and thicken mucus at the cervix, preventing sperm from passing. **Barrier methods** include male and female condoms, the diaphragm, caps and sponges. These work by stopping the sperm from reaching the egg.

Worked example

Give one advantage and one disadvantage of hormonal contraceptives compared with condoms.   **(2 marks)**

Hormonal contraceptives are more effective than condoms at preventing pregnancy. However, condoms protect against sexually transmitted diseases (STIs) but hormonal contraceptives do not.

Different methods have different success rates at preventing pregnancy when used correctly. Condoms = 98%, diaphragm/cap = 92–96%, hormonal methods = >99%.

Now try this

 1 Give a reason why failure to menstruate may be the first sign of pregnancy.   **(1 mark)**

 2 Some women who use hormonal contraception take a pill every day. Another method is to have an implant that releases hormones slowly over a longer period of time. Suggest **one** advantage and **one** disadvantage of an implant compared with a daily pill.   **(2 marks)**

Blood glucose regulation

Homeostasis maintains conditions inside the body at more or less constant levels, in response to internal and external changes. **Blood glucose** regulation is an example of homeostasis. The hormone **insulin** helps to control blood glucose concentration.

Pancreatic control

This is an example of **negative feedback** because a change away from the normal level (increase in blood glucose) triggers a response (release of insulin) that returns blood glucose to the normal level.

Worked example

The graph shows the changes in blood glucose concentration of a person who has just had a meal.

Describe what is happening.   **(3 marks)**

At A the person has just had a meal, so the carbohydrates are being digested and absorbed into the blood as glucose. This causes the blood glucose concentration to increase.

At B insulin has been secreted from the pancreas which converts glucose to glycogen. Therefore, the blood glucose concentration is falling.

Remember to refer to the graph when you answer a question like this.

Worked example

A doctor wanted to test a patient's blood glucose concentration. The patient was told to have nothing to eat, and only water to drink, for eight hours before the test. Explain why.

   (2 marks)

This makes sure that the glucose concentration in the blood is not affected by food or drink the person has recently consumed.

Now try this

 1 Name the endocrine gland that secretes insulin and the target organ that the hormone affects.   **(2 marks)**

 2 The control of blood glucose concentration is an example of negative feedback. Explain why.   **(2 marks)**

It may help to look back at page 57.

Diabetes

A person who cannot control their blood glucose concentration properly has a condition known as **diabetes**. There are two main types of diabetes.

Type 1 diabetes

- **Cause**: The immune system has damaged the person's insulin-secreting pancreatic cells, so the person does not produce **insulin**.
- **Control**: They have to inject insulin into the fat just below the skin. They have to work out the right amount of insulin to inject so that the blood glucose concentration is kept within safe limits.

Type 2 diabetes

- **Cause**: The person does produce insulin but their liver and muscle cells have become **resistant** to it.
- **Control**: Most people can control their blood glucose concentration by eating foods that contain less sugar, exercising and using medication if needed.

 Maths skills A person's **Body Mass Index (BMI)** is calculated using the equation:

$$BMI = \frac{\text{weight (kg)}}{(\text{height (m)})^2}$$

 You may be asked to evaluate data on the correlation between Type 2 diabetes and BMI or waist : hip ratio.

There are other factors that are linked to diabetes, apart from obesity. These include ethnic group, type of diet eaten and activity levels. The effect of exercise and diet is covered on page 46.

Worked example

Use the graph to evaluate the correlation between obesity and Type 2 diabetes. **(3 marks)**

 'Evaluate' here means that you have to say how strong the link is between these factors, giving reasons.

Sample sizes
men: 51 529
women: 114 281

The risk of developing Type 2 diabetes increases as BMI increases. It increases faster for women than for men. The large sample sizes and the smooth curves suggest that this is a strong correlation.

Now try this

1 Explain why the dose of insulin needed by a person with Type 1 diabetes will vary, depending on the food eaten and exercise. **(3 marks)**

2 Explain why Type 2 diabetes is not usually treated by giving insulin injections. **(2 marks)**

Extended response – Control and coordination

There will be one or more 6-mark questions on your exam paper. For these questions, you will need to think scientifically and structure your answer logically, showing how the points you make are related to each other. You can revise the topics for this question, which is about the **link between BMI and type 2 diabetes**, on page 60.

Worked example

The chart shows the results of a survey of adults in the UK who have Type 2 diabetes. The results are grouped by BMI category for men and for women.

Use the chart to explain how controlling weight could affect the occurrence of Type 2 diabetes.

(6 marks)

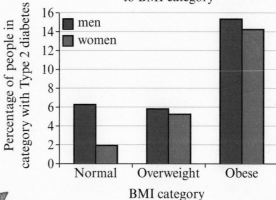

How Type 2 diabetes is related to BMI category

BMI is a measure of body mass (weight) and is calculated by dividing mass by height squared. As the amount of body fat increases, BMI increases. People with a BMI over 30 are said to be obese.

People with Type 2 diabetes are not able to control their blood glucose concentration properly because their pancreatic cells do not produce enough insulin, or because their muscle and liver cells do not respond properly to insulin.

A good start to answering this question is to show that you understand what terms in the question (BMI and Type 2 diabetes) mean.

The chart shows that the risk of developing Type 2 diabetes increases as BMI increases, both for men and for women. The risk for women increases more rapidly than for men when their BMI reaches the overweight category.

Before directly answering the question, you should explain what the graph shows. As well as describing trends shown by the bars on the graph, make sure you identify differences. Using values from the graph can show how well you understand the graph.

If people control their weight so they do not develop a high BMI, then they should keep their risk of developing Type 2 diabetes low. This beneficial effect will be greater for women than for men.

As there are two categories on the graph (men and women), you need to explain how they respond differently to controlling weight.

The chart shows men and women in the UK only. So this conclusion may not be the same for people in other countries, or different ethnic groups, or for other variables such as exercise or diet.

This point evaluates the link, showing why the the conclusion may not apply in different studies.

Now try this

Explain how blood glucose concentration is regulated in a healthy person.

(6 marks)

Exchanging materials

Substances such as oxygen, carbon dioxide, water, dissolved food molecules, mineral ions and urea need to be **transported** into and out of organisms.

How substances are exchanged

The table below shows different substances that need to be transported, where this happens and why.

More complex organisms

As organisms get **bigger**, their surface area to volume ratio gets **smaller**. This means they cannot rely on diffusion. They need to have specialised **exchange surfaces** and **transport systems**.

Substance	Site of exchange	Reason for exchange
oxygen	alveoli in lungs	needed for respiration
carbon dioxide	alveoli in lungs	waste product of metabolism
water	nephrons in kidney	needed for cells to function properly
dissolved food molecules	small intestine	needed for respiration
mineral ions	small intestine	needed for cells to function properly
urea	nephrons in kidney	waste product of metabolism

Worked example

(a) Complete the table to calculate some measurements relating to cubes of different side lengths. **(3 marks)**

Length of one side of cube (cm)	Surface area of cube (cm^2)	Volume of cube (cm^3)	Surface area : volume ratio
1	6	1	6
2	24	8	3
3	54	27	2
4	96	64	1.5

Adaptations for exchange

Special organs are adapted to make exchange efficient. For example, the **lungs** are adapted to exchange gases, and the **small intestine** is adapted to exchange solutes.

(b) Describe the pattern shown by these data. **(1 mark)**

As the length of one side of the cube increases, the surface area to volume ratio falls.

Maths skills Do not just talk about the surface area – it is the surface area to volume ratio that is important.

Now try this

1 Name **one** human organ that is specially adapted for exchanging substances with the environment. **(1 mark)**

2 The flatworm shown in this diagram is multicellular but it does not have an exchange system or a transport system. Explain why. **(3 marks)**

Look at the shape of the flatworm and think about its surface area to volume ratio.

Alveoli

Alveoli are adapted for **gas exchange** by diffusion between air in the lungs and blood in capillaries.

The lungs

The **lungs** are part of the breathing system. The breathing system takes air into and out of the body. In the lungs:
- oxygen diffuses from the air into the blood
- carbon dioxide diffuses from the blood into the air.

(There is more about diffusion on page 10.)

The lungs are **adapted** for efficient gas exchange.

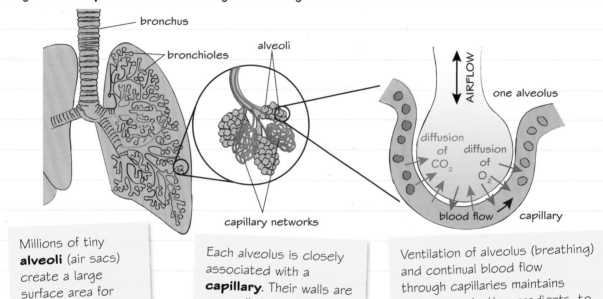

Millions of tiny **alveoli** (air sacs) create a large surface area for **diffusion** of gases.

Each alveolus is closely associated with a **capillary**. Their walls are one cell thick, minimising diffusion distance.

Ventilation of alveolus (breathing) and continual blood flow through capillaries maintains high concentration gradients, to maximise rate of diffusion.

Worked example

In some lung infections, fluid builds up inside the alveoli. Explain why this makes it harder for the person to breathe properly.   **(3 marks)**

This reduces the surface area of the alveoli over which diffusion can take place and so decreases the rate of gas exchange.

This question says 'Explain...', so your answer needs to specifically refer to how the function of the lung will be disrupted. You should try to use correct scientific language throughout.

Now try this

1   State **one** way in which the air breathed out is different from the air breathed in.   **(1 mark)**

2   People who smoke have fewer alveoli, and the alveoli are large. Explain why smokers may sometimes become short of breath.   **(2 marks)**

3   Explain the advantage of the alveoli having many capillaries around them.   **(2 marks)**

You need to consider both what the body needs to take in and what it needs to lose.

Blood

Blood is made of four main parts: **plasma**, **red blood cells**, **white blood cells** and **platelets**. Each part of the blood has a particular **function** (job).

Blood plasma

Plasma is the liquid part of blood:
- It carries the blood cells through the blood vessels.
- It contains many dissolved substances, such as carbon dioxide and glucose.

plasma (55%)

white blood cells and platelets (<1%)

red blood cells (45%)

White blood cells

White blood cells are larger than red blood cells, and they have a nucleus. All types of white blood cells are part of the **immune system**, which attacks pathogens in the body.

white blood cell

pathogen

Some white blood cells (**phagocytes**) surround (**ingest**) pathogens and destroy them.

antibodies

pathogen

Some white blood cells (**lymphocytes**) produce chemical **antibodies** that attach to pathogens and destroy them.

Platelets

Platelets are fragments of larger cells. They have no nucleus. Their function is to cause blood to clot when a blood vessel has been damaged. The clot blocks the wound and prevents pathogens getting into the blood.

Worked example

Explain how the structure of a red blood cell (erythrocyte) is related to its function.

(4 marks)

Red blood cells contain haemoglobin which carries oxygen. The biconcave shape of a red blood cell means it has a large surface area. This means it is easier for oxygen to diffuse into and out of the cell. The cell has no nucleus. This means the cell has room for more haemoglobin to carry more oxygen.

Biconcave means the cell is dimpled on both sides so that it is thinner in the middle than at the edges.

Now try this

1 Respiring cells need oxygen and glucose. State which parts of the blood carry each of these substances. **(2 marks)**

2 Describe **one** way in which the structure of a phagocyte is related to its function. **(2 marks)**

Blood vessels

There are three types of **blood vessels** – **arteries**, **veins** and **capillaries**. Their structure is related to their function.

Veins

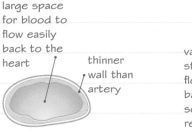

large space for blood to flow easily back to the heart

thinner wall than artery

valves to stop blood flowing backwards, so that it is returned to the heart

vein (cross-section)

vein (long section)

Arteries

space where blood flows

thick wall of muscle and elastic fibres

artery (cross-section)

Exchange in capillaries

Substances are exchanged between the body cells and blood in **capillaries**. Capillaries are **adapted** for their function of exchanging substances between the blood and body cells.

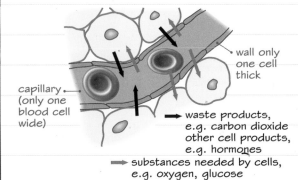

wall only one cell thick

capillary (only one blood cell wide)

→ waste products, e.g. carbon dioxide other cell products, e.g. hormones
⇒ substances needed by cells, e.g. oxygen, glucose

Worked example

Describe the role of arteries, veins and capillaries in the human circulatory system.   **(3 marks)**

Arteries carry blood away from the heart – all arteries except the pulmonary arteries carry oxygenated blood to the body. Veins carry blood towards the heart – all veins except the pulmonary veins carry deoxygenated blood from the body back towards the heart. Capillaries exchange materials, such as oxygen, glucose and carbon dioxide, with body tissues.

Remember: a key function of blood is to deliver oxygen and glucose to cells for respiration and to remove the carbon dioxide produced by respiration from cells.

Now try this

1 (a) Which is the narrowest blood vessel?

☐ **A** artery   ☐ **B** capillary   ☐ **C** heart   ☐ **D** vein   **(1 mark)**

(b) Which type of blood vessel has the thickest wall?

☐ **A** artery   ☐ **B** capillary   ☐ **C** vein   ☐ **D** all the same   **(1 mark)**

2 Explain why almost every body cell is very close to a capillary.   **(4 marks)**

Think carefully about the key function of blood, and what body cells need to survive.

The heart

The **heart** pumps blood round the body. The heart and the blood vessels together make up the **circulatory system**, which delivers oxygen and nutrients such as glucose to all parts of the body.

Structure and function of the heart

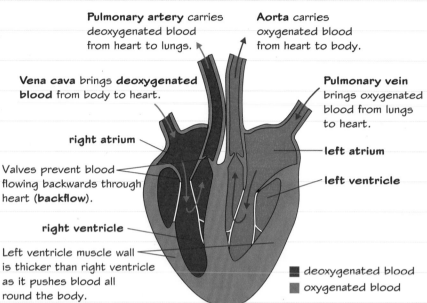

Pulmonary artery carries deoxygenated blood from heart to lungs.

Aorta carries oxygenated blood from heart to body.

Vena cava brings **deoxygenated blood** from body to heart.

Pulmonary vein brings oxygenated blood from lungs to heart.

right atrium

left atrium

Valves prevent blood flowing backwards through heart (**backflow**).

left ventricle

right ventricle

Left ventricle muscle wall is thicker than right ventricle as it pushes blood all round the body.

■ deoxygenated blood
■ oxygenated blood

The sides of the heart are labelled left and right as if you were looking at the person. So the left side of the heart is on the right side of the diagram.

Remember – arteries take blood away from the heart, veins bring it back in to the heart.

Blood circulation

Valves in the heart make the blood flow in the right direction.

| Blood enters the atria. | → | The atria contract, forcing blood into the ventricles. | → | The ventricles contract, forcing blood into the arteries. | → | Blood flows through arteries to the organs and returns to the heart through veins. |

There are two circulation systems: one through the lungs and one through all the other organs.

Worked example

Explain how the structure of the heart adapts it to circulate blood effectively to the lungs and body. **(4 marks)**

Blood returning to the heart from the body is low in oxygen. This enters the right side of the heart and is pumped to the lungs by the right ventricle. It becomes saturated with oxygen in the lungs. The blood then enters the left side of the heart

so it does not mix with the blood that is low in oxygen on the other side of the heart.

The left ventricle has a very thick muscular wall to pump the blood all the way round the body. There is a double circulation because blood passes through the heart twice to make a complete circulation round the body, making sure the pressure of the blood never falls too low.

Now try this

1 Give **one** reason why there are valves in the heart. **(1 mark)**

2 The muscular wall of the left ventricle of the heart is much thicker than that of the right ventricle. Explain the reason for this difference. **(3 marks)**

Aerobic respiration

Cellular respiration is a process that releases energy from glucose for use in cellular activities. The main type of cellular respiration is **aerobic respiration**, which uses oxygen.

Aerobic respiration

Aerobic respiration is a series of chemical reactions that take place mostly inside mitochondria in the cell. This is an **exothermic** process because it releases energy. This happens continuously in living cells. It is the main source of energy for cells.

Make sure you use the phrase 'releases energy' when describing the function of respiration.

broken down   releases energy

glucose + oxygen → carbon dioxide + water

a sugar   from air

The need for air makes this respiration 'aerobic'.

Use of energy from respiration

In animals:
• for metabolic processes to build larger molecules from smaller ones, e.g. proteins from amino acids, large carbohydrates (e.g. starch, glycogen) from small sugars (e.g. glucose), fats from fatty acids and glycerol
• to enable muscle contraction
• in birds and mammals, also to maintain steady body temperature in colder surroundings.

In plants and animals:
• to build larger molecules from smaller ones, e.g. sugars, nitrates and other nutrients into amino acids, which are then used to make proteins.

 Worked example

The graph shows the concentration of oxygen and carbon dioxide dissolved in the water of an aquarium that contains only pond weed. Explain the shape of the carbon dioxide curve. **(2 marks)**

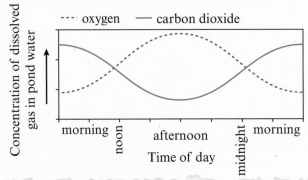

Carbon dioxide concentration increases during the evening and night because it is produced by respiration. Plants need to respire all the time. Carbon dioxide concentration falls during the hours of daylight when carbon dioxide is used in photosynthesis.

This question requires you to use knowledge about photosynthesis and respiration.

 Now try this

1 Define the term aerobic respiration. **(2 marks)**

 2 Give **two** processes that rely on energy from respiration. **(2 marks)**

Anaerobic respiration

During exercise, energy needed for muscle contraction comes from **aerobic respiration**. If there is not enough oxygen, or aerobic respiration is not possible, **anaerobic respiration** takes place.

How anaerobic respiration works

anaerobic respiration = incomplete breakdown of glucose to release energy

does not use oxygen → can supply energy to muscles when there is not enough oxygen for aerobic respiration

in muscle cells, produces lactic acid → blood flowing through muscles then removes the lactic acid

much less energy released per molecule of glucose than during aerobic respiration

extra oxygen is required to oxidise lactic acid to carbon dioxide and water after exercise

In **plants and fungal cells**, there is a different form of anaerobic respiration that produces ethanol. However, like anaerobic respiration in animals:

* it involves breakdown of glucose
* no oxygen is used
* less energy is released per glucose molecule.

Differences between aerobic and anaerobic respiration

Aerobic respiration	Anaerobic respiration
requires oxygen	does not require oxygen
releases a lot of energy	releases much less energy
glucose broken down completely	glucose only partly broken down to lactic acid
occurs mostly in mitochondria	does not occur in mitochondria

Worked example

The graph shows how the concentration of lactic acid in the blood varies with level of exercise.

Exercise output in watts

Explain what the graph shows. **(2 marks)**

As the exercise level increases up to point A, blood lactic acid concentration stays the same. This is because the energy for the exercise is coming from aerobic respiration.

As the exercise level increases beyond point A, blood lactic acid concentration increases. This is because aerobic respiration cannot supply enough energy and the rate of anaerobic respiration increases, producing more lactic acid.

Now try this

1 Explain why human muscle cells cannot function on anaerobic respiration alone. **(2 marks)**

2 State why anaerobic respiration releases much less energy than aerobic respiration. **(1 mark)**

Rate of respiration

 Practical skills You need to understand how **the rate of respiration in living organisms can be investigated.** This experiment can use small invertebrates (e.g. maggots, woodlice) or germinating peas. See page 67 for more information on respiration.

Worked example

The diagram below shows a **respirometer**, which is used for investigating rates of respiration.

screw clip – closed after 10 minutes

clamp

coloured liquid – this liquid moves as oxygen is taken up by the germinating seeds during respiration

soda lime – absorbs carbon dioxide

germinating seeds

stand

(a) Explain the function of the soda lime in the respirometer. **(2 marks)**

Soda lime absorbs carbon dioxide produced by the seeds during respiration, so that it does not affect the movement of the liquid blob.

(b) Explain why the liquid blob moves during the experiment. **(2 marks)**

Oxygen is absorbed from the surrounding air by the germinating seeds. This reduces the volume of air in the container, so the blob will move towards the container.

(c) Explain how this respirometer could be used to measure rate of respiration of the seeds. **(2 marks)**

The distance that the liquid blob moves over a particular time could be measured, and a rate calculated by dividing distance by time.

Safety and living organisms

You must consider the safe and ethical use of working with living organisms. You should minimise harm to small invertebrates, and return them to their natural environment as soon as possible. You should also wash your hands thoroughly after working with living organisms.

Factors affecting respiration

Remember that respiration is affected by environmental factors, particularly temperature, and that microorganisms also respire. So the investigation will need controls.

Control for temperature – e.g. by keeping respirometers in a water bath during the experiment.

Control for something other than the study organisms affecting the gas volume – e.g. by using the same volume of an inert substance as the organisms, such as glass beads instead of seeds.

 Maths skills $rate = \dfrac{change}{time}$

In this case the change measured could be the amount of oxygen absorbed. In other investigations, you might measure the amount of carbon dioxide produced.

Now try this

The table shows the results of an investigation in which respirometers containing woodlice were kept at different temperatures. The uptake of oxygen in each respirometer was measured at the end of 20 min.

(a) Calculate the rate of oxygen uptake per min for each respirometer. **(2 marks)**

(b) Draw a graph to show rate of oxygen uptake against temperature. **(4 marks)**

(c) Describe the relationship shown by this experiment. **(2 marks)**

Temperature (°C)	Volume of gas absorbed in 20 min (cm³)
5	0.6
10	1.0
15	1.7
20	2.4

Changes in heart rate

On this page you will revise the formula **cardiac output = stroke volume × heart rate**.

Effects of exercise

When you exercise, your **heart rate** increases. The harder you exercise, the more your heart rate increases. Heart rate can be measured by taking your **pulse** at the wrist. It is usually measured as number of **beats per minute**.

During exercise, muscle cells are respiring faster. This means that they need more oxygen and glucose, and release more carbon dioxide. A faster heart rate means that blood is pumped faster around the body. The blood takes oxygen and glucose to cells faster and removes carbon dioxide faster.

Exercise and the heart

When you exercise, your stroke volume increases. This is because the heart muscle pumps more strongly. As more deoxygenated blood passes back into the heart, this stretches the walls of the ventricles. In time, this causes the ventricles to become thicker and more powerful, so that the stroke volume is increased even when the person is not exercising. Therefore a trained athlete, when at rest, has a lower heart rate than a non-athlete.

Worked example

The table shows the stroke volume and heart rate for two people at rest.   **(2 marks)**

	Stroke volume (cm³)	Heart rate (beats per minute)
trained athlete	90	55
untrained person	60	70

Calculate the cardiac output for these two people.

athlete: 90 × 55 = 4950 cm³ per minute
untrained person: 60 × 70 = 4200 cm³ per minute

 Maths skills cardiac output = stroke volume × heart rate

Stroke volume is the volume of blood pumped by the heart in one beat.

Now try this

1 Describe how heart rate varies with level of exercise.   **(2 marks)**

2 A person has a cardiac output of 4500 cm³ per minute and a resting heart rate of 75 beats per minute.
Calculate their stroke volume.   **(2 marks)**

3 Suggest why a trained athlete may have a similar cardiac output to an untrained person but a lower resting heart rate.   **(2 marks)**

 Maths skills Rates are always how often something happens in a particular time period. So heart rate is how many times the heart beats in a minute.

Always show your working. This means the examiner can still give you credit for the right method even if your maths is wrong.

Extended response – Exchange

There will be one or more 6-mark questions on your exam paper. For these questions, you will need to think scientifically and structure your answer logically, showing how the points you make are related to each other. You can revise the topics for this question, which is about **aerobic respiration** and **anaerobic respiration**, on pages 67 and 68.

Worked example

Athletes who run a marathon race usually keep their rate of running within their 'aerobic zone' for most of the race, but sprint anaerobically as they get close to the end of the race. Compare and contrast the use of aerobic and anaerobic respiration in marathon racing.　**(6 marks)**

Aerobic respiration and anaerobic respiration both release energy from the breakdown of glucose. This energy can be transferred to muscle cells so that they can contract. Aerobic respiration requires oxygen from the air and produces carbon dioxide and water. Anaerobic respiration in muscle cells needs no oxygen and produces lactic acid.

In a long race, staying aerobic is important because more energy is released from each glucose molecule than in anaerobic respiration. This means the athlete has more energy for contracting muscle cells.

At the end of the race, aerobic respiration will not be able to supply extra energy for the sprint because there is a limit to how fast the heart and lungs can deliver oxygen to the muscle cells. So anaerobic respiration provides the extra energy needed for the sprint.

Command words: Compare and contrast

The answer to a **compare and contrast** question should identify similarities and differences between all the examples in the question. No conclusion needs to be drawn from the comparison.

This answer is well organised because it starts by identifying how aerobic and anaerobic respiration are similar, and then describes how they are different.

The question describes two stages of running, so the answer needs to describe what happens in both stages.

Remember that it is not a case of **either** aerobic **or** anaerobic respiration in human muscle cells. Aerobic respiration continues as fast as it can with the oxygen available, while anaerobic respiration provides the extra energy needed.

Answer the question using information in the diagrams and your own knowledge and understanding. You can revise blood vessels on page 65.

Now try this

Arteries carry blood from the heart, and veins carry blood towards the heart. The capillaries exchange substances with the body tissues. The diagram shows cross-sections through these blood vessels. Describe how the structure of each type of blood vessel is related to its function.　**(6 marks)**

artery　　vein　　capillary

lumen

5–20 μm diameter

Ecosystems and abiotic factors

Ecosystems are organised into different levels. At the level of **communities**, both **abiotic** (non-living) and **biotic** (living) factors can have an effect. You will look at abiotic factors on this page, and biotic factors on page 73.

Levels of organisation in an ecosystem

 organism ← **Organism** is a single living individual.

 population ← **Population** is all the organisms of the same species in an area.

 community ← **Community** is all the populations in an area.

 ecosystem ← **Ecosystem** is all the living organisms (the community) and the non-living components in an area.

All organisms in an ecosystem are **dependent** on other organisms for food, shelter and so on. Remember to think about the impact of this in questions about ecosystems.

Factors that affect distribution

Factors in the environment affect living organisms and their **distribution** (how widely spread they are). Changes in these factors may change their distribution.

environmental factors

living factors, e.g.
• prey
• competitor
• predator

non-living factors, e.g.
• light
• average temperature
• average rainfall
• oxygen levels in water
• pollution

A change in average temperature or rainfall may change the distribution of organisms in an area.

Oxygen levels are high in unpolluted water and low in polluted water.

A **pollutant** is energy or a chemical substance that has a harmful effect on living organisms.

Changes in non-living factors can be measured using equipment, e.g. oxygen meter, thermometer, rainfall gauge. For example, temperature affects the rates of reactions and light intensity affects the rate of photosynthesis.

Worked example

Nettle plants grow taller when they are under a large tree compared with those growing in open ground. Suggest a reason for this difference. **(2 marks)**

Under the tree, the light intensity is lower. Therefore, the plant grows taller so it has more leaves to trap available light.

There are other abiotic factors that you could suggest instead.

Now try this

The pygmy shrew is Britain's smallest mammal. It weighs only 2.3–5 g and its length (head and body) is only 40–55 mm. It can only live in southern Britain because the rest of the country is too cold. Explain why the pygmy shrew cannot survive in cold places. **(2 marks)**

This question is asking you to apply principles you have learned (for example, about surface area and volume ratios) to an unfamiliar example.

Biotic factors

You have seen how abiotic factors can affect communities. So can **biotic factors**. Biotic factors are factors that involve living organisms, e.g. **competition** and **predation**.

Deterring predators

Many organisms are the food of other organisms. Some animals and plants have special features that deter **predators**.

Some animals advertise that they are poisonous with very bright colours.

Some animals use colours to make them look more frightening, like these big 'eyes'.

Some plants have big thorns.

Other plants are poisonous.

Competition

Organisms need a supply of materials from their surroundings, and sometimes from other living organisms, so that they can survive and reproduce. This means there is **competition** between organisms for materials that are in limited supply.

... between plants

competition for light and space

competition for water and nutrients

... between animals

Animals may compete with each other for:
• food
• mates for reproduction
• **territory** (space for feeding, reproduction and rearing young).

Worked example

You will be expected to know the factors that organisms are competing for in a real-life situation.

(a) In spring, a male robin will sing loudly. Explain the role of singing in robins in terms of competition. **(2 marks)**

A male robin competes with other male robins for mates (females) and for territory. Singing loudly warns other males to keep out of the robin's territory and attracts females who choose to mate with him.

(b) The ground underneath the trees in a wood is mostly bare. Explain why very few plants can grow here. **(2 marks)**

There is very little light underneath the trees in a wood. Plants are unable to compete with the trees for the sunlight.

Now try this

1 A farmer plants the seeds of his crop plants so that they are well separated from each other. Explain why. **(2 marks)**

2 Milk snakes are non-poisonous snakes. Coral snakes are highly poisonous. Milk snakes that live in the same area as coral snakes have a bold red and black pattern that is similar to that of the coral snakes. Suggest the advantage to the milk snake of this patterning. **(2 marks)**

Remember to use technical vocabulary in your answer, for example, 'competition'.

Although you may be given an unfamiliar context like this you should be able to apply principles you already know to answer the question.

Parasitism and mutualism

Parasitism and **mutualism** are examples of **interdependence** where the survival of one species is closely linked with another species.

Parasitism

A **parasite** feeds on another organism (the **host**) while they are living together. This harms the host but benefits the parasite.

Parasite	Host	Description
flea (animal)	other animals, including humans	fleas feed by sucking the animal's blood after piercing its skin
head louse (animal)	humans	head lice feed by sucking blood after piercing the skin on the head
tapeworm (animal)	other animals, including humans	tapeworms live in the animal's intestine and absorb nutrients from the digested food in the intestine
mistletoe (plant)	trees, e.g. apple	mistletoe grows roots into the tree to absorb water and nutrients from the host

Mutualism

When two organisms live closely together in a way that benefits them both, they are called **mutualists**.

Remember to explain how **each** organism benefits in a mutualistic relationship.

Oxpecker bird benefits by getting food.

Herbivore benefits from loss of skin parasites.

The larger fish benefits from loss of dead skin and parasites.

Cleaner fish benefit by getting food.

Nitrogen-fixing bacteria in root nodules are protected from the environment and get food from the plant.

Legume plant gets nitrogen compounds for healthy growth from the bacteria.

Worked example

A tapeworm is a parasite that lives in the intestines of mammals. Explain why it is classed as a parasite.   **(3 marks)**

The tapeworm depends on the host for its food supply. It absorbs digested food from the host's intestines, so it benefits from the relationship. The host is harmed because it is losing some of the nutrients in the food it eats.

Remember mutualism is a 'win–win' relationship as both organisms benefit. Parasitism is a 'win–lose' relationship because one organism benefits but the other one is harmed.

Now try this

1 Define the term **parasite**.   **(1 mark)**

2 Describe what is meant by **mutualism**.   **(1 mark)**

3 Explain how the relationship between nitrogen-fixing bacteria and legumes is mutualistic.
    (2 marks)

Fieldwork techniques

The number of organisms in an area can be found using **fieldwork** techniques.

Sampling with quadrats

When studying organisms in the field, most areas are too large to count every individual organism. So we take **samples** and use them to draw conclusions about the whole area. Samples are often taken with square frames called **quadrats**.

- Quadrats are placed randomly in the area.
- The number of study organisms is counted in each quadrat.
- The number of organisms in the whole area is estimated using the equation:

number in whole area =

$$\text{mean number of organisms in one quadrat} \times \frac{\text{total area (m}^2)}{\text{area of one quadrat (m}^2)}$$

Belt transects

The effect of abiotic and biotic factors on where organisms live (their **distribution**) can be studied using **quadrats** placed along a **belt transect**.

1 m × 1 m quadrats placed at regular intervals along the transect

transect line – e.g. tape measure placed along the ground

Choosing the number of quadrat samples to take is usually a trade-off between taking more samples (more accurate) and taking fewer samples (quicker).

Examples:

pond ⟶ dry land

low tide on rocky shore ⟶ high tide

Changes in **factors** (such as temperature, light intensity, trampling) are also recorded at each quadrat position. This makes it easier to link a change in distribution with a change in physical factor.

Worked example

Ten 1 m² quadrats were placed randomly on a school field that was 100 m by 200 m. The number of daisies recorded in each quadrat was: 20, 6, 33, 0, 26, 21, 18, 7, 2, and 9. Estimate the total number of daisies on the field.   **(3 marks)**

Mean number of plants per quadrat

$$= \frac{\text{total daises sampled}}{\text{number of quadrats}} = 14.2$$

Estimated number of daisies $= \text{mean} \times \dfrac{\text{area of field}}{\text{area of quadrat}}$

$= 14.2 \times (20\,000/1) = 284\,000$ daisies

This is an estimate because if the quadrats were placed in different positions, the number sampled might be different.

Quadrats are only useful for sampling plants, or animals that do not move about much.

🖩 **Maths skills** To calculate the mean number of plants for one quadrat, divide the total number of plants by the number of quadrats.

Now try this

1 State when you would sample randomly with a quadrat.   **(1 mark)**

2 Describe the situation in which you would choose to sample along a transect rather than sample randomly.   **(2 marks)**

Organisms and their environment

🧪 **Practical skills** You can use **quadrats** and **belt transects** to investigate the relationship between organisms and their environment in the field. *See page 75 for more information on these techniques.*

Core practical

Aim

To investigate how the change in light intensity from inside a woodland to a nearby open meadow affects where cowslips grow.

Apparatus

- quadrat
- light meter
- long measuring tape

Method

1 Set out a measuring tape from inside the woodland out to the open meadow.
2 Take a quadrat sample at regular intervals.
3 At each quadrat sample, count the number of cowslips, and measure the light intensity.
4 Compare the number of plants with the light intensity along the transect to see how light affects where the plants live.

> Random sampling will not help here because you need to sample organisms in relation to how the environmental factor changes.

> An alternative to counting plants is estimating percentage coverage of the quadrat (e.g. 10%, 50%) by the species. This is useful if it is difficult to count individual plants, or if some plants are much bigger than others.

Results

The results were recorded in a table.

quadrat number	Q1	Q2	Q3	Q4	Q5
distance from woodland centre (m)	0	10	20	30	40
light intensity (lux)	2.3	2.1	3.5	9.5	13.5
number of cowslips	0	0	1	5	15

The results are displayed in this graph.

Conclusion

Cowslips seem to grow better in open meadow because the greater the light intensity the greater the number of cowslips.

> Repeating the transect several times and comparing the results for each transect would help to average out any random variation.

Now try this

In the woodland/meadow transect above, the number of primroses was also counted. The results were: Q1 2; Q2 4; Q3 7; Q4 1; Q5 0.

(a) Display these values, and the light intensity values, on one graph to show how they change over distance along the transect.
(2 marks)

(b) Describe what your graph shows about the relationship between light intensity and number of primroses.
(2 marks)

Human effects on ecosystems

Humans have positive and negative effects on **biodiversity** in ecosystems. Biodiversity is the variety of living organisms in an area.

Fish farming

Fish farming involves growing one kind of fish in an area. The fish are fed and the waste they produce is removed from their tanks.

👎 The waste can pollute the local area, changing conditions so that some local species die out.

👎 Diseases from the farmed fish (such as lice) can spread to wild fish and kill them.

👍 Farming fish reduces fishing of wild fish.

Non-indigenous species

Non-indigenous species (organisms that are not found naturally in the area) may be introduced on purpose or accidentally to an area.

👎 They may reproduce rapidly as they have no natural predators in the new area.

👎 They may **out-compete** native species for food or other resources.

👍 They may provide food for native species.

Eutrophication

Fertilisers added to fields for crops may get into streams and rivers. This adds phosphates and nitrates to the water, which is called **eutrophication**. Eutrophication can lead to loss of biodiversity in nearby water.

| Eutrophication causes water plants and algae to grow more quickly. | ➡ | Plants and algae cover the water surface, and block light to deeper water. | ➡ | Deeper plants cannot get light, so they die. | ➡ | Bacteria decompose dying plants and take oxygen from the water. | ➡ | There is not enough oxygen left in the water for fish, so they die. |

Worked example

Unionid mussels are found in many waters in the USA. Zebra mussels are small freshwater mussels that are non-indigenous species introduced to the Hudson River in 1991. The graph shows the changes in population sizes of both kinds of mussel over a 20-year period in the Hudson River.

 (a) Describe the changes in the unionid mussel population between 1991 and 2009. **(2 marks)**

The population falls rapidly until 1994 then more slowly until 1998. After this the population stays at approximately the same low level.

 (b) The zebra mussels do not eat the unionid mussels. Suggest another reason why the zebra mussels have caused this reduction in the unionid mussel population. **(2 marks)**

They may outcompete the unionid mussels for a resource, such as food supply or breeding places.

Now try this

Focus on giving the stages that cause a decrease.

Explain how eutrophication can lead to a decrease in biodiversity. **(3 marks)**

Biodiversity

Maintaining **biodiversity** is very important, at both the **local** and **global** levels, because many organisms have important roles in ecosystems and can be useful to humans.

Reasons for maintaining biodiversity

- Moral reasons: Humans should respect other living organisms.
- Aesthetic reasons: People enjoy seeing the variety of living organisms that live in different habitats.
- Ecosystem structure: Some organisms have an important role in ecosystems, such as microorganisms in decay processes and nutrient recycling. If this planet loses species, food chains become more unstable.
- Usefulness: Some species are particularly useful to humans, for example plants that produce life-saving drugs, or wild varieties of plants grown for crops (as a source of genes if the environment changes).

Reforestation

Reforestation is replanting forests where they have been destroyed, for example to create farmland.

Advantages include:

- ✓ Restores habitat for species that are endangered. Restoring rain forest, for example, helps to conserve many species.
- ✓ Reduces the concentration of carbon dioxide in the air as the trees photosynthesise.
- ✓ Tree roots bind the soil together and reduce the effects of soil erosion.
- ✓ Affects local climate, for example reducing the range of temperature variation.

Conservation is important so that we do not lose valuable species. We can conserve organisms by protecting their habitat, preventing poaching, or keeping insurance populations in zoos and seed banks.

Worked example

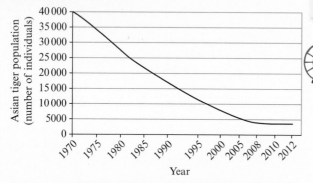

The graph shows the decline in the Asian tiger population.

(a) Calculate the percentage decrease in the population between 1970 and 2008. Show your working.   **(2 marks)**

decrease = 40 000 − 3500 = 36 500

% decrease = (36 500 ÷ 40 000) × 100

= 91.25%

(b) During this time the human population in tiger regions has increased significantly. Explain how this could be linked to the decrease in tiger population.   **(1 mark)**

The tigers' habitat might be being destroyed.

Another suggestion would be hunting by humans.

(c) Suggest why scientists monitor the populations of top predators such as the tiger very closely when they are assessing the biodiversity in an area.   **(2 marks)**

If there are plenty of top predators, then there is plenty of energy being transferred through the food web in that ecosystem, which suggests high biodiversity.

Now try this

Farmers in the UK are encouraged to keep hedges around their fields.
Explain how keeping hedges around fields can help maintain biodiversity.   **(2 marks)**

The carbon cycle

Living organisms need substances from the environment. As the amount of these on Earth is limited, they are recycled through both living (**biotic**) and non-living (**abiotic**) parts of the ecosystem. The **carbon cycle** shows how the element carbon passes between the environment and living organisms.

Controls of the carbon cycle

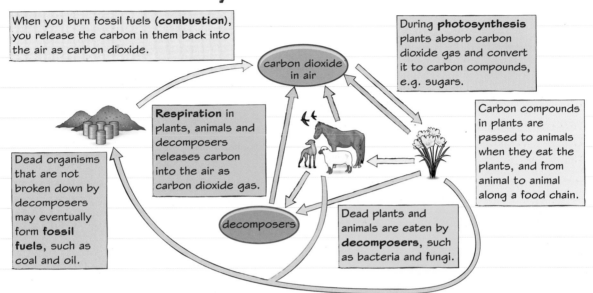

When you burn fossil fuels (**combustion**), you release the carbon in them back into the air as carbon dioxide.

During **photosynthesis** plants absorb carbon dioxide gas and convert it to carbon compounds, e.g. sugars.

carbon dioxide in air

Respiration in plants, animals and decomposers releases carbon into the air as carbon dioxide gas.

Carbon compounds in plants are passed to animals when they eat the plants, and from animal to animal along a food chain.

Dead organisms that are not broken down by decomposers may eventually form **fossil fuels**, such as coal and oil.

decomposers

Dead plants and animals are eaten by **decomposers**, such as bacteria and fungi.

In the air, carbon is part of carbon dioxide gas. In organisms, it is part of complex carbon compounds. The carbon cycle is important because it recycles carbon dioxide released in respiration to be taken in by plants in photosynthesis, to make organic molecules in living organisms.

Worked example

A large forest is cleared by burning. What effects will this have on the amount of carbon dioxide in the air (a) immediately, and (b) over a longer period? (**4 marks**)

(a) Large amounts of carbon dioxide will be released into the air by the burning (combustion) of the trees.

(b) Less carbon dioxide will be removed from the air than before because the trees would have used some for photosynthesis. So the amount of carbon dioxide in the air is likely to remain high.

Two key processes in the carbon cycle are **respiration** and **photosynthesis**. These processes are important in maintaining oxygen and carbon dioxide concentrations in the air. Combustion can change this balance.

Remember that plants photosynthesise in the light but, like all other living organisms, they respire all the time.

Now try this

1 Describe the importance of decomposers in the carbon cycle.   (**1 mark**)

Decomposers respire using dead plant and animal matter, releasing carbon dioxide into the atmosphere.

2 Explain the effect of respiration, photosynthesis and combustion in the carbon cycle in transferring carbon dioxide to and from the atmosphere.   (**3 marks**)

In each case, explain whether these release carbon dioxide into the atmosphere, or remove it.

The water cycle

The **water cycle** describes how water moves between different parts of our planet.

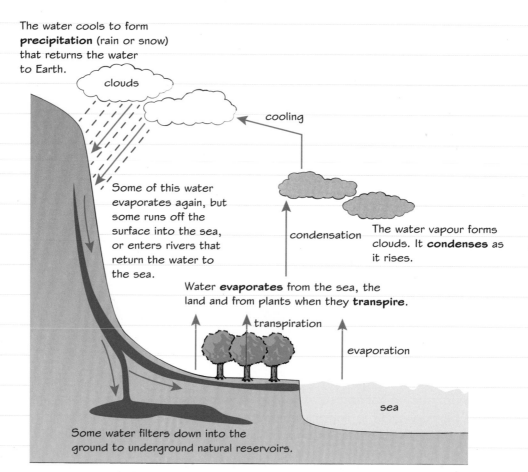

The water cools to form **precipitation** (rain or snow) that returns the water to Earth.

clouds

cooling

Some of this water evaporates again, but some runs off the surface into the sea, or enters rivers that return the water to the sea.

condensation

The water vapour forms clouds. It **condenses** as it rises.

Water **evaporates** from the sea, the land and from plants when they **transpire**.

transpiration

evaporation

sea

Some water filters down into the ground to underground natural reservoirs.

Desalination

Some areas of the world where it is hot and dry suffer **drought**. They do not get enough precipitation to use as their source of **potable** water (that is, fit to drink). If they are close to the sea, they can produce drinking water from salty water by **desalination**. One way to do this is **distillation**.

Worked example

Explain how distillation can be used to produce potable water in a village that is close to the sea. **(4 marks)**

- Salty water is heated until the water evaporates, forming steam.
- The steam is condensed in another container to give pure water.
- The salt and other impurities are left behind in the salty water.
- If renewable energy, such as sunlight, is used this saves electricity costs and avoids pollution.

Now try this

You need to describe each stage in turn.

 1 Describe the processes that take place in the water cycle. **(4 marks)**

 2 Suggest the effect on the water cycle of planting a large number of trees. **(3 marks)**

The nitrogen cycle

Plants need **nitrates** to grow well. They can get nitrates in several different ways, including through the **nitrogen cycle**.

Controls of the nitrogen cycle

A diagram of the **nitrogen cycle** shows how the element nitrogen moves between living organisms and the environment.

Worked example

Plants grow well in fertile soil. Explain how bacteria help to keep soil fertile.   **(4 marks)**

Plants need nitrogen for making proteins but they can only take in nitrogen in the form of nitrogen compounds such as nitrates. Soil bacteria act as decomposers, releasing ammonia from proteins in dead bodies and from urea. Bacteria in the soil make nitrates. Plants can then use the nitrates to make proteins. Nitrogen-fixing bacteria in the soil and roots of some plants convert nitrogen gas from the air into nitrogen compounds that the plant can use.

In the nitrogen cycle it is important to focus on the role of bacteria.

Fertilisers and crop rotation

Farmers add **nitrates** to crop plants in **fertiliser** to help the plants grow better.

Crop rotation means growing different crops each year, on a rotation basis. This improves soil fertility (the amount of nutrients in the soil) because:

- different crops remove different nutrients from the soil
- plants such as clover have nitrogen-fixing bacteria in their roots, and can be ploughed back into the soil, to add nitrates.

The roots of clover plants contain nitrogen-fixing bacteria.

Now try this

1 Explain why a farmer might decide one year to grow clover plants in a field instead of a crop.
   (2 marks)

Explain why this could be an advantage to a farmer.

2 Farmers plough crop stubble back into the soil after harvesting. Explain how this helps to improve soil fertility.   **(4 marks)**

Extended response – Ecosystems and material cycles

There will be one or more 6-mark questions on your exam paper. For these questions, you will need to think scientifically and structure your answer logically, showing how the points you make are related to each other. You can revise the topic for this question, which is about **human effects on ecosystems**, on page 77.

Worked example

edge of field
lake

There is a small lake in one corner of a farmer's field. The lake's surface is green.

A scientist tells the farmer that the lake is green because of eutrophication, how it happens and its effects on the lake.

Describe how eutrophication occurs, and explain the problems it causes to living things in the lake.
(6 marks)

The farmer has used fertilisers to help his crops grow well. These fertilisers contained nitrates, which washed from the field into the lake when it rained. Eutrophication is the accumulation of nitrates in the lake.

The extra nitrates in the lake cause algae to grow faster. This is why the lake's surface looks green. The algae stop sunlight reaching plants in the bottom of the lake. Without sunlight, these plants cannot photosynthesise. They die and start to decompose.

Decomposers break down the dead plants. The decomposer organisms use oxygen to respire while they do this. The amount of oxygen in the water decreases, so there is not enough oxygen for fish. The fish in the lake die because of lack of oxygen.

Command words: Describe

You need to give an account in your answer to a **describe** question. **Explain** needs a reason or justification but **describe** does not.

 Nitrate fertilisers provide plants with nitrogen, needed for healthy growth. Nitrate compounds dissolve easily in water.

 This part of the answer explains the problems that eutrophication can cause to plants in the lake.

 This part of the answer explains the problems that eutrophication can cause to animals in the lake. Insects and other aquatic animals are also affected, leading to a loss of biodiversity.

You should think clearly about how to present your ideas before you start. Aim for a clear and logical structure. You can support this with scientific information and ideas. You should leave out information or ideas that are unnecessary to answer the question.

Remember to include at least one example of each type of relationship in your answer. You can revise parasitism and mutualism on page 74.

Now try this

The survival of some organisms depends on the presence of other species.
Using examples, compare and contrast mutualism and parasitism.   **(6 marks)**

Command words: Compare and contrast

The question is looking for the similarities and differences between two or more things, without needing a conclusion.

Formulae

You should be able to recall the formulae of elements, simple compounds and ions.

Elements

An **element** is a substance made from atoms with the same number of protons in the nucleus. Each element has its own **chemical symbol**, which:

- consists of one or two letters
- starts with a capital letter
- has any other letters in lower case.

For example, mercury is Hg. You can find the symbols for the elements in the periodic table.

Atoms and molecules

An **atom** is the smallest particle of an element that still has its chemical properties.

A **molecule** consists of two or more atoms chemically joined together.

Most elements that are gases at room temperature exist as molecules with two atoms. They are shown by **chemical formulae**, e.g. H_2, N_2, O_2, F_2, Cl_2.

Compounds

A **compound** consists of two or more different elements chemically joined together.

carbon　hydrogen
$$CH_4$$
one　　four

The chemical formula for methane is CH_4. Each methane molecule has:

- one carbon atom (no number in the formula)
- four hydrogen atoms (4 in the formula)
- atoms of two elements joined together
- $(1 + 4) = 5$ atoms in total.

Remember: you will not find the formulae for any compounds in the periodic table.

Worked example

(a) Give the meaning of the term **ion**. **(2 marks)**

An ion is a charged particle formed when an atom, or group of atoms, loses or gains electrons.

(b) An ion is represented as Na^+.
   Explain what this shows. **(2 marks)**

The ion has one positive charge, and it is formed from a sodium atom.

(c) An ion is represented as SO_4^{2-}.
   Explain what this shows. **(2 marks)**

The ion has two negative charges, and it is formed from one sulfur atom and four oxygen atoms chemically joined together.

(d) Write the formula for sodium sulfate. **(1 mark)**

Na_2SO_4

In general:
- metal atoms lose electrons to form positive ions
- non-metal atoms gain electrons to form negative ions.

Look at page 86 for help with the atomic structure. For a reminder about how ions form, look at page 91.

Write the charge as a superscript at the top right of the symbol.

You should show a single positive charge as + and a single negative charge as −.

A sodium ion has a single positive charge and a sulfate ion has two negative charges. Two sodium ions balance the charge on one sulfate ion.

Now try this

Use the periodic table on page 89 to help you answer these questions.

1　The formula for bromine is Br_2.
   Explain what this shows. **(2 marks)**

2　In copper carbonate, there is one carbon atom and three oxygen atoms for every copper atom. State the formula for copper carbonate. **(1 mark)**

3　The formula for magnesium hydroxide is $Mg(OH)_2$.
   Explain what this tells you about the number and type of each atom or ion present.
   (2 marks)

Multiply the numbers of each atom inside the brackets by 2.

Equations

Chemical **equations** are used to model the changes that happen in chemical reactions.

Word equations

In a chemical reaction:
- **reactants** are the substances that undergo a chemical change in a reaction
- **products** are the new substances formed.

In general: reactants → products

Two or more reactants or products are separated by a + sign. In a **word equation**, you write the name of each substance, not its formula.

An example word equation

Iron oxide reacts with carbon to form iron and carbon monoxide:

iron oxide + carbon → iron + carbon monoxide

reactants on the left   products on the right

Write it all on one line if possible. If you are going to run out of space, write words below others as shown here.

Balanced equations

- All substances are shown by their formulae.
- The numbers of atoms of each element in the reactants and products are the same.
- You may need to write a number in front of a reactant or product to balance an equation. For example, hydrogen reacts with chlorine to form hydrogen chloride.

1 Write all the symbols and formulae:
$H_2 + Cl_2 \rightarrow HCl$

2 Count the atoms of each element on each side, and write numbers if needed:

$$H_2 + Cl_2 \rightarrow 2HCl$$

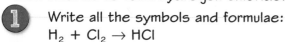

2HCl in the equation means two HCl molecules.

An example balanced equation

The balanced chemical equation for the reaction between iron oxide and carbon is:

$$Fe_2O_3 + 3C \rightarrow 2Fe + 3CO$$

It shows that one unit of iron oxide reacts with three carbon atoms. The products are two iron atoms and three carbon monoxide molecules:

Element	On left	On right
Fe	2	2
O	3	3
C	3	3

State symbols

State symbols show the physical state of each substance in a balanced equation:

- ✓ solid (s)
- ✓ liquid (l)
- ✓ gas (g)
- ✓ aqueous solution (aq).

dissolved in water

Worked example

Aluminium reacts with hot dilute sulfuric acid, H_2SO_4. Aluminium sulfate, $Al_2(SO_4)_3$, and hydrogen, H_2, are formed.

Write a balanced equation for this reaction and include state symbols. **(2 marks)**

$2Al(s) + 3H_2SO_4(aq) \rightarrow Al_2(SO_4)_3(aq) + 3H_2(g)$

The unbalanced equation is:

$$Al + H_2SO_4 \rightarrow Al_2(SO_4)_3 + H_2$$

- There are two Al atoms on the right, so a **2** is placed in front of the Al on the left.
- There are three units of SO_4 on the right, so a **3** is placed in front of the H_2SO_4 on the left.
- There are now $3 \times H_2$ on the left, so a **3** is placed in front of the H_2 on the right.

Now try this

1 Balance these chemical equations:
(a) ...... $Mg + O_2 \rightarrow$ ...... MgO **(1 mark)**
(b) $N_2 +$ ...... $H_2 \rightarrow$ ...... NH_3 **(1 mark)**
(c) $CH_4 +$ ...... $O_2 \rightarrow CO_2 +$ ...... H_2O **(1 mark)**

2 (a) Copper oxide reacts with nitric acid, forming copper nitrate and water. Write the word equation. **(1 mark)**

(b) Iron filings react with chlorine gas, forming iron chloride powder. Balance this equation and add state symbols.
...... $Fe +$ ...... $Cl_2 \rightarrow$ ...... $FeCl_3$ **(2 marks)**

Hazards, risks and precautions

You should be able to evaluate the risks in a practical procedure. You should also be able to suggest suitable precautions.

Hazards

A **hazard** is something that could cause:
- damage or harm to someone or something
- negative health effects, which may occur immediately or later on.

For example, ethanol is flammable. This is a hazard. If the ethanol ignited, it could cause burns or a fire.

Practical skills Risks

A **risk** is the chance that someone or something will be harmed if exposed to a hazard. The amount of risk depends on factors such as:
- ✓ how much someone is exposed to a hazard
- ✓ the way in which exposure happens
- ✓ how serious the effects of exposure are.

The risk from heating ethanol using a hot water bath is less than when using a Bunsen burner.

Hazard symbols

The labels on containers of hazardous substances include **hazard symbols**. These are intended to:
- warn about the dangers of the substance in the container
- let people know about the precautions to take when they use the substance.

Some common hazard symbols

 harmful or irritant   flammable   respiratory sensitiser

 toxic   corrosive   oxidising

Precautions

A **precaution** is something that you can do to reduce the risk of harm from a hazard. Precautions include:
- using smaller amounts of a hazardous substance
- using protective clothing, such as gloves and eye protection
- using a different method or apparatus.

The answer is specific to this activity.

It is not a general lab rule such as not running or not drinking the solution.

Other suitable precautions that could be mentioned, if linked to the activity, include:
- wearing gloves if toxic substances are used
- tying hair back or tucking in a tie if a Bunsen burner is used for heating.

Worked example

A student is preparing a dry sample of copper sulfate. She heats some copper sulfate solution in an evaporating basin. She then allows it to cool. Crystals of copper sulfate appear.
Describe and explain one safety precaution she should use.
(3 marks)

She should heat the solution gently. This reduces the risk that it will spit out of the evaporating basin. The hot solution could cause skin burns or eye damage.

Now try this

1 State **one** reason why hazard symbols are used. **(1 mark)**
2 A student carries out electrolysis on a concentrated sodium chloride solution. Toxic chlorine gas and flammable hydrogen gas are produced.
Describe **two** precautions the student could take to reduce the risk of harm in this experiment. **(2 marks)**

85

Atomic structure

Dalton's simple model has changed over time because of the discovery of subatomic particles.

A brief atomic timeline

When	Who	What
1803	Dalton	Solid atom model: all atoms of an element are identical; different elements have different atoms
1897	Thomson	Discovers the electron
1904	Thomson	Plum pudding model: atoms are spheres of positive charge with negative electrons dotted around inside
1911	Rutherford	Solar system model: atoms have a positive nucleus surrounded by negative electrons in orbits
1913	Bohr	Electron shell model: electrons occupy shells or energy levels around the nucleus
1918	Rutherford	Discovers the proton
1932	Chadwick	Discovers the neutron

Atomic structure

An **atom** consists of a central **nucleus**, which:
- contains **protons** and **neutrons**
- is surrounded by electrons in shells.

shell · electron · proton · neutron · nucleus

▦ Maths skills Relative values

Atoms and their subatomic particles are very small. Their diameters, masses and electrical charges are expressed as **relative values**. For example, the diameter of a hydrogen nucleus is 1.75×10^{-15} m. The diameter of a hydrogen atom is 1.06×10^{-10} m.

The diameter of the nucleus relative to the atom:

$$= \frac{1.75 \times 10^{-15} \text{ m}}{1.06 \times 10^{-10} \text{ m}} = \frac{1}{60\,600}$$

The nucleus is very small compared with the overall size of the atom.

Worked example

Complete the table with the names and properties of subatomic particles. **(3 marks)**

Particle	Relative charge	Relative mass
proton	+1	1
neutron	0	1
electron	−1	$\frac{1}{1836}$

- Atoms have equal numbers of protons and electrons. They have equal numbers of positive and negative charges, and so are neutral overall.
- Electrons have very little mass compared with protons and neutrons. Most of the mass of an atom is concentrated in its nucleus.

Now try this

1 Describe the structure of an atom.   **(4 marks)**

2 Explain why atoms have no charge overall.   **(2 marks)**

3 State where most of the mass of an atom is concentrated. Explain your answer.   **(3 marks)**

Isotopes

The atoms of an element have identical chemical properties, but can exist as different isotopes.

Numbers of particles

Each atom can be described by its:
- **mass number**, the total number of protons and neutrons in the nucleus
- **atomic number**, the number of protons in the nucleus.

These are in full chemical symbols:

mass number → $^{23}_{11}\text{Na}$ ← atomic number

Atoms of a given element have the same number of protons in the nucleus:
- all have the same atomic number
- this number is unique to that element.

Calculating particle numbers

Use the atomic number and mass number to calculate the number of subatomic particles in an atom.

For example, for sodium, Na:

① atomic number = 11
number of protons = 11
number of electrons = 11   (equal numbers of protons and electrons)

② mass number = 23
neutrons = mass number – atomic number
= 23 – 11 = 12

Isotopes

Isotopes are atoms of an element with:
- the same number of protons
- different numbers of neutrons.

You can recognise isotopes of the same element because they will have the same atomic number, but different mass numbers.

Isotopes of an element have the same chemical properties because they have the same number of electrons.

You can revise electronic configurations on page 90.

Relative atomic mass

Take care not to confuse **relative atomic mass**, A_r, with mass number:

A_r values take into account the **relative abundance** or percentage of each isotope in a sample of an element. The existence of isotopes means that the A_r values of elements may not be whole numbers. Mass numbers can only be whole numbers. This is because you cannot have parts of protons or neutrons in an atom.

Worked example

The relative atomic mass of copper is 63.5 but the mass number of most copper atoms is 63. Explain this difference. **(3 marks)**

Mass number is the total number of protons and neutrons in an atom. All copper atoms have the same number of protons, but different isotopes of copper have different numbers of neutrons. Relative atomic masses are averages, so there must also be an isotope of copper that has a mass number greater than 63.

Copper has two isotopes: 69% is $^{63}_{29}\text{Cu}$ (copper-63) and 31% is $^{65}_{29}\text{Cu}$ (copper-65). The existence of isotopes results in a relative atomic mass between 63 and 65.

Now try this

 1 Describe what the atoms of any element have in common. Your description should be in terms of particles. **(2 marks)**

 2 Calculate the number of protons, neutrons and electrons in an atom of chlorine-35, $^{35}_{17}\text{Cl}$. **(3 marks)**

Mendeleev's table

Dmitri Mendeleev's **periodic table** was successful and developed into the modern periodic table. In 1869, Mendeleev arranged all the elements known at the time into a table:

- Mendeleev put the elements in order of the relative atomic masses.
- He checked the properties of the elements and their compounds.
- He swapped the places of some elements so that elements with similar properties lined up.
- He left gaps where he thought there were other elements, and predicted their properties.
- When these elements were discovered, Mendeleev's predictions fitted the properties very well.

Pair reversals

At first Mendeleev arranged the elements in order of relative atomic mass. However he reversed the position of some pairs of elements. For example, Mendeleev put tellurium in group 6 and iodine in group 7. This matched the properties of the elements and their compounds.

However, according to their relative atomic masses, iodine should have been first:

A$_r$ of Te = 128   A$_r$ of I = 127

Iodine naturally exists only as ^{127}I. ^{126}Te exists, but ^{128}Te and ^{130}Te are its most abundant isotopes. Their high relative abundance gives tellurium a greater A$_r$ than iodine.

Group 6 and 7 elements

Group 6 elements	Group 7 elements
do not react with water	all react with water
all react with oxygen (except oxygen itself)	do not react with oxygen
all form compounds with hydrogen with the general formula: H_2X	all form compounds with hydrogen with the general formula: HX
6 electrons in their atom's outer shell	7 electrons in their atom's outer shell

This information was not available in Mendeleev's time. See page 90 to revise electronic configurations.

Worked example

Mendeleev published another table in 1871. Part of this is shown on the right. Mendeleev left gaps in his table, shown as * here.
Explain the importance of doing this. **(3 marks)**

The gaps were for elements not discovered then. Mendeleev used his table to predict the properties of these elements. When they were discovered later, their properties closely matched his predicted properties. This supported the ideas behind his table.

One of the gaps was for 'eka-silicon'. This was discovered in 1886 and named germanium.

	Group						
1	2	3	4	5	6	7	
H							
Li	Be	B	C	N	O	F	
Na	Mg	Al	Si	P	S	Cl	
K / Cu	Ca / Zn	* / *	Ti / *	V / As	Cr / Se	Mn / Br	
Rb / Ag	Sr / Cd	Y / In	Zr / Sn	Nb / Sb	Mo / Te	* / I	

Now try this

 1 Describe how Mendeleev arranged the elements known to him. **(2 marks)**

 2 Suggest **one** reason why other scientists at the time thought that Mendeleev's table was not correct. **(1 mark)**

The periodic table

The modern periodic table is useful for describing and predicting properties of elements.

Atomic number

In Mendeleev's periodic table, atomic number was just the position of an element in the table.

Later discoveries showed that:
- atomic number is actually the number of protons in the nucleus of an atom
- each element has a unique atomic number
- if the elements are arranged in order of increasing atomic number, Mendeleev's pair reversals are explained.

Explaining pair reversals

Iodine should be placed before tellurium according to its relative atomic mass, but after tellurium using its atomic number:

Relative atomic mass	128	127
Element symbol	Te	I
Atomic number	52	53

Mendeleev did not know about atomic structure. He could explain the pair reversal only in terms of the elements' properties.

Features of the modern periodic table

The elements in the modern periodic table are arranged in order of their atomic numbers.

The horizontal rows are called **periods**.

Metals are on the left-hand side and in the centre.

Elements with similar properties are placed in the same vertical **groups**.

Non-metals are on the right-hand side.

relative atomic mass
atomic number

Group 1	2											3	4	5	6	7	0
Period 1								1 H 1									4 He 2
2	7 Li 3	9 Be 4											11 B 5	12 C 6	14 N 7	16 O 8	19 F 9	20 Ne 10
3	23 Na 11	24 Mg 12											27 Al 13	28 Si 14	31 P 15	32 S 16	35.5 Cl 17	40 Ar 18
4	39 K 19	40 Ca 20	45 Sc 21	48 Ti 22	51 V 23	52 Cr 24	55 Mn 25	56 Fe 26	59 Co 27	59 Ni 28	63.5 Cu 29	65 Zn 30	70 Ga 31	73 Ge 32	75 As 33	79 Se 34	80 Br 35	84 Kr 36
5	85 Rb 37	88 Sr 38	89 Y 39	91 Zr 40	93 Nb 41	96 Mo 42	(98) Tc 43	101 Ru 44	103 Rh 45	106 Pd 46	108 Ag 47	112 Cd 48	115 In 49	119 Sn 50	122 Sb 51	128 Te 52	127 I 53	131 Xe 54
6	133 Cs 55	137 Ba 56	139 La 57	178 Hf 72	181 Ta 73	184 W 74	186 Re 75	190 Os 76	192 Ir 77	195 Pt 78	197 Au 79	201 Hg 80	204 Tl 81	207 Pb 82	209 Bi 83	(209) Po 84	(210) At 85	(222) Rn 86
7	(223) Fr 87	(226) Ra 88	(227) Ac 89	(261) Rf 104	(262) Db 105	(266) Sg 106	(264) Bh 107	(277) Hs 108	(268) Mt 109	(271) Ds 110	(272) Rg 111							

Worked example

The table shows information about cobalt and nickel. Their positions in the periodic table were difficult to determine in Mendeleev's time.

Explain how knowledge of atomic structure helps to determine the positions of cobalt and nickel in the periodic table. **(2 marks)**

Relative atomic mass	58.9	58.7
Element symbol	Co	Ni
Atomic number	27	28

Elements are arranged in order of increasing atomic number (number of protons) in the modern table. The atomic number of cobalt is lower than that of nickel.

The answer uses the modern definition of the term **atomic number**. This is the number of protons in the nucleus of an atom. Mendeleev used a different definition.

Now try this

1 State the name given to vertical columns in the periodic table. **(1 mark)**

2 Describe how the elements are arranged in the periodic table. **(3 marks)**

Electronic configurations

An **electronic configuration** describes the arrangement of electrons in shells in an atom.

Modelling the arrangement of electrons

In an atom:
- electrons occupy electron **shells**
- shells are filled, starting with the innermost shell
- different shells hold different maximum numbers of electrons.

The diagram shows the electronic configuration of sodium, which has 11 electrons in its atoms.

You can also show it in writing as 2.8.1 (each dot separates two occupied shells).

symbol for the element

Electrons are shown using dots or crosses.

Circles represent electron shells.

1st (inner) shell holds 2 electrons.

2nd shell holds 8 electrons.

3rd shell holds 8 electrons (there is only 1 shown here, because sodium atoms only have 11 electrons).

Electronic configurations and the periodic table

The electronic configuration of hydrogen is 1. Below is a 'short form' of the periodic table for the remaining first 20 elements (He to Ca). In general, for these 20 elements:
- metal atoms have up to two electrons in their outer shell (the exception is Al which has three)
- non-metal atoms (not boron or helium) have four or more electrons in their outer shell.

The number of occupied shells is the same as the period number.

The number of electrons in the outer shell is the same as the group number (except for elements in group O, which have full outer shells).

Elements in a group have the same number of electrons in their outer shell, except for helium in group O.

Worked example

The electronic configuration of phosphorus is 2.8.5. Describe how this electronic configuration shows the position of phosphorus in the periodic table, in terms of its group and period. **(2 marks)**

There are five electrons in the outer shell of a phosphorus atom, so it is in group 5. There are three occupied shells, so phosphorus is in period 3.

You need to be able to predict the electronic configurations of the first 20 elements.

The total number of electrons in a phosphorus atom is 15 (2 + 8 + 5).

This means that a phosphorus atom also has 15 protons. Its atomic number is 15, so phosphorus is placed between element 14 (silicon) and element 16 (sulfur).

Now try this

1 Draw the electronic configuration of chlorine, atomic number 17. **(2 marks)**

2 Describe the links between the electronic configuration of an element and its position in the periodic table. **(2 marks)**

Ions

An **ion** is an atom or a group of atoms with a positive or negative charge.

Cations

A **cation** is:

- ✓ a positively charged ion
- ✓ formed when an atom or group of atoms loses one or more electrons.

Cations usually form from hydrogen or metals:

- ✓ Group 1 atoms lose 1 electron to form ions with one positive charge, +.
- ✓ Group 2 atoms lose 2 electrons to form ions with two positive charges, 2+.

sodium atom, Na — electron lost →

sodium ion, Na⁺

Anions

An **anion** is:

- ✓ a negatively charged ion
- ✓ formed when an atom or group of atoms gains one or more electrons.

Anions usually form from non-metals:

- ✓ Group 7 atoms gain 1 electron to form ions with one negative charge, −.
- ✓ Group 6 atoms gain 2 electrons to form ions with two negative charges, 2−.

electron gained → chlorine atom, Cl

chloride ion, Cl⁻

🖩 Maths skills 2D models of 3D objects

In these 2D **dot-and-cross diagrams** each dot or cross represents an electron. Electrons are 3D.

 Worked example

Calculate the number of protons, neutrons and electrons in a sodium ion, $^{23}_{11}Na^+$. **(3 marks)**

number of protons = 11

number of neutrons = (23 − 11) = 12

number of electrons = 11 − 1 = 10

Remember that neutral atoms have equal numbers of protons and electrons.

Reduce the number of electrons for positive ions and increase it for negative ions.

For example, for $^{16}_{8}O^{2-}$:

- number of protons = 8
- number of electrons = 8 + 2 = 10

In which groups are these elements found?

Look at the periodic table on page 89.

 Now try this

1 Give the formula for the ions formed by atoms of the following elements:
   (a) lithium **(1 mark)**
   (b) magnesium **(1 mark)**
   (c) sulfur **(1 mark)**
   (d) bromine. **(1 mark)**

2 F⁻ ions have 9 protons in their nucleus. Calculate the number of electrons in an F⁻ ion. **(1 mark)**

3 Al³⁺ ions have 13 protons in their nucleus. Calculate the number of electrons in an Al³⁺ ion. **(1 mark)**

Formulae of ionic compounds

You should be able to write the formulae of ionic compounds from the formulae of their ions.

Naming ions

An ion's name depends on the charge, and whether the ion also contains oxygen. **Compound ions** contain atoms of two different elements.

- Positively charged ions formed from hydrogen or metal atoms take the name of the element:

Formula	Name	
H^+	hydrogen	
Li^+	lithium	
Na^+	sodium	group 1
K^+	potassium	
Mg^{2+}	magnesium	
Ca^{2+}	calcium	group 2
Ba^{2+}	barium	
Al^{3+}	aluminium	group 3
Ag^+	silver	
Cu^{2+}	copper	
Zn^{2+}	zinc	transition metals
Fe^{2+}	iron(II)	
Fe^{3+}	iron(III)	
NH_4^+	ammonium	compound ion

- Negatively charged ions formed from single non-metal atoms take the name of the element, but end in -**ide**.
- Negatively charged ions in compounds containing three or more elements, one of which is oxygen, end in -**ate**:

Formula	Name	
F^-	fluoride	
Cl^-	chloride	
Br^-	bromide	group 7
I^-	iodide	
O^{2-}	oxide	group 6
S^{2-}	sulfide	
NO_3^-	nitrate	
CO_3^{2-}	carbonate	
SO_4^{2-}	sulfate	compound ions
OH^-	hydroxide	

OH^- does not follow the -ate rule.

Worked example

Write down the formulae of these ionic compounds:
(a) sodium fluoride **(1 mark)**
NaF
(b) magnesium oxide **(1 mark)**
MgO
(c) iron(III) oxide **(1 mark)**
Fe_2O_3
(d) sodium nitrate **(1 mark)**
$NaNO_3$
(e) barium nitrate. **(1 mark)**
$Ba(NO_3)_2$

If a compound ion is present **and** more than one of these ions is needed in the formula:
- put the compound ion in brackets, with the number after the closing bracket.

Maths skills **Balancing charges**

This is simple if both ions have:
- ✓ 1 charge, as in NaF (Na^+ and F^-), or
- ✓ 2 charges, as in MgO (Mg^{2+} and O^{2-}).

If the ions have different numbers of charges, it may help to multiply them together. For example, for Fe^{3+} and O^{2-}, $(3 \times 2) = 6$. This means that you need:
- ✓ 2 Fe^{3+} ions to get 6 positive charges,
- ✓ 3 O^{2-} ions to get 6 negative charges.

So the formula of iron(III) oxide is Fe_2O_3.

Now try this

You can use the tables on this page to help you.

Give the formulae of these ionic compounds:
(a) calcium sulfide **(1 mark)**
(b) iron(II) chloride **(1 mark)**
(c) ammonium hydroxide **(1 mark)**
(d) ammonium carbonate **(1 mark)**
(e) sodium sulfate. **(1 mark)**

Properties of ionic compounds

You can explain physical properties of ionic compounds in terms of bonding and structure.

Bonding

Ionic bonds are strong **electrostatic forces** of attraction between oppositely charged ions. For example, when sodium reacts with chlorine to form sodium chloride, NaCl:
- electrons transfer from sodium atoms to chlorine atoms
- Na^+ ions and Cl^- ions form
- Na^+ and Cl^- ions attract each other.

Structure

The ions in an ionic compound form a **lattice** structure which has:
- a regular arrangement of ions
- ionic bonds between oppositely charged ions.

Melting and boiling points

Ionic compounds usually have:
- high melting points
- high boiling points.

As a result, they are in the **solid** state at room temperature. You can explain this in terms of bonding and structure:
- There are many strong ionic bonds.
- Large amounts of energy must be transferred to the lattice structure to break these bonds.

Solubility in water

Ionic compounds are often **soluble** in water. They **dissolve** to form **aqueous solutions**.

You can revise more about this on page 118.

▦ Maths skills 3D models

The diagram above models an ionic lattice in two dimensions. However, the lattice extends in three dimensions. It is called a **giant** lattice because it involves very many ions.

The structure of sodium chloride can be modelled in three dimensions as follows:

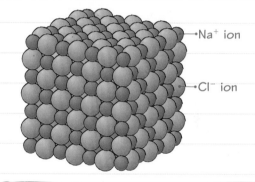

→Na⁺ ion

→Cl⁻ ion

Worked example

(a) State why sodium chloride does **not** conduct electricity when it is in the solid state.   **(1 mark)**

The ions are not free to move around in a solid.

(b) Explain why sodium chloride **does** conduct electricity when it is molten or in aqueous solution.   **(2 marks)**

The ions are free to move around when sodium chloride is liquid or when it is dissolved in water. This means they can carry electric charge from place to place.

Although ions are electrically charged, they are held in fixed positions in the lattice structure.

An electric current is a flow of charge. A substance will conduct electricity if:
- it contains charge carriers (such as ions)
- these charge carriers are free to move through the substance.

Now try this

Aluminium oxide is an insoluble ionic compound.
(a) State why solid aluminium oxide cannot conduct electricity.   **(1 mark)**
(b) Describe how you could make aluminium oxide conduct electricity.   **(2 marks)**

(c) Suggest why the method described in **(b)** may be expensive.   **(2 marks)**

Covalent bonds

A **covalent bond** is formed when a pair of electrons is shared between two atoms.

A shared pair of electrons

Covalent bonds:
- are strong
- form between non-metal atoms
- often produce **molecules**, which can be elements or compounds.

A hydrogen atom can form one covalent bond. Usually, for atoms of other non-metals:
- number of bonds = (8 – group number)

Group	Example	Covalent bonds
4	carbon, C	4
5	nitrogen, N	3
6	oxygen, O	2
7	chlorine, Cl	1
0	helium, He	none

Helium and other elements in group 0 have full outer shells. They do not transfer or share electrons, so they are unreactive.

Modelling covalent bonds

There are three ways you can represent a covalent bond, e.g. hydrogen, H_2:

 dot-and-cross (with shells)

 dot-and-cross (without shells)
H ● H
  ×

structural formula
H–H

Maths skills The size of atoms is around 1×10^{-10} m and the size of simple molecules is around 1×10^{-9} m.

Some examples of dot-and-cross diagrams

hydrogen chloride, H–Cl

water, H–O–H

carbon dioxide, O=C=O (two double bonds)

non-bonding pair of electrons

When you draw diagrams like these:
- draw overlapping circles to represent the outer shells
- draw a dot to represent an electron from one atom, and a cross to represent an electron from the other atom (make sure each bonding pair of electrons is between the two atoms)
- make sure that each atom (apart from hydrogen) has eight electrons in its outer shell.

Worked example

Methane, CH_4, can be represented by this structure:
Draw a dot-and-cross diagram to represent methane. **(1 mark)**

Hydrogen atoms do not have non-bonding pairs of electrons, but other atoms may do.

The molecule contains a double bond (two shared pairs of electrons).

Now try this

1 Describe covalent bonding. **(2 marks)**

2 Draw a dot-and-cross diagram to represent a molecule of oxygen, O_2. **(2 marks)**

Simple molecular substances

You can explain the physical properties of simple molecular substances in terms of their bonding and structure.

Bonding

A **simple molecule** consists of just a few atoms, joined to each other by strong covalent bonds. Simple molecular substances can be:
- non-metal elements, such as H_2, O_2, Cl_2
- compounds of non-metals, such as HCl, H_2O, CH_4.

Simple molecular substances usually have:
- low melting points
- low boiling points.

They are usually in the **gas** or **liquid** state at room temperature because of this.

Simple molecular substances with relatively large molecules, such as wax, are in the solid state at room temperature.

Melting and boiling points

There are weak attractive forces between molecules, called **intermolecular forces**.

When a simple molecular substance such as oxygen, O_2 or O=O, melts or boils:

☑ intermolecular forces are overcome

☑ covalent bonds do not break.

strong covalent bonds between atoms

not broken in state changes

weak intermolecular forces between molecules

overcome in state changes

Non-conductors of electricity

Simple molecular substances do not conduct electricity when solid, liquid or gas. This is because their molecules:
- are not electrically charged, and
- do not contain electrons that are free to move.

Conducting in solution

Most simple molecular substances do not conduct electricity when in solution. However:

☑ some of them, such as acids, break down when they dissolve forming ions

☑ these ions can move around, so the solution conducts electricity.

Solubility in water

Many simple molecular substances are **insoluble** in water. The intermolecular forces between water and these substances are weaker than those between:
- water molecules
- molecules of the substance itself.

Simple molecular substances dissolve in water if they can form strong enough intermolecular forces with water molecules:
- Hydrogen and oxygen are **sparingly soluble** (very little dissolves).
- Chlorine, carbon dioxide, sulfur dioxide and ammonia are soluble.
- Ethanol and ethanoic acid are soluble.
- Sugar is soluble.

Worked example

Nitrogen is a colourless, unreactive gas at room temperature.
Explain why it is suitable for use as an insulator in high-voltage electrical transformers.   **(2 marks)**

Nitrogen is unreactive. So, it will not react with the materials used in the transformer. Nitrogen can insulate the parts in the transformer because it does not conduct electricity.

A nitrogen molecule consists of two nitrogen atoms joined together by a triple covalent bond: N≡N

A lot of energy must be transferred to break this very strong bond. This is why nitrogen is unreactive.

The answer includes only the properties of nitrogen that make it useful in transformers.

Now try this

1 Ammonia, NH_3, is a simple molecular substance. Explain, in terms of intermolecular forces, why it is a gas at room temperature.   **(2 marks)**

2 Petrol and water are simple molecular substances. Explain why petrol does not dissolve in water.   **(3 marks)**

95

Giant molecular substances

Giant molecules contain very many atoms, rather than just a few.

Bonding and structure

A **giant molecule** consists of many atoms. In giant molecules, the atoms are:
- joined by strong covalent bonds
- arranged in a regular lattice structure.

Giant molecular substances can be:
- non-metal elements, such as carbon
- compounds, such as silica.

Giant molecular substances usually have:
- high melting points
- high boiling points.

They are solids at room temperature. A lot of energy must be transferred to break the many strong covalent bonds during melting and boiling. Giant molecular substances are insoluble in water.

Modelling giant molecules

There are many atoms in an entire giant molecule. You cannot represent an entire giant molecule using displayed formulae or dot-and-cross diagrams.

This is a **ball-and-stick model** of a small part of a silica molecule (found in sand):

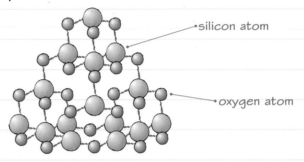

- silicon atom
- oxygen atom

The formula of silica is SiO_2. As with other giant molecular substances, this is its **empirical formula** (see page 101).

Diamond

Each atom is bonded to four others.

strong covalent bonds between atoms

Graphite

Each atom is bonded to three others.

weak intermolecular forces between layers

strong covalent bonds between atoms in a layer

Diamond and graphite are both forms of carbon. They are giant molecular substances.

Worked example

Graphite is used to make electrodes because it conducts electricity. Explain why graphite conducts electricity. **(3 marks)**

A carbon atom can form four covalent bonds. But in graphite each carbon atom only forms three covalent bonds. The non-bonding outer electrons become delocalised. This means they can move through the structure, so graphite conducts electricity.

Graphite is also used as a lubricant because it is slippery. The weak intermolecular forces between its layers let the layers slide over each other.

Diamond does not have delocalised electrons, so it does not conduct electricity. However, it is very hard because it has a rigid lattice structure with strong bonds, so diamond is useful for cutting tools.

Now try this

Your answer must include at least one similarity and one difference.

1 Compare and contrast the structure and bonding of diamond and graphite. **(4 marks)**

2 Silica has a similar structure to diamond. Explain whether it should conduct electricity. **(2 marks)**

Other large molecules

Graphene and fullerenes are forms of carbon that exist as giant molecules.

Graphene

Graphene is a giant molecular substance. Its structure resembles a single layer of graphite:

- Each carbon atom is covalently bonded to three other carbon atoms.
- It has a regular lattice structure.

interlocking hexagonal rings of carbon atoms

Properties of graphene

Graphene conducts electricity:
- ✓ The non-bonding outer electrons become delocalised.
- ✓ They can move through the structure.

Graphene is very strong and flexible:
- ✓ It contains many strong covalent bonds.

Graphene is almost transparent:
- ✓ Its layers are just one atom thick.

Fullerenes

Fullerenes resemble a sheet of graphene rolled to form:

- hollow balls, often called **buckyballs**

- hollow tubes, called carbon **nanotubes**.

Buckminsterfullerene, C_{60}, has carbon atoms arranged in pentagons as well as hexagons. Materials made from buckyballs:
- conduct electricity because they have delocalised electrons
- are soft when in the solid state because they have weak intermolecular forces.

Nanotubes have closed ends or open ends. They can be several mm long. Nanotubes:
- conduct electricity because they have delocalised electrons
- are very strong because the structure has many strong covalent bonds.

Worked example

The diagram shows a section of a molecule of poly(ethene), a simple polymer.

Describe the structure of poly(ethene).   **(2 marks)**

Poly(ethene) consists of large molecules containing chains of carbon atoms. These atoms are joined to each other, and to hydrogen atoms, by covalent bonds.

Polymers are large molecules made from many smaller molecules, called **monomers**, joined together.

Poly(ethene) is not a fullerene:
- It is a **hydrocarbon** (a compound of carbon and hydrogen).

Polymer molecules are described as **macromolecules** rather than giant covalent molecules.

Now try this

1 Describe the properties of graphene that make it suitable for use in flexible touch screens.   **(2 marks)**

2 Explain why buckminsterfullerene has a much lower melting point than diamond.   **(3 marks)**

Metals

Most elements are metals, and are placed on the left-hand side of the periodic table.

Metals versus non-metals

Some typical physical properties:

Property	Metals	Non-metals
appearance	shiny	dull
electrical conduction	good conductors	poor conductors
density	high	low
melting point	high	low

Mercury is liquid at room temperature.

Diamond and graphite have very high melting points. Graphite conducts electricity.

In addition:
* metals are **malleable** – they can be pressed into shape without shattering
* non-metals are **brittle** in the solid state – they shatter when bent or hit.

Metallic structure and bonding

A metal:

✓ consists of a giant lattice of positively charged metal ions

✓ has a 'sea' of delocalised electrons.

The delocalised electrons come from the outer shells of the atoms.

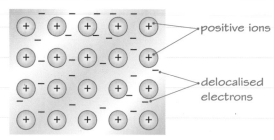

positive ions

delocalised electrons

Metallic bonds are strong electrostatic forces of attraction between positive metal ions and delocalised electrons.

Malleable metals

If a force is applied to a metal:
* layers of positive ions slide over each other
* the metal changes shape without shattering.

Insoluble metals

Metals are insoluble in water. However, some metals do seem to dissolve in water.

This is because they react with the water to produce soluble metal hydroxides. These dissolve, exposing more metal to the water.

For example, sodium reacts with water, forming sodium hydroxide solution and hydrogen:

$$2Na(s) + 2H_2O(l) \rightarrow 2NaOH(aq) + H_2(g)$$

You can revise the reactions of sodium and other group 1 metals on page 133.

metals on page 133.

Worked example

Copper is used in electricity cables. Explain, in terms of structure and bonding, why metals are good conductors of electricity. **(2 marks)**

Metals contain delocalised electrons which can move through the structure of the metal.

Copper is also **ductile**. It can be pulled to make wires without breaking. This is because its layers of positive ions can slide over each other.

The answer makes it clear that the delocalised electrons, not the metal ions, move through the structure.

Now try this

1 Aluminium is used to make overhead mains electricity cables. In terms of its structure and bonding, explain why aluminium is:
   (a) ductile **(2 marks)**
   (b) a good conductor of electricity. **(2 marks)**

2 Mercury is a liquid metal at room temperature. State whether it should conduct electricity, giving a reason for your answer. **(1 mark)**

Limitations of models

The structure and bonding of different substances are represented using **models**. Different models have different features and limitations. All the examples on this page refer to ethanoic acid.

Written formulae

The formula for a substance can be written as:
- an empirical formula
- a molecular formula
- a **structural** formula.

Empirical	Molecular	Structural
CH_2O	$C_2H_4O_2$	CH_3COOH

This is the simplest whole number ratio of atoms of each element. This does not show how the atoms are arranged, or (usually) the actual number of atoms.

This is the number of atoms of each element. This does not show how the atoms are arranged.

This is the number of atoms of each element. This does give an idea of how they are arranged.

Drawn structures

When you draw a structure, you should show all the covalent bonds in the molecule.

This carbon atom is covalently bonded to three hydrogen atoms. It is also covalently bonded to another carbon atom.

This carbon atom is covalently bonded to two oxygen atoms. It has a double bond to one of them.

This model does not show:
- the molecule's three-dimensional shape
- the bonding and non-bonding electrons.

Ball-and-stick models

You can draw **ball-and-stick models**. You can also make them using plastic modelling kits.

These models show:
- how each atom is bonded to other atoms
- the molecule's three-dimensional shape.

They do not show the bonding and non-bonding electrons, or each element's chemical symbol.

Space-filling models

Similar to ball-and-stick models but more accurately represent:

✓ the sizes of atoms relative to their bonds.

You may not be able to see all the atoms in a complex space-filling model.

The diagram below is a dot-and-cross diagram.

Describe the information it provides. State a limitation of this model.   **(4 marks)**

Dot-and-cross diagrams are two-dimensional models. This one may lead you to think incorrectly that ethanoic acid molecules are flat.

The diagram shows the symbol for each atom in the molecule. It also shows how each atom is bonded to other atoms. The pairs of electrons in each covalent bond are shown by dots and crosses. Non-bonding pairs of electrons in the outer shells are included.

It does not show the three-dimensional shape of the molecule.

Now try this

State **one** limitation of each model described on this page.   **(7 marks)**

Relative formula mass

You should be able to calculate relative formula masses when given relative atomic masses.

Calculating relative formula mass

Relative formula mass has the symbol M_r.

To calculate the M_r of a substance, add together the relative atomic masses of all the atoms shown in its formula:

oxygen molecule – formula O_2
relative atomic mass of oxygen = 16
relative formula mass = 2×16
= 32

No units

M_r values are just numbers.

This is because an M_r value is the mass of a molecule or unit of a substance compared with 1/12th the mass of a ^{12}C atom. The M in M_r stands for 'molecular'.

You might see or hear the term 'relative molecular mass'. This really applies only to covalent substances.

Worked example

Calculate the relative formula mass of aluminium oxide, Al_2O_3. **(1 mark)**
(relative atomic masses: Al = 27, O = 16)

atoms in Al_2O_3:
$(2 \times Al) + (3 \times O)$
$M_r = (2 \times 27) + (3 \times 16)$
= 54 + 48
= 102

You do not need to learn any relative atomic masses. You will be given them in questions or you can find them on the periodic table.

This answer shows you the working out needed to obtain the answer.

If you show the working for steps in the calculation you may gain some marks even if your final answer is incorrect.

Worked example

Calculate the relative formula mass of calcium nitrate, $Ca(NO_3)_2$. **(1 mark)**
(relative atomic masses: Ca = 40, N = 14, O = 16)

atoms in $Ca(NO_3)_2$:
$(1 \times Ca) + (2 \times 1 \times N) + (2 \times 3 \times O)$
$M_r = (1 \times 40) + (2 \times 14) + (6 \times 16)$
= 40 + 28 + 96
= 164

Maths skills You may find it easier if you first add up the A_r values for the atoms inside the brackets:

M_r of $NO_3 = 14 + (3 \times 16)$
= 14 + 48
= 62

Then multiply your answer by the number outside, and add that to the remaining A_r values:

M_r of $Ca(NO_3)_2 = 40 + (2 \times 62)$
= 40 + 124
= 164

Now try this

relative atomic masses: H = 1, C = 12, O = 16, Na = 23, Al = 27, S = 32, Cl = 35.5, Cu = 63.5

Calculate the relative formula masses, M_r, of the following substances.
(a) H_2O **(1 mark)**
(b) CO_2 **(1 mark)**
(c) NaOH **(1 mark)**

(d) CCl_4 **(1 mark)**
(e) $CuCl_2$ **(1 mark)**

(f) Na_2SO_4 **(1 mark)**
(g) $Al(OH)_3$ **(1 mark)**
(h) $Al_2(CO_3)_3$ **(1 mark)**

Empirical formulae

An **empirical formula** is the simplest whole-number ratio of atoms of each element in a compound.

Calculating an empirical formula

A 10 g sample of a compound **X** contains 8 g of carbon and 2 g of hydrogen.

		C	H
1	Write the symbol of each element as a header	C	H
2	Write down the mass of each element in g	8	2
3	Write down the A_r of each element	12	1
4	For each element, calculate: mass ÷ A_r	$\frac{8}{12} = 0.667$	$\frac{2}{1} = 2$
5	Divide each answer by the smallest answer (0.667 here)	$\frac{0.667}{0.667} = 1$	$\frac{2}{0.667} = 3$
6	You may then need to multiply all the numbers to remove fractions, then write out the empirical formula	CH_3	

Finding a molecular formula

You can find the molecular formula of a compound from its empirical formula:
• if you know its relative formula mass, M_r.

The M_r of **X** in the example above is 30:

1 Calculate the M_r of the empirical formula:

M_r of $CH_3 = 12 + (3 \times 1) = 15$

2 Divide the M_r of **X** by answer 1:

$\frac{30}{15} = 2$

3 Multiply each number in the empirical formula by answer 2:

CH_3 becomes C_2H_6 – the molecular formula

Practical skills — Determining empirical formula

You need to be able to describe an experiment to determine an empirical formula.

The apparatus below can be used to obtain results to do this for magnesium oxide.

- crucible and lid
- magnesium ribbon
- pipeclay triangle
- tripod

HEAT

The crucible and its contents are weighed before and after heating the magnesium.

Worked example

The table shows the results of an experiment to find the empirical formula of magnesium oxide.

Object	Mass (g)
empty crucible and lid	19.06
crucible, lid and Mg before heating	19.42
crucible, lid and Mg after heating	19.66

(a) Calculate the mass of magnesium used. **(1 mark)**

mass of magnesium = 19.42 – 19.06
= 0.36 g

(b) Calculate the mass of oxygen gained. **(1 mark)**

mass of oxygen = 19.66 – 19.42
= 0.24 g

Now try this

Use the masses given in the Worked example to determine the empirical formula of magnesium oxide. (relative atomic masses: O = 16, Mg = 24) **(3 marks)**

Set out your calculations as shown at the top of the page.

Conservation of mass

According to the **law of conservation of mass**, the total mass of reactants and products stays constant during a chemical reaction. The total mass before and after a reaction is the same.

Closed systems

A **closed system** is a situation in which no substances can enter or leave during a reaction.

Closed systems include:
* reactions in a sealed container, such as a flask fitted with a bung
* precipitation reactions in a beaker.

In a **precipitation reaction**, two **soluble** reactants form an **insoluble** product – the **precipitate**. For example:

$NaCl(aq) + AgNO_3(aq) \rightarrow$ forms a cloudy white
$NaNO_3(aq) + AgCl(s)$ precipitate

The total mass of the beaker and its contents stays the same during the formation of the silver chloride precipitate.

Non-enclosed systems

A **non-enclosed system** is a situation in which substances can enter or leave during a reaction.

Non-enclosed or 'open' systems include:
* reactions in an open flask, where a substance in the gas state may enter or leave.

Mass is conserved, but you will observe the following:
* The mass of a reactive metal **increases** if it is heated in air. This is because oxygen atoms combine with metal atoms to form a metal oxide.
* The mass of a reactive non-metal or a fuel **decreases** if it is heated in air. This is because products in the gas state escape from the container.
* The mass of a metal carbonate **decreases** if it is heated. This is because carbon dioxide gas is produced and this escapes from the container.

Mass calculations

Always start with the balanced equation. You do not need state symbols.

Work out the relative masses and multiply by the balancing numbers. You only need to do this for the substances asked for in the question.

Divide by the number for lithium to find the mass of hydrogen produced for each gram of lithium.

Multiply by the mass of lithum given in the question.

Worked example

0.5 g of lithium metal is added to water. Calculate the mass of hydrogen gas produced.
(4 marks)

(relative atomic masses: Li = 7, H = 1)

$2Li + 2H_2O \rightarrow 2LiOH + H_2$

$2 \times 7 \qquad\qquad 1 \times (1 + 1)$

$= 14 \qquad\qquad\qquad = 2$

14 g of Li $\rightarrow$ 2 g of H_2

1 g $\rightarrow \dfrac{2}{14}$ g = 0.143 g

0.5 g $\rightarrow$ 0.143 g × 0.5

$= 0.072$

0.072 g of hydrogen is produced.

Now try this

1 Methane, CH_4, burns in oxygen to form carbon dioxide and water.
$CH_4 + 2O_2 \rightarrow CO_2 + 2H_2O$
Calculate the mass of oxygen used when 10 g of methane burns.
(relative atomic masses: C = 12, H = 1, O = 16)
(4 marks)

2 Potassium reacts with chlorine to form potassium chloride, KCl. Calculate the mass of potassium needed to produce 20.0 g of potassium chloride.
(relative atomic masses: K = 39, Cl = 35.5)
(4 marks)

Concentration of solution

You need to be able to calculate the concentration of solutions in g dm^{-3}.

Solute, solvent and solution

A **solution** is a mixture of a solute in a solvent:
- The **solute** is the substance that dissolves.
- The **solvent** is the substance that the solute dissolves in.

Water is the solvent in an **aqueous solution**. The state symbol for an aqueous solution in balanced equations is (aq). The symbol (l) is for substances in the liquid state.

Mass and volume

To calculate the **concentration** of a solution, you need to know:
- the mass of solute in **grams**, g, and
- the volume of solution in **cubic decimetres**, dm^3.

If you are making a solution, you can use the volume of the solvent instead.

dm³ and cm³

Measuring cylinders and other lab apparatus show volumes in cubic centimetres, cm^3. You need to convert these measurements into cubic decimetres, dm^3, when you calculate concentrations. It helps to know that:

✓ 1 dm^3 = 10 × 10 × 10 = 1000 cm^3

✓ to convert cm^3 to dm^3, divide by 1000.

Mass, volume and concentration

You use this equation to calculate the concentration of a solution in g dm^{-3}:

$$\text{concentration (g dm}^{-3}） = \frac{\text{mass of solute (g)}}{\text{volume of solution (dm}^3）}$$

 LEARN IT! IT'S NOT ON THE EQUATIONS LIST

 Units

The unit g dm^{-3} means 'grams per cubic decimetre'. You may also see it written as g/dm^3.

 Rearranging equations

You need to be able to change the subject of an equation. For example:

✓ mass of solute = concentration × volume

✓ volume = $\dfrac{\text{mass of solute}}{\text{concentration}}$

Worked example

2.50 g of sodium hydroxide is dissolved in 250 cm^3 of water. Calculate the concentration of the solution formed in g dm^{-3}. **(2 marks)**

$$250 \text{ cm}^3 = \frac{250}{1000} = 0.250 \text{ dm}^3$$

$$\text{concentration} = \frac{2.50 \text{ g}}{0.250 \text{ dm}^3} = 10 \text{ g dm}^{-3}$$

Remember to convert the volume to dm^3 if it is given to you in cm^3.

The units are shown in the concentration calculation here. This makes it easier for you to see how it is done. You do not need to show units in your working out, but you must show the units in your final answer.

Now try this

1 Calculate the concentrations of the following solutions formed:
  (a) 0.40 g of glucose dissolved in 0.50 dm^3 of water. **(1 mark)**
  (b) 1.25 g of copper chloride dissolved in 100 cm^3 of water. **(2 marks)**

2 Calculate the mass of sodium hydroxide needed to make 150 cm^3 of a 40 g dm^{-3} solution. **(2 marks)**

Extended response – Types of substance

There will be one or more 6-mark questions on your exam paper. For these questions, you will need to think scientifically and structure your answer logically, showing how the points you make are related to each other. You can revise the topics for this question, which is about the **structure and bonding** of different types of substance, on pages 83–98.

Worked example

Sodium chloride is an ionic compound produced in the reaction between sodium and chlorine. The table shows information about how well these three substances conduct electricity at room temperature.

Substance	Ability to conduct
sodium	conducts
chlorine	does not conduct
sodium chloride	does not conduct

Explain, in terms of structure and bonding, the differences in the ability to conduct electricity.

(6 marks)

Sodium is a metal. It consists of a regular lattice of positively charged sodium ions attracted to a sea of delocalised electrons. These electrons are free to move, so solid sodium conducts electricity.

On the other hand, chlorine is a simple molecular substance. Its molecules are attracted to each other by weak intermolecular forces. Even though its molecules are free to move they are uncharged, so chlorine does not conduct.

Sodium chloride is an ionic compound. In the solid state, it contains oppositely charged ions held together strongly in a regular lattice. Therefore, even though it contains charged particles, these are not free to move. This is why solid sodium chloride does not conduct electricity.

Command word: Explain

When you are asked to **explain** something, it is not enough just to state or describe it. Your answer **must** contain some reasoning or justification of the points you make. Your explanation **can** include mathematical explanations, if calculations are needed.

In this example Extended response question, no calculations are needed.

 You should give a description of the structure of a solid metal, making it clear that solid sodium contains sodium ions. You should also give the reason why sodium conducts electricity.

 You should use **connectives** as you move from one idea to the next. Here the use of 'on the other hand' shows that this part of the answer is in contrast to the first part of the answer.

 This part of the answer includes another connective: 'therefore' indicates that the sentence before has a consequence. In this case the lattice structure prevents the conduction of electricity.

You need to show comprehensive knowledge and understanding using relevant scientific ideas to support your explanations. You should consider each substance in turn, giving clear lines of reasoning. Leave out any information or ideas that are unnecessary to answer the question.

Now try this

Mercury is a metal and paraffin oil is a simple molecular compound. Both exist as liquids at room temperature. Paraffin oil does not conduct electricity but mercury does.

Explain, in terms of structure and bonding, the differences in the ability to conduct electricity.

(6 marks)

States of matter

The **particle theory** models the states of matter, with particles described as hard spheres.

	Solid	Liquid	Gas
Particle diagram	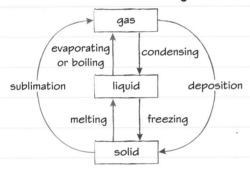		
Arrangement of particles	close together regular pattern	close together random	far apart random
Movement of particles	vibrate about fixed positions	move around each other	fast in all directions
Relative energy of particles	least stored energy	→→→	most stored energy

State changes

The interconversions between states of matter are called **state changes**.

```
              gas
        ↗           ↘
evaporating      condensing
or boiling   ↓        ↓
sublimation  liquid   deposition
        ↑        ↓
  melting      freezing
        ↖    ↓    ↙
            solid
```

During a state change:
- energy is transferred to or from the particles
- the arrangement of particles changes
- the movement of particles changes.

Melting and boiling points

At its **melting point**, a substance begins to:
- ✓ melt if energy is transferred to the particles
- ✓ freeze if energy is transferred to the surroundings.

At its **boiling point**, a substance begins to:
- ✓ boil if energy is transferred to the particles
- ✓ condense if energy is transferred to the surroundings.

A substance evaporates if it changes from a liquid to a gas below its boiling point:
- ✓ Particles with high enough energy leave the surface of the liquid.
- ✓ The remaining particles have less energy.
- ✓ The liquid cools down unless it is heated.

Worked example

The table shows some data about bromine.

Melting point (°C)	Boiling point (°C)
−7	59

(a) Predict the state of bromine at 25 °C. **(1 mark)**

liquid

(b) Describe, in terms of the particle theory, what happens when bromine boils. **(3 marks)**

Forces of attraction between bromine particles are overcome and the particles move far apart. The particles no longer just move around each other, but move quickly in all directions.

A substance is a:
- solid below its melting point
- gas above its boiling point
- liquid between its melting and boiling points.

See pages 91–98 to revise the different types of bonds and forces. Some forces of attraction are overcome during melting, and the remainder during boiling.

State changes are **physical changes** because the particles themselves are unchanged.

Chemical reactions cause **chemical changes** – the particles are changed by rearranging atoms.

Now try this

Naphthalene is a solid that can change directly from a solid to a gas at room temperature. Name this change of state. Describe what happens to the particles. **(5 marks)**

Pure substances and mixtures

Elements and compounds

An **element** is a substance that consists only of atoms with the same atomic number (the same number of protons in their nucleus), e.g.

- Hydrogen is an element because its atoms all have one proton in their nucleus.
- Oxygen is a different element because its atoms all have eight protons.

A **compound** is a substance that consists of atoms of two or more different elements, chemically joined together.

For example, water is a compound. This is because it consists of hydrogen atoms and oxygen atoms chemically joined together.

You can revise **ionic bonds** on page 93 and **covalent bonds** on page 94.

Atoms and molecules

Elements exist as atoms or molecules.

Argon is in group 0. It has no tendency to gain, lose or share electrons. It exists as single atoms (that is, it is **monatomic**).

Hydrogen and oxygen exist as simple molecules.

Carbon exists as giant molecules (diamond, graphite and graphene).

Compounds exist as:

✓ molecules, such as water, H_2O

✓ ionic structures.

Pure substances and mixtures

In everyday use, the word 'pure' usually means that nothing has been added to a substance.

In chemistry, a **pure** substance contains only one element or compound, e.g.

- pure hydrogen contains only hydrogen molecules
- pure water contains only water molecules.

Most substances are **mixtures** because they contain different elements and/or compounds. Mixtures are impure substances.

The parts of a mixture are not chemically joined together.

Air

Air is a mixture of:

✓ elements, such as nitrogen, N_2, oxygen, O_2, and argon, Ar

✓ compounds, such as water, H_2O, and carbon dioxide, CO_2.

Worked example

A student heats a sample of solid hexadecanol in a hot-water bath. She measures its temperature at regular intervals until after it melts. The graph shows her results.

Explain how the results show whether the hexadecanol is pure or impure. **(2 marks)**

The hexadecanol is pure because it has a sharp melting point, shown by the horizontal part of the heating curve. A mixture would melt over a range of temperatures instead.

The melting point of hexadecanol is 49 °C.

Now try this

1 The label on a bottle describes the contents as 'pure mineral water'.
Explain why the water is not pure in the scientific sense. **(3 marks)**

2 When it is heated, 18 carat gold melts between 915 °C and 963 °C.
Explain why its melting point is not a single temperature. **(2 marks)**

Distillation

You can separate liquids from mixtures using **distillation**.

 Simple distillation

You use **simple distillation** to separate:

☑ a solvent from a solution.

For example, you can separate water from seawater (a mixture of water and dissolved compounds) using this method.

The **condenser** has two tubes, one inside the other:

☑ Cold water runs through the space between the two tubes, keeping the condenser cold.

The cooling water does not mix with the substance being separated.

 Fractional distillation

You use **fractional distillation** to separate:

☑ a liquid from a mixture of **miscible** liquids (liquids that mix completely with each other).

For example, you can separate ethanol from a mixture of ethanol and water using this method.

The **fractionating column** used in fractional distillation has a **temperature gradient**:

☑ hottest at the bottom, coldest at the top.

Explaining simple distillation

Simple distillation works because the solute in the solution has a much higher boiling point than the solvent.

When the solution is heated:
• the solvent boils
• solvent vapour passes into the condenser
• the vapour is cooled and condensed back to the liquid state.

The solution becomes more **concentrated** during simple distillation because the solute stays behind.

Explaining fractional distillation

Fractional distillation works because the liquids in the mixture have different boiling points.

When the mixture is heated:
• the mixture boils
• hot vapour rises up the fractionating column
• vapour condenses when it hits the cool surface of the column and drips back
• the fraction with the lowest boiling point reaches the top of the column first
• its vapour passes into the condenser.

If you carry on heating, vapours from fractions with higher boiling points pass to the condenser.

 Now try this

(a) Explain the function of a condenser in distillation. **(2 marks)**

(b) State the physical property that allows substances to be separated by distillation. **(1 mark)**

(c) Describe the temperature gradient in a fractionating column. **(1 mark)**

Filtration and crystallisation

Filtration and crystallisation are two important techniques for separating mixtures.

 Filtration

You use **filtration** to separate an insoluble substance from a liquid or a solution. There are two reasons for doing this:

 to purify a liquid or a solution by removing solid impurities from it, e.g. sand from water

 to separate the solid you want from the liquid it is mixed with, e.g. to separate crystals from a solution after crystallisation.

mixture of solution and insoluble solid · filter funnel
residue · filter paper
· filtrate

 Crystallisation

You use **crystallisation** to produce:

✓ solid crystals from a solution.

In crystallisation:

✓ the solution is heated to remove enough solvent to produce a **saturated** solution (one that cannot hold any more solute)

✓ the saturated solution is allowed to cool

✓ **crystals** form in the solution

✓ the crystals are separated from the liquid and dried.

· solution
· hot water

A hot-water bath gives you more control over heating than using a Bunsen burner flame directly on the evaporating basin.

Explaining filtration

Filtration works because the filter paper has tiny holes called pores. These are:
- large enough to let water molecules and dissolved substances through
- small enough to stop insoluble solid particles going through.

Explaining crystallisation

Solubility is the mass of solute that dissolves in a given volume of solvent at a given temperature. Crystallisation works because:
- the solubility of the solute goes down as the saturated solution cools
- crystals form from the excess solute.

Worked example

A student wants to produce some copper sulfate crystals from copper sulfate solution. She heats the solution in an evaporating basin to remove some of the water.

Describe the steps that she should then take to obtain dry crystals of copper sulfate. **(3 marks)**

She should let the solution cool down so that crystals form. She should then decant the remaining liquid and dry the crystals in an oven.

It is safer to make a concentrated or saturated solution than to remove all the water. The crystals will be a better size and shape, and will not spit out of the evaporating basin.

Decanting means pouring the liquid away carefully so that the solid stays behind. The student could use filtration instead to separate the crystals from the liquid. She could pat them dry using filter paper.

Now try this

Glass and dust are insoluble in water but copper chloride is soluble.

Outline a method to produce dry copper chloride from a mixture of broken glass, dust and copper chloride powder. **(4 marks)**

Paper chromatography

Paper chromatography is used to separate mixtures of soluble substances.

Practical skills — Paper chromatography

lid (to stop evaporation of solvent)

paper

Drops of the different samples are put onto the paper and allowed to dry. The bottom of the paper is then dipped into a solvent.

solvent (this can be water or some other liquid that the samples will dissolve in)

solvent front (the solvent has reached this level)

The different compounds in a sample dissolve to different extents in the solvent.

More soluble compounds are carried up the paper faster than less soluble ones, so the compounds separate out.

Explaining chromatography

In chromatography, there are two phases:

   a **stationary phase** (a substance that does not move)

   a **mobile phase** (a substance that moves through the stationary phase – the solvent).

During chromatography:

• each soluble substance in the mixture forms bonds with the two phases
• substances that form stronger attractive forces with the stationary phase stay near the bottom
• substances that form stronger attractive forces with the mobile phase move towards the top.

Using a chromatogram

You can use a **chromatogram** to:

✓ distinguish between pure and impure substances (a pure substance will produce only one spot)

✓ identify a substance by comparing its pattern of spots with those of a known substance

✓ identify substances using R_f values.

Maths skills — R_f values

$$R_f = \frac{\text{distance travelled by spot}}{\text{distance travelled by solvent}}$$

R_f values have no units. They vary from 0 (spot stays on baseline) to 1 (spot travels with solvent front).

Worked example

What is the R_f value of the lowest spot for sample C in this chromatogram? **(1 mark)**

☐ **A** 0.20
☒ **B** 0.40 $R_f = \dfrac{4\ cm}{10\ cm} = 0.4$
☐ **C** 0.44
☐ **D** 0.90

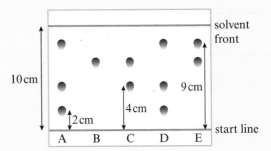

Now try this

1 Calculate the R_f values for the lowest spot in A and the highest spot in E (see above). **(2 marks)**

2 Explain, in terms of attractive forces, why a spot travels far up the paper. **(2 marks)**

Investigating inks

 Practical skills You can use **simple distillation** and **paper chromatography** to investigate the composition of inks.

Core practical

Paper chromatography

> You can revise paper chromatography on page 109.

Aim

> Ink is a mixture of coloured substances dissolved in a solvent.

To investigate the composition of inks using paper chromatography.

Apparatus

> Eye protection is important because you should treat all substances in the lab (apart from water straight from the tap) as potentially harmful.
>
> You could use a narrow glass **capillary tube** instead of a pipette to obtain tiny drops of ink.

- eye protection
- chromatography paper
- boiling tube with bung
- dropping pipette
- pencil and ruler
- solvent for mobile phase.

Method

> The solvent used depends on the type of ink. For ballpoint pen ink, you may need to use propanone rather than water.
>
> If you write a **risk assessment**, remember to include hazardous substances and procedures. For example, propanone is flammable and it has a harmful vapour, so you would need to keep it away from Bunsen burner flames and make sure that the lab is well ventilated.

Draw a pencil line near the bottom of the chromatography paper. Apply a small spot of ink to the line, and then place the paper into a boiling tube containing a little solvent. Replace the bung and allow the solvent to travel through the paper.

chromatography paper

rising solvent

final height of solvent

ink spot

level of solvent

Results

Measure:
- the distance from the pencil line to the solvent front
- the distance from the pencil line to the centre of each spot.

Record the colour of each spot and its R_f value.

Simple distillation

You can use simple distillation to separate the solvent in the ink from the coloured substances. The method you use will depend on the apparatus available to you in school.

> Revise simple distillation on page 107.

> **Maths skills** You could use a suitable table to record the results. Remember:
>
> $$R_f = \frac{\text{distance travelled by spot}}{\text{distance travelled by solvent}}$$
>
> Measure distances in millimetres rather than centimetres.

Now try this

A student uses simple distillation to purify the solvent in a sample of ink. The method that he uses is as follows:

- Add some ink to a boiling tube, then fit a delivery tube and bung.
- Hold the boiling tube with a test-tube holder.
- Heat the ink using a roaring Bunsen burner flame until it is dry.
- Collect the vapour in a test tube.

State **two** ways of improving his method using the same essential equipment. **(2 marks)**

> You could suggest different ways of working. You could also suggest additional apparatus to improve the safety or efficiency of the practical activity.

Drinking water

Waste water and ground water is treated to make it **potable** (safe to drink).

Drinking water

Potable drinking water must have:
- low levels of contaminating substances
- low levels of microbes.

Fresh water can come from reservoirs, lakes and rivers. It is likely to contain:
- objects such as leaves and twigs
- insoluble solids such as particles of soil
- microbes, which may cause disease.

The water must be treated to remove these.

Safe but not pure

Tap water is potable but it is not a pure substance. It contains:
- ✓ dissolved salts
- ✓ dissolved chlorine.

Stages in water treatment

The main stages are as follows:

1. **sedimentation** – large insoluble particles sink to the bottom of a tank
2. **filtration** – small insoluble particles are removed by filtering through beds of sand
3. **chlorination** – chlorine gas is bubbled through the water to kill microbes.

Sea water and distillation

Sea water contains dissolved salts. Their concentration is too high to drink it safely. Sea water can be made potable by simple distillation:
- Filtered sea water is boiled.
- The water vapour is cooled and condensed to form **distilled water**.

Distilled water does not contain dissolved salts, but it contains dissolved gases from the air.

Evaluating distillation

Simple distillation of sea water:
- 👍 uses a plentiful raw material
- 👍 produces pure water
- 👍 kills microbes in the sea water
- 👎 needs a lot of energy to heat the water.

Distillation is rarely used in the UK, which has high fuel costs. It is suitable for countries with low fuel costs, little fresh water, or plentiful sunshine to evaporate the water without using a fuel.

Worked example

Explain why water used for a chemical analysis must not contain any dissolved salts. **(3 marks)**

Dissolved salts could react with the substances used in the analysis. A product formed in the reaction could interfere with the analysis, giving a false result. If the water used does not contain any dissolved salts, this will not happen.

Many substances used for chemical analysis are used in aqueous solution (dissolved in water).

Dissolved salts may react with a sample, forming insoluble precipitates. Analytical instruments may detect the dissolved salts, giving a false result.

Now try this

1 Describe what is meant by 'potable'. **(1 mark)**

2 In the UK, fresh water is piped from reservoirs so that it can be treated to make it safe to drink.
Name and describe the three main stages in water treatment. **(3 marks)**

Extended response – Separating mixtures

There will be one or more 6-mark questions on your exam paper. For these questions, you will need to think scientifically and structure your answer logically, showing how the points you make are related to each other. You can revise the topics for this question, which is about **states of matter** and **separation techniques**, on pages 105–109.

Worked example

Nitrogen and oxygen are useful substances in air.
They can be separated from air by:
- cooling air until water vapour and carbon dioxide solidify
- filtering the chilled air
- further cooling the filtered air to –200 °C
- carrying out fractional distillation.

Substance	Melting point (°C)	Boiling point (°C)
nitrogen	–210	–196
oxygen	–219	–183
water vapour	0	100
carbon dioxide	–78.5	–78.5

The table gives information about four substances found in air. Use the information above, and your knowledge and understanding of separation methods, to explain how nitrogen and oxygen may be separated in this way. **(6 marks)**

If the air is cooled to below –78.5 °C but above –183 °C, the water vapour and carbon dioxide will become solid. The nitrogen and oxygen will stay as gases, so the solid water and carbon dioxide could then be filtered to remove them. This will stop them contaminating the oxygen and nitrogen later in the process.

 Use data from the table to suggest the range of temperatures needed to solidify water and carbon dioxide. Use your knowledge and understanding of separation techniques to suggest how they could be separated from oxygen and nitrogen.

When the filtered air is cooled to –200 °C, the oxygen and nitrogen will condense to form a mixture of liquids. This mixture can then be piped into a fractionating column. The column should be warmer at the bottom and colder towards the top.

 Use data from the table to describe what happens to the oxygen and nitrogen at –200 °C. Use your knowledge and understanding of fractional distillation to describe the temperature gradient needed in the column.

In the fractionating column, the nitrogen will boil more easily than the oxygen, because it has the lower boiling point. Nitrogen gas can leave from the top of the column and oxygen from the bottom of the column. Depending on the temperature at the bottom, the oxygen could leave as a liquid or a gas.

 Use data from the table to explain why oxygen and nitrogen can be separated by fractional distillation. Use your knowledge and understanding to describe where each substance will leave the fractionating column.

You need to show comprehensive knowledge and understanding. Be prepared to apply what you know to a new context. Use the data given to you in a structured way with clear lines of reasoning.

Now try this

Calcium carbonate is effectively insoluble.

Substance	Solubility at 25 °C (g dm⁻³ water)
sodium carbonate	307
calcium carbonate	0.013

Sodium carbonate and calcium carbonate are both white powders at room temperature. The table shows some information about them. A student accidentally makes a mixture of the two powders. Use the information in the table, and your knowledge and understanding of separation methods, to explain how the student could produce separate, dry samples of sodium carbonate and calcium carbonate from this mixture. **(6 marks)**

Acids and alkalis

You can recognise acids and alkalis by their effects on indicator solutions.

Acids

Acids have these properties:
- The pH of their aqueous solutions is less than 7.
- They are a source of **hydrogen ions**, $H^+(aq)$ in solution.

Hydrochloric acid releases H^+ ions:
$$HCl(aq) \rightarrow H^+(aq) + Cl^-(aq)$$

Ethanoic acid releases H^+ ions:
$$CH_3COOH(aq) \rightarrow CH_3COO^-(aq) + H^+(aq)$$

- The more strongly acidic a solution is, the lower its pH.

Alkalis

Alkalis have these properties:
- The pH of their aqueous solutions is more than 7.
- They are a source of **hydroxide ions**, $OH^-(aq)$ in solution.

Sodium hydroxide releases OH^- ions:
$$NaOH(aq) \rightarrow Na^+(aq) + OH^-(aq)$$

Ammonia produces OH^- ions in solution:
$$NH_3(g) + H_2O(l) \rightarrow NH_4^+(aq) + OH^-(aq)$$

- The more strongly alkaline a solution is, the higher its pH.

The pH scale

The **pH scale** is a measure of the **acidity** or **alkalinity** of a solution (how acidic or alkaline it is). It goes from 0 to 14. **Neutral** solutions are pH 7.

Indicators are substances that have different colours, depending on their pH. Universal indicator solution or paper is often used to estimate the pH of a solution.

0 1 2 3 4 5 6 7 8 9 10 11 12 13 14

← increasingly acidic   neutral   increasingly alkaline →

The indicator colour is matched to a colour chart, which shows the pH of each colour.

Worked example

Litmus and phenolphthalein are single indicators. Complete the table to show their colours in acidic and alkaline solutions.   **(4 marks)**

Indicator	In acidic solution	In alkaline solution
litmus	red	blue
phenolphthalein	colourless	pink

Methyl orange is another single indicator (unlike universal indicator, which is a mixed indicator). Single indicators are useful in **titrations**. You can revise titrations on page 117.

Methyl orange is:
- red in acidic solutions
- yellow in alkaline solutions.

You will see an orange colour at the end-point of a titration.

Now try this

The paper can change colour (as litmus solution does) or stay the same colour.

1 Explain why sodium chloride, NaCl, dissolves in water to produce a solution with a pH of 7, but hydrogen chloride, HCl, dissolves in water to produce a solution with a pH below 7.   **(3 marks)**

	Acidic solution	Alkaline solution
Red litmus		
Blue litmus		

2 Potassium reacts with water:
$$2K(s) + 2H_2O(l) \rightarrow 2KOH(aq) + H_2(g)$$
State and explain the effect that the solution formed has on phenolphthalein.   **(2 marks)**

3 Copy and complete this table to show the colours of litmus paper in different solutions.   **(2 marks)**

Bases and alkalis

An **alkali** is a soluble **base** – one that will dissolve in water.

Reactions of acids with bases

A **base** is:
- any substance that reacts with an acid to form a salt and water **only**.

Bases are metal oxides and metal hydroxides. In general:

$$\text{base} + \text{acid} \rightarrow \text{salt} + \text{water}$$

For example:

$$NaOH + HCl \rightarrow NaCl + H_2O$$
$$CuO + 2HNO_3 \rightarrow Cu(NO_3)_2 + H_2O$$

Naming salts

A **salt** forms when hydrogen ions in an acid are replaced by metal ions or ammonium ions. The name of a salt consists of two parts:
- first part – the metal in the base
- second part – from the acid used.

Acid used	Second part
hydrochloric acid, HCl	chloride
nitric acid, HNO_3	nitrate
sulfuric acid, H_2SO_4	sulfate

Reactions of acids with metals

Reactive metals react with acids to produce a salt and hydrogen **only**. In general:

$$\text{metal} + \text{acid} \rightarrow \text{salt} + \text{hydrogen}$$

For example:

$$Mg + 2HCl \rightarrow MgCl_2 + H_2$$
$$2Al + 3H_2SO_4 \rightarrow Al_2(SO_4)_3 + 3H_2$$

Reactions of acids with metal carbonates

Metal carbonates react with acids to produce a salt, water **and** carbon dioxide. In general:

$$\text{metal carbonate} + \text{acid} \rightarrow \text{salt} + \text{water} + \text{carbon dioxide}$$

For example:

$$CaCO_3 + 2HCl \rightarrow CaCl_2 + H_2O + CO_2$$

🧪 Practical skills Hydrogen

A **lighted splint** ignites hydrogen with a 'pop'.

gas collected in upturned test tube

'pop' sound

hydrogen made in reaction

lighted splint

🧪 Practical skills Carbon dioxide

Carbon dioxide turns **limewater** milky or cloudy white.

carbon dioxide

limewater

turns milky

Neutralisation

A **neutralisation** reaction is a reaction between an acid and a base. When an acid reacts with an alkali, hydrogen ions (H^+) from the acid react with hydroxide ions (OH^-) from the alkali to form water.

Now try this

 1 Explain why all alkalis are bases but not all bases are alkalis. **(2 marks)**

 2 Give the formulae, and names, for the five salts formed in the reactions shown on this page. **(5 marks)**

Neutralisation

Core practical

Investigating neutralisation

Aim

To investigate the change in pH when powdered calcium hydroxide, a base, is added to a fixed volume of dilute hydrochloric acid.

Calcium hydroxide is an irritant but calcium oxide is corrosive, so calcium hydroxide is safer to use.

Apparatus

- eye protection
- beaker
- measuring cylinder
- balance
- spatula
- stirring rod
- white tile
- universal indicator paper and pH colour chart
- dilute hydrochloric acid
- calcium hydroxide powder.

You should choose appropriate apparatus for your practical work. If you are using a measuring cylinder, choose one that is closest to the volume of liquid you need. For example, to measure 50 cm³, choose a 50 cm³ measuring cylinder. Do not choose a 25 cm³ or 100 cm³ one.

Method

Add some dilute hydrochloric acid to the beaker. Measure and record the pH of the contents of the beaker. Add a small mass of calcium hydroxide powder, stir, and then measure and record the pH again. Repeat until the pH no longer changes.

You could use a pH meter instead of universal indicator paper. This produces a more precise reading. It will be accurate only if you calibrate it first using standard pH solution.

Results

Use a table to record your results. For example:

Mass of Ca(OH)$_2$ added (g)	pH of mixture
0	
0.3	

Maths skills Make sure that any units, such as g, go in the column headings only. Do not include units in the main body of the table. Do not forget to take a reading before you add anything!

Analysis

Plot a **titration curve** – a line graph with:
- mass (or volume) added on the horizontal axis
- pH on the vertical axis.

Draw a smooth curve best fit, ignoring **anomalous** results (results that are too high or low).

 Label each axis with the quantity and unit (if there is one), e.g. 'mass of Ca(OH)$_2$ (g)'.

 Choose scales so that the plotted points occupy at least 50% of the graph area.

Use a sharp pencil for your graph.

 Plot each point with × (but you might find it more accurate to use + instead).

What pH values do you expect at the start, middle and end? Why?

A student adds portions of a powdered soluble base to dilute hydrochloric acid. She estimates the pH each time using universal indicator paper.

 (a) Describe **two** ways she can ensure that her measurements are precise. **(2 marks)**

(b) Describe how she should use the universal indicator paper to estimate the pH. **(3 marks)**

 (c) The student added the base until it was in excess.
Explain the changes in pH during her experiment. **(6 marks)**

Salts from insoluble bases

🧪 **Practical skills** You can make pure, dry, hydrated copper sulfate crystals, starting from copper oxide.

Core practical

Preparing copper sulfate

Aim

To make a sample of pure, dry, hydrated copper sulfate crystals using copper oxide and sulfuric acid:

$$CuO(s) + H_2SO_4(aq) \rightarrow CuSO_4(aq) + H_2O(l)$$

'Hydrated' copper sulfate crystals are the familiar blue ones. Their structure includes water molecules as **water of crystallisation**.

Apparatus

- eye protection
- beakers
- spatula
- stirring rod
- Bunsen burner
- heat-resistant mat
- tripod and gauze mat
- filter funnel and filter paper
- evaporating basin
- dilute sulfuric acid
- copper oxide powder.

The apparatus is used in the three main stages of this practical:

stage 1: reacting warm sulfuric acid with excess copper oxide powder

stage 2: filtering the reaction mixture to remove excess (unreacted) copper oxide

stage 3: producing hydrated copper sulfate crystals by crystallisation with the help of a hot water bath.

You can revise filtration and crystallisation on page 108.

Method

The diagrams describe the main steps needed.

spatula
insoluble copper oxide
sulfuric acid

unreacted copper oxide
copper sulfate solution

copper sulfate crystals formed by evaporating the water

1. Add excess base to the acid.

2. Filter to remove unreacted copper oxide.

3. Crystallise the copper sulfate solution by heating it or leaving it to stand in a warm place.

The same method works using a metal but hydrogen, $H_2(g)$, is made rather than water. However, copper does not react with sulfuric acid.

Results

Record your observations at each stage and the appearance of the crystals at the end. This could include the dry mass of the crystals, and their colour, sizes and shapes.

Record your observations as you go, rather than trying to remember them afterwards.

Now try this

Devise means that you need to plan or invent a procedure from existing ideas.

Calcium carbonate is an insoluble white solid. It reacts with dilute nitric acid to form calcium nitrate solution:

$$CaCO_3(s) + 2HNO_3(aq) \rightarrow Ca(NO_3)_2(aq) + H_2O(l) + CO_2(g)$$

(a) Describe what you will see when excess calcium carbonate is used in the reaction. **(3 marks)**

(b) Devise a method to prepare a sample of pure, dry, hydrated calcium nitrate crystals. **(6 marks)**

Had a look ☐   Nearly there ☐   Nailed it! ☐

Salts from soluble bases

You should be able to describe how to carry out a **titration** to prepare a pure, dry salt.

Using a soluble base

The flow chart shows the three main steps needed to make a soluble salt from a soluble base.

| Use an acid–base titration to find the exact volume of the soluble base that reacts with the acid. | → | Mix the acid and soluble base in the correct proportions, producing a solution of the salt and water. | → | Warm the salt solution to evaporate the water – this will leave crystals of the salt behind. |

Practical skills **Doing a titration**

To carry out a typical titration:

✓ Put acid into a **burette**.

✓ Use a **pipette** to put a known volume of alkali into a conical flask.

✓ Put a few drops of a suitable **indicator** solution, such as phenolphthalein or methyl orange, into the alkali.

✓ Record the burette start reading.

✓ Add acid to the alkali until the colour changes – the **end-point**.

✓ Record the burette end reading.

Maths skills **Mean titres**

The **titre** is the volume of acid added to exactly neutralise the alkali:

titre = (end reading) – (start reading)

Concordant titres are identical to each other, or very close together (usually within 0.10 cm³).

You normally calculate the **mean** titre using your concordant results only:

$$\text{mean titre} = \frac{\text{sum of concordant titres}}{\text{number of concordant titres}}$$

Worked example

> Potassium hydroxide is a soluble base (an alkali) and the salt (potassium chloride) is also soluble. You can revise solubility rules on page 118.

(a) Explain why titration must be used to produce a salt from dilute hydrochloric acid and potassium hydroxide solution.   **(1 mark)**

Titration lets you find the correct proportions of acid and alkali to mix together to produce a solution that contains only a salt and water.

(b) Describe **three** steps needed to obtain an accurate titre during a titration.   **(3 marks)**

Swirl the flask continuously during the titration to mix the acid and alkali thoroughly. Near the end-point, add the acid drop by drop, pausing between each addition. Rinse the inside of the flask to make sure all the acid mixes with the alkali.

Obtain accurate readings by clamping the burette vertically and reading it at eye level.

> When you are making a salt, you find the mean titre, then use the burette to add this volume of acid to the alkali without the indicator.

Apparatus

burette
stand, boss and clamp
pipette with filler

Now try this

In a titration, a dilute acid is added to a dilute alkali solution in a conical flask. Name a suitable piece of apparatus to:

(a) add the acid to the alkali   **(1 mark)**

(b) measure an accurate volume of the alkali.   **(1 mark)**

Making insoluble salts

You need to be able to predict, using solubility rules, whether a precipitate will be formed when named solutions are mixed together. If a precipitate is formed, you should be able to name it.

General rules

This is why solutions in practicals are often sodium compounds.

This is very useful to remember.

This follows the first rule at the top.

Soluble	Insoluble
all common sodium, potassium and ammonium salts	
all nitrates	
common chlorides	silver chloride lead chloride
common sulfates	lead sulfate barium sulfate calcium sulfate
sodium hydroxide potassium hydroxide ammonium hydroxide	common hydroxides
sodium carbonate potassium carbonate ammonium carbonate	common carbonates

Worked example

(a) Predict whether a precipitate forms when silver nitrate and sodium chloride solutions are mixed. Name any precipitate formed. **(1 mark)**

A precipitate will form – silver chloride.

(b) Name **two** substances that could be used to produce insoluble barium sulfate. **(2 marks)**

barium nitrate and sodium sulfate

Two products form, sodium nitrate and silver chloride, but only silver chloride is insoluble. It forms a cloudy **precipitate** in the mixture:

$AgNO_3(aq) + NaCl(aq) \rightarrow NaNO_3(aq) + AgCl(s)$

All nitrates, and all sodium salts, are soluble. So, to make an insoluble salt **XY**, choose:
- **X** nitrate, and
- sodium **Y**

as your two soluble reactants.

Practical skills   Making insoluble salts

1 Mix solutions of two substances that will form the insoluble salt.

2 Filter the mixture. The insoluble salt will be trapped in the filter paper.

3 Wash the salt with distilled water.

4 Leave the salt to dry on the filter paper. It could be dried in an oven.

Now try this

Predict if a precipitate forms when these solutions are mixed, naming any precipitate formed.
(a) sodium carbonate and calcium chloride   **(1 mark)**
(b) ammonium nitrate and potassium hydroxide   **(1 mark)**
(c) lead nitrate and sodium sulfate.   **(1 mark)**

Extended response – Making salts

There will be one or more 6-mark questions on your exam paper. For these questions, you will need to think scientifically and structure your answer logically, showing how the points you make are related to each other. You can revise the topics for this question, which is about **acids, alkalis and salts**, on pages 113–118.

Worked example

Soluble salts can be made by the reactions of acids with insoluble metal compounds. The salt produced depends on the reactants chosen.

Devise a method to prepare pure, dry crystals of zinc sulfate, $ZnSO_4$, from a zinc compound and a suitable acid. Begin your answer by choosing suitable reactants.

I would use zinc carbonate and sulfuric acid. The reaction produces zinc sulfate, water and carbon dioxide.

I would put some of the acid into a beaker and warm it with a Bunsen burner, tripod and gauze.

I would then use a spatula to add a little zinc carbonate to the warm acid and stir it with a stirring rod. I would repeat this until all the bubbling stopped and some solid was left in the bottom of the beaker.

Next, I would filter the mixture to remove the excess zinc carbonate, using a filter funnel and filter paper. I would collect the zinc sulfate solution in a conical flask.

I would pour the solution into an evaporating basin and leave it on a windowsill for water to evaporate and crystals to form. I would carefully pour away the excess liquid and dry the crystals with filter paper.

Command word: Devise

When you are asked to **devise** something, you need to plan or invent a procedure from existing principles or ideas. These may include familiar chemistry in an unfamiliar context, so make sure that you study carefully any information given to you in the question.

Zinc oxide and zinc hydroxide would also work. Each react with dilute sulfuric acid to produce zinc sulfate and water.

You should describe how to make sure that all the acid has reacted. You would not see bubbling if you chose zinc oxide or zinc hydroxide, but you would see unreacted solid left in the beaker when all the acid had reacted.

If you were asked to prepare an insoluble salt by precipitation, you could wash the salt in the filter paper with distilled water at this stage.

In this part of the answer, you could mention heating the solution to evaporate most of the water instead. You would then leave the crystals in a warm place to dry, such as an oven.

You should make sure that your plan is thought out well, with a clear and logical structure. Aim to support it with scientific information and ideas. You could write a method in continuous prose, as here, or you could write it in numbered steps instead. You should apply your knowledge and understanding of the necessary techniques, and use this to answer the question even if you have not made the required salt in school. Include appropriate apparatus without going into irrelevant detail.

Now try this

An insoluble salt can be made by mixing two suitable solutions together to form a precipitate.
Devise a method to prepare a pure, dry sample of insoluble lead(II) chloride, $PbCl_2$.
Begin your answer by choosing suitable solutions and precautions needed for safe working. **(6 marks)**

Electrolysis

Electrolysis is used to decompose ionic compounds in the molten state or dissolved in water.

Some key words

An **electrolyte** is:

* an ionic compound in the **molten** state (liquid) or **dissolved** in water.

Electrolysis is:

* a process in which **electrical energy**, from a **direct current** (d.c.) supply, decomposes an electrolyte.

Anions are:

* negatively charged ions that move to the positive **electrode** (anode).

Cations are:

* positively charged ions that move to the negative electrode (cathode).

Moving charges

The ions in an electrolyte are charged particles. An electric current will pass through the electrolyte only if the ions are free to move from place to place.

Remember that ions:

👍 can move about in liquids

👍 can move about in solutions

👎 cannot move about in solids.

You can revise the arrangement and movement of particles in solids and liquids on page 105.

Electrolysis of molten lead bromide

The electrolysis of hot, molten lead bromide produces lead and bromine: $PbBr_2(l) \rightarrow Pb(l) + Br_2(g)$

During electrolysis positive charged ions are attracted to the negative electrode and move to it.

Positively charged ions gain electrons and are **reduced**.

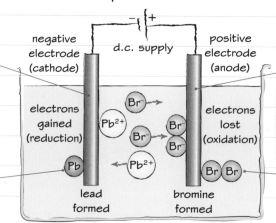

Negatively charged ions are attracted to the positive electrode and move to it.

Remember that ions move towards the oppositely charged electrode.

Negatively charged ions lose electrons and are **oxidised**.

Worked example

Molten zinc chloride is electrolysed.

(a) Predict the products formed at each electrode. **(2 marks)**

Zinc forms at the negative electrode and chlorine at the positive electrode.

(b) Explain why zinc chloride conducts electricity when molten, but not when solid. **(2 marks)**

The ions in liquid zinc chloride are free to move about, but they can only vibrate about fixed positions in solid zinc chloride.

Zinc chloride (and lead bromide) is a **binary** ionic compound. This means that it consists of two elements only. You must be able to predict the products of electrolysis of such compounds in the molten state.

Zinc chloride solution conducts electricity too, because its ions are free to move about.

Now try this

Predict the products formed at each electrode during the electrolysis of the following substances:

(a) molten potassium iodide **(2 marks)**

(b) molten aluminium oxide. **(2 marks)**

Electrolysing solutions

You need to be able to explain products formed by the electrolysis of compounds in solution.

Ions in a solution

Water is a covalent compound. Some of its molecules naturally form ions:

$$H_2O(l) \rightleftharpoons H^+(aq) + OH^-(aq)$$

You can revise reversible reactions and the use of the $\rightleftharpoons$ symbol on page 132.

The presence of these ions means that a solution of an ionic compound contains:
- cations and anions from the dissolved ionic compound, and
- H^+ and OH^- ions from the water.

Competing ions

During electrolysis of an aqueous solution, all the ions in the electrolyte compete to be discharged (gain or lose electrons) to form products.

 Hydrogen gas is produced if H^+ ions are discharged.

 Oxygen gas is produced if OH^- ions are discharged.

At the cathode

metal or hydrogen given off | Ions gain electrons. (+)

At the negative electrode:
- ✓ hydrogen is produced, **unless**
- ✓ the compound contains ions from a metal less reactive than hydrogen.

In that case:
- ✓ the metal is produced instead.

Copper and silver are below hydrogen in the reactivity series (revise this series on page 124).

At the anode

non-metal (except hydrogen) given off | Ions lose electrons. (−)

At the positive electrode:
- ✓ oxygen is produced (from OH^- ions) **unless**
- ✓ the compound contains halide ions (Cl^-, Br^- or I^-).

In that case:
- ✓ chlorides produce chlorine, Cl_2
- ✓ bromides produce bromine, Br_2
- ✓ iodides produce iodine, I_2.

Worked example

Predict the products formed at each electrode during the electrolysis of the following concentrated aqueous solutions.

(a) Copper chloride solution. **(1 mark)**

copper at the cathode, chlorine at the anode

Copper is less reactive than hydrogen, so copper is produced. Chloride ions are present, so chlorine is produced.

(b) Sodium chloride solution. **(1 mark)**

hydrogen at the cathode, chlorine at the anode

Sodium is more reactive than hydrogen, so hydrogen is produced instead of sodium.

(c) Sodium sulfate solution. **(1 mark)**

hydrogen at the cathode, oxygen at the anode

Halide ions are not present, so oxygen is produced when OH^- ions are discharged.

Now try this

Which four ions are present, which are discharged and which stay in solution?

 Dilute sulfuric acid, $H_2SO_4(aq)$, is an electrolyte.
(a) Give the formulae of all the ions in the electrolyte, and where each comes from.
(3 marks)

 (b) Predict the product formed at each electrode.
(2 marks)

Practical skills # Investigating electrolysis

Copper can be purified by the electrolysis of copper sulfate solution using copper electrodes.

Core practical

Electrolysis of copper sulfate

Aim

To investigate the change in mass of the anode and the cathode when copper sulfate solution is electrolysed using copper electrodes.

 The cathode gains mass as copper ions gain electrons.
The anode loses mass as the copper atoms lose electrons.

Apparatus

- eye protection
- beaker
- two strips of copper
- crocodile clips and leads
- d.c. power supply
- copper sulfate solution
- filter paper
- ±0.01 g balance.

 You could bend the strips of copper over the edge of the beaker. Hold them in place using crocodile clips. You can measure the current if you connect an ammeter in series with one of the electrodes.

Method

Measure and record the mass of each electrode. Connect the apparatus as shown below.

Allow the experiment to run as directed by your teacher, or by your own preliminary experiments. Disconnect the two electrodes, carefully dry them with filter paper, and then weigh them again.

pure copper cathode

Copper ions move to the copper electrode, gain electrons and are discharged as pure copper.

copper sulfate solution

d.c. supply

impure copper anode

Ions are replaced by copper ions from the impure copper anode.

Impurities form a 'sludge' below the anode.

Results

Record the masses of each electrode at the start and end. A table is one way to do this neatly.

 Make sure your table has columns to record which electrode is being weighed (at the start and the end) and the mass recorded.

Analysis

Calculate the change in mass of each electrode. Compare these two values and discuss reasons for any difference observed.

 The gain in mass of the cathode should equal the loss in mass of the anode, if the anode were pure copper.

Now try this

During the electrolysis of copper sulfate solution with copper electrodes, the cathode gains 0.19 g and the anode loses 0.43 g.

(a) The electrodes are rinsed with ethanol, which boils at 78 °C, before being dried and weighed. Suggest why they dry more quickly than if water is used. **(1 mark)**

(b) Give **two** reasons why the change in mass of the cathode is less than expected. **(2 marks)**

Extended response – Electrolysis

There will be one or more 6-mark questions on your exam paper. For these questions, you will need to think scientifically and structure your answer logically, showing how the points you make are related to each other. You can revise the topics for this question, which is about **electrolysis**, on pages 120–122.

Worked example

Potassium iodide is an ionic compound. It contains potassium ions, K^+, and iodide ions, I^-. When molten potassium iodide is electrolysed, potassium metal and iodine vapour are formed. Explain how the potassium ions and iodide ions in solid potassium iodide are converted into potassium and iodine by electrolysis. **(6 marks)**

The potassium iodide must be heated. This is so that its ionic bonds break and it becomes molten. Electrolysis cannot happen in the solid state because the ions are not free to move. It happens in the liquid state because the ions are free to move.

Potassium ions are attracted to the oppositely charged electrode, the negatively charged cathode. At the cathode, the potassium ions gain electrons and become potassium atoms.

Iodide ions are attracted to the positively charged electrode, the anode. Here they lose electrons to form iodine atoms. Pairs of iodine atoms join together to form an iodine molecule.

Your answer should show comprehensive knowledge and understanding. Use relevant scientific ideas to support your explanations, including appropriate balanced equations. You should include why potassium iodide must be melted first, then what happens at each electrode. You should leave out information or ideas that are unnecessary to answer the question.

Command word: Explain

When you are asked to **explain** something, it is not enough just to state or describe it. Your answer **must** contain some reasoning or justification of the points you make. Your explanation **can** include mathematical explanations, if calculations are needed.

In this example Extended response question, no calculations are needed.

You need to remember what the starting point in the question is. In this case it is solid potassium iodide, not molten potassium iodide. Remember to explain how to melt the compound, and why this is needed.

You should include knowledge and understanding about what happens at the cathode.

You should include knowledge and understanding about what happens at the anode. You could also mention that a covalent bond forms between two iodine atoms when they share a pair of electrons.

Now try this

Remember to explain whether the lithium and chloride ions will be free to move in the molten potassium chloride. Also explain why this matters.

Lithium-ion batteries are found in many consumer products, including smartphones and electric cars. Lithium chloride contains lithium ions, Li^+, and chloride ions, Cl^-. Lithium is manufactured by the electrolysis of lithium chloride dissolved in molten potassium chloride. During this process, molten lithium rises to the surface and chlorine gas bubbles off.

Explain how the lithium ions and chloride ions in solid lithium chloride are converted into lithium and chlorine by electrolysis.

(6 marks)

The reactivity series

You can find the relative **reactivity** of a metal by comparing its reactions with other metals.

Reactions with water

Hydrogen is produced if a metal reacts with water:

metal + water → metal hydroxide + hydrogen

For example:

sodium + water → sodium hydroxide + hydrogen

$$2Na(s) + 2H_2O(l) \rightarrow 2NaOH(aq) + H_2(g)$$

In general, the more reactive the metal, the greater the rate of bubbling.

Reactions with acids

Hydrogen is produced if a metal reacts with a dilute acid:

metal + acid → salt + hydrogen

These reactions, and the lab test for hydrogen, are explained in more detail on page 114.

- The rate of reaction is greater in warm acid than in cold acid.
- In general, the more reactive the metal, the greater the rate of bubbling.

Some exceptions

Some reactive metals react unexpectedly slowly with water or acids.

1 Aluminium has a layer of aluminium oxide that stops water reaching the metal below.

2 In the reaction of calcium with dilute sulfuric acid, a layer of insoluble calcium sulfate forms, slowing the reaction.

3 In the reaction of magnesium with water, a layer of sparingly soluble magnesium hydroxide forms, slowing the reaction.

Magnesium reacts vigorously with steam:

$$Mg(s) + H_2O(g) \rightarrow MgO(s) + H_2(g)$$

Metals less reactive than hydrogen do not react with water or dilute acids.

A reactivity series

A **reactivity series** shows elements arranged in order of their reactivity.

	Reaction with	
	Water	**Dilute acid**
potassium	reacts quickly with cold water	violent reaction
sodium		
calcium		
magnesium	very slow	reaction becoming less vigorous
aluminium	none	
zinc	reacts with steam	
iron		
hydrogen		
copper	no reaction with water or steam	no reaction with dilute acids
silver		
gold		

Remember that hydrogen is not a metal.

Worked example

The diagram shows how five metals react with cold dilute hydrochloric acid and with cold water. Deduce the order of reactivity, starting with the least reactive. **(2 marks)**

copper, iron, zinc, magnesium, calcium

The rate of bubbling from both diagrams is used to list the metals in the order asked for.

dilute acid

magnesium   calcium   iron   zinc   copper

water

Now try this

 Using the information in the Worked example:
(a) Name **one** metal that reacts with cold water. **(1 mark)**

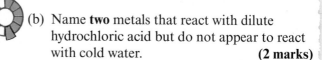 (b) Name **two** metals that react with dilute hydrochloric acid but do not appear to react with cold water. **(2 marks)**

Metal displacement reactions

You can work out the relative reactivity of metals using displacement reactions.

Displacement

A more reactive metal will **displace** a less reactive metal from its salts in solution. Magnesium is more reactive than copper. It can displace copper from copper sulfate solution:

$$Mg(s) + CuSO_4(aq) \rightarrow MgSO_4(aq) + Cu(s)$$

In this reaction, you observe:

 the colour of the solution fading as blue copper sulfate is replaced by colourless magnesium sulfate

 an orange–brown coating of copper forming on the surface of the magnesium

 an increase in temperature because the reaction is **exothermic** (see page 142).

magnesium + copper sulfate

magnesium sulfate + copper

 Method for deducing a reactivity series

You can work out a reactivity series for metals by observing what happens when you mix different combinations of metals and their salt solutions. To do this:

✓ add a powdered metal to a test tube or beaker of a metal salt solution (as above right), or

✓ dip a small piece of metal into a metal salt solution on a spotting tile.

Then look for evidence of a reaction, such as a change in colour or temperature.

Some example results

Here are the results of an experiment with three metals and their salt solutions. A ✓ shows where a coating forms on the metal.

	MgSO$_4$(aq)	ZnSO$_4$(aq)	CuSO$_4$(aq)
Mg(s)	X	✓	✓
Zn(s)	X	X	✓
Cu(s)	X	X	X

From the results:

✓ magnesium is the most reactive

✓ copper is the least reactive

✓ a metal does not displace itself.

Worked example

A student adds a spatula of powdered metal to 10 cm³ of copper sulfate solution in boiling tubes. He stirs the mixtures and records the maximum increases in temperature. The table shows his results.

Metal	Temperature increase (°C)	Metal	Temperature increase (°C)
copper	0.0	magnesium	12.5
iron	5.0	zinc	9.5

 (a) Explain, using the results, which metal was the most reactive of the four metals tested. **(2 marks)**

Magnesium was the most reactive because its reaction gave the greatest temperature rise.

 (b) Explain the results for copper. **(2 marks)**

There was no temperature change because there was no reaction. A metal does not displace itself from its compounds.

Metals less reactive than copper would also have no reaction with copper sulfate solution.

Use the table in the Worked example.
Deduce a reactivity series for the four metals and explain your answer. **(2 marks)**

Explaining metal reactivity

You can explain the reactivity of metals in terms of how easily they form cations.

Forming cations

Metal atoms lose electrons to form **cations** (positively charged ions). For example:

A full outer shell is obtained when a metal atom loses electrons. The electronic configuration of Na is 2.8.1, but it is 2.8 for Na^+.

sodium atom, Na

sodium ion, Na^+

Metals in reactions

Metal atoms form cations when metals react with water or dilute acids.

 Metals react with water to form metal hydroxides, e.g.

$$2Na + 2H_2O \rightarrow 2NaOH + H_2$$

NaOH contains Na^+ and OH^- ions.

 Metals react with dilute acids to form salts, e.g.

$$2Na + 2HCl \rightarrow 2NaCl + H_2$$

NaCl contains Na^+ and Cl^- ions.

Oxidation and reduction

Displacement reactions involve oxidation and reduction. You can see this in a reaction between a reactive metal and the oxide of a less reactive metal:

$$Mg + CuO \rightarrow MgO + Cu$$

✓ the atoms of the more reactive metal are **oxidised** – they gain oxygen

✓ the oxide of the less reactive metal is **reduced** – it loses oxygen.

The oxide ions, O^{2-}, are unchanged.

Worked example

The list shows four metals arranged in order of decreasing reactivity from left to right.

sodium, aluminium, iron, copper

Which atoms form cations most easily?   **(1 mark)**

☒ **A** sodium atoms
☐ **B** aluminium atoms
☐ **C** iron atoms
☐ **D** copper atoms

The reactions of metals (with water, dilute acids and salt solutions) show the **relative tendency** of metal atoms to form cations. The more easily a metal atom loses electrons, the more reactive the metal is.

Remember that sodium and iron react with water but aluminium, placed between them in the reactivity series, does not. It is protected by a layer of aluminium oxide.

Now try this

One way of joining two pieces of railway line together involves the 'thermite reaction'. A mixture of powdered aluminium and iron(III) oxide, Fe_2O_3, is heated. Aluminium oxide, Al_2O_3, and molten iron are produced. Use the description of the thermite reaction to help you to explain the difference in reactivity of aluminium and iron.   **(3 marks)**

Metal ores

Most metals are extracted by the reduction of ores found in the Earth's crust.

Ores

Rocks contain metals or their compounds. An **ore** is a rock that contains enough of a metal to make its extraction economical.

Rocks may contain too little metal to make extraction worthwhile (if the cost of extracting the metal is greater than the value of the metal itself). Over time, metal prices may rise and these **low-grade ores** may become useful.

Unreactive metals

Unreactive metals such as gold are placed at the bottom of the reactivity series. They are found in the Earth's crust. They are in their 'native state' uncombined with other elements:

✓ they are not found as **compounds**

but

✓ they may occur naturally as **alloys** (mixtures of metals).

Oxidation

Oxidation is the gain of oxygen by a substance. For example, magnesium is **oxidised** to magnesium oxide in air:

$$2Mg + O_2 \rightarrow 2MgO$$

Reduction

Reduction is the loss of oxygen by a substance. For example, zinc oxide is **reduced** to zinc when it is heated with carbon:

$$ZnO + C \rightarrow Zn + CO$$

Worked example

Copper can be produced from copper oxide, CuO, by heating it with hydrogen gas. Water, H_2O, is also formed:

copper oxide

hydrogen →

HEAT

Explain which substance is oxidised and which substance is reduced in the reaction. **(2 marks)**

Hydrogen gains oxygen so it is oxidised. Copper oxide loses oxygen so it is reduced.

Resistance to corrosion

Metals **corrode** when they react with substances around them, such as air and water. How easily a metal corrodes depends upon how reactive it is:

easily corrodes | potassium | Aluminium is protected by an oxide layer.
sodium
calcium
magnesium
(aluminium)
zinc
iron
copper
corrodes slowly | silver
does not corrode | gold

1 Explain which metal is more resistant to corrosion – calcium or copper. **(2 marks)**

2 Iron can be produced from iron(III) oxide by heating it with carbon:
$$2Fe_2O_3 + 3C \rightarrow 4Fe + 3CO_2$$

Explain which substance is reduced and which substance is oxidised in the reaction. **(2 marks)**

3 Explain why platinum is found in its native state in the Earth's crust. **(2 marks)**

Iron and aluminium

Most metals are extracted by the reduction of ores found in the Earth's crust.

Metal extraction

The method used to extract a metal from its ore is related to:
- the **cost** of the extraction process
- the metal's position in the **reactivity series** (shown on the right).

In principle, all metals can be extracted from their compounds using electrolysis. But:
- electricity is needed, which is expensive
- reduction by heating with carbon can be used if a metal is less reactive than carbon
- chemical reactions may be needed to separate silver and gold from other metals.

most reactive	potassium	electrolysis of a molten compound
	sodium	
	calcium	
	magnesium	
	aluminium	
carbon →	zinc	reduction of its oxide using carbon
	iron	
hydrogen →	copper	
	silver	found as the element
least reactive	gold	

Hydrogen can reduce copper oxide to copper, but this is hazardous.

Iron extraction

Iron is less reactive than carbon, so it is produced by reducing iron oxide using carbon. This happens in industrial equipment called a **blast furnace**.
You do not need to know any details about the furnace itself, but at the high temperatures inside it:

 Iron oxide is reduced by carbon:

iron oxide + carbon → iron + carbon monoxide

$$Fe_2O_3(s) + 3C(s) \rightarrow 2Fe(l) + 3CO(g)$$

 It is also reduced by carbon monoxide:

iron oxide + carbon monoxide → iron + carbon dioxide

$$Fe_2O_3(s) + 3CO(g) \rightarrow 2Fe(l) + 3CO_2(g)$$

③ Molten iron (iron in the liquid state) is produced.

Aluminium extraction

Aluminium is more reactive than carbon. It is produced by reducing aluminium oxide in an **electrolytic cell**.

 Aluminium oxide is dissolved in molten **cryolite**. This reduces the temperature needed for electrolysis to happen, when an electric current passes through the mixture.

 At the **cathode**, aluminium ions gain electrons and form aluminium atoms:

$$Al^{3+} + 3e^- \rightarrow Al$$

 At the **anode**, oxide ions lose electrons and form oxygen gas:

$$2O^{2-} \rightarrow O_2 + 4e^-$$

 Oxygen reacts with the graphite anodes, so these must be replaced every few weeks.

Worked example

A student tries to extract the metals from magnesium oxide and lead oxide. He heats each oxide with powdered carbon. Explain why he can extract lead but not magnesium. **(3 marks)**

Carbon is above lead in the reactivity series but below magnesium. This means that carbon can reduce lead oxide but not magnesium oxide.

Lead and its compounds are toxic. Using a fume cupboard reduces the chance of breathing these in during the experiment.

It is not enough to write that magnesium is more reactive than lead. You need to include the role of carbon as a **reducing agent**.

Now try this

1 Suggest why tin oxide, but not calcium oxide, can be reduced by carbon. **(3 marks)**
2 Explain why electrolysis is not used to extract iron from iron oxide. **(2 marks)**

Recycling metals

Recycling metals rather than extracting them from ores has economic implications. It can also preserve the environment and the supply of limited raw materials.

Extracting metals

Extracting metals from their ores:

- 👎 uses up limited resources
- 👎 uses a lot of energy
- 👎 damages the environment.

Recycling reduces these disadvantages. Used metal items are collected. Rather than throwing them away, these are taken apart. The metal is melted down to make new items.

 VS

Recycling

Recycling metals means:

- 👍 metal ores will last longer
- 👍 less energy is needed
- 👍 fewer quarries and mines are needed
- 👍 less noise and dust are produced
- 👍 less land is needed.

Worked example

The flow chart shows the main stages in extracting aluminium from its ore.

Use it to suggest the benefits of recycling aluminium. **(3 marks)**

Less waste rock will be produced from mining.

Aluminium oxide will not need separating and purifying from aluminium ore, which will save energy. Less carbon dioxide will be emitted because less fuel will be needed for heat and electricity and because carbon dioxide is produced from the electrolysis.

You need to be specific in your answer. To write that recycling is 'better for the environment' does not give enough detail.

aluminium ore obtained by mining → waste rock

aluminium oxide separated from ore and purified

electrolysis at 950 °C to extract aluminium → waste carbon dioxide

aluminium metal

Drawbacks of recycling

- 👎 Used metal items must be collected and transported to the recycling centre.
- 👎 Different metals must be removed from used items and sorted.
- 👎 Recycling saves different amounts of energy, depending on the metal involved.

Recycling metals saves energy

Different amounts of energy are saved by recycling metals compared with extracting them from ores:

Metal	Percentage energy saved
aluminium	94
copper	86
iron and steel	70

Now try this

1 Describe **two** ways in which recycling copper, rather than extracting it from copper ores, can reduce pollution. **(2 marks)**

2 Suggest **two** reasons why more energy is saved when aluminium is recycled than when steel is recycled. **(2 marks)**

3 Explain why recycling metals conserves the supplies of metal ores. **(2 marks)**

Life-cycle assessments

You need to be able to describe the basic principles involved in carrying out a life-cycle assessment.

Cradle to grave

A **life-cycle assessment** (LCA) of a product is a 'cradle-to-grave' analysis of its impact on the environment. It includes these stages:

Data for an LCA

An LCA is likely to need data on these factors at most or all stages:
- ✓ the use of energy
- ✓ the release of waste materials
- ✓ transport and storage.

An LCA is also likely to need data on:
- ✓ whether the raw materials needed are renewable or non-renewable
- ✓ whether any of the product can be recycled or re-used
- ✓ how the product is disposed of.

An example of a life cycle

There are many detailed stages in the life cycle of a product, e.g. for a car.

Worked example

The table shows information about the energy needed in the life cycle of a polyester shirt.

Stage	Percentage of lifetime energy used
obtaining raw materials	5
manufacturing the shirt	14
using the shirt	80
disposing of the shirt	1

Discuss the use of energy in the life cycle of the shirt, and suggest how it may be improved.   **(4 marks)**

Almost one-fifth of the energy used is to do with making the shirt. Very little is to do with disposing of it at the end of its life. Most of the energy used is to do with using the shirt, probably due to washing and ironing it. Energy use could be reduced by washing at low temperatures and drying it outside and not ironing it.

The question shows only part of the data that should be available to make a life-cycle assessment, e.g. no information is given about the environmental impact of each stage, or the lifespan of the shirt.

Now try this

1 State the four main stages in a life-cycle assessment.   **(1 mark)**

2 Life-cycle assessments may identify alternative materials that can be used with less impact. Give one other reason for carrying out a life-cycle assessment.   **(1 mark)**

Extended response – Reactivity of metals

There will be one or more 6-mark questions on your exam paper. For these questions, you will need to think scientifically and structure your answer logically, showing how the points you make are related to each other. You can revise the topics for this question, which is about **metal reactivity** and **metal extraction**, on pages 124–128.

Worked example

Some metals are found as uncombined elements, but most metals are extracted from ores found in the Earth's crust. Different metals are extracted using different methods.

Explain how the method used to obtain a metal is related to its position in the reactivity series and to the cost of the extraction process. In your answer, refer to aluminium, iron and gold as examples.

(6 marks)

Gold is placed at the bottom of the reactivity series because it is an unreactive metal. It is found in the Earth's crust uncombined with other elements so the cost of extracting gold is low.

Aluminium is placed near the top of the reactivity series, because it is a very reactive metal. It is found combined with other elements, such as oxygen. Aluminium is more reactive than carbon, so it must be extracted using electrolysis. A lot of electricity is used in electrolysis, which makes it expensive to extract aluminium from its ore.

Iron is placed in the middle of the reactivity series, because it is less reactive than aluminium but more reactive than gold. Iron is also less reactive than carbon. Iron can be extracted by heating its ore with carbon. Although electrolysis could be used instead, carbon is cheaper than electricity.

The stem of the question

Make sure that you read the question carefully before starting to write your answer. It can be easy to ignore information given in the stem of the question (the part at the beginning).

In this question, you are given two factors to consider. You are also given the identity of three metals to write about.

You could begin your answer with any of the metals. The extraction of gold is simple to explain so it is covered first here. In your answer, refer clearly to the position of gold in the reactivity series, and also to the cost of extracting it.

You should include knowledge and understanding about why aluminium must be extracted using electrolysis. You should also include why this is expensive. You need to explain why heating with carbon is unsuitable. You can do this by referring to the position of carbon in the reactivity series.

You might point out that electrolysis could still be used to extract iron. You can then explain that heating with carbon is cheaper.

You should think clearly about how to present your ideas before you start. Aim for a clear and logical structure. You can support this with scientific information and ideas. You should leave out information or ideas that are unnecessary to answer the question.

Now try this

You are provided with these metal powders and solutions:

Metal powder	Solution
copper	copper sulfate
magnesium	magnesium sulfate
zinc	zinc sulfate

Explain how you could use these substances in displacement reactions to find the order of reactivity of the three metals. In your answer, include the expected results and how you would use them to show the correct order of reactivity. You may use equations if you wish. **(6 marks)**

The Haber process

Reversible reactions

Chemical reactions are **reversible**. The direction of some reversible reactions can be altered by changing the reaction conditions.

Ammonium chloride decomposes when heated: $NH_4Cl(s) \rightarrow NH_3(g) + HCl(g)$

Ammonia and hydrogen chloride combine when cool:
$NH_3(g) + HCl(g) \rightarrow NH_4Cl(s)$

These changes can be modelled using $\rightleftharpoons$, the **reversible symbol**:

$$NH_4Cl(s) \rightleftharpoons NH_3(g) + HCl(g)$$

Dynamic equilibrium

In a **closed system**, a container where no reacting substances can enter or leave, a reversible reaction can reach **equilibrium**. At equilibrium:

✓   rate of forward reaction $=$ rate of backward reaction

✓   the concentrations of the reacting substances stay constant (do not change).

A chemical equilibrium is a **dynamic** equilibrium:

✓   the forward and backward reactions keep going – they do not stop at equilibrium.

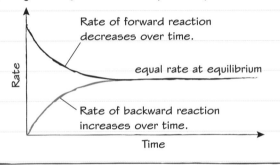

The Haber process

The **Haber process** is a reversible reaction between nitrogen and hydrogen to form ammonia.

$$N_2(g) + 3H_2(g) \rightleftharpoons 2NH_3(g)$$

Nitrogen can be obtained by fractional distillation of liquefied air.

Methane in natural gas reacts with steam to produce carbon dioxide and hydrogen:

$$CH_4(g) + 2H_2O(g) \rightarrow CO_2(g) + 4H_2(g)$$

The Haber process requires nitrogen and hydrogen. State the raw materials needed to obtain these two reactants.   **(2 marks)**

Nitrogen is extracted from the air and hydrogen is obtained from natural gas.

Now try this

Hydrated copper sulfate crystals turn from blue to white when they are heated:

hydrated copper sulfate $\rightleftharpoons$ anhydrous copper sulfate   +   water
        (blue)   (white)

(a) State why the word equation contains the symbol $\rightleftharpoons$.   **(1 mark)**

(b) Describe how anhydrous copper sulfate could be used to test for water.   **(2 marks)**

The alkali metals

The elements in group 1 of the periodic table are known as the **alkali metals**.

Physical properties

The alkali metals have some properties typical of metals. For example, they are:
- good conductors of heat and electricity
- shiny when freshly cut.

However, compared with most other metals, they:
- are soft (you can cut them with a knife)
- have relatively low melting points (but all are solid).

Group 1
alkali metals

Reactions with water

The alkali metals react with water, producing an alkaline metal hydroxide and hydrogen, e.g.

sodium + water → sodium hydroxide + hydrogen

$$2Na(s) + 2H_2O(l) \rightarrow 2NaOH(aq) + H_2(g)$$

Reactivity

The **reactivity** of the alkali metals increases down the group. For example, when reacted with water:
- Lithium fizzes steadily.
- Sodium melts into a ball from the heat released in the reaction and fizzes rapidly.
- Potassium gives off sparks and the hydrogen produced burns with a lilac-coloured flame.

Density

Lithium, sodium and potassium are less dense than water, so they float.

Storage

Lithium, sodium and potassium are stored in oil. This is to keep air and water away.

Worked example

(a) Rubidium is placed below potassium in the periodic table.
Predict what is seen in the reaction of rubidium with water. **(2 marks)**

Rubidium will react very vigorously with water, producing sparks and bursting into flames explosively.

(b) Explain why sodium is more reactive than lithium. **(2 marks)**

Sodium atoms are larger than lithium atoms. So the outer electron in a sodium atom is further from the nucleus than the outer electron in a lithium atom. This means that the force of attraction is weaker. So the outer electron is lost more easily from sodium than from lithium.

You need to be able to:
- describe the pattern of reactivity of lithium, sodium and potassium, and
- use it to predict the reactivity of other alkali metals (rubidium, caesium and francium).

The alkali metals all have one electron in the outer shell of their atoms. They lose this electron in reactions to form ions with a 1+ charge, e.g. Li^+ and Na^+. The more easily the outer electron is lost, the more reactive the metal.

Going down the group, the number of occupied shells in an atom increases. The electrons in the inner shells **shield** the outer electron, reducing its attraction for the nucleus.

Now try this

Look at the balanced equation above for the reaction of sodium with water.

Caesium, Cs, is placed below rubidium in group 1 of the periodic table.
(a) Write a balanced equation for the reaction of caesium with water. **(2 marks)**

(b) Predict what is seen in the reaction of caesium with water. **(2 marks)**

(c) State **two** physical properties that rubidium and caesium have in common. **(2 marks)**

The halogens

The elements in group 7 of the periodic table are non-metals known as the **halogens**.

Appearance

Element	State at room temperature	Colour
fluorine, F_2	gas	pale yellow
chlorine, Cl_2	gas	yellow–green
bromine, Br_2	liquid	red–brown
iodine, I_2	solid	dark grey

covalent molecules,
each with two atoms

forms a purple vapour
when warmed

Group 7
halogens

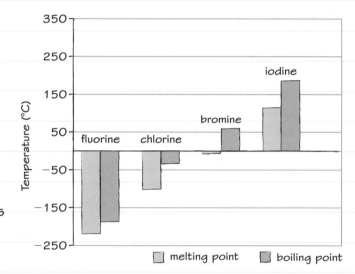

Melting and boiling points

Going down group 7:
- melting points increase
- boiling points increase.

When simple molecular substances melt or boil:
- weak intermolecular forces are overcome
- the strong covalent bonds joining atoms together in each molecule do not break.

Going down group 7:
- the intermolecular forces between molecules become stronger
- more heat energy is needed to overcome these forces.

You can revise simple molecular substances on page 95 and physical states on page 105.

You can revise simple molecular substances on page 95 and physical states on page 105.

 Worked example

Chlorine is manufactured on an industrial scale by the electrolysis of concentrated sodium chloride solution.
Describe a simple laboratory test for the presence of chlorine. **(2 marks)**

Put a piece of damp blue litmus paper into the container. If chlorine is present, the litmus paper turns red, then is bleached white.

Practical skills When you describe a laboratory test, say what you would do and what you would observe.

In a different test, damp **starch iodide paper** turns blue–black in the presence of chlorine. The colour change happens because chlorine displaces iodine, which then reacts with starch. You can revise halogen displacement reactions on page 136.

 Now try this

Use evidence from the table and bar chart to explain your answer.

Astatine is a rare, radioactive element placed immediately below iodine in group 7.

(a) Suggest why astatine is thought to be dark in colour, even though no one has seen it. **(1 mark)**

(b) Predict the melting point of astatine, and justify your answer. **(2 marks)**

Reactions of halogens

The reactivity of the elements decreases down group 7 (the opposite trend to group 1).

Reactions with metals

The halogens react with metals to produce compounds called metal halides, e.g.

sodium + chlorine → sodium chloride

$$2Na(s) + Cl_2(g) \rightarrow 2NaCl(s)$$

The sodium burns with an orange flame, forming white sodium chloride.

Iron wool reacts with the halogens when it is heated, e.g.

iron + chlorine → iron(III) chloride

$$2Fe(s) + 3Cl_2(g) \rightarrow 2FeCl_3(s)$$

The iron burns to form a dark purple solid.

Halide ions, halides

The elements in group 7 are called **halogens**. In reactions with metals, halogen atoms gain electrons and are reduced, e.g.

$$Cl_2 + 2e^- \rightarrow 2Cl^-$$

The ions formed:

✓ have a 1– charge, e.g. Cl^-, Br^- and I^-

✓ are called **halide ions**.

Halides are compounds of metals or hydrogen with halogens, such as sodium chloride.

Explaining reactivity

A halogen atom has seven electrons in its outer shell. When a halogen reacts with a metal or hydrogen, each halogen atom gains one electron to complete its outer shell. The less easily a halogen atom gains an electron, the less reactive the halogen is.

Going down group 7:
- the outer shell gets further from the nucleus
- there is more shielding by inner electrons
- the force of attraction between the nucleus and outer shell electrons gets weaker
- electrons are gained less easily
- the elements become less reactive.

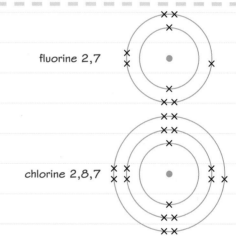

fluorine 2,7

chlorine 2,8,7

Fluorine is more reactive than chlorine – its atoms gain electrons more easily.

Worked example

Hydrogen reacts vigorously with bromine vapour to produce hydrogen bromide gas:

$$H_2(g) + Br_2(g) \rightarrow 2HBr(g)$$

What happens if this gas is added to water? **(1 mark)**

- ☐ **A** It does not dissolve.
- ☐ **B** It dissolves to form a neutral solution.
- ☐ **C** It dissolves to form an alkaline solution.
- ☒ **D** It dissolves to form an acidic solution.

Hydrogen reacts with the halogens to produce hydrogen halides. The reactions become less vigorous down group 7:
- Fluorine reacts explosively in the dark.
- Chlorine reacts explosively in sunlight.
- Bromine reacts vigorously in a flame.

The hydrogen halides all dissolve in water to produce acidic solutions, e.g.
- hydrogen chloride gas, HCl(g), produces hydrochloric acid, HCl(aq).

Now try this

1 Hydrogen and fluorine react together explosively. Name the product of the reaction. Predict what happens when this product is added to water. **(3 marks)**

2 Explain, in terms of the size of its atoms and the ease of gaining electrons, why chlorine is more reactive than bromine. **(2 marks)**

Halogen displacement reactions

A more reactive halogen can displace a less reactive halogen from its compounds.

🧪 Practical skills Investigating displacement

The halogens dissolve in water to form aqueous solutions, such as 'chlorine water', $Cl_2(aq)$.

You can demonstrate **displacement reactions** by adding a few drops of a halogen solution to a metal halide solution, then seeing if the mixture darkens. For example:

✓ Chlorine is more reactive than bromine.

✓ Chlorine in 'chlorine water' displaces bromine from aqueous sodium bromide solution.

✓ word equation: chlorine + sodium bromide → sodium chloride + bromine

✓ balanced equation: $Cl_2(aq) + 2NaBr(aq) \rightarrow 2NaCl(aq) + Br_2(aq)$

chlorine water

The reddish-brown colour is due to the bromine that has been displaced.

sodium chloride solution + bromine

sodium bromide solution

Worked example

A student adds a few drops of halogen solutions to small volumes of potassium halide solutions on a spotting tile. Put a tick (✓) in the table below to show where she sees the mixture turning darker.   **(2 marks)**

	Chloride	Bromide	Iodide
Chlorine	not done	✓	✓
Bromine		not done	✓
Iodine			not done

The halogens are toxic. It is safer to use small volumes of dilute halogen solutions.

Potassium salts form colourless solutions. They darken if bromine or iodine is produced. A halogen cannot displace itself so, for example, chlorine water is not added to potassium chloride solution in the investigation.

Fluorine

Fluorine is the most reactive halogen:

✓ Fluorine gas can displace all the other halogens from aqueous solutions of their salts.

Fluorine reacts violently with water:

✗ You cannot easily carry out displacement reactions in solution using fluorine.

Now try this

Astatine, At, is placed at the bottom of group 7 in the periodic table.

1 Write a word equation for the reaction of bromine with potassium iodide solution. **(1 mark)**

2 Potassium bromide solution changes from colourless to orange when a few drops of chlorine solution are added to it. Explain this observation. **(3 marks)**

3 State and explain whether astatine will react with potassium iodide solution. **(2 marks)**

The noble gases

The elements in group O of the periodic table are known as the **noble gases**.

Chemical properties

The noble gases are chemically **inert**. Their lack of reactivity is because:
- their atoms have full outer shells of electrons, so
- they do not lose, gain or share electrons.

Group O noble gases

Element	He	Ne	Ar
Electronic configuration	2	2.8	2.8.8

Uses of the noble gases

You need to be able to explain how use of a noble gas depends on a particular property. The table shows some typical uses of noble gases.

Noble gas	Use	Property needed		Reason for use
		Low density	Inertness	
helium	**lifting gas** in party balloons and airships	✓	✓	• Helium is less dense than air so the balloons and airships rise. • It is **non-flammable** so does not ignite.
argon krypton xenon	**filling gas** in filament lamps		✓	• The metal filament becomes hot enough to glow. • The inert gases stop it burning away.
argon	**shield gas** during welding		✓	• Argon is denser than air so it keeps air away from the metal. • It is inert so the metal does not oxidise.

Worked example

The table shows the densities and boiling points of some of the noble gases. Describe the trends in these properties. Use them to predict the missing numbers. **(4 marks)**

Element	Density (kg/m³)	Boiling point (°C)
helium, He	0.15	−269
neon, Ne	1.20	
argon, Ar		−186
krypton, Kr	2.15	−152

The densities increase as you go down the group. The boiling points get higher as you go down the group.

The density of argon could be about 1.7 or 1.8 kg/m³.

The boiling point of neon could be about −230°C.

⬅ These numbers are about halfway between the numbers above and below in the table.

You need to be able to answer questions like this one that ask you to identify a trend, and use the trend to predict missing values.

Now try this

1 The density of air is 1.225 kg/m³.
Explain why helium and neon can be used as lifting gases, but argon and krypton cannot.
(2 marks)

Look at the data in the Worked example.

2 Give **two** reasons why argon may be used in some fire-extinguishing systems. **(2 marks)**

3 The electronic configuration of neon is 2.8. Explain why neon is inert. **(2 marks)**

Extended response – Groups

There will be one or more 6-mark questions on your exam paper. For these questions, you will need to think scientifically and structure your answer logically, showing how the points you make are related to each other. You can revise the topics for this question, which is about **groups in the periodic table**, on pages 133–137.

Worked example

Lithium and potassium react with cold water. Similar products form in these reactions.

Compare and contrast the way in which these two elements react with water. Explain your answers in terms of electronic configurations, reactions and products. **(6 marks)**

Both elements are in group 1 of the periodic table, the alkali metals. Their atoms have one electron in their outer shells, which is why they react in a similar way (lithium is 2.1 and potassium is 2.8.8.1).

Both metals float on water and both produce hydrogen. They also produce soluble metal hydroxides when they react with water, forming alkaline solutions.

However, potassium is more reactive than lithium, so its reaction with water is more vigorous. This is because potassium atoms lose their outer electron more easily. Potassium atoms have more filled electron shells, so their outer electron is further from the nucleus and more shielded, so has a weaker attraction to it.

Lithium fizzes slowly when it reacts with water, gradually becoming smaller until it disappears. Potassium reacts more vigorously. It immediately ignites with a lilac flame when it reacts with water, and disappears with sparks.

Command words: Compare and contrast

The question is looking for the similarities and differences between two or more things, without needing a conclusion. The answer must relate to all things mentioned in the question. It must include at least one similarity and one difference.

 You should mention which group the elements are placed in. Their electronic configurations are important in explaining why their reactions are similar.

 You should be clear about what is similar in the reactions of lithium and potassium with water.

 Your answer should compare the reactivity of the two metals, and explain this in terms of how easily the outer electrons are lost in reactions.

 You need to be able to describe the reactions of the alkali metals with water. The key differences in the reactions of lithium and potassium are mentioned here.

Your answer should show comprehensive knowledge and understanding of the topic covered. Take care to cover both similarities and differences. Make sure that you use any information given to you to support your explanations. Organise your explanations in a structured way with clear lines of reasoning.

Now try this

The command word **devise** means that you need to plan or invent a procedure from existing principles or ideas.

The elements in group 7 of the periodic table include chlorine, bromine and iodine. Devise an experiment to determine the order of reactivity of these elements using displacement reactions.

In your answer, assume that you are given dropping pipettes, test tubes and these solutions:
- chlorine solution, bromine solution, iodine solution
- potassium chloride solution, potassium bromide solution, potassium iodide solution.

Describe suitable safety precautions. Include the expected results and explain how you would use them to show the order of reactivity. **(6 marks)**

Rates of reaction

The greater the frequency of successful collisions, the greater the rate of reaction.

Colliding particles

For a reaction to happen:
- reactant particles must collide with each other **and**
- the collisions must have enough energy.

The **activation energy** of a reaction is the minimum energy needed by reactant particles for a reaction to happen. A **successful collision** has the activation energy or more.

Rate and time

The greater the **rate of reaction**, the lower the **reaction time**:
- ✓ A fast reaction happens in a short time, such as combustion.
- ✓ A slow reaction happens over a long time, such as rusting.

Take care not to confuse the two quantities.

Concentration and pressure

The rate of reaction increases if the **concentration** of a dissolved reactant increases, or if the **pressure** of a reacting gas increases:
- There are more particles in the same volume.
- The frequency of successful collisions increases.

Surface area : volume ratio

The rate of reaction increases when the **surface area:volume ratio** of a solid reactant increases, e.g. when lumps are made into a powder:
- more particles of reactant are available
- the frequency of successful collisions increases.

Temperature

The rate of reaction increases when the **temperature** increases because the particles gain energy, and:
- the particles move faster
- the frequency of collisions increases **and**
- the energy of collisions increases, so a greater proportion of collisions are successful.

larger piece   smaller pieces

smaller surface area   larger surface area
slower reaction   faster reaction

Worked example

(a) Describe three features of a catalyst.   **(3 marks)**

Catalysts are substances that speed up the rate of a reaction without altering the products. They are unchanged chemically and in mass at the end of the reaction.

(b) Explain how a catalyst works.   **(2 marks)**

Catalysts provide an alternative reaction pathway with a lower activation energy.

Catalysts are often transition metals or their compounds, such as iron in the Haber process.

Enzymes are **biological** catalysts. Enzymes found in yeast catalyse the conversion of glucose to ethanol and carbon dioxide. Enzymes are used in the production of wine and other alcoholic drinks.

With a lower activation energy, a greater proportion of collisions have the necessary activation energy or more. So the frequency of successful collisions is greater at a given temperature.

Now try this

Marble chips react with hydrochloric acid: $CaCO_3(s) + 2HCl(aq) \rightarrow CaCl_2(aq) + H_2O(l) + CO_2(g)$
State and explain the effect of the following on the rate of the reaction:
(a) crushing the chips   **(3 marks)**
(b) diluting the acid.   **(3 marks)**

Practical skills

Investigating rates

Core practical

Effect of surface area on rate

Aim

To investigate the effect on the rate of reaction with hydrochloric acid of changing the surface area of calcium carbonate.

> You could also investigate the effect of changing the concentration of the hydrochloric acid.

Apparatus

- eye protection
- conical flask
- measuring cylinder
- marble chips (small, medium, large)
- cotton wool
- dilute hydrochloric acid
- ±0.01 g balance
- stop clock.

> You could use powdered marble. However, the rate of reaction may be so great that it becomes difficult to measure the mass at a given time.
>
> Instead of recording the change in mass, you could use a gas syringe to measure the volume of carbon dioxide produced.

Method

1 Prepare three sets of marble chips on folded paper, one for each size of chip. Adjust the numbers so that each set has the same mass.

2 Add a measured volume of dilute acid to the conical flask. Plug the flask with cotton wool.

3 Place the flask and a set of marble chips on the balance. Record the reading.

4 Remove the cotton wool. Add the chips to the acid. Start the stop clock, and replace the cotton wool and folded paper.

5 Record the mass each 30 s for a few minutes.

Repeat steps 2 to 5 with the other sets of chips.

cotton wool to stop acid 'spray' escaping

dilute hydrochloric acid

marble chips

balance

70.00 g

Results

Time (s)	Mass (g)	Change in mass (g)
0	70.00	0.00
30	69.90	0.10
60	69.83	0.17

> You should record your results for each set of chips in a suitable table. Include a column for the change in mass at each time. Make sure that you have enough rows for all your readings.

Analysis

Calculate the change in mass at each time, t:

- change in mass = mass at start – mass at t

For each set of chips, calculate the mean rate of reaction over the same amount of time:

$$\text{mean rate of reaction} = \frac{\text{change in mass}}{\text{chosen time}}$$

> You could also plot line graphs:
> - change in mass in g on the vertical axis
> - time in s on the horizontal axis
> - smooth line of best fit, ignoring anomalous results.
>
> You can revise how to interpret the results from experiments similar to this on page 141.

Now try this

A student investigates the effect of acid concentration on the rate of this reaction:

$$Na_2S_2O_3(aq) + 2HCl(aq) \rightarrow 2NaCl(aq) + H_2O(l) + SO_2(g) + S(s)$$

The reaction mixture becomes cloudy as sulfur forms. The student measures the time taken for it to become too cloudy to see a cross drawn on a piece of paper underneath the flask. In each experiment, he uses the same volume and concentration of sodium thiosulfate solution. He uses the same volume of diluted acid each time. Explain three steps that the student takes to obtain results that allow a fair comparison. **(4 marks)**

Skills – Rates of reaction

There may be opportunities to draw or complete graphs and to interpret them. You can revise the topics for this question, which is about **rates of reaction**, on pages 139 and 140.

Worked example

Hydrogen peroxide solution decomposes to form water and oxygen: $2H_2O_2(aq) \rightarrow 2H_2O(l) + O_2(g)$
Manganese dioxide powder, MnO_2, is a catalyst for this reaction. A student investigates the rate of the catalysed reaction. He measures the volume of oxygen produced over 2 minutes at 20 °C.

Time (s)	0	15	30	45	60	75	90	105	120
Volume of oxygen (cm³)	0	20	34	43	47	49	50	50	50

(a) Plot these results on the grid. **(3 marks)**

Command word: Plot

You need to produce a graph by marking points accurately on a grid using given data. Then draw a line of best fit through these points. You must include a suitable scale and labelled axes if these are not given to you.

You should aim to plot each point to at least half the correct square. A line of best fit need not be a straight line (it could be a smooth curve), but:

✓ draw it in one go, not in bits.

(b) Calculate the mean rate of reaction, giving your answer to two significant figures. **(2 marks)**

volume of oxygen produced = 50 cm³

reaction time = 90 s

mean rate = $\dfrac{\text{volume}}{\text{time}} = \dfrac{50\,cm^3}{90\,s} = 0.56\ cm^3/s$

Line C, the answer to (**c**), lies to the left of the first line and ends at the same volume.

No more oxygen is produced after 90 s, so the reaction time is 90 s, not the duration of the investigation.

(c) On the same axes, sketch the curve you would expect if the student used the same volume of hydrogen peroxide solution at 40 °C.
Label this curve **C**. **(2 marks)**

Command word: Sketch

You need to do a freehand drawing or graph. You may need labelled axes (not to scale), a line and to identify key features.

Now try this

(a) Use the student's results to calculate the mean rate of reaction between 0 s and 45 s, and between 45 s and 90 s. **(4 marks)**

(b) Describe how the student could show that the mass of catalyst is unchanged in the reaction. **(4 marks)**

Heat energy changes

Temperature changes

Most reactions involve temperature change:
- In **exothermic reactions**, heat energy is given **out**, and the reaction mixture or the surroundings increase in temperature.
- In **endothermic reactions**, heat energy is taken **in**, and the reaction mixture or the surroundings decrease in temperature.

Reaction	Exothermic	Endothermic
neutralisation	✓	
displacement	✓	
precipitation	✓	✓
dissolving	✓	✓

Temperature can go up or down depending on the precipitate or salt.

Practical skills — Measuring temperature changes

You can use this apparatus to investigate the temperature changes in reactions.

- thermometer
- lid with hole
- polystyrene cup
- beaker for support
- reaction mixture

The beaker and air inside are further insulation to reduce energy transfer.

Bonds and energy

When a chemical reaction happens, the bonds that hold the atoms together in the molecules of the reactants are broken. The atoms then come together in new arrangements to form the products.

- Breaking bonds is endothermic (energy is needed).
- Making bonds is exothermic (energy is released).

exothermic reaction

Energy is released to the surroundings because more heat energy is released making bonds in the products than is needed to break bonds in the reactants.

reactants → products (Energy down)

Overall energy is released to surroundings and this makes the reaction exothermic.

endothermic reaction

Energy is taken in from the surroundings because less heat energy is released making bonds in the products than is needed to break bonds in the reactants.

reactants → products (Energy up)

Overall energy is taken in to the reaction and this makes the reaction endothermic.

Worked example

Calcium chloride is added to water and stirred. Explain why the mixture warms up. **(3 marks)**

An exothermic change happens. More heat energy is released in forming bonds in the products than is needed to break bonds in the reactants. So, overall, heat energy is given out.

The temperature does not always go up when solutions form. For example, the temperature goes down when ammonium nitrate dissolves.

The temperature increases so this must be an exothermic change. Remember:
- exothermic = energy out or 'energy exits'
- endothermic = energy in or 'energy enters'

Now try this

Copy and complete the table by putting a tick (✓) in each correct box.   **(4 marks)**

	Breaking bonds	Making bonds	Temperature of reaction mixture	
			Increases	Decreases
Exothermic process				
Endothermic process				

Reaction profiles

Energy profile diagrams model the energy changes that happen during reactions.

Exothermic reactions

The diagram shows a typical **reaction profile** for an exothermic reaction.

You should see that:

- ✓ the **energy level** of the reactants is greater than the energy level of the products

- ✓ the **energy change** of the reaction is negative (energy is transferred to the surroundings).

The **activation energy** is the minimum energy needed to start a reaction. It may be supplied by, for example:

- ✓ heating the reaction mixture
- ✓ applying a flame or a spark.

Endothermic reactions

The diagram shows a typical reaction profile for an endothermic reaction.

You should see that:

- ✓ the energy level of the reactants is lower than the energy level of the products

- ✓ the energy change of the reaction is positive (energy is transferred from the surroundings).

The activation energy may be supplied by, for example:

- ✓ continually heating the reaction mixture
- ✓ passing an electric current through an electrolyte (as in electrolysis).

Worked example

The reaction profile represents an exothermic reaction.

(a) Explain what the energy change shown as A represents. **(2 marks)**

the activation energy, which means that this is the energy needed to start the reaction

(b) Draw a line to represent the reaction profile for when a catalyst is added. **(1 mark)**

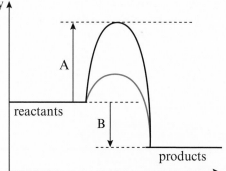

In this diagram, B represents the overall energy change. A catalyst provides an alternative pathway with a lower activation energy for the chemical reaction.

Now try this

1 Explain the term 'activation energy'. **(2 marks)**

2 Sketch reaction profiles for the following reactions:

(a) $CH_4 + 2O_2 \rightarrow CO_2 + 2H_2O$ (exothermic)
(4 marks)

(b) $CaCO_3 \rightarrow CaO + CO_2$ (endothermic)
(4 marks)

Crude oil

Crude oil is a fossil fuel, formed over millions of years from ancient remains of marine plants and animals.

Hydrocarbons

Hydrocarbons are compounds of carbon and hydrogen atoms **only**. Carbon atoms can form four covalent bonds. In a hydrocarbon molecule, these bonds can be:
- carbon–carbon bonds
- carbon–hydrogen bonds.

Hydrocarbon molecules can consist of:
- chains (with or without branches) or rings of carbon atoms.

Hydrocarbons in crude oil

Crude oil is:
- a complex mixture of hydrocarbons, with their carbon atoms in chains or rings
- an important source of useful substances
- a finite resource.

Finite resources

Finite resources:

✓ are no longer being made, or

✓ are being made extremely slowly.

Crude oil takes millions of years to form.

Worked example

(a) Hydrocarbons are found in crude oil. Which of the following formulae represents a hydrocarbon? **(1 mark)**

☐ **A** C_2H_5OH

☒ **B** C_2H_6

☐ **C** $C_6H_{12}O_6$

☐ **D** CCl_4

(b) Describe **two** ways in which crude oil is an important source of useful substances.

(2 marks)

Hydrocarbons from crude oil are useful as fuels and as feedstock for the petrochemical industry.

The chemical symbols you see in the formulae for hydrocarbon molecules are:
- C for carbon
- H for hydrogen.

In **ball-and-stick models** (similar to the ones above), atoms are usually modelled as:
- black for carbon atoms
- white for hydrogen atoms.

Familiar fuels such as petrol and diesel oil (used in cars) come from crude oil.

A **feedstock** is a starting material for an industrial chemical process.

The **petrochemical** industry involves the use and manufacture of substances from crude oil.

Now try this

1 (a) Explain the meaning of the term 'hydrocarbon'. **(2 marks)**

(b) State the type of chemical bond found in a hydrocarbon molecule. **(1 mark)**

2 Explain why crude oil is described as a **finite** resource. **(2 marks)**

3 Describe the possible arrangements of carbon atoms in hydrocarbon molecules. **(2 marks)**

4 (a) Give an example of a fuel obtained from crude oil. **(1 mark)**

(b) Give an example of a substance manufactured using crude oil as a feedstock. **(1 mark)**

Fractional distillation

Fractional distillation is used to separate crude oil into simpler, more useful mixtures.

Fractional distillation

Crude oil can be separated by fractional distillation because its different hydrocarbons have different **boiling points**. During fractional distillation:

- oil is heated to evaporate it
- vapours rise in a fractionating column
- the column has a **temperature gradient** – hot at the bottom, cool at the top
- each fraction condenses where it becomes cool enough, and is piped out of the column.

The **gases** fraction does not condense and leaves at the top.

The **bitumen** fraction does not evaporate and leaves at the bottom.

The other fractions are liquid at room temperature and are useful as fuels.

Fractions

A **fraction** is a mixture of hydrocarbons with **similar** boiling points and numbers of carbon atoms. There are trends in the properties of the different fractions from crude oil:

Number of C and H atoms	Boiling point	Ease of ignition	Viscosity
smallest	lowest	most flammable	least viscous
⬆	⬆	⬆	⬆
largest	highest	least flammable	most viscous

Substances with a low viscosity are runny, and those with a high viscosity are 'thick'.

Alkanes

Most of the hydrocarbons from crude oil are **alkanes**, a **homologous series** of compounds.

You can revise alkanes and homologous series on page 146.

Boiling point and molecule size

As the number of carbon and hydrogen atoms in a hydrocarbon molecule increases:

- ✓ the strength of the **intermolecular forces** increases
- ✓ more energy must be transferred to overcome these forces
- ✓ the boiling point increases.

Worked example

Draw one straight line from the name of each fraction to its correct typical use. **(5 marks)**

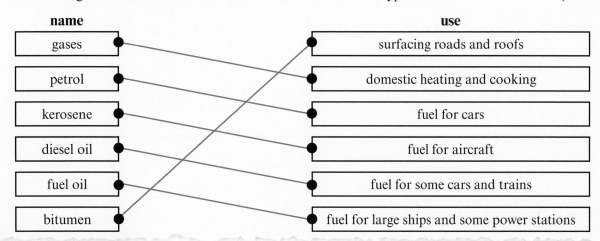

name	use
gases	surfacing roads and roofs
petrol	domestic heating and cooking
kerosene	fuel for cars
diesel oil	fuel for aircraft
fuel oil	fuel for some cars and trains
bitumen	fuel for large ships and some power stations

Now try this

1 Suggest **two** reasons to explain why bitumen is not suitable for use as a fuel. **(2 marks)**

2 Describe how crude oil is separated into fractions by fractional distillation. **(3 marks)**

Alkanes

The **alkanes** are a homologous series of hydrocarbons.

Features of a homologous series

A **homologous series** is a series of compounds:
- in which **molecular formulae** of neighbouring members differ by CH_2
- that show a gradual variation in physical properties, such as boiling points
- that have similar chemical properties.

Chemical properties of alkanes

The alkanes undergo **complete combustion**. If there is lots of oxygen, they react to form carbon dioxide and water vapour.

For example, methane (from natural gas):

methane + oxygen → carbon dioxide + water

$$CH_4(g) + 2O_2(g) \rightarrow CO_2(g) + 2H_2O(g)$$

Alkanes

Names
end in ane

Structure
single bonds only

Formulae and reactions
Their general formula is C_nH_{2n+2}.
They are flammable and form carbon dioxide and water when they burn completely.

ethane C_2H_6

propane C_3H_8

Worked example

The molecular formula shows the number of carbon atoms (and hydrogen atoms) in the molecule.

The table shows the boiling points of some alkanes.

Molecular formula of alkane	CH_4	C_2H_6	C_4H_{10}	C_6H_{14}	C_8H_{18}	$C_{10}H_{22}$	$C_{16}H_{34}$
Boiling point of alkane (°C)	−162	−89	0	69	126	174	287

Complete the graph below, and draw a line of best fit. **(3 marks)**

The boiling point increases as the number of carbon atoms in the alkane molecule increases.

This is why each fraction contains hydrocarbon molecules that have similar numbers of carbon atoms, and similar boiling points.

Now try this

1 State three features of a homologous series. **(3 marks)**

2 The molecular formula for icosane is $C_{20}H_{42}$. Predict the molecular formula for heneicosane, the next member of the alkane homologous series. **(1 mark)**

3 Use the Worked example graph to predict the boiling point of propane, C_3H_8. **(1 mark)**

Incomplete combustion

Incomplete combustion happens when the supply of oxygen to a burning fuel is limited.

Complete versus incomplete combustion

During **complete combustion** of a hydrocarbon fuel, such as petrol, kerosene or diesel oil:

- hydrogen is oxidised to water vapour, H_2O
- carbon is oxidised to carbon dioxide, CO_2
- energy is given out (transferred to the surroundings by radiation as heat and light).

During **incomplete combustion**, hydrogen is still oxidised to water vapour, but:

- carbon may be partially oxidised to carbon monoxide, CO
- carbon may be released as carbon particles or **soot**
- less energy is given out.

During incomplete combustion, different amounts of the different carbon products form, depending on how much oxygen is available for oxidation. For example, if the supply of oxygen is only slightly limited, some carbon dioxide may also be produced. If the supply of oxygen is very limited, the products will mostly be carbon and carbon monoxide.

Cars and appliances

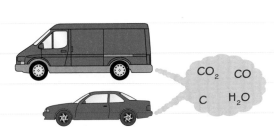

There is always incomplete combustion in vehicle engines.

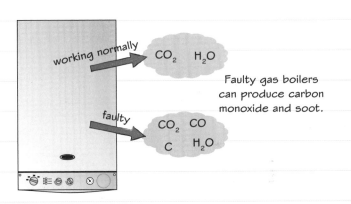

working normally → CO_2 H_2O

faulty → CO_2 CO C H_2O

Faulty gas boilers can produce carbon monoxide and soot.

Worked example

 (a) Explain how carbon monoxide behaves as a toxic gas. **(2 marks)**

Carbon monoxide attaches to haemoglobin in red blood cells, preventing oxygen attaching instead. This reduces the amount of oxygen carried around the body by the bloodstream.

Carbon monoxide can cause unconsciousness and even death. It is:

- colourless
- odourless (has no smell).

Electronic carbon monoxide detectors are used to warn us when the gas is present.

(b) Describe **two** problems caused by soot. **(2 marks)**

Soot can build up in chimneys where it may eventually cause fires; it also blackens buildings.

Tiny soot particles can be breathed in. This may cause lung diseases such as bronchitis, or make existing lung disease worse.

Now try this

When are soot and carbon monoxide produced, and are they always formed together?

1 Explain why soot and carbon monoxide are produced during incomplete combustion of a hydrocarbon fuel. **(3 marks)**

2 Explain why carbon monoxide is difficult for our bodies to detect. **(2 marks)**

3 A householder sees soot marks around his gas boiler. He thinks that this shows that carbon monoxide is being produced. Comment on the accuracy of this thought. **(2 marks)**

Acid rain

Rainwater is naturally acidic, but **acid rain** is more acidic than normal.

Sulfur dioxide

Hydrocarbon fuels may contain impurities such as sulfur compounds. When the fuel burns, the sulfur in these impurities is oxidised to form sulfur dioxide:

sulfur + oxygen → sulfur dioxide

$$S(s) + O_2(g) \rightarrow SO_2(g)$$

Sulfur dioxide is a non-metal oxide:

- It dissolves in rainwater to form an acidic solution.

Reducing environmental damage

The problems caused by acid rain can be reduced in several ways, including:

- ✓ removing sulfur from petrol, diesel oil and fuel oil at the oil refinery before selling it
- ✓ preventing sulfur dioxide leaving power station chimneys – 'flue gas desulfurisation'
- ✓ adding calcium carbonate or calcium hydroxide to fields and lakes to neutralise excess acid from acid rain.

The effects of acid rain

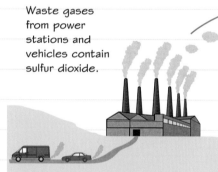

Waste gases from power stations and vehicles contain sulfur dioxide.

Sulfur dioxide dissolves in water in the air.

Rain is more acidic than normal.

Acid rain speeds up the weathering of buildings and statues.

Trees are damaged.

Rivers, lakes and soils are more acidic, which harms organisms living in them.

Worked example

Oxides of nitrogen, NO_x, are atmospheric pollutants. They may contribute to acid rain.

(a) Explain why oxides of nitrogen are produced when hydrocarbon fuels are used in vehicle and aircraft engines. **(2 marks)**

Air goes into the engine so that the fuel can burn. Nitrogen and oxygen from the air react together at the high temperatures in the engine to produce oxides of nitrogen.

(b) Balance the equation below to represent the production of nitrogen dioxide. **(1 mark)**

$$N_2(g) + \underline{2}\,O_2(g) \rightarrow \underline{2}\,NO_2(g)$$

Unlike sulfur dioxide, oxides of nitrogen are **not** produced from impurities in the hydrocarbon fuel.

NO_2 is a non-metal oxide that dissolves in rainwater to form an acidic solution.

Nitrogen dioxide is a toxic, orange-brown gas. Unlike carbon monoxide (produced during incomplete combustion), nitrogen dioxide has a sharp smell. You can revise incomplete combustion on page 147.

Now try this

1 State **two** environmental problems caused by acid rain. **(2 marks)**

Look at the diagram to help you.

2 Explain why, when hydrocarbon fuels are used:
(a) sulfur dioxide is produced **(2 marks)**
(b) oxides of nitrogen are produced. **(2 marks)**

Choosing fuels

Most cars use petrol or diesel oil, but hydrogen may also be used as a fuel for cars.

Fossil fuels

These **fossil fuels** are obtained from crude oil:

- petrol (for cars)
- diesel oil (for some cars and trains)
- fuel oil (for large ships and some power stations).

This fossil fuel is obtained from natural gas:

- methane (for domestic cooking and heating).

Non-renewable resources

Non-renewable resources are used up faster than they are formed.

Crude oil and natural gas take millions of years to form (see page 144 for more about this). The fossil fuels obtained from these resources are being used up very quickly, so they are non-renewable fuels.

Hydrogen

The combustion of hydrogen produces only water vapour:

hydrogen + oxygen → water

$$2H_2(g) + O_2(g) → 2H_2O(g)$$

Hydrogen is manufactured in several ways, including:

- electrolysis of water (the reverse of the reaction above)
- cracking of oil fractions (for more about cracking, see page 150)
- reaction of natural gas with steam:

$$CH_4(g) + 2H_2O(g) → CO_2(g) + 4H_2(g)$$

Worked example

Describe three features of a good fuel. **(3 marks)**

A good fuel should:

- burn easily – it should be easy to ignite and stay alight
- not produce soot, smoke or ash
- release a lot of energy when it burns.

A good fuel should also be easy to store and transport safely.

Petrol versus hydrogen

Petrol	Hydrogen
👍 burns easily	👍 burns easily
👍 does not produce ash	👍 does not produce ash or smoke
👎 produces carbon dioxide and carbon monoxide as well as water when it burns	👍 only produces water when it burns
👍 releases more energy per kg when it burns than fuels such as coal or wood	👍 releases nearly three times as much energy per kg as petrol
👍 is a liquid, so it is easy to store and transport	👎 is a gas, so it has to be stored at high pressure
	👎 Filling stations would need to be adapted for hydrogen to be used in cars.

Now try this

1 Explain why the combustion of petrol produces carbon dioxide, but the combustion of hydrogen does not. **(3 marks)**

2 (a) Suggest reasons to explain why hydrogen produced from crude oil or natural gas may not be renewable. **(2 marks)**

Look at the ways hydrogen can be manufactured.

(b) Carbon dioxide is a greenhouse gas linked to global warming and climate change.
Hydrogen is often regarded as a 'carbon-neutral fuel', a fuel with production, transport and use that have no overall emission of carbon dioxide.
Suggest reasons to explain why hydrogen may not actually be carbon neutral. **(2 marks)**

Cracking

Cracking is a process carried out on fractions in oil refineries after fractional distillation.

Making fractions more useful

Cracking involves breaking down larger alkanes into smaller, more useful alkanes and **alkenes**.

| The long molecules are not very useful. | **Cracking** breaks down molecules by heating them. | Cracking produces shorter-chain alkanes, which are useful as fuels. | Cracking also produces **alkenes**, which are used to make **polymers**. |

Cracking in the lab

Paraffin is an alkane. Liquid paraffin can be cracked in the laboratory using this apparatus.

✓ The porous pot catalyst is heated strongly.

✓ The liquid paraffin is heated and evaporates.

✓ The paraffin vapour passes over the hot porous pot and the hydrocarbon molecules break down.

✓ One of the products is ethene, which is a gas and collects in the other tube.

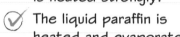

liquid paraffin on mineral wool · broken porous pot · delivery tube · ethene gas · HEAT · HEAT · water

---

Worked example

The bar chart shows the supply and demand of different fractions from crude oil.

Explain how cracking helps to balance supply with demand. **(2 marks)**

Some larger alkanes, such as bitumen, are in greater supply than their demand. Cracking converts these alkanes into smaller hydrocarbons, such as petrol, which are in greater demand than can be supplied by fractional distillation alone.

The supply is the amount that the oil refinery can produce. The demand is the amount that customers want to buy.

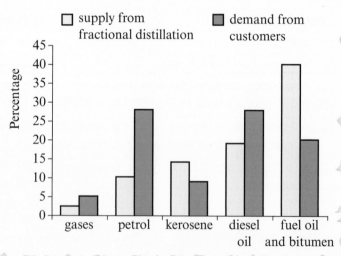

□ supply from fractional distillation   ■ demand from customers

---

Now try this

(a) Give the formula of the substance needed to balance this equation (which represents a cracking reaction):
$$C_8H_{18} \rightarrow C_6H_{14} + \ldots\ldots\ldots\ldots$$ **(1 mark)**

(b) State a use for the hydrocarbon in your answer to (a), other than as a fuel. **(1 mark)**

Study the diagram at the top of the page.

Extended response – Fuels

There will be one or more 6-mark questions on your exam paper. For these questions, you will need to think scientifically and structure your answer logically, showing how the points you make are related to each other. You can revise the topics for this question, which is about **fuels**, on pages 144–149.

Worked example

Crude oil is a complex mixture of hydrocarbons. Most belong to the alkane homologous series. Diesel oil is a fuel produced from crude oil.

gases

diesel oil

crude oil →

bitumen

Explain how diesel oil is separated from crude oil. Use your knowledge and understanding, and the diagram above, in your answer. **(6 marks)**

Crude oil is separated into different fractions by fractional distillation. The crude oil is heated to around 350 °C to evaporate it. Some of the hydrocarbons stay in the liquid state and leave at the bottom of the column. The other hydrocarbons rise inside the fractionating column in the gas state.

The fractionating column has a temperature gradient inside it. The column becomes cooler towards the top, so the hydrocarbons cool down as they rise. They condense to the liquid state when they reach a part of the column that is cool enough.

The gases do not condense and they leave at the top. Diesel oil leaves through a pipe as a liquid fraction when it condenses.

Command word: Explain

When you are asked to **explain** something, it is not enough just to state or describe it.

Your answer must contain some reasoning or justification of the points you make.

 The labelled diagram in the stem of the question helps you in two ways:
- It may remind you that crude oil is separated by fractional distillation (not, for example, by cracking).
- It shows approximately where diesel oil leaves the fractionating column.

 You should state clearly which separation method is involved, and outline what happens to the crude oil immediately after heating it.

 The temperature gradient inside a fractionating column is important to the process. You could also mention that the hydrocarbons condense when they cool to their boiling point, because this is an important feature too.

 Your answer could also explain that smaller hydrocarbons have lower boiling points because they have weaker intermolecular forces.

Your answer should show comprehensive knowledge and understanding of the topic covered. Take care to use the information given to you in support of your explanations. Organise your answer in a structured way with clear lines of reasoning.

Now try this

Diesel oil is used as a fuel for some cars and trains. Scientists and engineers are researching ways to use hydrogen as a fuel for cars instead of diesel oil. Compare and contrast the use of hydrogen and diesel oil as fuels for cars. **(6 marks)**

You need to include at least one similarity and one difference between these two fuels. You do not need to make a conclusion.

The early atmosphere

Gases produced by volcanic activity formed the Earth's early atmosphere.

Gases in the early atmosphere

Scientists believe that the Earth's early atmosphere, billions of years ago, contained:
• little or no oxygen
• a large amount of carbon dioxide
• water vapour
• small amounts of other gases.

Evidence for this includes:
• the mixture of gases released by volcanoes
• the atmospheres of other planets in our solar system today, which have not been changed by living organisms.

Today's atmosphere

Nitrogen and oxygen are the main gases in the modern atmosphere.

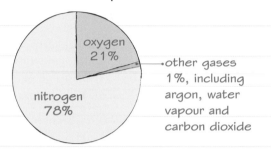

oxygen 21%

other gases 1%, including argon, water vapour and carbon dioxide

nitrogen 78%

Decreasing carbon dioxide and increasing oxygen

The Earth was very hot to start with. As it cooled, water vapour condensed and fell as rain to form the oceans.

Earth is very hot

Earth cools and oceans form.

Oxygen builds up in the oceans.

Forms of plant life evolve in the oceans and **photosynthesis** begins.

Oxygen builds up in the atmosphere.

Carbon dioxide dissolves in the oceans.

The shells of dead marine organisms fall to the sea bed and become part of the **sediment**.

Marine organisms used the dissolved carbon dioxide to make calcium carbonate for shells.

Over millions of years the layers of sediment become squashed and form **sedimentary rocks**.

Worked example

Some rocks contain iron. Very old rocks do not contain iron oxides but later ones do.

(a) Explain how these rocks provide evidence for changes to the Earth's atmosphere.   **(3 marks)**

The very old rocks are evidence that the early atmosphere contained little or no oxygen, because they do not contain iron oxides. Later rocks do contain iron oxides, which is evidence that oxygen was released into the atmosphere and reacted with iron in the rocks.

(b) Describe a simple test for oxygen.   **(2 marks)**

A glowing wooden splint relights in oxygen.

When you describe a laboratory test, say what you would do, and what you would observe.

Remember:
• a lighted wooden splint ignites hydrogen with a pop
• limewater turns milky in the presence of carbon dioxide.

When oxygen was first produced, it reacted with iron in rocks to produce iron oxides. This meant that, even though primitive plants were photosynthesising, oxygen levels in the atmosphere did not begin to rise straight away.

Now try this

1 (a) State how the formation of oceans was a cause of decreasing carbon dioxide levels.   **(1 mark)**

  (b) Describe why the levels of oxygen in the atmosphere increased.   **(2 marks)**

2 Suggest a reason that explains why scientists cannot be certain about the Earth's early atmosphere.   **(1 mark)**

Greenhouse effect

The greenhouse effect helps to keep the Earth warm enough for living organisms to exist.

Reducing radiation to space

In the **greenhouse effect**:

• **Greenhouse gases** in the atmosphere absorb heat radiated from the Earth.
• The greenhouse gases then release energy in all directions.

This reduces the amount of heat radiated into space, keeping the Earth warm.

Sun
heat radiated from the Earth
Gases absorb heat.
Gases release energy.
energy from the Sun
(not to scale)

Greenhouse gases

The table shows gases that are particularly good at absorbing and emitting energy by radiation.

Greenhouse gas	Typical source
carbon dioxide	burning fossil fuels
methane	livestock farming, e.g. cattle
water vapour	evaporation from oceans

This is not seen as a problem because excess water vapour leaves the atmosphere as rain and snow.

Global warming and climate change

The accumulation of greenhouse gases in the atmosphere:

• increases the greenhouse effect.

This:

• increases the warming effect in the atmosphere – **global warming**.

Global warming is associated with:

• long-term changes to weather patterns – **climate change**
• rising sea levels due to melting ice and expanding ocean water.

Worked example

Evaluate how far the graph provides evidence for global warming.   **(2 marks)**

The graph shows that both temperature and carbon dioxide concentration have been rising since 1950. There is a correlation but this does not <u>prove</u> that rising carbon dioxide levels are causing the warming.

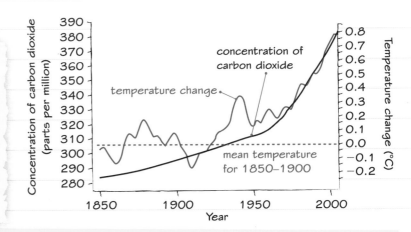

concentration of carbon dioxide
temperature change
mean temperature for 1850–1900

Concentration of carbon dioxide (parts per million)
Temperature change (°C)
Year

Many scientists believe that carbon dioxide is the main cause of global warming, but this opinion is based on computer modelling and other information, not just on graphs like this.

Now try this

1 (a) Name two greenhouse gases, other than water vapour.   **(2 marks)**
  (b) State one typical source for each gas named in your answer to **(a)**.   **(2 marks)**

2 Describe how the greenhouse effect keeps the Earth warm.   **(2 marks)**

3 Explain how the increased use of fossil fuels, which contain carbon and carbon compounds, may lead to global warming.   **(4 marks)**

Extended response – Atmospheric science

There will be one or more 6-mark questions on your exam paper. For these questions, you will need to think scientifically and structure your answer logically, showing how the points you make are related to each other. You can revise the topics for this question, which is about **the atmosphere**, on pages 152 and 153.

Worked example

The graph shows the mean annual release of carbon dioxide from burning fossil fuels during each decade from the 1900s to the 2000s. It also shows the mean change in global temperature during that time.

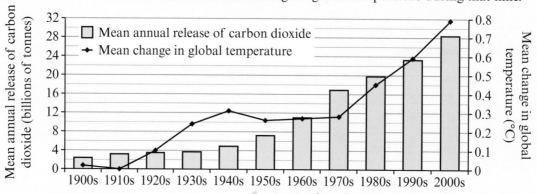

Evaluate this evidence of human activity as a cause of global warming.   **(6 marks)**

The mass of carbon dioxide released increased each decade from the 1900s to the 2000s. For example, in the 1900s about 2.5 billion tonnes was released on average each year, but by the 2000s it was over 28 billion tonnes, more than 10 times greater.

Over the same period, the mean global temperature increased by nearly 0.8 °C. As the carbon dioxide was released by burning fossil fuels, this shows that there is a positive correlation between the consumption of fossil fuels and temperature change.

However, the temperature increased more rapidly in the 1930s and 1940s than the release of carbon dioxide. It also went down in the 1950s and then barely changed until the 1980s, whereas the release of carbon dioxide increased greatly. By itself, the evidence given does not show that human activity caused the global warming observed, but it strongly suggests that it did.

Command word: Evaluate

When you are asked to **evaluate** something, you need to review information given to you, and then bring it together to form a conclusion. You should include evidence such as strengths and weaknesses, and arrive at a judgement.

You should use the information in your answer, e.g. by interpreting the bar chart.

A **correlation** between two sets of data means that they are connected in some way. In this case, there is a **positive correlation** – as one variable increases, the other one does too.

You should point out evidence for weaknesses as well as strengths for the main argument.

A **causal** relationship means that a change in one variable causes a change in another variable.

Now try this

The concentration of carbon dioxide in the atmosphere increased by about 35% between 1900 and 2015.

Describe the processes that remove carbon dioxide from the atmosphere, and suggest reasons to explain the observed increase in its concentration.   **(6 marks)**

Key concepts

You need to know the SI units of physical quantities, as well as their multiples and sub-multiples, how to convert between units and how to use significant figures and standard form.

Base SI units

There are six main **base SI units** you need to know.

Name	Unit	Abbreviation
length	metre	m
mass	kilogram	kg
time	second	s
current	ampere or amp	A
temperature	kelvin	K
amount of a substance	mole	mol

Derived SI units

There are nine derived SI units you need to know.

Name	Unit	Abbreviation
frequency	hertz	Hz
force	newton	N
energy	joule	J
power	watt	W
pressure	pascal	Pa
electric charge	coulomb	C
electric potential difference	volt	V
electric resistance	ohm	Ω
magnetic flux density	tesla	T

Multiples and sub-multiples

For values of physical quantities, you need to know the values of these multiples or **prefixes**.

$$10^9 \quad 10^8 \quad 10^7 \quad 10^6 \quad 10^5 \quad 10^4 \quad 10^3 \quad 10^2 \quad 10^1 \quad 10^0 \quad 10^{-1} \quad 10^{-2} \quad 10^{-3} \quad 10^{-4} \quad 10^{-5} \quad 10^{-6} \quad 10^{-7} \quad 10^{-8} \quad 10^{-9}$$

giga-	mega-	kilo-	centi-	milli-	micro-	nano-
prefix **G**	prefix **M**	prefix **k**	prefix **c**	prefix **m**	prefix **μ**	prefix **n**
× 1 000 000 000	× 1 000 000	× 1000	÷ 100	÷ 1000	÷ 1 000 000	÷ 1 000 000 000
e.g. 5 GHz	e.g. 5 MW	e.g. 2 km	e.g. 8 cm	e.g. 6 mA	e.g. 7 μs	e.g. 2 nm

Significant figures

Significant figures are either non-zero digits (i.e. the digits 1 to 9) or zeroes between non-zero digits.

- The number **543 563** has 6 significant figures.
- The number 0.**23** has two significant figures.
- The number 0.000 000 000 **254** has 3 significant figures. The zeroes before the '2' are not significant figures.
- The number **30 340 000** has 4 significant figures.

The number 30 339 900 rounded to 5 significant figures is 30 340 000.

Standard form

It is useful to write very large and very small numbers in **standard form**.

This is a number between 1 and 10.

This is an integer – a whole number that can be positive or negative.

$$A \times 10^B$$

You also need to be able to convert between units such as kilometres to metres, or hours to seconds.

Now try this

1 State the number of significant figures in each number.
   (a) 4.56   **(1 mark)**
   (b) 0.000 564 5   **(1 mark)**
   (c) 3.0046   **(1 mark)**

2 Convert:
   (a) 12 hours to seconds   **(2 marks)**
   (b) 64 km/h to m/s   **(2 marks)**

3 Convert 58.3 MW to watts. Give your answer in standard form.   **(2 marks)**

4 The diameter of an atom is 0.000 000 000 1 m. Write this in standard form.   **(2 marks)**

Scalars and vectors

All physical quantities can be described as either a scalar or a vector quantity.

Scalar quantities

Scalar quantities have a size or a magnitude but no specific direction.

Examples include:
- mass
- speed
- distance
- energy
- temperature.

Vector quantities

Vector quantities have a size or magnitude and a specific direction.

Examples include:
- force or weight
- velocity
- displacement
- acceleration
- momentum.

Speed and velocity

The girl is running to the right so she has a velocity of 5 m/s to the right.

5 m/s

Both the girl and the boy are running at 5 m/s. They have the same speed.

5 m/s

If we take 'to the right' as the positive direction, then the girl has a velocity of +5 m/s and the boy has a velocity of −5 m/s.

The boy is running to the left so he has a velocity of 5 m/s to the left.

Speed has a size but velocity has a size AND a direction.

Velocity is speed in a stated direction.

Worked example

(a) Describe the difference between a scalar and a vector. **(2 marks)**

A scalar has a size, whereas a vector has a size and a specific direction.

(b) Describe an example which shows the difference between a scalar and a vector. **(2 marks)**

Speed is a scalar quantity and may have a value of 5 m/s. Velocity may also have a value of 5 m/s but a direction of north.

All vector quantities can be given positive and negative values to show their direction. Examples include:

1 A force of +4 N may be balanced by a force acting in the opposite direction of −4 N.

2 A car that accelerates at a rate of +2 m/s² could decelerate at −2 m/s².

3 If a distance walked to the right of 20 m is a displacement of +20 m, then the same distance walked to the left from the same starting point is a displacement of −20 m.

Now try this

1 State what is meant by
   (a) a scalar quantity **(1 mark)**
   (b) a vector quantity. **(1 mark)**

2 (a) Which of these quantities is a scalar? **(1 mark)**
      ☐ **A** velocity   ☐ **B** acceleration   ☐ **C** mass   ☐ **D** weight
   (b) Which of these quantities is a vector? **(1 mark)**
      ☐ **A** temperature   ☐ **B** energy   ☐ **C** speed   ☐ **D** electric field

3 A boy has a speed of 4 m/s when running. State his (a) speed and (b) velocity when he is running in the opposite direction. **(2 marks)**

Speed, distance and time

Speed is the distance that a moving object covers each second.

Calculating speed

When an object covers the same distance per second throughout its journey, you can use this equation to calculate its speed:

$$\text{speed (m/s)} = \text{change in distance (m)} \div \text{time taken (s)}$$

The greater the change in distance per second, the faster the object is moving.

When the change in distance over a period of time is zero, the speed is zero and the object is stationary.

Average speed

LEARN IT! IT'S NOT ON THE EQUATIONS LIST

Objects often change speed during a journey, so it is better to use average speed:

$$\text{average speed (m/s)} = \text{total distance travelled (m)} \div \text{total time taken (s)}$$

You can also write this as:

$$\text{distance travelled (m)} = \text{average speed (m/s)} \times \text{time taken (s)}$$

Distance/time graphs

Distance/time graphs have distance on the y-axis and time on the x-axis. The gradient or slope of the graph tells us about the motion of the object.

A — Constant or steady speed   B — Accelerating (speeding up)   C — Decelerating (slowing down)   D — Stationary

Journeys and distance/time graphs

This distance/time graph tells you about a student's journey.

Steep line: the student is moving much faster than before.

Horizontal line: the student is stationary.

Sloping line: shows that the student is moving. The gradient of the line is shallow, showing that the student is moving slowly.

Worked example

(a) Calculate the speed for each part of the journey shown in the graph on the left. **(3 marks)**

speed between 0 and 60s = 80m ÷ 60s = 1.33 m/s

speed between 60s and 120s = 0m ÷ 60s = 0 m/s

speed between 120s and 140s = 160m ÷ 20s = 8 m/s

(b) Calculate the average speed for the whole journey. **(2 marks)**

average speed = 240m ÷ 140s = 1.7 m/s

(c) The student then travels at 4m/s for 25 seconds. Calculate how far the student travels in this time.

Distance = speed × time = 4 m/s × 25s = 100m

Now try this

1. Calculate the average speed of a motorbike that travels 120 m in 8 s. **(3 marks)**
2. A cyclist rides a bike at an average speed of 9 m/s for 30 seconds. Calculate the distance that the cyclist travels in this time. **(3 marks)**
3. A car accelerates from 0 m/s to 12 m/s in 5 s. **Sketch** a distance/time graph to show this. **(3 marks)**

Equations of motion

You can use equations to work out the velocity and acceleration of moving bodies.

Acceleration

Acceleration is a change in velocity per second. Acceleration is a vector quantity.

$$\text{acceleration (m/s}^2) = \frac{\text{change in velocity (m/s)}}{\text{time taken (s)}}$$

$$a = \frac{(v - u)}{t}$$

LEARN IT!
IT'S NOT ON THE EQUATIONS LIST

- a is the acceleration
- v is the final velocity
- u is the initial velocity
- t is the time taken

Velocity

Velocity is the change in distance per second.

Velocity is a vector quantity.

$$(\text{final velocity})^2 - (\text{initial velocity})^2 = 2 \times \text{acceleration} \times \text{distance}$$

$$v^2 - u^2 = 2 \times a \times x$$

x is the distance travelled.

You can also write this as:

$$v^2 = u^2 + 2ax$$

If a vehicle is said to be 'starting from rest' then its initial velocity, u, will be zero, so the equation simplifies to $v^2 = 2ax$.

 Worked example

A cat changes its speed from 2.5 m/s to 10.0 m/s over a period of 3.0 s. Calculate the cat's acceleration. **(3 marks)**

$v = 10$ m/s, $u = 2.5$ m/s, $t = 3$ s, $a = ?$

$a = (v - u) \div t$

$a = (10.0$ m/s $- 2.5$ m/s$) \div 3.0$ s

$a = 7.5$ m/s $\div 3.0$ s

$a = 2.5$ m/s^2

Write down all the quantities you know and the one you need to work out. Then decide which equation you need to use.

Watch out! When using this equation, the value for $(v - u)$ may be negative.

 Worked example

A motorcyclist passes through green traffic lights with an initial velocity of 4 m/s and then accelerates at a rate of 2.4 m/s^2, covering a total distance of 200 m. Calculate the final velocity of the motorcycle. **(4 marks)**

Final velocity^2 = initial velocity^2 + 2 × acceleration × distance travelled

final velocity^2 = $(4)^2 + 2 \times 2.4 \times 200$

$= 16 + 960 = 976$

$= \sqrt{976} = 31.2$ m/s

 Maths skills When working out x using this equation, you will need to rearrange it. Subtract u^2 from both sides and then divide both sides by $2a$, to give $x = \dfrac{v^2 - u^2}{2a}$. Substitute the other values and work out the value of x.

Watch out! When you substitute the values for initial velocity, acceleration and distance, you get a value for final velocity^2. So you need to find the square root of this value to get the value for the final velocity.

 Now try this

1. A dog changes its speed from 2 m/s to 8 m/s in 5 s. Calculate the acceleration of the dog. **(3 marks)**

2. A motorcycle changes its speed from 18 m/s to 6 m/s in 4 s. Calculate the acceleration of the motorcycle in this time. **(3 marks)**

3. A car passes through traffic lights with an initial velocity of 5 m/s and accelerates at a rate of 2 m/s^2 over a distance of 180 m. Calculate the final velocity of the car. **(4 marks)**

Velocity/time graphs

Velocity/time graphs show how the velocity of a vehicle changes with time. You can also work out acceleration and distance travelled from the graph.

Interpreting velocity/time graphs

Velocity/time graphs have velocity plotted on the y-axis and time plotted on the x-axis. The graph shows you how the velocity changes with time.

- The **slope** or **gradient** of the graph tells us the acceleration of the vehicle.
- The **area under the graph** tells us the **distance** travelled.

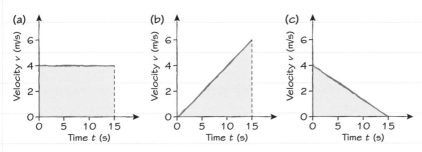

Maths skills Acceleration (gradient) = change in velocity/change in time. For distance travelled (area) use the formulae for the area of a rectangle (base × height, $b \times h$) and area of a triangle ($\frac{1}{2} \times b \times h$). The area will have units of metres, as m/s × s = m.

(a) Acceleration is zero, distance travelled is 60 m.

(b) Acceleration is 0.4 m/s^2, distance travelled is 45 m.

(c) Acceleration is −0.27 m/s^2, distance travelled is 30 m.

Velocity/time graphs

This velocity/time graph shows how the velocity of a train along a straight track changes with time.

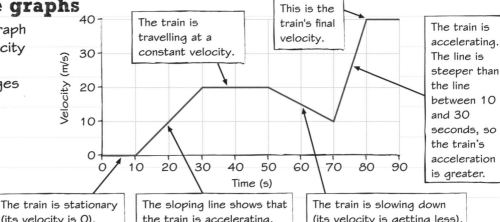

The train is travelling at a constant velocity.

This is the train's final velocity.

The train is accelerating. The line is steeper than the line between 10 and 30 seconds, so the train's acceleration is greater.

The train is stationary (its velocity is 0).

The sloping line shows that the train is accelerating.

The train is slowing down (its velocity is getting less).

Worked example

Use the velocity/time graph of the train to calculate:

(a) the distance travelled between 10 s and 30 s. **(3 marks)**

Distance travelled is the area of the triangle beneath the line between 10 s and 30 s.

Distance travelled = area
= ½ × (30 − 10)s × 20 m/s = 200 m

(b) the acceleration of the train between 10 s and 30 s. **(3 marks)**

Acceleration = gradient or slope of the line between 10 s and 30 s

= change in velocity ÷ change in time
= (20 − 0) m/s ÷ (30 − 10) s = 1 m/s^2

Now try this

1 State what can be determined from the (a) gradient and (b) area beneath a velocity/time graph. **(2 marks)**

2 A car travels a distance of 200 m in 8 s before stopping at traffic lights for 20 s. It then moves off and travels another 100 m in 5 s. Draw a distance/time graph to show this journey. **(4 marks)**

3 An athlete in a race changes her velocity from 0 m/s to 10 m/s over a time of 4 s. She then runs at a constant velocity of 10 m/s for the next 8 seconds.

(a) Draw a velocity/time graph for this race. **(4 marks)**

(b) Calculate how far she has run in this time. **(3 marks)**

Determining speed

You can measure speeds of objects in the lab by using light gates connected to a computer or data logger.

The speed is found from length of card ÷ time.

card

vehicle

The vehicle is released from its starting position and it moves down the slope.

light gate (attached to laptop)

When the card leaves the light gate, the light beam stops the timer.

`00:00:00`

The beam remains cut until the back of the card passes out of the light gate.

The light beam is cut by the card as it enters the light gate and the timer starts.

Speed and average speed

The **speed** of an object is how fast it is moving at a given point in time. For example, the speedometer on a car tells the driver the speed at that point in time.

The speed of a car may change regularly over a journey. You can calculate the **average speed** which is the total distance travelled divided by the total time taken to cover that distance.

Typical speeds

Different activities occur at different speeds.

Activity	Typical speed
walking	1.5 m/s
running	3.0 m/s
cycling	6.0 m/s
driving	14 m/s
speed of sound in air	330 m/s
airliner	250 m/s
commuter train	55 m/s
gale-force wind	16 m/s

Worked example

Describe how you can determine the average speed of a moving trolley as it moves down a slope.   **(3 marks)**

When you know the distance that a body moves, and the time taken for the body to move that distance, you can use the equation speed = distance ÷ time to determine its speed. This can be done by measuring the distance between two points that the trolley moves past and dividing it by the time taken to travel between those points, or by using light gates to measure the time for which a known length of card breaks a light beam.

Now try this

1 State what you need to measure to determine the speed of an object.   **(2 marks)**

2 Explain why using light gates is better than using a stopwatch when determining the average speed of a trolley in the lab.   **(2 marks)**

3 Explain why the speed of the trolley at the bottom of the slope is greater than its speed at the top of the slope.   **(3 marks)**

Newton's first law

A body will remain at rest or continue in a straight line at a constant speed as long as the forces acting on it are balanced.

Stationary bodies

The forces acting on a stationary body are balanced.

The forces acting on the object are balanced

tension 25 N

weight 25 N

A common mistake is to think that when the resultant force on an object is zero, the object is stationary. The object may also be travelling at a constant speed.

Bodies moving at a constant speed

The forces acting on a body moving at a constant speed, and in a straight line, are balanced.

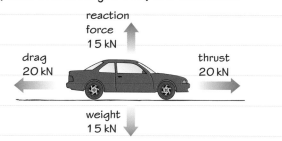

reaction force 15 kN

drag 20 kN

thrust 20 kN

weight 15 kN

The forces on the car are balanced. The car will continue to move at a constant speed in a straight line until another external force is applied.

Unbalanced forces

5 N   10 N

This body will accelerate to the right, since there is a resultant force of 5 N acting to the right.

Worked example

Explain the effect that each of these forces will have on a car.

(a) 300 N forward force from the engine, 200 N drag. **(3 marks)**

Resultant force = 300 N − 200 N = 100 N. The car will accelerate in the direction of the resultant force. Its velocity will increase.

A resultant force acting in the opposite direction to the movement of a body will slow it down. It can also reverse the direction of motion.

(b) 200 N forward force from the engine, 400 N friction from brakes. **(3 marks)**

Resultant force = 200 N − 400 N = −200 N (200 N acting backwards). The car will accelerate in the direction of the resultant force. This is in the opposite direction to its velocity, so the car will slow down.

(c) 300 N forward force, 300 N drag. **(3 marks)**

Resultant force = 0 N. The car will continue to move at the same velocity.

Now try this

1 State what forces act on a body that is moving at a constant speed. **(2 marks)**

2 Explain how the direction of a moving body can be made to change. **(2 marks)**

3 Draw diagrams to show how two forces of 100 N acting on a mass can make it:
   (a) stationary **(2 marks)**
   (b) move at a constant speed **(2 marks)**
   (c) accelerate to the left. **(2 marks)**

Newton's second law

When a resultant force acts on a mass then there will be a change in its velocity. The resultant force determines the size and direction of the subsequent acceleration of the mass.

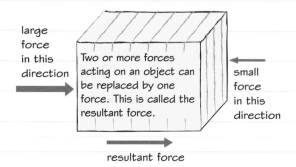

large force in this direction → Two or more forces acting on an object can be replaced by one force. This is called the resultant force. ← small force in this direction

resultant force →

Forces have direction, so a force of -1 N is in the opposite direction to a force of 1 N.

When two or more forces act on the same straight line or are parallel, they can be added together to find the **resultant force**.

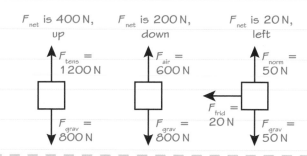

F_{net} is 400 N, up
$F_{tens} = 1200$ N
$F_{grav} = 800$ N

F_{net} is 200 N, down
$F_{air} = 600$ N
$F_{grav} = 800$ N

F_{net} is 20 N, left
$F_{norm} = 50$ N
$F_{frid} = 20$ N
$F_{grav} = 50$ N

Force, mass and acceleration

You can calculate the acceleration of an object when you know its mass and the resultant force acting on it using the equation:

$$\text{acceleration (m/s}^2) = \frac{\text{force (N)}}{\text{mass (kg)}}$$

$$a = \frac{F}{m}$$

Rearrange the equation to give the force:

$$F = m \times a$$

LEARN IT!
IT'S NOT ON THE EQUATIONS LIST

- The acceleration is in the same direction as the force.
- When the resultant force is zero, the acceleration is zero.
- A negative force means that the object is accelerating backwards or is slowing down.

Worked example

The diagram shows the horizontal forces acting on a boat. The boat has a mass of 400 kg.

drag 600 N   thrust 900 N

Calculate the acceleration of the boat at the instant shown in the diagram.   **(3 marks)**

resultant force on boat = 900 N – 600 N
= 300 N forwards

mass = 400 kg

acceleration $= \dfrac{F}{m} = \dfrac{300 \text{ N}}{400 \text{ kg}}$

F / $m \times a$

= 0.75 m/s².

Make sure you include minus signs in your calculations where necessary.

Worked example

A resultant force of 6 N acts on a toy car, giving it an acceleration of 2 m/s². Calculate the mass of the toy car.   **(3 marks)**

Force = mass × acceleration

Mass = force ÷ acceleration = 6 N ÷ 2 m/s²

= 3 kg

Now try this

1 Calculate the resultant force that causes a 1.2 kg mass to accelerate at 8 m/s².   **(3 marks)**

2 Calculate the size of the mass that will accelerate at 2 m/s² when a resultant force of 24 N acts on it.   **(3 marks)**

3 Calculate the acceleration of a car of mass 1200 kg when a resultant force of 6000 N acts on it.   **(3 marks)**

Weight and mass

It is important that you understand the difference between weight and mass. These words are often used interchangeably but are actually different things.

Weight

Weight is the **force** that a body experiences due to its mass and the size of the gravitational field that it is in.

Weight is a **vector** quantity and is measured in **newtons** (N).

The weight of a body on the surface of the Earth acts inwards towards the Earth's centre.

Mass

Mass is a measure of the **amount of matter** that is contained within a three-dimensional space.

Mass is a **scalar** quantity and is measured in **kilograms** (kg).

The mass of a body is not affected by the size of the gravitational field that it is in.

Connection between mass and weight

To find the weight of an object, use the equation:

weight (N) = mass (kg) × gravitational field strength (N/kg)

$W = m \times g$

LEARN IT!
IT'S NOT ON THE EQUATIONS LIST

The weight of an object is directly proportional to the value of g, so a mass will weigh more on Earth than it does on the Moon.

Gravitational field strength

When a body has a large mass and a small radius, it will have a large gravitational field strength.

The units of gravitational field strength are newtons per kilogram (N/kg), but it can also be given as m/s².

Astronomical body	Value for g
Earth	10 N/kg
Moon	1.6 N/kg
Jupiter	26 N/kg
Neptune	13.3 N/kg
Mercury	3.6 N/kg
Mars	3.75 N/kg
neutron star	10^{12} N/kg

The value of g on Jupiter is nearly twice that of the value of g on Neptune. This means that the weight of a body on Jupiter will be nearly twice that of the same body when it is on Neptune.

Worked example

An astronaut has a mass of 58 kg on Earth. State the astronaut's mass and weight:

(a) on the surface of the Moon   **(3 marks)**

Mass does not change so it is still 58 kg.

weight = 58 kg × 1.6 N/kg = 92.8 N

(b) on the surface of Jupiter.   **(3 marks)**

Mass does not change, so it is still 58 kg.

weight = 58 kg × 26 N/kg = 1508 N

Measuring weight

Weight is measured using a newtonmeter.

The greater the mass attached, the more weight it will experience due to gravity and the more the spring will stretch.

Reading the scale tells you the weight of the mass in newtons.

A 2 kg mass has twice the weight on Earth as a 1 kg mass, so the extension of the spring will be twice as big.

Now try this

1 Calculate the weight of a 50 kg mass when it is placed on
   (a) Earth   **(2 marks)**
   (b) Jupiter.   **(2 marks)**

2 A body has a weight of 480 N on Earth. Calculate its mass.   **(3 marks)**

3 Calculate the value for g on the surface of a planet where a mass of 18 kg experiences a weight of 54 N.   **(3 marks)**

Force and acceleration

Practical skills You can determine the relationship between force, mass and acceleration by varying the masses added to a trolley and measuring the time it takes to pass between two light gates that are a small distance apart.

Core practical

There is more information about the relationship between force, mass and acceleration on pages 162 and 163.

Investigating force and acceleration

Aim

To investigate the effect of mass on the acceleration of a trolley.

Apparatus

- trolley, light gates, data logger, card of known length, slope or ramp, masses

Method

1 Set up the apparatus as shown.

trolley   light gate   light gate

2 Set up the light gates to take the velocity and time readings for you.

3 Record velocity and time for different values of mass on the trolley.

4 Work out acceleration by dividing the difference in the velocity values by the time taken for the card to pass between both gates.

5 If you are changing the mass, the slope or gradient needs to remain the same throughout the investigation.

Results

The results for a slope of 20° to the horizontal and a card width of 10 cm are shown in the table below.

Mass (g)	Δv (m/s)	Δt (s)	a (m/s²)
200	7.0	2.2	3.2
400	6.7	2.1	3.2
600	6.8	2.2	3.1
800	6.9	2.1	3.3

Conclusion

The acceleration of the trolley does not depend on the mass of the trolley and will remain fairly constant throughout.

An accelerating mass of greater than a few hundred grams can be dangerous, and may hurt somebody if it hits them at speed. Bear this in mind when designing your investigation.

It is better to use light gates and other electronic equipment to record values as this is more accurate than using a ruler and a stopwatch.

Maths skills

Velocity and acceleration

Key points to remember for this investigation are:

Acceleration is change in speed ÷ time taken, so two velocity values are needed, along with the time difference between these readings, to obtain a value for the acceleration of the trolley.

Velocity is the rate of change of displacement and acceleration is the rate of change of velocity. The word rate means 'per unit time':

$$v = \Delta x \div \Delta t \quad \text{and} \quad a = \Delta v \div \Delta t$$

Now try this

1 Explain why it is better to use light gates and a data logger than a stopwatch to record time values. **(3 marks)**

2 Suggest how the investigation described above could be improved to obtain better results. **(4 marks)**

3 Design a similar experiment to determine how acceleration depends on the gradient of the slope. **(5 marks)**

Newton's third law

Newton's third law relates to bodies in equilibrium and can be applied to collisions when considering the conservation of momentum.

Action and reaction

Newton's third law states that for every action there is an equal and opposite reaction.

The action force and the reaction force **act on different bodies**.

100 N from the man

100 N from the wall

The man and wall are in equilibrium because the forces in the system are all balanced. There is no overall force in any direction.

Newton's third law examples

Watch out! Just because two forces are equal and opposite it does not always mean that they are an example of Newton's third law.

$R = -F = -mg$

$F = mg$

The reaction force of the table pushing up on the book, and the force of gravity acting downwards, are both acting on the same object – the book – so this is **not** an example of Newton's third law.

The gravitational pull of the Earth on the book and the gravitational pull of the book on the Earth **are** an example of Newton's third law, since they act on different objects, and are equal and opposite.

Worked example

Identify five action–reaction pairs that are present in the diagram. **(5 marks)**

1 The elephant's feet push backward on the ground; the ground pushes forward on its feet.

2 The right end of the right rope pulls leftward on the elephant's body; its body pulls rightward on the right end of the right rope.

3 The left end of the right rope pulls rightward on the man; the man pulls leftward on the left end of the right rope.

4 The right end of the left rope pulls leftward on the man; the man pulls rightward on the right end of the left rope.

5 The tractor pulls leftward on the left end of the left rope; the left end of the left rope pulls rightward on the tractor.

Now try this

 1 State Newton's third law. **(3 marks)**

 2 A goalkeeper catches a football from a penalty kick. Explain how Newton's third law applies to the goalkeeper's gloves in this situation. **(3 marks)**

Human reaction time

Human reaction time is the time between a **stimulus** occurring and a **response**. It is related to how quickly the human brain can process information and react to it.

Human reaction time

It takes a typical person between 0.20s and 0.25s to react to a stimulus. Some people, such as international cricketers, 100m sprinters and fighter pilots, train themselves to have improved reaction times.

For example, a top cricketer has a total time of 0.5s to play a batting stroke. The first 0.2s of this is the reaction time, the next 0.2s is the batsman's preparation to play the shot and the final 0.1s involves hitting the ball.

Reaction times and driving

Drivers have to react to changes in the traffic when driving. This may involve reacting to traffic lights changing colour, traffic slowing on a motorway or avoiding people or animals that may have walked in front of the vehicle.

The reaction time of humans may be affected by:

- ☑ tiredness   ☑ distractions
- ☑ alcohol and drugs ☑ age.

Measuring reaction time

You can determine human reaction time by using the ruler drop test.

The reaction time is determined from the equation:

$$\text{reaction time} = \sqrt{\frac{2 \times \text{distance ruler falls}}{\text{gravitational field strength}}}$$

Repeats can be used to get a mean value for the reaction time.

A metre ruler is held, by a partner, so that it is vertical and exactly level with the person's finger and thumb, with the lowest numbers on the ruler at the bottom.

The ruler is dropped and then grasped by the other person.

A person sits with their index finger and thumb opened to a gap of about 8 cm.

Worked example

A ruler drop test is conducted five times with the same person. The results show that the five distances fallen are: 0.16m, 0.17m, 0.18m, 0.16m and 0.15m.

(a) Calculate the mean distance that the ruler drops. **(3 marks)**

mean = (0.16 + 0.17 + 0.18 + 0.16 + 0.15) ÷ 5 = 0.16m

(b) Calculate the person's reaction time. **(3 marks)**

reaction time = $\sqrt{\frac{2 \times 0.16}{10}}$ = 0.18s

Worked example

A driver moving at 30km/h in her car has a reaction time of 0.25s. Calculate the distance the car travels between seeing a hazard in the road and then applying the brakes. **(4 marks)**

distance (m) = speed (m/s) × time(s)

30km/h = 30000m ÷ 3600s = 8.3m/s

distance travelled = 8.3m/s × 0.25s = 2.1m

This distance for a driver is called the thinking distance. Read more about it on page 167.

Now try this

1 (a) Define human reaction time. **(1 mark)**

(b) Give three factors that can cause reaction times to increase. **(3 marks)**

2 A ruler drops a distance of 0.24m before being caught by a person. Calculate the person's reaction time. **(3 marks)**

Stopping distances

Stopping distance is the **total distance** over which a vehicle comes to rest.

It takes time for a moving car to come to a stop, and the car is still moving during this time. Understanding the factors that affect stopping distance is important for road safety.

Danger appears.   Driver brakes.   Car has stopped.

thinking distance = the distance the car travels while the driver reacts to the danger and applies the brakes

braking distance = the distance the car travels while it is slowing down, once the brakes have been applied

stopping distance = thinking distance + braking distance

Factors affecting thinking distance

Thinking distance increases when the driver's reaction time increases. This can be due to:
- the driver being **tired**
- the driver being **distracted**
- the driver having taken **alcohol** or **drugs**.

Thinking distance also increases if the car's speed increases. If the thinking distance at 20mph is 6 m, at 40 mph it will double to 12 m.

Cars can experience large decelerations when they slow down, and this means that typical forces, of around 10,000 N, can be exerted on the vehicles.

Factors affecting braking distance

Braking distance is the distance the car travels once the brakes have been applied. It increases when:
- the amount of **friction** between the **tyres** and the **road** decreases, such as when the road is **icy** or **wet**
- the **brakes** are worn
- the **tyres** are worn
- the **mass** of the car is bigger.

Braking distance also increases as the speed of the car increases. If at 20 mph it is 6m, at 40 mph it will be 24 m.

Worked example

A car is moving at a constant speed. Explain how and why the stopping distance changes when:
(a) the speed of the car increases   **(2 marks)**
(b) the car has more passengers   **(2 marks)**
(c) the driver has been drinking alcohol. **(2 marks)**

(a) The stopping distance increases because the thinking distance and braking distance increase.

(b) The mass of the car will be greater so the braking distance will increase, which means the stopping distance will increase.

(c) The stopping distance will increase because the thinking distance will increase.

Now try this

1 State **two** factors that affect:
   (a) thinking distance   **(2 marks)**
   (b) braking distance.   **(2 marks)**

2 Explain why icy and wet roads lead to a greater stopping distance.   **(3 marks)**

Extended response – Motion and forces

There will be one or more 6-mark questions on your exam paper. For these questions, you will need to think scientifically and structure your answer logically, showing how the points you make are related to each other. You can revise the topics for this question, which is about **motion and forces**, on pages 156–167.

Worked example

The diagram shows a trolley, ramp and light gates being used to investigate the relationship between the acceleration of a trolley on a slope and the angle that the slope makes with the horizontal.

Describe a simple investigation to determine how the acceleration of the trolley depends on the angle of the slope.

trolley   light gate   light gate

(6 marks)

I will start with the ramp at an angle of 10° and roll the trolley down the slope from the same starting position along the slope each time. The mass of the trolley needs to be kept constant, and a suitable value would be 500 g. I will then increase the ramp angle by 5° each time until I have at least 6 readings. I will repeat readings to check for accuracy and precision.

The speed of the trolley at each light gate is calculated using the equation, speed = distance ÷ time, where the distance recorded is the length of the card that passes through the light gates. The acceleration of the trolley is calculated by finding the difference in the speed values at the two light gates and then dividing this by the time it takes the trolley to pass between the gates.

I would expect the acceleration of the trolley to increase as the angle increases, although the relationship may not be linear. This is because as the slope angle increases, you increase the component of the trolley's weight that is acting down the slope, which is the force responsible for the trolley's acceleration.

Command word: Describe

When you are asked to **describe** something, you need to write down facts, events or processes accurately.

Your answer should refer to the equations needed to calculate the velocity and acceleration of the trolley, as well as how you will show the relationship between acceleration and angle of slope.

You need to be careful when stating what you will vary and what you will keep the same. Since the dependent variable is acceleration and the independent variable is angle of slope, you will need to keep the mass of the trolley and its starting point the same each time.

Be clear when referring to how the speed of the trolley will be measured by referring to the card that passes through the light gates, and mention that the length of the card needs to be known if the light gates are recording time values. You need two speed and time values to calculate the acceleration.

You can also refer to the increase in gravitational potential energy as the slope angle increases. This means more is transferred to kinetic energy and so a greater change in velocity per second.

Now try this

The distance taken for vehicles to stop on roads depends on a number of factors. Discuss what these factors are and how they affect stopping distance.

(6 marks)

Energy stores and transfers

Energy can be stored in different ways, and can be transferred from one **energy store** to another.

Examples of energy stores

There are eight main energy stores.

Energy store	Example
chemical	fuel, food, battery
kinetic	moving objects
gravitational potential	raised mass
elastic	stretched spring
thermal	hot object
magnetic	two magnets
electrostatic	two charges
nuclear	radioactive decay

Closed systems

When there are **energy transfers** in a closed system, there is no net change to the total energy in the system.

A **closed system** is one where energy can flow in or out of the system, but there is no transfer of mass. An example of a closed system is a pan of water being heated that has a lid on it so that no steam can escape.

Energy transfers

Energy is transferred from one store to another in four different ways:

- **mechanically** – by a force moving through a distance
- **electrically** – by the use of electric current
- **thermally** – because of a difference in temperature
- by **radiation** – by waves such as electromagnetic or sound.

Some of the energy will be usefully transferred, and some will be wasted or **dissipated**.

Mechanical processes become wasteful when they lead to a rise in the temperature of the surroundings through heating. In all system changes, energy is stored in less useful ways. For example, the light and sound energy from a TV will eventually be absorbed by the walls and by people, leading to a rise in their temperature.

Examples of energy transfers

Energy transfers from one store to another can be shown on an energy flow diagram. This one shows a battery being used to lift a mass above the ground.

Worked example

Draw a flow diagram to show the useful and wasted energy transfers for a camping gas stove. **(4 marks)**

In all flow diagrams, there must be energy stores and energy transfers present to show how the energy is transferred from one store to others.

Based on the law of conservation of energy, the total energy present in the original stores must be equal to the energy present in the stores after the transfers have taken place, since you cannot create or destroy energy in any given system.

Now try this

You could be asked to analyse other energy changes such as for boiling water or for moving objects.

1 Draw an energy store flow diagram for a car driving up a hill. **(4 marks)**

2 Analyse the changes involved in the energy stores when a car accelerates with a constant force. **(4 marks)**

Efficient heat transfer

The rate at which a material transfers thermal energy depends on a number of factors. The **efficiency** of a device is a measure of how much **useful** energy it transfers.

Thermal energy transfer

The rate at which thermal energy is transferred through a wall of a house depends on:

1 the difference in temperature between the warmer interior and the colder exterior

2 the thickness of the walls

3 the material that the walls are made from.

outside: 2°C inside: 22°C outside: 2°C inside: 22°C

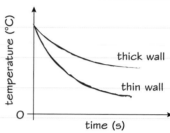

Efficiency

All machines **waste** some of the **energy** they **transfer**. Most machines waste energy as **heat** energy. The **efficiency** of a machine is a way of saying how good it is at transferring energy into **useful** forms.

A very efficient machine has an efficiency that is nearly 100%. The higher the efficiency, the better the machine is at transferring energy to useful forms.

Unwanted energy transfers can be reduced by thermal insulation and lubrication.

Lubrication involves placing a liquid, such as oil, between moving parts to reduce friction. This leads to less energy being wasted as thermal energy to the surroundings.

Thermal conductivity

A material with a high thermal conductivity is a better conductor of energy than one with a lower thermal conductivity. The rate at which the blue wall transfers energy is greater than that of the red wall. Different materials have different **relative thermal conductivities**.

outside: 2°C inside: 22°C

house walls made of different materials

outside: 2°C inside: 22°C

Worked example

A motor transfers 100 J of energy by electricity. 60 J are transferred as kinetic energy, 12 J as sound energy and 28 J as thermal energy. Calculate the efficiency of the motor. **(3 marks)**

efficiency = (useful energy transferred by the machine) / (total energy supplied to the machine) × 100% ◀ Efficiency does not have units.

total useful energy = 60 J

LEARN IT! IT'S NOT ON THE EQUATIONS LIST

efficiency = $\frac{60 J}{100 J}$ × 100%
= 60%

No machine is ever 100% efficient. If you calculate an efficiency greater than 100% you have done something wrong!

Now try this

 1 Calculate the efficiency of a lamp that transfers 14 J of energy into useful light energy for every 20 J of electrical energy input. **(2 marks)**

 2 Describe how you could reduce the rate of transfer of thermal energy through a wall. **(2 marks)**

Energy resources

The main energy resources include both **renewable** and **non-renewable** resources.

Renewable energy resources

5 **Solar cells** convert solar energy (energy from the Sun) directly to electricity. Solar energy can also be used directly to cook food or to heat water.

1 **Bio-fuels** are animal or plant matter used to produce thermal energy, electrical energy or used to power cars.

2 **Hydroelectricity** generates electricity from water behind a dam flowing down a pipe and turning a turbine to generate electricity.

Renewable energy resources will not run out. Most do not cause pollution or emit carbon dioxide.

4 **Tidal power** uses the rise and fall of the tide or tidal currents to generate electricity.

3 **Wind turbines** use kinetic energy from the wind to generate electricity.

Non-renewable energy resources

1 **Nuclear fuels** such as uranium are used:
• to generate electricity
• as energy sources in spacecraft.

Non-renewable resources are available all the time, unlike some renewable resources.

2 **Fossil fuels** are **coal**, **oil** and **natural gas**. They are used:
• to generate electricity
• to power transport
• to heat homes and for cooking.

Worked example

Describe how different renewable and non-renewable resources are used for transport. **(4 marks)**

Renewable and non-renewable energy resources can both be used in power stations, leading to the production of electricity which is used to power trains. Electrical energy can also be supplied from other renewable sources such as solar, hydroelectric and wind.

Biofuel, in the form of methanol, is an example of how renewable fuel can be used to power cars, and solar power is also being developed to do more of this. Petrol and diesel, from oil, are examples of non-renewable fuels that are used to power cars.

Now try this

1 Draw diagrams to show the energy transfers that take place
  (a) in hydroelectricity   **(3 marks)**
  (b) when biofuels are used for transport.   **(3 marks)**

2 Suggest the advantages and disadvantages of using biofuels to power cars compared with using solar power to power cars.   **(4 marks)**

Patterns of energy use

The patterns and trends in how humans have used energy resources have changed over time.

Patterns and trends in energy use

The use of energy resources has changed over the years. This is because of several factors.

1. **The world's population:** in the past 200 years, the population of the world has risen from 1 billion to 7 billion people.

2. **The development of technology:** vehicles such as cars, trains and planes and other devices have increased in number and these all require energy.

3. **Electrical energy:** power stations require fuels in order to generate electricity.

Growth in world population

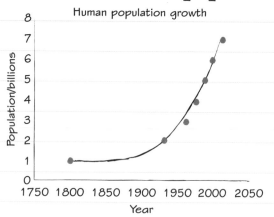

Human population growth

Trends in the world's energy use

As the graph shows, most of the world's energy use has been fossil fuels. Before about 1900, biomass in the form of wood was the major source of fuel and its use has remained constant over time.

In more recent years, there has been an increase in the use of nuclear fuel and hydroelectric power.

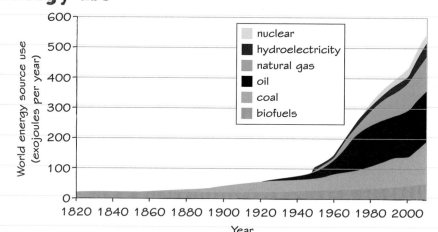

Worked example

Compare the shape of the world's population graph with that of the energy use graph. **(4 marks)**

They are similar in that as the population has increased, the total energy used has increased. They differ in that the total energy use has increased faster than the population. As societies develop, they use more technology that requires energy to run it. This means that the average amount of energy used per person also increases.

The future

It is not possible to continue using the Earth's non-renewable energy reserves to the extent that they are being used now. They are a finite reserve, so will run out and not be replaced.

Greater use of fossil fuels will lead to more carbon dioxide in the atmosphere. This could cause greater global warming, leading to severe weather, flooding and threats to food supplies.

Now try this

1 Describe the main issues with using the Earth's energy supplies. **(2 marks)**

2 Wood is a biofuel. Suggest why wood has been used constantly for many years, whereas other fuels have only been used much more recently. **(3 marks)**

Potential and kinetic energy

You can calculate the **kinetic** and **gravitational potential energy** of objects using the equations on this page.

Gravitational potential energy

Gravitational potential is the energy possessed by a body due to its height above the Earth. The value of the gravitational potential energy stored depends on:
- the mass of the body
- the gravitational field strength
- the height the body is raised.

The change in gravitational potential energy is given by the equation:

change in gravitational potential energy (J) = mass (kg) × gravitational field strength (N/kg) × change in vertical height (m)

$$\Delta GPE = m \times g \times \Delta h$$

LEARN IT! IT'S NOT ON THE EQUATIONS LIST

The gravitational field strength on Earth is 10 N/kg. It can also be given in m/s^2.

Kinetic energy

Kinetic energy is stored in moving objects and is calculated using the equation:

kinetic energy (J) = $\frac{1}{2}$ × mass (kg) × (speed)² (m/s)²

$$KE = \frac{1}{2} \times m \times v^2$$

LEARN IT! IT'S NOT ON THE EQUATIONS LIST

 Maths skills Kinetic energy is directly proportional to the mass of the moving object: doubling the mass doubles the kinetic energy of the moving object.

KE is directly proportional to the square of the speed, so doubling the speed means the KE increases by a factor of four.

Worked example

(a) A mass of 5 kg is moving at 8 m/s. Calculate its kinetic energy. **(3 marks)**

Kinetic energy = ½ × mass × velocity²

= ½ × 5 kg × (8 m/s)² = 160 J

(b) A mass of 800 g is moving at 14 m/s. Calculate its kinetic energy. **(3 marks)**

KE = $\frac{1}{2}$ × m × v²

KE = $\frac{1}{2}$ × 0.8 × 14² = 78.4 J

 Remember to square the value of speed when calculating the kinetic energy. The term v^2 means $v \times v$. Make sure the mass is in kg and the velocity is in m/s.

Worked example

(a) A body of mass 73 kg is lifted through a vertical height of 26 m. Calculate how much gravitational potential energy it has gained. **(3 marks)**

$\Delta GPE = m \times g \times \Delta h$

= 73 kg × 10 N/kg × 26 m = 18 980 J

(b) A book of 600 g is lifted through a vertical height of 3 m and placed on a shelf. Calculate how much gravitational potential energy the book has gained. **(3 marks)**

Change in gravitational potential energy = mass × gravitational field strength × change in height

= 0.6 kg × 10 N/kg × 3 m = 18 J

Now try this

1 A mass of 5 kg is raised through a vertical height of 18 m. Calculate the change in gravitational potential energy. **(3 marks)**

2 A girl of mass 60 kg is running with a velocity of 5 m/s. Calculate her kinetic energy. **(3 marks)**

3 A motorbike of mass 80 kg is moving at 30 km/h. Calculate its kinetic energy. **(4 marks)**

Extended response – Conservation of energy

There will be one or more 6-mark questions on your exam paper. For these questions, you will need to think scientifically and structure your answer logically, showing how the points you make are related to each other. You can revise the topics for this question, which is about **the principle of the conservation of energy**, on pages 169–172.

Worked example

Figure 1 shows the arrangement of apparatus for a simple pendulum. Figure 2 shows how the kinetic energy of the pendulum changes with time.

Describe the energy transfers taking place during the motion of the simple pendulum. Your answer should refer to the energy stores and energy transfers that are involved.

(6 marks)

Figure 1

Figure 2

Initially, the pendulum has to be raised through a small angle, so it will gain gravitational potential energy. Once released, this gravitational potential energy store will be transferred mainly to a kinetic energy store, with some energy being dissipated as sound and heat by thermal transfer from friction due to air resistance.

The principle of conservation of energy states that the total energy of the system at any time must be the same, since energy cannot be created nor destroyed. Initially, this was all in the gravitational potential energy store, but this is then mechanically transferred to the kinetic energy store once the pendulum starts to swing. At the bottom of the swing, the gravitational potential store will be greatly reduced and the energy will be mostly in the kinetic store. Some energy is also transferred to the surroundings as heat and sound by thermal transfer from friction due to air resistance, which must also be taken into consideration as part of the total energy of the system.

Eventually, the pendulum will stop swinging, so the gravitational energy has been transferred to kinetic energy and it has eventually all ended up in the surroundings by friction due to air resistance, leading to the surroundings becoming slightly warmer. The useful energy store has been dissipated to the surroundings.

Command word: Describe

When you are asked to **describe** something, you need to write down facts, events or processes accurately.

It is a good idea to state what the principle of conservation of energy is, so that the examiner knows that you understand it. You can then apply this idea to the changes in the energy stores and transfers in the system. It is also worth noting that the way we talk about energy at GCSE now has changed – you need to refer to energy stores as well as energy transfers. In this example, the main stores are gravitational and kinetic, and the motion of the pendulum is via mechanical transfer, with energy transfer to the surroundings by thermal transfer.

In energy transfers, the energy stores are usually dissipated to the surroundings, which become warmer. In a perfect situation, with no frictional forces or energy wasted, the pendulum would swing forever, but in reality this does not happen.

Refer to *energy stores* and *energy transfers* in your answer. There are eight energy stores and four energy transfers that you need to know. See page 169 to remind yourself of these.

Now try this

The people on a small island want to use either wind power, on hills and out at sea, or its reserves of coal to generate electrical energy. Compare the advantages and disadvantages of each resource.

(6 marks)

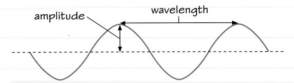
Waves

Waves transfer energy and information without transferring matter. Evidence of this for a water wave can be seen when a ball dropped into a pond bobs up and down, but the wave energy travels outwards as ripples across the surface of the pond.

Waves can be described by their
- **frequency** – the number of waves passing a point each second, measured in **hertz (Hz)**
- **speed** – measured in **metres per second (m/s)**
- **wavelength** and **amplitude**
- **period** – the time taken for one wavelength to pass a point
  period = 1/frequency.

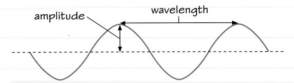

amplitude   wavelength

Watch out! Remember that the amplitude is *half* of the distance from the top to the bottom of the wave. Students often get this wrong.

Longitudinal waves

Sound waves and **seismic P waves** are **longitudinal** waves. The particles in the material the sound is travelling through move back and forth along the same direction that the sound is travelling.

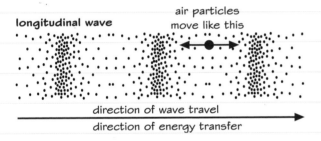

longitudinal wave

air particles move like this

direction of wave travel
direction of energy transfer

Particles in a **longitudinal** wave move **along** the same direction as the wave.

Transverse waves

Waves on a **water surface, electromagnetic waves** and **seismic S waves** are all **transverse** waves. The particles of water move in a direction at right angles to the direction the wave is travelling.

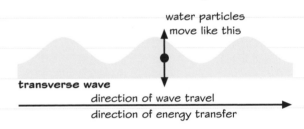

water particles move like this

transverse wave
direction of wave travel
direction of energy transfer

Particles in a transverse wave move **across** the direction the wave is travelling.

Worked example

Give two ways in which longitudinal and transverse waves are
(a) similar   **(2 marks)**

They both transfer energy without transferring matter and have an amplitude, speed, wavelength and frequency.

(b) different.   **(2 marks)**

Particles in longitudinal waves vibrate along the direction of movement, whereas particles in transverse waves move at 90 degrees to the direction of travel. They can also have different speeds, frequencies and wavelengths.

Now try this

1 (a) Sketch a transverse wave and mark the amplitude and wavelength on it. **(3 marks)**
  (b) Draw an arrow to show which way the wave moves. **(1 mark)**
  (c) Draw a small particle on the wave, with arrows to show which way it moves. **(1 mark)**

2 Describe how a particle moves in a longitudinal wave. **(2 marks)**

3 The graph shows a wave. Each vertical square represents 1 mm. Work out the amplitude of the wave. **(1 mark)**

Wave equations

Both of these equations can be used to find the **speed** or **velocity** of a wave.

Speed, frequency and wavelength

$v = f \times \lambda$ v = wave speed (metres per second, m/s)

f = frequency (hertz, Hz)

λ = wavelength (metres, m)

LEARN IT!
IT'S NOT ON THE EQUATIONS LIST

Speed, distance and time

$v = \dfrac{x}{t}$ v = wave speed (metres per second, m/s)

x = distance (metres, m)

t = time (seconds, s)

LEARN IT!
IT'S NOT ON THE EQUATIONS LIST

Worked example

A seismic wave has a frequency of 15 Hz and a wavelength of 270 m. Calculate the wave speed of the seismic wave. **(3 marks)**

Wave speed
= frequency × wavelength
= 15 Hz × 270 m
= 4050 m/s

Maths skills To calculate wavelength, start with the equation $v = f \times \lambda$ and rearrange it to make λ the subject.

Divide both sides of the equation by f, to get

$$\lambda = \frac{v}{f}$$

Substitute the values for v and f to calculate the value for the wavelength, λ.

The units for v are m/s and the units for f are Hz (or per second), so the units for λ are $\dfrac{\text{m/s}}{1/\text{s}}$ = m.

Always state the correct units as part of your answer.

Worked example

A wave on the sea travels 20 m in 5 s. Calculate the speed of the water wave. **(3 marks)**

Speed = distance travelled ÷ time
= 20 m ÷ 5 s
= 4 m/s

Maths skills To calculate time, rearrange the equation $v = \dfrac{x}{t}$ to give $t = \dfrac{x}{v}$.

You can also find this easily by covering the letter t in the triangle at the top of the page.

When dividing the units, m ÷ (m/s), you get m × s/m = s, which is the correct unit for time.

Again, always include the correct unit in your answer.

Now try this

1 (a) A sound wave has a wavelength of 3.3 m and a frequency of 100 Hz. Calculate its speed. **(3 marks)**

   (b) Another sound wave, with the same speed as in (a), has a frequency of 1650 Hz. Calculate its wavelength. **(3 marks)**

2 A wave in the sea travels at 25 m/s. Calculate the distance it travels in one minute. **(4 marks)**

Measuring wave velocity

You need to be able to **calculate** the speed of sound in air or the speed of ripples on the surface of water.

Calculating the speed of sound in air

Method 1: using an echo.

1. Measure the distance from the source of the sound to the reflecting surface (the wall).

2. Measure the time interval, with a stopwatch, between the original sound being produced and the echo being heard.

3. Use $\frac{\text{speed}}{\text{(m/s)}} = \frac{\text{distance}}{\text{(m)}} \div \frac{\text{time}}{\text{(s)}}$ to calculate the speed of sound in air.

Repeating the experiment a number of times over a range of distances will allow you to obtain accurate and precise results.

Method 2: using two microphones and an oscilloscope.

1. Set up the microphones one in front of the other at different distances in a straight line from a loudspeaker.

2. Set the frequency of the sound from the loudspeaker to a known, audible value.

3. Display the two waveforms on the oscilloscope. Measure the distance between the microphones.

4. Move the microphones apart so that the waveforms move apart by 1 wavelength.

5. Calculate the speed of sound using the equation:
$$\frac{\text{wavespeed}}{\text{(m/s)}} = \frac{\text{frequency}}{\text{(Hz)}} \times \frac{\text{wavelength}}{\text{(m)}}$$

Calculating the speed of ripples on water surfaces

You can work out the speed of ripples on the surface of water using a ripple tank and a strobe.

Set the power supply to vibrate the paddle at a known frequency.

lamp
water
plane waves
image of waves on screen

Use a strobe light to 'freeze' the water waves so that you can measure the wavelength.

strobe light

Use the equation *wave speed = frequency × wavelength* to calculate the speed or velocity of the water waves on the surface of the ripple tank.

Worked example

(a) A hand clap is made 480 m from a wall and the echo is heard 3 seconds later. Calculate the speed of sound. **(3 marks)**

speed = distance ÷ time = 960 m ÷ 3 s = 320 m/s

(b) Method 2 is used to determine the speed of sound. The distance between the two microphones is 35 cm and it represents one wavelength. The frequency of the sound is 1 kHz. Calculate the speed of sound in air. **(3 marks)**

wave speed = frequency × wavelength = 1000 Hz × 0.35 m = 350 m/s

Now try this

1. A wave on the sea travels 30 m in 5 s. Calculate the speed of the wave. **(3 marks)**
2. The frequency of a ripple tank paddle is 4 Hz and the wavelength of the ripples is 8 cm. Calculate the speed of the water waves in m/s. **(3 marks)**
3. Describe how you could obtain an accurate value for the speed of sound in air. **(4 marks)**

Waves and boundaries

Refraction

Whenever a sound wave, light wave or water wave reaches the boundary between two materials, the wave can be **refracted**. Refraction is the change in the direction of a light ray that happens when it travels from one transparent material into another. The direction does not change if the wavefronts travel perpendicular to the normal. See page 182 to investigate refraction.

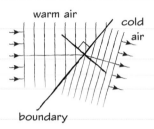

Sound waves travel faster in warmer air than in cooler air, as the molecules move faster in warmer air.

Water waves change direction and bend towards the normal when they move from deep water to shallow water.

Light waves bend towards the normal when they move from air into glass. They bend away from the normal when they move from glass back into air.

Refraction special case

When light, sound or water waves move from one material into another their **direction does not change** if they are moving along the normal.

Notice that the ray of light bends *towards* the normal as it enters the glass and *away* from the normal when it leaves the glass.

Worked example

Describe what happens when light enters water from air. **(3 marks)**

The direction of the wave changes unless it is travelling along the normal. The light wave will bend towards the normal. This is called refraction.

Now try this

Describe what happens when a light ray moves from glass into air. **(3 marks)**

Waves in fluids

 Practical skills You can **determine the wave speed, frequency and wavelength** of waves by using appropriate apparatus.

Core practical

See pages 175–177 for the properties of waves, including the relationship between wave speed, frequency and wavelength.

Investigating waves

Aim

To investigate the suitability of apparatus to measure the speed, frequency and wavelength of waves in a fluid.

Apparatus

- ripple tank, motor, plane wave generator, stroboscope, ruler, A3 paper and pencil

Water and electricity are being used here, both of which can be dangerous. Be careful to take this into consideration when planning your practical.

Method

1 Set up the apparatus as shown.
2 Calculate the frequency of the waves by counting the number of waves that pass a point each second. Do this for a minute and then divide by 60 to get a more accurate value for the frequency of the water waves.
3 Use a stroboscope to 'freeze' the waves and find their wavelength by using a ruler. The ruler can be left in the tank or the waves can be projected onto a piece of A3 paper under the tank and the wave positions marked with pencil marks on the paper.
4 Calculate the wave speed.

To obtain accurate results for the wavelength of the water wave, it is best to find the distance between a large number of waves and then divide this value by the number of waves. This will reduce the percentage error in your value when determining a value for the wavelength of the wave.

Results

Wavelength (m)	Frequency (Hz)	Wave speed (m/s)
0.05	10.0	5.0
0.10	5.0	5.0
0.15	3.0	4.5
0.20	2.5	5.0

Waves in water

Water waves will travel at a constant speed in a ripple tank when generated at different frequencies if the depth of the water is constant at all points. This means that the equation wave speed = frequency × wavelength will give the same wave speed – if the frequency increases, then the wavelength will decrease in proportion.

Conclusion

A ripple tank can be used to determine values for the wavelength, frequency and wave speed of water waves. It is a suitable method, provided that small wavelengths and frequencies are used.

Now try this

1 State the two equations that can be used to calculate wave speed. **(2 marks)**

2 When a water wave moves from shallow water to deep water its wavelength increases. Explain why the wave velocity will also increase. **(3 marks)**

Extended response – Waves

There will be one or more 6-mark questions on your exam paper. For these questions, you will need to think scientifically and structure your answer logically, showing how the points you make are related to each other. You can revise the topics for this question, which is about **waves**, on pages 175–179.

 Worked example

Waves transfer energy without there being any overall transfer of matter.

These waves can be modelled using a slinky spring, as shown in Figure 1 and Figure 2.

Explain how the wave motion that occurs is related to the disturbance that is causing it and the material that it is moving in.

Your answer should refer to real-life examples of both types of waves.   **(6 marks)**

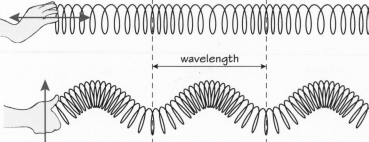

Figure 1

Figure 2

wavelength

Figure 1 shows a longitudinal wave. A longitudinal wave is produced when the vibration is parallel to the direction of energy transfer.

> The wave in Figure 1 has correctly been identified as a longitudinal wave. A simple description of how it is produced is also given.

Figure 2 shows a transverse wave. A transverse wave is produced when the vibration or oscillation is at right angles to the direction of energy transfer.

> The wave in Figure 2 has correctly been identified as a transverse wave. There is also a simple description of how it is produced.

Sound waves, infrasound and ultrasound waves are all examples of longitudinal waves, as are seismic P waves. These waves can only transfer energy if there is a medium (a solid, liquid or gas) for them to travel through. Some transverse waves also travel through matter, with examples including water waves and seismic S waves.

Unlike longitudinal waves, some transverse waves can travel through a vacuum and do not need a medium. This is the case for all electromagnetic waves.

> **Command word: Explain**
>
> When you are asked to **explain** something, it is not enough to just state or describe something. Your answer **must** contain some reasoning or justification of the points you make.

> After identifying the waves correctly, examples are given of these waves and the fact that longitudinal waves require a medium. Transverse waves can also do this, but one distinct difference is that transverse electromagnetic waves can travel through space.

> All electromagnetic waves are transverse and all sound waves are longitudinal in nature. In terms of seismic waves, think of the letter 's' – a **s**eismic **S**-wave is tran**s**ver**s**e. These **S** waves will only travel through **s**olids. Unlike P waves, they will **not** travel through liquids such as the Earth's liquid outer core.

 Now try this

Describe an experiment to show that with water and sound waves it is the wave, and not the water or air, itself that travels.   **(6 marks)**

Electromagnetic spectrum

Infrared radiation, **visible light** and **ultraviolet radiation** are all part of the **electromagnetic spectrum**.

All electromagnetic waves...

- are **transverse waves** (the electromagnetic vibrations are at right angles to the direction the wave is travelling – see page 175)
- travel at the **same speed** (3×10^8 m/s) in a **vacuum**
- **transfer energy** to the observer.

The electromagnetic spectrum

As the **frequency** of the radiation **increases**, the **wavelength decreases**.

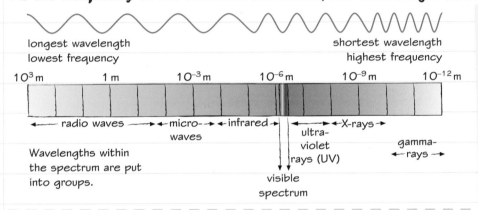

longest wavelength
lowest frequency

shortest wavelength
highest frequency

10^3 m   1 m 10^{-3} m 10^{-6} m 10^{-9} m 10^{-12} m

radio waves — micro-waves — infrared — X-rays — ultra-violet rays (UV) — gamma-rays

Wavelengths within the spectrum are put into groups.

visible spectrum

All electromagnetic waves transfer energy from a source to the observer. For example, radio waves are sent from a transmitting antenna to a TV where they are 'seen' as TV images; microwaves are sent from mobile phones and received by another person; and infrared radiation can be 'seen' by infrared cameras when given off by hot bodies.

Worked example

(a) List the main groups of electromagnetic waves from longest to shortest wavelength.   **(1 mark)**

radio, microwave, infrared, visible, ultraviolet, X-rays, gamma

(b) A wave has a wavelength of 100 m and a frequency of 3 000 000 Hz in a vacuum. Calculate its wave speed.
    (3 marks)

Wave speed = frequency × wavelength = 3 000 000 Hz × 100 m = 300 000 000 m/s

(c) Explain why this wave must be an electromagnetic wave.
    (1 mark)

Electromagnetic waves all travel at 300 000 000 m/s in a vacuum.

You can use a mnemonic to help you to remember the order. A mnemonic is a sentence or phrase whose words have the same initial letters as the list you are trying to remember. For example:
Red **M**onkeys **I**n **V**ans **U**se **X**-ray **G**lasses.

You can find the wave equation on page 176.

Now try this

1 State the type of electromagnetic radiation that has the (a) longest wavelength, (b) highest frequency.
    (2 marks)

2 Calculate the speed of a radio wave in air if it has a wavelength of 3000 m and a frequency of 100 000 Hz.
    (2 marks)

3 Calculate the frequency of a microwave that has a wavelength of 5 cm in air. Take the speed of light in air to be 300 000 000 m/s.
    (4 marks)

Investigating refraction

 Practical skills You can investigate refraction in rectangular glass blocks in terms of the interaction of light waves with matter. Look back at page 178 to remind yourself about refraction.

Core practical

Aim

To investigate the nature of how light waves change direction when they move from air into glass.

Apparatus

- ray box and slits, 12 V power supply, glass block, protractor, A3 paper, sharp pencil

Method

1 Place the rectangular block on the A3 paper and draw around it with the sharp pencil.

2 Draw the normal line, which will be at right angles to the side of the block towards which the light ray will be shone.

3 Using the protractor and pencil, mark on the paper angles of incidence of 0° through to 80° in 10° intervals.

4 Starting with the 0° angle (the light ray travelling along the normal line), direct the light ray towards the block and mark its exit point from the block with a sharp pencil dot.

5 Remove the glass block and join the dot to the point of incidence by drawing a straight line. Measure and record this angle, which is the angle of refraction.

6 Repeat for all of the other angles from 10° to 80°.

glass box

normal

ray box

When carrying out the investigation, make sure that you direct a thin beam of light towards the point at which the normal makes contact with the glass block. Clearly mark the angles from 0° to 80° with a sharp pencil and ruler.

Refraction

The refraction of a light ray involves a change in:

✓ the direction of the light ray.

The only time when the direction does not change is when the beam is travelling along the normal.

Remember that the angle of incidence is measured with respect to the normal line.

Light will change direction more when it travels from air into glass than it will when it travels from air into water. This is because the 'optical density' of glass is greater than that of air.

Results

Angle of incidence	Angle of refraction
0°	0°
10°	7°
20°	13°
30°	19°
40°	25°
50°	31°
60°	35°

Conclusion

When a light ray travels from air into a glass block, its direction changes and the angle of refraction will be less than the angle of incidence unless it is travelling along the normal.

 Now try this

1 State what changes when a light ray is refracted. **(1 mark)**

2 Draw a table of results for a light ray travelling from air into a block of water instead of a block of glass. **(2 marks)**

Dangers and uses

The amount of **energy** that is transferred by an electromagnetic wave is dependent on its **wavelength** or **frequency**. The **highest frequencies** (shortest wavelengths) are the most energetic and the **most dangerous** waves.

Dangers

X-rays and gamma-rays can cause **mutations** (changes) to the DNA in cells in the body. This may kill the cells or cause **cancer**.

UV in sunlight can damage skin cells, causing **sunburn**. Over time, exposure to UV can cause **skin cancer**. UV can also damage the **eyes** leading to eye conditions.

Infrared radiation transfers thermal energy. Too much infrared radiation can cause **skin** burns.

Microwaves heat water – so they can heat the water inside our bodies. Heating cells can damage or kill them.

high frequency

- gamma-rays
- X-rays
- ultraviolet
- visible light
- infrared
- microwaves
- radio waves

low frequency

Uses

- to sterilise food and medical equipment
- in scanners to detect cancer
- to treat cancer

- to look inside objects, including medical x-rays to look inside bodies
- in airport security scanners, to see what people have in their luggage

- to detect security marks made using special pens
- inside fluorescent lamps
- to detect forged banknotes (real banknotes have markings that glow in UV light)
- to disinfect water

- allows us to see, lights up rooms and streets, buildings and roads (illumination)
- photography

- in cooking (by grills and toasters)
- to make thermal images (images using heat), used by police and rescue services
- in short-range communications, such as between laptops or other small computers
- in remote controls for TVs and other appliances, where the signal only has to travel short distances
- to send information along optical fibres
- in security systems such as burglar alarms, to detect people moving around

- in mobile phones, and to communicate by satellite transmissions
- for cooking (in microwave ovens)

- broadcasting radio and TV programmes
- communicating with ships, aeroplanes and satellites

Worked example

State which type(s) of electromagnetic radiation are:

(a) used for communicating **(4 marks)**

radio waves, microwaves, infrared and visible light

(b) used for cooking **(2 marks)**

microwave and infrared

(c) used for cleaning things **(2 marks)**

ultraviolet and gamma

(d) most dangerous. **(3 marks)**

ultraviolet, X-rays and gamma

Radio waves can be produced by, or can themselves induce, oscillations in electrical circuits.

The different types of electromagnetic radiation share uses and dangers. For example, more than one type can be used for communicating and cooking, and there are three main types of electromagnetic radiation that can cause humans serious harm.

Now try this

1 State the dangers associated with ultraviolet radiation. **(3 marks)**

2 Explain how X-rays are useful to doctors but can also be harmful to patients. **(3 marks)**

3 Explain how gamma-rays can be used to detect cancer even though they can also cause it. **(2 marks)**

Changes and radiation

Radiation is **absorbed** or **emitted** when **electrons** jump between **energy levels**.

Energy levels

Electrons can only exist in atoms at certain, well-defined energy levels. These **energy levels** depend on the atom, and the electrons inside the atom can move between the shells or leave the atom completely.

Electromagnetic radiation is **emitted** or **absorbed** by atoms based on whether energy is given out or taken in.

Electrons move up energy levels when they absorb energy and they fall down to lower energy levels when they emit energy.

Electrons move from a lower energy level to a higher energy level when the correct amount of energy is absorbed.

Electromagnetic radiation is emitted when electrons fall down from a higher to a lower energy level.

The electromagnetic radiation can have a **wide frequency range**, from **infrared** through to **ultraviolet** and beyond.

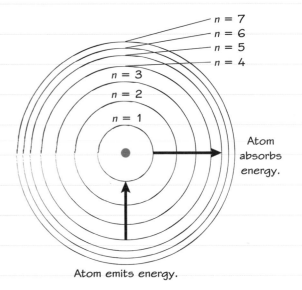

Nuclear radiation

Energy is also emitted from the **nuclei** of **unstable** atoms. **Protons** and **neutrons** also occupy **energy levels** in the nucleus, in the same way that electrons do in the atom.

When energy changes occur in the nucleus, high-energy **gamma-rays** are emitted.

Gamma-rays can be emitted over a large range of frequencies, depending on the energy levels within the nucleus.

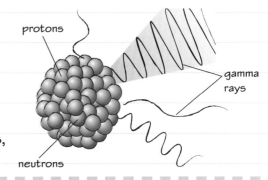

Worked example

Explain the energy changes that occur within the electron levels of the atom.   **(3 marks)**

Electrons can move between energy levels if they absorb or emit electromagnetic radiation. When they absorb electromagnetic radiation they move up energy levels and when they emit electromagnetic radiation they move down energy levels.

The energy of electromagnetic radiation that is emitted or absorbed has to **match** the difference between the **energy levels** that the **electron** is moving between.

Energy changes in the **nucleus** are far greater than those seen between electron energy levels.

Now try this

1 Name the two places in the atom where energy levels are found.   **(2 marks)**

2 Describe what happens when electrons
   (a) absorb electromagnetic radiation **(2 marks)**
   (b) emit electromagnetic radiation.   **(2 marks)**

Extended response – Light and the electromagnetic spectrum

There will be one or more 6-mark questions on your exam paper. For these questions, you will need to think scientifically and structure your answer logically, showing how the points you make are related to each other. You can revise the topics for this question, which is about **light and the electromagnetic spectrum**, on pages 181–184.

Worked example

Exposure to certain types of electromagnetic radiation can have harmful effects on the human body.

Describe how exposure to electromagnetic radiation can be harmful.

Your answer should refer to the types of electromagnetic radiation and the damage that they may cause. **(6 marks)**

long wavelength, low frequency   short wavelength, high frequency

radio waves · microwaves · infrared · visible light · ultraviolet · X-rays · gamma-rays

Apart from radio waves and visible light, which are not deemed to cause damage to humans, the other five members of the electromagnetic spectrum do cause harmful effects.

Microwaves are absorbed by water molecules and can lead to internal heating of body cells, which can be harmful. Infrared radiation can cause burns to the skin.

Ultraviolet radiation can damage the eyes, leading to eye conditions. It can also cause skin cancer as surface cells are affected. X-rays and gamma-rays can both lead to cellular damage and mutations, which can lead to diseases such as cancer.

The initial sentence states which types of electromagnetic wave are dangerous and which are not. This will help to structure the rest of the answer.

Two of the low-energy members of the electromagnetic spectrum are commented on next.

The three higher-energy electromagnetic waves are then commented on. The energy of electromagnetic radiation is related directly to its frequency, so as frequency increases, so does the energy and so does the extent of the damage.

UV, X-rays and gamma-rays are examples of **ionising radiation**. This can lead to tissue damage and possible mutations in cells. Although not mentioned here, you could be asked a question that relates specifically to the dangers of ionising radiation. Of the three types mentioned here, only gamma-rays come from the nucleus of the atom. You can read more about this on pages 186–197.

Command word: Describe

When you are asked to **describe** something, you need to write down facts, events or processes accurately.

Now try this

Describe how the electromagnetic spectrum is useful to humans. Refer to specific members of the EM spectrum in your answer. **(6 marks)**

Structure of the atom

There is a very big difference in the sizes of **atoms**, **nuclei** and **molecules**.

Structure of the atom

Atoms have a **nucleus** containing **protons** and **neutrons**. Electrons move around the nucleus of an atom. An atom has the same number of protons and electrons, so the **+** and **– charges** balance and the atom has no overall charge.

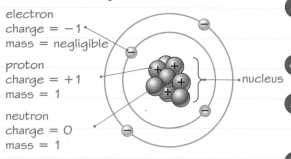

electron
charge = −1
mass = negligible

proton
charge = +1
mass = 1

neutron
charge = 0
mass = 1

nucleus

The atom and the nucleus

1. All atoms have a **nucleus**. The **nucleus** is always **positively charged** as it contains **protons** which have a positive charge and neutrons which do not have a charge.

2. The **nucleus** contains more than **99%** of the **mass** of the atom.

3. The total number of **protons** in an atom's **nucleus** must be the same as the total number of **electrons** in the shells.

4. Electrons in atoms always orbit the **nucleus** and have a **negative charge**.

5. Atoms are always **neutral** because the positive charge from the **protons** cancels out the negative charge from the **electrons**.

6. The **nucleus** of an atom of an element may contain **different numbers of neutrons**.

Atom, nucleus and molecule

A **molecule** is two or more atoms bonded together. A **molecule** is about 10 times the diameter of an atom and about 10^6 times the diameter of a nucleus.

10^{-9} m 10^{-10} m $10^{-15} - 10^{-14}$ m

molecule   atom   nucleus

Gases such as oxygen and carbon dioxide are **molecules**. Water is also a **molecule**.

The diameter of an atom is about 10^{-10} m. The diameter of the nucleus is about 10^{-15} m.

Diagrams of atoms are always incorrect in terms of the scale. In reality, if the nucleus were the size shown here, the nearest electron would be at least 1000 m away.

Worked example

A molecule has a length of 4.8×10^{-9} m. A nucleus has a diameter of 1.2×10^{-15} m. How many nuclei would need to be placed side by side in a line to have the same length as the molecule?   **(3 marks)**

4.8×10^{-9} m $\div$ 1.2×10^{-15} m

    $= 4 \times 10^6$ or 4 million nuclei.

Maths skills Beware! A number written as 19.3 $\times 10^3$ is not written in standard form. The first number needs to be between 1 and 10, so the proper way to write this would be 1.93×10^4. Notice how the power has increased from 3 to 4 as the number at the front has become 10 times smaller.

Remember, $-9 - (-15)$ is equal to 6 because two minuses make a plus, so $-9 + 15 = 6$.

Now try this

How many times bigger than the diameter of the nucleus is:

(a) the diameter of the atom   **(2 marks)**
(b) the diameter of a molecule?   **(2 marks)**

Atoms and isotopes

Atoms of the same **element** can be **different** based on the composition of their **nuclei**.

Atoms

Atoms are made up of **protons**, **neutrons** and **electrons**. The **protons** and **neutrons** are in the nucleus of the atom, and the **electrons** move around the outside.

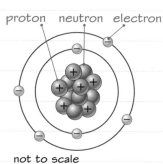

proton neutron electron

not to scale

Describing atoms

All the atoms of a particular element have the same number of **protons**. The number of protons in each atom of an element is called the **atomic number**, or **proton number**.

The total number of protons and neutrons in an atom is the **mass number**, or **nucleon number**.

The atomic number and mass number of an element can be shown like this:

mass number ⟶ $^{16}_{8}O$ ⟵ atomic number

Isotopes

Atoms of a particular element always have the **same number of protons**, but they can have **different numbers of neutrons**. Atoms with the **same number of protons** but **different numbers of neutrons** are **isotopes** of the same element.

As the number of protons determines the element, you can also say that the nuclei of different elements have their own characteristic charge. In this example, a carbon nucleus always has a charge of +6.

6 protons
6 neutrons

6 protons
7 neutrons

6 protons
8 neutrons

● proton (atomic mass = 1)
● neutron (atomic mass = 1)
○ electron (atomic mass = 0)

Carbon atoms can contain different numbers of neutrons.

Worked example

The symbol represents an atom of sodium.

$^{23}_{11}Na$

Explain what these numbers tell you about the structure of the sodium nucleus.   **(2 marks)**

The atomic number shows that sodium contains 11 protons. The mass number shows that it contains (23 − 11) = 12 neutrons.

Worked example

Explain how these atoms are similar and different:

$^{6}_{3}Li$, $^{7}_{3}Li$, $^{8}_{3}Li$ **(3 marks)**

They all contain the same number of protons and the same number of electrons (three of each). They have different numbers of neutrons, so they are different isotopes of lithium.

Now try this

1 Explain which two of these atoms are isotopes. **(2 marks)**

	Number of protons	Number of neutrons
Atom A	6	6
Atom B	6	7
Atom C	7	6

2 An atom of boron (B) has 5 protons and 6 neutrons. Show the atomic number and mass number as a symbol for the isotope.   **(1 mark)**

Atoms, electrons and ions

Electrons can **move** between energy levels, or they can **leave** the atom completely.

Electrons in orbit

In all atoms, electrons orbit the nucleus in different orbits or energy levels, at different, fixed distances from the nucleus.

6 protons + 6 neutrons

– electron

○ neutron

+ proton

carbon atom

Moving between energy levels

An **electron** will move from a **lower to a higher orbit** if it **absorbs** electromagnetic radiation.

An **electron** will move from a **higher to a lower orbit** if it **emits** electromagnetic radiation.

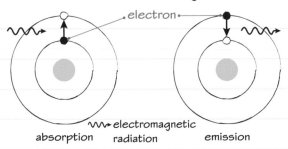

electron

electromagnetic radiation

absorption   emission

Forming positive ions

Atoms become positively charged particles called **positive ions** when they **lose electrons**. There are now more protons present in the nucleus than there are electrons in the shells.

Electrons can leave an atom by:

1. absorbing electromagnetic radiation of enough energy so that they can escape the pull of the nucleus; the three types of electromagnetic radiation that have enough energy to do that are UV, X-rays and gamma-rays
2. being hit by a particle such as an alpha particle or beta particle.

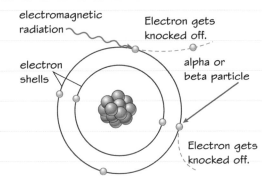

electromagnetic radiation

Electron gets knocked off.

electron shells

alpha or beta particle

Electron gets knocked off.

Worked example

State the overall charge of

(a) an atom   **(1 mark)**

neutral or 0

(b) a sodium atom that has lost an electron   **(1 mark)**

+1

(c) an atom where an electron has moved from a higher to lower orbit.   **(1 mark)**

neutral or 0

All atoms have a neutral overall charge. Positive ions are formed when an atom loses an electron.

Atoms can also gain electrons. They become negative ions with an overall negative charge.

No electron has been lost from the atom so there is no net change in the amount of charge present within the atom.

Now try this

1 State where
   (a) protons   **(1 mark)**
   (b) neutrons   **(1 mark)**
   (c) electrons   **(1 mark)**
   are found in atoms.

2 Explain how ions are different from atoms.
                                   (4 marks)

3 Determine what the overall charge of an atom would be if it:
   (a) lost two electrons   **(2 marks)**
   (b) gained one electron.   **(2 marks)**

Ionising radiation

Alpha, **beta**, **gamma** and **neutron** radiation are **emitted** by **unstable nuclei**. The process is **random**, which means it is not possible to determine exactly **when** any nucleus will decay next.

Alpha, beta, gamma and neutron radiation

Some elements are **radioactive** because their nuclei are **unstable**. This means that they will undergo radioactive decay and change into other elements. Unstable nuclei will decay when alpha, beta, gamma or neutron radiation is emitted.

An **alpha particle** is a helium nucleus. It is composed of two protons and two neutrons. It has a charge of +2 and is the heaviest of

the particles emitted by unstable atoms. A **beta particle** is an electron. It has a charge of −1. A **positron** is an anti-electron and has a charge of +1.

A **gamma-ray** is a form of high-energy electromagnetic radiation. It has no mass or charge.

A **neutron** has zero charge.

Properties of radiation

Alpha and beta particles and gamma-rays can collide with atoms, ionising them by causing them to lose electrons.

Neutrons:
- are not directly ionising
- have a very high penetrating power due to them having no charge and not interacting strongly with matter

1 (α) Alpha particles:
- will travel around 5 cm in air
- very ionising
- can be stopped by a sheet of paper.

2 (β) Beta particles:
- will travel a few metres in air
- moderately ionising
- can be stopped by 3 mm thick aluminium.

3 (γ) Gamma-rays:
- will travel a few kilometres in air
- weakly ionising
- need thick lead to stop them.

- can travel through humans and buildings for long distances before being stopped.

Worked example

Complete the table to show the properties of alpha, beta, gamma and neutron radiation. **(5 marks)**

Type of radiation emitted	Relative charge	Relative mass	Ionising power	Penetrating power	Affected by magnetic fields?
alpha, α (helium nucleus, two protons and two neutrons)	+2	4	heavily ionising	very low, only ~5 cm in air	yes
beta, β− (an electron from the nucleus)	−1	1/1840	weakly ionising	low, stopped by thin aluminium	yes, but in the opposite direction to α and β+
positron, β+ (a particle with same size as electron but an opposite charge)	+1	1/1840	weakly ionising	low, stopped by thin aluminium	yes
neutron, n	0	1	not directly ionising	high	no, since neither are charged
gamma, γ (waves)	0	0	not directly ionising	very high, stopped only by thick lead	

Now try this

1 State which is the most ionising type of radiation. **(1 mark)**

2 Explain why radioactive decay is a random process. **(2 marks)**

Background radiation

Low levels of **radiation** are present around you all the time. This radiation is both **natural** and **man-made** and is called **background radiation**.

Background radiation

We are always exposed to ionising radiation. This is called **background radiation**. This radiation comes from different sources, as shown in the pie chart.

Radon is a radioactive gas that is produced when **uranium** in rocks decays. Radon decays by emitting an alpha particle. The radon can build up in houses and other buildings. The amount of radon gas varies from place to place, because it depends on the type of rock in the area.

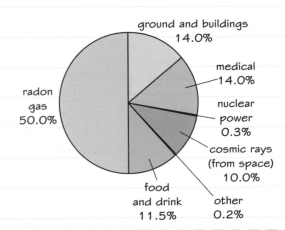

ground and buildings 14.0%
medical 14.0%
nuclear power 0.3%
cosmic rays (from space) 10.0%
other 0.2%
food and drink 11.5%
radon gas 50.0%

☐ up to 1%
▨ 1–2.99%
▨ 3–4.99%
▨ 5–9.99%
■ 10–29.99%
■ 30% and over

Norfolk

Cornwall

Percentage of houses where radon is a potential problem.

Now try this

1 Which one of these is a source of artificial background radiation?

☐ **A** soil
☐ **B** rock
☐ **C** cosmic rays
☐ **D** medical X-rays   **(1 mark)**

2 Explain what is meant by the term background radiation.   **(3 marks)**

3 Look at the map above. How would the pie chart above change if you lived in
(a) Norfolk
(b) Cornwall?   **(2 marks)**

Measuring radioactivity

Photographic film and a **Geiger–Müller tube** can both be used to **measure** and **detect** radiation.

The Geiger–Müller tube

The Geiger–Müller (GM) tube is used to detect nuclear radiation. It is connected to a counter or ratemeter which shows the amount of radiation that has been detected.

The text in red shows what is happening inside the GM tube, but you do not need to remember this in detail.

The GM tube contains argon gas. When radiation enters the tube, the atoms of argon are ionised and electrons travel towards the thin wire.

source Am-241

The GM tube has a thin wire in the middle which is connected to a voltage of +400 V.

As the electrons travel towards the thin wire, more electrons are knocked from atoms and an avalanche effect occurs.

The amount of radiation detected is shown by the ratemeter.

ratemeter

Detecting radiation

In 1896, Henri Becquerel discovered that uranium salts would lead to the darkening of a photographic film, even if it was wrapped up so that no light could reach it.

Radiation was being emitted from the uranium nuclei and this was responsible for the darkening of the film. This is now made use of in the nuclear industry as workers will wear a film badge to determine if they are being exposed to different forms of nuclear radiation.

photographic film inside

thin and thick plastic windows or aluminium – stop some beta particles

open window

lead between the plastic case and the film – stops beta and most gamma radiation

This dosimeter is a film badge used to monitor the radiation received by its wearer.

Worked example

(a) Explain why there is an open window in the film badge. **(3 marks)**

Light rays will darken the film. Since the film badge is designed to detect nuclear radiation, this acts as a control so that you know that the film is working.

(b) Explain why the film badge has aluminium and lead sheets inserted in it. **(3 marks)**

Aluminium absorbs beta particles and lead absorbs gamma-rays. If there is darkening behind these sheets, then high-energy beta- or gamma-rays may have got through and so the nature of the radiation can be determined and the risk identified.

You should use your knowledge of the penetrating powers of the different types of radioactivity to answer the question.

Now try this

1 State the two types of device that are used to detect and measure radiation. **(2 marks)**

2 The photographic film behind the lead sheet darkens in the film badge worn by a worker in a nuclear power plant. Explain why the worker is concerned. **(3 marks)**

Models of the atom

The **model of the atom** has changed over time, based on **evidence** of its structure that became available from **experiments**.

Plum pudding model

J. J. Thomson's model of the atom was that the atom was like a 'plum pudding' with negatively charged 'electron plums' embedded in a uniform, positively charged 'dough' – a bit like the way currants look in a Christmas pudding.

This model showed that both positive and negative charges existed in atoms and accounted for the atom being neutral.

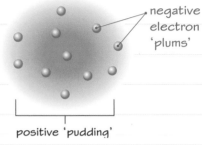

negative electron 'plums'

positive 'pudding'

plum pudding model of the atom

Rutherford's model

Rutherford proposed that the atom must contain a very **small, positively charged nucleus** which electrons orbit – a bit like planets orbiting the Sun.

Rutherford's hypothesis was proved to be correct by Geiger and Marsden, who fired alpha particles at gold film.

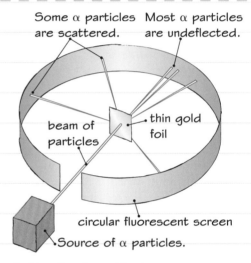

Some α particles are scattered. Most α particles are undeflected.

beam of particles

thin gold foil

circular fluorescent screen

Source of α particles.

Rutherford scattering

The Bohr model

Niels Bohr showed that **electrons** had to orbit a **positive nucleus** in well-defined **energy levels** or orbits, but could move between energy levels if they gained or lost energy.

electron energy levels

nucleus

electron

Worked example

Which model of the atom is being described?

(a) The atom is mostly empty space, in which electrons orbit randomly, and has a small positive nucleus. **(1 mark)**

Rutherford's model

(b) Electrons can only orbit the atom in certain energy levels or orbits. **(1 mark)**

the Bohr model of the atom

(c) The atom is neutral with negative 'plums' embedded in a positive 'dough'. **(1 mark)**

the plum pudding model

Now try this

Refer to page 188 for more information on electron levels.

1 Describe the three models of the atom. **(3 marks)**

2 Explain how Rutherford's work led to the conclusion that the atom had a small, positive nucleus. **(4 marks)**

3 Explain how new models of the atom become accepted over time. **(3 marks)**

Beta decay

One way in which unstable nuclei can undergo radioactive decay is by **beta decay**. There are two types – one where an **electron is emitted**, the other where a **positron is emitted**.

Beta-minus (β⁻) decay

In β⁻ decay, a **neutron** in the nucleus of an unstable atom decays to become a **proton** and an **electron**. The proton stays within the nucleus, but the **electron**, which is the β⁻ **particle**, is emitted from the nucleus at high speed as a fast-moving electron.

$$n \longrightarrow p + \beta^-$$

The decay of **carbon-14** into **nitrogen-14** by the emission of a β⁻ particle is an example of β⁻ decay. The mass number does not change, but the proton number **increases** by 1.

$$^{14}_{6}C \longrightarrow {}^{14}_{7}N + {}^{0}_{-1}\beta$$

Beta-plus (β+) decay

In β⁺ decay, a **proton** in the nucleus decays to become a **neutron** and a **positron**. The neutron stays in the nucleus. The **positron**, which is the β⁺ **particle**, is emitted from the nucleus at a very high speed, carrying away a positive charge and a very small amount of the nuclear mass.

$$p \longrightarrow n + \beta^+$$

The decay of **sodium-22** into **neon-22** by the emission of a positron is an example of β⁺ decay. The mass number does not change, but the proton number **decreases** by 1.

$$^{22}_{11}Na \longrightarrow {}^{22}_{10}Ne + {}^{0}_{+1}\beta$$

Worked example

Complete each equation and state whether it is β⁻ or β⁺ decay:

(a) $^{131}_{53}I \rightarrow {}^{131}_{54}Xe + ?$ **(2 marks)**

Add $_{-1}^{0}\beta$. β⁻ decay

(b) $^{23}_{12}Mg \rightarrow {}^{23}_{11}Na + ?$ **(2 marks)**

Add $^{0}_{1}\beta$. β⁺ decay

Uses of beta decay

Carbon-14 is an unstable isotope of carbon and emits β⁻ particles – it has a half-life of over 5700 years. This means that it can be used for radiocarbon dating, which involves finding the ages of materials that are thousands of years old. Positrons can be used in hospitals to form images of patients by the use of PET scans.

Now try this

1 Describe the changes that take place in the nucleus when it undergoes:
   (a) β⁻ decay   **(2 marks)**
   (b) β⁺ decay.   **(2 marks)**

2 Describe how a β⁻ particle is different from an electron that is found in a stable atom.   **(2 marks)**

3 Fill in the missing numbers in the decay equation and state the type of decay.   **(2 marks)**

$$^{66}_{28}Ni \rightarrow {}^{-}_{29}Cu + {}^{0}_{-}\beta$$

Radioactive decay

When unstable nuclei decay, the changes that occur depend on the **radiation** that is emitted from the **nucleus**.

Changes to the nucleus

Type of radiation	Effect on the mass of the nucleus	Effect on the charge of the nucleus
alpha α	nuclear mass reduced by 4 [−4]	positive charge reduced by 2 [−2]
beta $\beta-$	no change [0]	positive charge increased by 1 [+1]
beta $\beta+$	no change [0]	positive charge reduced by 1 [−1]
gamma	no effect on either the mass or the charge of a nucleus	
neutron	mass reduced by 1	no change of nuclear charge

Balancing nuclear decay equations

In any nuclear decay, the total mass and charge of the nucleus are conserved – they are the same before and after the decay. So the masses and charges on each side of the equation must balance.

When uranium-238 undergoes alpha decay, mass and charge are conserved. Nuclei that have undergone radioactive decay also undergo a rearrangement of their protons and neutrons. This involves the loss of energy from the nucleus in the form of gamma radiation. The mass and charge of the gamma-ray must be zero for the equation to balance:

$$^{238}_{92}\text{U} \longrightarrow \,^{234}_{90}\text{Th} + \,^{4}_{2}\alpha + \gamma$$

uranium   thorium   alpha   gamma-
                             particle   ray

When neutron decay occurs, mass and charge are also conserved:

$$^{13}_{4}\text{Be} \longrightarrow \,^{12}_{4}\text{Be} + \,^{1}_{0}\text{n}$$

Neutron decay results in another isotope of the same element being formed.

When beryllium decays by neutron emission, the mass and charge are both conserved. The nuclear charge is +4 on both sides of the decay equation and the total mass is 13.

Worked example

Balance the nuclear equations for these decays:

(a) Iodine-121 undergoes β^+ decay to form tellurium. **(2 marks)**

$^{121}_{53}\text{I} \rightarrow \,^{121}_{52}\text{Te} + \,^{0}_{+1}\beta$

 $^{0}_{+1}\beta$ is the emitted β^+ particle

(b) An isotope of carbon undergoes β^- decay to form nitrogen-14. **(2 marks)**

$^{14}_{6}\text{C} \rightarrow \,^{14}_{7}\text{N} + \,^{0}_{-1}\beta$

 $^{0}_{-1}\beta$ is the emitted β^- particle

(c) Radon-220 undergoes α decay to form an isotope of polonium. **(2 marks)**

$^{220}_{86}\text{Rn} \rightarrow \,^{216}_{84}\text{Po} + \,^{4}_{2}\text{He}$

 $^{4}_{2}\text{He}$ is the emitted α particle.

Now try this

1 Balance the nuclear equations for these decays and state the type of decay.

(a) $^{-}_{6}\text{C} \rightarrow \,^{10}_{-}\text{B} + \,^{0}_{1}\beta$ **(2 marks)**

(b) $^{232}_{-}\text{Th} \rightarrow \,^{-}_{88}\text{Ra} + \,^{4}_{-}\text{He}$ **(2 marks)**

2 A uranium nucleus contains 92 protons and 146 neutrons.

(a) State the mass number and atomic number of this uranium isotope. **(3 marks)**

(b) Determine what the mass number and atomic number will be if this uranium atom emits two alpha particles and a beta$^-$ particle. **(4 marks)**

Half-life

The **activity** of a radioactive source is the number of atoms that **decay** every second. The unit for activity is the **becquerel (Bq)**. When an atom decays it emits radiation but changes into a more stable isotope.

Unstable atoms

The activity of a source depends on how many **unstable** atoms there are in a sample, and on the particular isotope. As more and more atoms in a sample decay, there are fewer unstable ones left, so the activity decreases. The **half-life** of a radioactive isotope is the time it takes for **half** of the **unstable** atoms to **decay**. This is also the time for the activity to go down by half.

We cannot predict when a particular nucleus will decay. But when there is a very large number of nuclei, the half-life gives a good prediction of the proportion of nuclei that will decay in a given time.

Radioactive decay and half-life

The number of radioactive nuclei present in a sample will halve after each successive half-life. After 1 half-life there will be 50% of the radioactive atoms left; after 2 half-lives there will be 25% of the radioactive atoms left, and so on.

Half-life example

The activity of a radioactive source is 240 Bq and its half-life is 6 hours.

After 1 half-life, the activity will halve to 120 Bq.

After 2 half-lives it will halve again to 60 Bq.

After 3 half-lives it will halve again to 30 Bq.

After 4 half-lives (one day) it will be 15 Bq.

 Maths skills

Be careful when multiplying fractions:

After **1 half-life**, $\frac{1}{2}$ of the initial radioactive atoms are left.

After **2 half-lives**, $\frac{1}{2} \times \frac{1}{2}$ or $\frac{1}{4}$ are left.

After **3 half-lives**, $\frac{1}{2} \times \frac{1}{2} \times \frac{1}{2}$ or $\frac{1}{8}$ are left.

Worked example

The graph shows how the activity of a sample changes over 24 hours. What is the half-life of the sample?   **(3 marks)**

Activity at time 0 = 1000 Bq

Half of this is 500 Bq. The activity is 500 Bq at 8 hours.

The half-life is 8 hours.

As the activity of a radioactive source decreases, the gradient of the graph will get less and less steep.

Now try this

1 The half-life of a radioactive source with an initial activity of 4000 Bq is known to be 2 days. Calculate the activity of the source after
   (a) 2 days   **(2 marks)**
   (b) 4 days   **(2 marks)**
   (c) 8 days.   **(2 marks)**

2 The activity of a source is 120 Bq. Four hours later it is found to be 30 Bq. Calculate the half-life of the source.
   (2 marks)

3 The half-life of a source is 15 minutes. Calculate the fraction that will remain after one hour.   **(3 marks)**

Dangers of radiation

Ionising radiation can knock electrons out of atoms, turning the atoms into **ions**. This can be very **harmful** to humans.

Ionisation and cellular mutation

The energy transferred by ionising radiation can remove electrons from atoms to form **ions**. Ions are very reactive and can cause mutations to the **DNA** in **cells**. This can lead to **cancer**.

Energy transferred by ionising radiation removes electrons from atoms to form ions. → Ions are reactive and can cause mutations to the DNA in cells. → Damaged DNA can lead to cancer.

Ionising radiation can also cause damage to cell tissue in the form of radiation burns. When its energy is high enough it can also kill cells.

Precautions and safety

People who come into contact with ionising radiation need to be protected. They are protected by:

1. **limiting the time of exposure** – keep the time that a person needs to be in contact with the ionising radiation as **low** as possible

2. **wearing protective clothing** – wearing a **lead apron** will **absorb** much of the ionising radiation

3. **increasing the distance from the person to the radioactive source** – the **further** a person is from the ionising radiation, the **less damage** it will do.

To determine how much radiation a person has been exposed to, a film badge may be worn. See page 191 for more details.

Precautions

People using radioactive material take precautions to make sure they stay safe.

radioactive source

The radioactive source is being moved using tongs to keep it as far away from the person's hand as possible. The source is always kept pointing away from people.

Worked example

Describe two precautions taken by dentists and dental nurses to reduce their exposure to ionising radiation while taking an X-ray. **(2 marks)**

1. They go out of the room in which the X-ray is taking place.
2. They keep the X-ray pulse as short as possible. (This also minimises the patient's exposure.)

The amount of energy that the human body is exposed to from a radioactive source is referred to as the **dose**. The dose needs to be big enough to obtain the X-ray image, but low enough to be safe for the patient and the dentist.

Now try this

1 State two ways in which ionising radiation can be dangerous to humans. **(2 marks)**

2 Explain why ionising radiation is more dangerous than non-ionising radiation. **(3 marks)**

3 Describe how people who work with radioactive materials decrease the risk of being exposed to high levels of ionising radiation. **(3 marks)**

Contamination and irradiation

You may be exposed to the effects of radioactive materials by being **irradiated** or **contaminated**.

Irradiation

Irradiation is ionising radiation from an external radioactive source travelling to the body – it is not breathed in, eaten or drunk.

Irradiation does not refer to non-harmful rays from televisions, light bulbs or other non-ionising sources.

Irradiation is the exposure of a person to ionising radiation from outside the body. This could be in the form of harmful gamma-rays, beta particles or X-rays.

Alpha particles are unlikely to be harmful outside the body as they have a very short range in air (5 cm) and are unlikely to reach a person.

When ionising radiation reaches the body, cells may be damaged or killed, but you will not become radioactive.

Contamination

External contamination occurs when radioactive materials **come into contact with a person's hair, skin or clothing.**

Internal contamination occurs when a **radioactive source is eaten or drunk.** Some nuts, plants, fruits and alcoholic drinks have low levels of radioactivity. This is due to the radioactive minerals that they are exposed to during their growth or manufacture.

Worked example

State what type of contamination the following examples are describing:
(a) eating radioactive strontium-90 that is found in some foods **(1 mark)**
internal contamination
(b) being exposed to cosmic rays from the Sun **(1 mark)**
irradiation
(c) having an X-ray to find if a bone is broken **(1 mark)**
irradiation
(d) radioactive dust comes into contact with the skin. **(1 mark)**
external contamination

Remember that with contamination, the radioactive source comes into contact with the skin or is taken into the body. This can be through the mouth or nose, or through a cut in the skin. With irradiation, the source does not come into contact with the skin.

Now try this

1 Define
  (a) irradiation **(2 marks)**
  (b) contamination. **(2 marks)**

2 Explain why alpha particles are more likely to cause damage inside the body rather than outside the body. **(3 marks)**

3 Describe how background radiation is a mixture of contamination and irradiation. **(2 marks)**

Extended response – Radioactivity

There will be one or more 6-mark questions on your exam paper. For these questions, you will need to think scientifically and structure your answer logically, showing how the points you make are related to each other. You can revise the topics for this question, which is about **radioactivity**, on pages 186–197.

Worked example

Unstable nuclei emit **ionising** radiation which can cause damage to human tissue.

Explain the precautions that need to be taken to reduce the potential danger of ionising radiation to humans.

Your answer should refer to the nature of ionising radiation and how it may be dangerous both inside and outside the body.

(6 marks)

Ionising radiation is radiation that has enough energy to knock electrons from the outer shells of atoms, turning them from neutral atoms to positively charged ions. There are three types of ionising radiation that are emitted from the nucleus – alpha and beta particles and gamma rays. Alpha particles are the most ionising and gamma rays are the least ionising.

Since ionising radiation can damage human tissue and cause mutations in cells, leading to cancer, it is necessary to take precautions. These precautions include wearing lead aprons to absorb the radiation, being exposed to as low a radiation energy as possible, being as far from the radioactive source as possible and being exposed for as short a period of time as possible. All of these help to reduce the exposure to ionising radiation.

Inside the body, alpha particles are easily absorbed and can cause cellular mutations which can lead to cancer. Beta particles and gamma rays tend to pass out of the body. Alpha particles are not dangerous outside the body as they will not reach the body due to their short range, but beta particles and gamma rays can reach the body and can cause damage to cells.

Command words: Explain

When you are asked to **explain** something, it is not enough to just state or describe something. Your answer **must** contain some reasoning or justification of the points you make based on the physics being addressed. This needs to be communicated clearly with good spelling, punctuation, grammar and sentence structure.

 The answer starts with an explanation of what ionising radiation is as well as a description of the three main types of ionising radiation and their relative ionising abilities.

 The second paragraph addresses the dangers and the precautions that need to be taken to ensure that exposure does not lead to adverse health issues.

Contamination and irradiation

Although not mentioned here specifically in the answer, you could state that material emitting ionising radiation can be breathed into the body or eaten, in which case the person is **contaminated**, and that the radiation could reach them as beta particles or gamma rays from an external source, in which case the person is being **irradiated**.

 The final paragraph looks at which type of radiation is most dangerous inside the body as well as which types of radiation are most dangerous when the radioactive source is outside the body.

Now try this

Describe how and why the atomic model has changed over time. Your answer should refer to three different models of the atom.

(6 marks)

Work, energy and power

The **work** done by a force is the same as the **energy** transferred by the force. **Power** is the **rate of work** being done or the **rate at which energy is transferred**. You should already be familiar with some of the content about **energy** for this topic which is covered on pages 169, 170 and 172.

Work done and energy

Work done is the amount of energy transferred, and is measured in **joules (J)**.

Work done is calculated using this formula:

$$\text{work done (J)} = \text{force (N)} \times \text{distance moved in the direction of the force (m)}$$

$$E = F \times d$$

LEARN IT!
IT'S NOT ON THE EQUATIONS LIST

$$\boxed{\dfrac{E}{F \times d}}$$

You can measure the work done by recording the size of the force and the distance moved in the direction of the force. Multiply these values together to find the value for the work done.

Power

Power is the rate of doing work (how fast energy is transferred). Power is measured in **watts (W)**. 1 watt is 1 joule of energy being transferred every second.

$$\text{power (W)} = \dfrac{\text{work done (J)}}{\text{time taken (s)}}$$

$$P = \dfrac{E}{t}$$

LEARN IT!
IT'S NOT ON THE EQUATIONS LIST

$$\boxed{\dfrac{E}{P \times t}}$$

A hairdryer with a power of 1800W transfers 1800J each second.

Changing the energy of a system

The energy of a system can be changed by:

1 **work done through forces:** a body can be lifted through a vertical height by a force. This will increase the store of gravitational potential energy.

2 **electrical equipment:** a cell in a circuit provides a potential difference so that components in the circuit can transfer energy into other forms, such as thermal energy.

3 **heating a material:** supplying thermal energy to a system will increase the kinetic energy of the particles in the material. Its temperature will increase if it is not changing state.

Worked example

(a) Dan uses a force of 100 N to push a box across the floor. He pushes it for 3 m. Calculate the work done. **(3 marks)**

Work done = 100 N × 3 m = 300 J

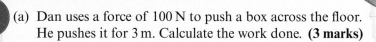

(b) A kettle converts 360 000 J of electrical energy into thermal energy in 3 minutes whilst heating a mass of water. Calculate the power of the kettle. **(3 marks)**

Power = energy ÷ time

= 360 000 J ÷ (3 × 60 s) = 2000 W

Don't get work and power mixed up. Remember:

Work = energy transferred, measured in joules.

Power = **rate** of energy transfer, measured in watts.

Always make sure that energy is in J and time is in s before substituting to find an answer in W.

Now try this

1 Calculate how much work is done when 350 N pushes an object through 30 m along the floor. **(3 marks)**

2 Calculate how much energy an 1800 W hairdryer transfers when used for 8 minutes. **(3 marks)**

3 Calculate the power of a light bulb that transfers 3600 J of energy in one minute. **(3 marks)**

Extended response – Energy and forces

There will be one or more 6-mark questions on your exam paper. For these questions, you will need to think scientifically and structure your answer logically, showing how the points you make are related to each other. You can revise the topics for this question, which is about **energy and forces**, on pages 169, 170 and 199.

Worked example

You can find more information on efficiency on page 170.

56 J   56 J   kinetic energy

27 J

17 J

17 J   27 J

thermal energy in the surroundings   thermal energy in the motor

Energy stores and energy transfers can be shown on energy transfer diagrams.

An energy transfer diagram is shown for a battery-operated fan. Explain how this energy transfer diagram can be used to determine the efficiency of the fan.

Your answer should refer to the term efficiency, the equation for efficiency and a calculation. **(6 marks)**

For the energy transfer diagram shown, the input is in the form of a chemical energy store, which is transferred to kinetic energy, sound energy (although not shown in the diagram) and thermal energy.

For the energy transfer diagram shown, for every 100 J of energy transferred from the chemical energy store of the battery, there will be 56 J transferred to the kinetic energy, 17 J to the thermal energy store in the surroundings and 27 J to the thermal energy store in the motor.

Since a battery-operated fan is designed to transfer the chemical energy store to kinetic energy as a useful form, 56 J of the 100 J of chemical energy can be deemed to be useful, and 44 J can be assumed to be wasted.

The efficiency of a device is the proportion of the input energy that is usefully transferred and is calculated using the equation:

$$\text{Efficiency} = \frac{\text{(useful output energy)}}{\text{(total input energy)}} \times 100\%$$

For the battery-operated fan, the efficiency is 56 J ÷ 100 J × 100% which is an efficiency of 56%.

The answer starts by simply stating what the energy transfer diagram is showing in terms of energy stores and transfers.

This part of the answer explains which energy store is useful as an output energy store and which of the stores are wasted energy stores. It also states the amounts that are useful and wasted.

Command word: Explain

When you are asked to **explain** something, it is not enough just to state or describe it.

Your answer must contain some reasoning or justification of the points you make.

Your explanation can include mathematical explanations, if calculations are needed.

The term efficiency is explained, an equation for calculating the efficiency is provided and a value is calculated for the fan's efficiency.

The question expects you to talk about **energy stores** and **energy transfers**. There are eight types of energy store and four types of energy transfer, which you can read more about on page 169.

Now try this

Describe an experiment to determine how powerful three weightlifters are.

Your answer should refer to the equations for calculating changes in gravitational potential energy and power.

(6 marks)

Interacting forces

Pairs of forces can interact **at a distance** or by **direct contact**.

Non-contact forces

Forces can be exerted between objects without them being in contact with one another. There are three **non-contact forces** that you need to know about.

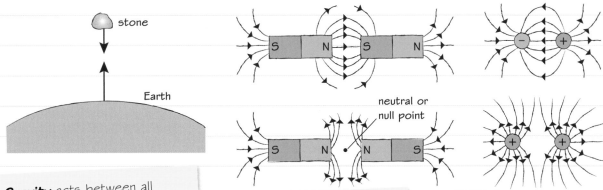

Gravity acts between all masses. It is always attractive.

Magnetism acts between magnetic poles. Unlike poles attract and like poles repel.

Electrostatic charges exert forces on each other at a distance. Unlike charges attract and like charges repel.

Contact forces

Forces can be exerted between objects due to them being in contact. In each case there is an interaction pair of forces that act in opposite directions. The forces can be represented by vectors.

The **normal contact force** acts upwards in opposition to the weight of the object. The interaction pair is the force of the ground on the box and the force of the box on the ground.

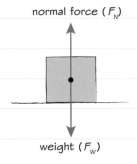

The **force of friction** acts in opposition to the pushing force that is trying to change its motion. Friction always acts to slow a moving object down. The interaction pair is the force of the object on the surface and the force of the surface on the object.

Other examples of contact forces include tension, upthrust and drag. Upthrust is the force acting upwards on a floating body or a body in a fluid.

Worked example

An archer fires an arrow from a bow. Describe the contact and non-contact forces involved in firing the arrow. **(2 marks)**

Contact forces include the normal force acting on the arrow, friction as it moves through the air and the tension in the string. Non-contact forces include gravity once it has been released.

Now try this

1 State how gravity is different from magnetism and the electrostatic force. **(1 mark)**

2 State how the forces of friction and drag are similar. **(1 mark)**

3 Describe the contact and non-contact forces acting on a moving ship. **(3 marks)**

Circuit symbols

Electric circuit diagrams are drawn using agreed symbols and conventions that can be understood by everybody across the world.

Circuit symbols

You need to know the symbols for these components.

Component	Symbol	Purpose
cell (battery)	positive terminal / negative terminal	provides a potential difference
switches		allows the current flow to be switched on or off
voltmeter	(V)	measures potential difference across a component
ammeter	(A)	measures the current flowing through a component
fixed resistor		provides a fixed resistance to the flow of current
variable resistor		provides a variable (changeable) resistance
filament lamp	(X)	converts electrical energy to light energy as a useful form
motor	(M)	converts electrical energy to kinetic energy as a useful form
diode		allows current to flow in one direction only
thermistor		resistance decreases when the temperature increases
LDR		resistance decreases when the light intensity increases
LED		a diode that gives out light when current flows through it

---

Worked example

Name four components that are commonly used to change or control the amount of resistance in a circuit.

(2 marks)

thermistor, LDR, fixed resistor, variable resistor

> 2 marks for all correct, I mark for 3 correct and zero marks for less than 3 correct.

Worked example

Describe how an LED is different from a filament lamp.   **(1 mark)**

An LED will only allow electrical current to pass through it in one direction.

Now try this

1 State which components above are output devices.   **(3 marks)**

2 State how ammeters and voltmeters should be arranged with components in circuits.   **(2 marks)**

3 Design a circuit to turn on a lamp when it goes dark.   **(3 marks)**

Series and parallel circuits

Components in circuits can be arranged in **series** or **parallel**. The rules for current and potential difference in these two types of circuits are different.

Series circuits

A **series circuit** contains just one loop, around which an electric current can flow.

Electrons do not flow through any of the voltmeters.

Electrons flow clockwise in this circuit, through the cell, wires, three ammeters and two resistors.

Ammeters have a very low resistance so the current can flow through them and be measured accurately.

Ammeters are always connected in series with components.

The size of the current in a series circuit is the same at every point in the circuit. All three ammeters in this circuit will show the same value for the current.

The potential difference across components that are arranged in series must add up to give the cell voltage, so $V_1 = V_2 + V_3$.

Voltmeters have a very high resistance so that no current will flow through them.

Parallel circuits

A **parallel circuit** contains more than one loop and the current will split up or recombine at the junctions.

The potential difference across the components in each branch of a parallel circuit must add to give the cell voltage. The voltmeter readings across the two resistors will both have the same value as the potential difference across the cell.

The sum of the currents in each of the branches must equal the current leaving the cell. For this example,
$A_1 = A_4 = A_2 + A_3$.

Worked example

What are the missing values in this parallel circuit if the bulbs are identical?   **(2 marks)**

Both the ammeter readings A_3 and $A_4 = 1$ A. The voltmeter readings V_3 and V_4 will both be 6 V.

1   Describe the differences for current and potential difference in series and parallel circuits.   **(4 marks)**

2   Explain why car lights are connected in parallel and not in series.   **(3 marks)**

3   Explain why a cell goes flat more quickly when lamps are arranged in parallel.   **(4 marks)**

4   The bulbs in this circuit are identical. What are the missing values in this series circuit for A_1, A_2, V_1 and V_2?   **(2 marks)**

Current and charge

An **electric current** is the **rate of flow of charge**. In a metal, electric current is the flow of electrons.

Charge and current

The size of a current is a measure of how much charge flows past a point each second. It is the rate of flow of charge. The unit of charge is the **coulomb** (C). One ampere, or amp (A), is one coulomb of charge per second. You can calculate charge using the equation:

Charge (C) = current (A) × time (s)

$$Q = I \times t$$

LEARN IT!
IT'S NOT ON THE EQUATIONS LIST

Watch out! Don't get the units and quantities confused. The units have sensible abbreviations (C for coulombs, A for amps). The symbols for the quantities are not as easy to remember (Q stands for charge, I for current).

You also need to know how to rearrange the equation using the triangle shown so that you can calculate Q, I and t using values provided in questions.

Measuring current

Electric current will flow in a closed circuit when there is a source of potential difference. To measure the size of the current flowing through a component, an ammeter is connected in series with the component.

The current flowing is the same at all points in a series circuit. In this example, the current is 0.5 A.

The cell is the source of potential difference.

Conventional current flows this way, from + to − in a circuit.

Electrons flow this way, from − to +.

The three ammeters are connected in series with the two filament lamps.

Worked example

(a) Describe how ammeters should be connected with components in circuits. **(1 mark)**

Ammeters should always be arranged in series with the component to be measured.

(b) Describe what happens to the size of the current in a series circuit. **(1 mark)**

The current is the same value at any point in a series circuit.

Worked example

(a) A current of 1.5 A flows for 2 minutes. Calculate how much charge flows in this time. **(3 marks)**

$$Q = I \times t$$
$$= 1.5\,A \times 120\,s = 180\,C$$

(b) A charge of 1200 C flows through a filament lamp for 4 minutes. Calculate the average current in the filament lamp. **(3 marks)**

$$I = Q \div t$$
$$= 1200\,C \div 240\,s = 5\,A$$

Now try this

There are 60 × 60 seconds in one hour.

1 State the units of current and charge. **(2 marks)**

2 Calculate the charge that flows in one hour when there is a current of 0.25 A in a circuit. **(3 marks)**

3 A charge of 3000 C is transferred by a current of 0.25 A. Calculate the length of time for which the current flows. **(4 marks)**

Energy and charge

Energy, **charge** and **potential difference** are closely related when dealing with electrical circuits.

Energy, charge and potential difference

Energy, charge and potential difference are related by the equation:

energy transferred = charge moved × potential difference
(J)   (C)   (V)

$$E = Q \times V$$

Calculate the charge, Q, from the current reading on the ammeter using the equation $Q = I \times t$ (see page 204).

LEARN IT! IT'S NOT ON THE EQUATIONS LIST

 Maths skills Cover up the quantity you want to find with your finger. The position of the other two quantities tells you the formula.

Remember that for this circuit, the value obtained for the energy transferred will be for this bulb, since the potential difference being measured is across this bulb only.

The potential difference, V, across the bulb is measured with a voltmeter. Voltmeters are always connected in parallel with components and ammeters are always connected in series.

Worked example

(a) A charge of 25 C passes through a motor. The potential difference across the motor is 6 V. Calculate how much energy is transferred. **(3 marks)**

$E = Q \times V$, so $E = 25C \times 6V = 150J$

(b) A current of 1.2 A flows through a bulb for 2 minutes. The potential difference across the bulb is 12 V. Work out how much energy is transferred. **(3 marks)**

$E = Q \times V$ and $Q = I \times t$, so $E = I \times t \times V$
$E = 1.2A \times 120s \times 12V = 1728J$

For some calculations, you just need to substitute the numbers straight into the equation $E = Q \times V$.

For other calculations, there may be two steps. Here you need to calculate Q first by using $Q = I \times t$ and then substitute this value into $E = Q \times V$.

Worked example

A charge of 18 C transfers 364 J of electrical energy through a resistor. Calculate the potential difference across the resistor. **(3 marks)**

Rearrange $E = Q \times V$ to give $V = E \div Q$.
$V = 364J \div 18C = 20.2V$

Now try this

1 A charge of 24 C flows through an LED and the potential difference across it is 6 V. Calculate how much energy is transferred. **(3 marks)**

2 Explain why the volt, V, can also be described as a 'joule per coulomb'. **(3 marks)**

3 400 J of energy are transferred through a lamp by 50 C of electric charge. Calculate the potential difference across the lamp. **(4 marks)**

205

Ohm's law

Ohm's law states how the **current** through a component relates to its **resistance** and the **potential difference** across it.

Resistance

The **resistance** of a component is a way of measuring how hard it is for electricity to flow through it. The units for resistance are **ohms (Ω)**.

The resistance of a whole circuit depends on the resistances of the different components in the circuit. The higher the total resistance, the smaller the current.

resistance UP, current DOWN

The resistance of a circuit can be changed by putting different **resistors** into the circuit, or by using a **variable resistor**. The resistance of a variable resistor can be changed using a slider or knob.

Ohm's law

Ohm's law states that the size of the current, *I*, flowing through a component of resistance, *R*, is directly proportional to the potential difference, *V*, across the component at constant temperature.

The equation for Ohm's law is:

potential difference (V) = current (A) × resistance (Ω)

$$V = I \times R$$

LEARN IT!
IT'S NOT ON THE EQUATIONS LIST

Components that obey Ohm's law are said to be ohmic conductors whereas those that do not obey Ohm's law are non-ohmic. Examples of both of these can be found on page 208.

Worked example

(a) Resistor A has a current of 3 A flowing through it when the potential difference across it is 15 V. What is the size of its resistance? **(3 marks)**

From $V = I \times R$ you obtain $R = V / I$

Substituting gives $R = 15V / 3A = 5Ω$

(b) Sketch a circuit that could be used to plot current against potential difference for this resistor. **(4 marks)**

The variable resistor can be used to collect numerous values for *I* and *V* so that an I–V graph can be plotted.

(c) Resistor A is then replaced with resistor B. A graph of current against potential difference is plotted.

Explain what the graph tells you about the two resistors. **(2 marks)**

The steeper line shows that resistor A has a lower resistance than resistor B.

Both resistors are ohmic because the graphs are straight lines.

Now try this

1 A current of 3.2 A flows through a lamp of resistance 18 Ω. Calculate the size of the potential difference across the lamp. **(3 marks)**

2 The potential difference across a resistor is 28 V when the current flowing through it is 0.4 A. Calculate the resistance of the resistor. **(3 marks)**

Resistors

The arrangement of resistors in **series** or **parallel** determines whether the **resistance** in a circuit **increases** or **decreases**.

Resistors in series

Calculating series resistance

For resistors arranged in series:

① The current through each resistor is the same value.

② The sum of the voltages across the resistors must add up to equal the cell voltage.

The total resistance in this series circuit is $12\,\Omega$. The total potential difference from the battery is $6\,V$. Using $I = V \div R$ the current, I, flowing in resistors P and Q, is $6\,V \div 12\,\Omega = 0.5\,A$.

Resistors in parallel

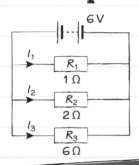

Calculating parallel resistance

For resistors arranged in parallel:

① The total current leaving the battery is equal to the sum of the current flowing in the separate branches.

② The potential difference across the resistors in each branch is equal to the potential difference of the battery.

Worked example

In the series circuit in the diagram, resistor X is known to have a resistance of $16\,\Omega$.

(a) Calculate the missing potential difference value across resistor Y.   **(2 marks)**

8 V, since the values across X and Y must add up to 12 V.

(b) Calculate the current flowing through resistor X.   **(3 marks)**

$I = V \div R = 4\,V \div 16\,\Omega = 0.25\,A$

Worked example

Two resistors are arranged in parallel as shown in the circuit below. Calculate:

(a) the resistance of Y   **(2 marks)**

$R = V \div I = 12\,V \div 0.3\,A = 40\,\Omega$

(b) the current through resistor X   **(2 marks)**

$I = V \div R = 12\,V \div 20\,\Omega = 0.6\,A$

(c) the total current supplied by the battery.   **(2 marks)**

total current = $0.3\,A + 0.6\,A = 0.9\,A$

Now try this

Two resistors, each of resistance 60 ohms, are arranged in series and connected to a 12 V cell. Calculate the size of the current flowing in the circuit.   **(3 marks)**

I–V graphs

An **I–V graph** shows how the **current** flowing through a component varies as the **potential difference** across it varies. You need to know the characteristics of these I–V graphs.

① Fixed resistor

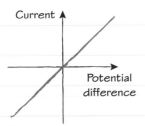

The temperature remains constant so the resistance remains constant. The slope or gradient is constant and the line remains straight throughout.

② Filament lamp

As the potential difference increases, the filament gets hotter, and atomic vibration increases. This leads to greater resistance. The slope or gradient decreases as the potential difference increases since resistance is increasing.

③ Diode

The current only flows in one direction. There is a **threshold** in the forward direction, which is why the graph is flat initially. A diode behaves like a fixed resistor – the resistance does not change. A diode has a very high resistance in the reverse direction.

Drawing an I–V graph

You can use a circuit like this to collect data about current and potential difference.

☑ When the switch is closed you can read current from the ammeter and potential difference from the voltmeter.

☑ Varying the value of the variable resistor allows you to record the current for different potential differences.

☑ You can reverse the cell to obtain negative values for potential difference.

Component to be tested is placed here

Worked example

A student is testing the resistance of a component. She draws an I–V graph.

The component being tested is a

☐ **A** diode

☐ **B** filament lamp

☒ **C** fixed resistor

☐ **D** cell

(1 mark)

An I–V graph always has the current (I) plotted on the vertical y-axis and the potential difference (V) plotted on the horizontal x-axis. To find the resistance of a component from an I–V graph, you will need to divide the x-axis value by the corresponding y-axis value. That is, the gradient is not the resistance, the gradient = I/resistance.

Now try this

Amy is testing the resistance of a filament lamp. She varies the potential difference across the lamp and records the current that flows.

(a) Sketch a graph of potential difference (V) against current (I) for Amy's experiment.
(2 marks)

(b) Explain the shape of your graph.   **(3 marks)**

Electrical circuits

Practical skills You can investigate the relationship between **potential difference**, **current** and **resistance** for a filament lamp and a resistor by arranging them in series and parallel circuits.

Core practical

Aim

To determine the relationship between potential difference, current and resistance for a filament lamp and a resistor when arranged in series and parallel.

Apparatus

- cell or battery, ammeters, voltmeters, filament lamps, resistors, connecting wires

Method 1: Investigating V, I and R

Set up the circuit so that the current through the filament lamp and the potential difference across it can be measured. Adjust the variable resistor setting to obtain a number of readings for current and potential difference. Plot a graph of I against V. Repeat for the resistor.

Results

Your results can be recorded in a table.

Potential difference (V)	Current (I)
−2.0	−0.20
−1.5	−0.18
−1.0	−0.15
−0.5	−0.10
0	0
0.5	0.10
1.0	0.16
1.5	0.18
2.0	0.20

Method 2: Testing series and parallel circuits

Set up the circuits in both parallel and series arrangements and use these to verify the rules for the behaviour of current and potential difference in both types of circuits.

There is more information relating to current, potential difference, resistance and series and parallel circuits on pages 203–208.

Be careful when using electrical circuits as electric current can produce heat and cause burns.

Data collected in an investigation are accurate if close to the true value. The data are precise if the repeat readings of a certain variable are close to one another. The best data is both accurate and precise.

In order to improve the accuracy of your results, place a switch in your circuit so that the current does not get too large. Too large a current leads to a greater value of the resistance being recorded, due to thermal energy causing extra vibrations of the ions in the metal lattice.

Now try this

1 Explain why a series or parallel arrangement will still lead to the same shape of I–V graph for both components. **(4 marks)**

2 Explain why the I–V graph for a filament lamp has the shape that it does. **(5 marks)**

Conclusion

Current is the same at any point in a series circuit, but will split up at a junction in a parallel circuit.

The sum of the potential difference across components in any loop in a series or parallel circuit equals the potential difference of the cell.

The LDR and the thermistor

The resistance of **light-dependent resistors (LDRs)** and **thermistors** changes according to light conditions (LDR) or temperature (thermistor).

Light-dependent resistors

The resistance of a **light-dependent resistor (LDR)** is large in the dark. The resistance gets less if light shines on it. The brighter the light, the lower the resistance.

brightness **UP**, resistance **DOWN**

Thermistors

The resistance of a **thermistor** depends on its temperature. The higher the temperature, the lower the resistance.

temperature **UP**, resistance **DOWN**

Worked example

A 6V battery is connected in series with an LDR, a 300Ω fixed resistor and an ammeter, as shown.

(a) Describe how the circuit shown can be used to explore the variation in resistance as the light levels change. **(2 marks)**

The amount of light being shone on the LDR can be changed by varying the intensity of the light it is exposed to from a torch or a lamp. The size of the current flowing in the circuit can then be recorded for each of these light levels and the resistance can be calculated from R = V ÷ I.

(b) Describe the results you would expect. **(2 marks)**

The output current will be highest when the light level is greatest. As the brightness increases, the LDR's resistance decreases.

(c) How could a voltmeter be used in the circuit to show how the resistance changes with light levels? **(3 marks)**

Connect a voltmeter across the LDR. As the light level increases, the potential difference across the LDR will decrease since the resistance has decreased and a greater share of the 6V will be across the fixed resistor.

Worked example

A 3V battery is connected in series with a thermistor, as shown.

(a) Explain how the circuit can be used to explore how the resistance of the thermistor changes. **(2 marks)**

The thermistor could be immersed in a beaker of cold water, or a water bath, which is then heated from 10°C to 80°C. The current flowing in the circuit is recorded at each temperature over this range and the resistance can be calculated from R = V ÷ I.

(b) Describe what your results would show. **(2 marks)**

As the temperature increases, the current increases. This is because the thermistor's resistance decreases as it gets warmer.

If a buzzer was placed in this circuit then it could be used as a simple fire alarm, with the buzzer sounding when the current reached a certain value. This could be controlled or calibrated by using a variable resistor.

Now try this

1 State what affects the resistance of (a) a thermistor and (b) an LDR. **(2 marks)**

2 Describe how an LDR and a thermistor could be used together in a circuit. **(4 marks)**

Current heating effect

When a **current** flows in a circuit it has a **heating** effect. This can have **advantages** and **disadvantages**.

Energy transfers in a resistor

When there is an electric current flowing through a resistor, energy is transferred which heats the resistor.

Electrical energy is **dissipated** as thermal energy in the surroundings when an electrical current does work against electrical resistance.

Unwanted thermal energy transfers can be reduced by using low-resistance wires. Wires that are better conductors, shorter or thicker will waste less energy as heat compared with longer, thinner wires of a poorer electrical conductor.

Energy and collisions

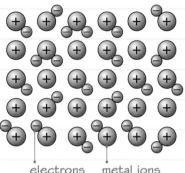

electrons   metal ions

Electrons flow through a metal lattice when a potential difference is applied across the ends of the metal. Collisions between the electrons and the ions in the lattice lead to the kinetic energy of the electrons being dissipated as thermal energy.

Advantages of the heating effect

Some appliances such as the iron, the heater and the fuse are designed to transfer energy to thermal energy by the heating effect of a current.

The heating effect of a current passing through a resistor is useful for:

- heating water in a kettle
- radiant heaters
- toasters, grills and ovens
- underfloor heating.

Disadvantages of the heating effect

If too much current flows in a circuit, then the heating effect can lead to the appliance catching fire or the user becoming burned.

Too much current can flow if too many appliances are being used at the same time. Safety features such as correct fuses, circuit breakers and earthing need to be in place. See page 214.

In many devices, the heating effect of a current means that some energy is wasted. For example, a light bulb and a TV screen transfer some energy to thermal energy by the heating effect of a current.

Worked example

Give three examples of appliances in the home where the heating effect of the current causes energy to be wasted as thermal energy.

(1 mark)

a computer, computer monitor and a mobile phone screen

Worked example

Explain how energy is transferred to thermal energy in a resistor. **(3 marks)**

Collisions between the moving electrons and the fixed metal ions in a lattice result in the kinetic energy of the electrons being transferred to thermal energy. The thermal energy is dissipated into the surroundings.

Now try this

1   Name three household devices that usefully transfer electrical energy to thermal energy.

(3 marks)

2   Explain why it might be dangerous to have many electrical appliances being used at the same time. **(3 marks)**

3   Explain how electrical energy is dissipated as thermal energy when a potential difference is applied across the ends of a metal wire.

(4 marks)

Dissipated means energy lost to surroundings.

211

Energy and power

Electrical energy is **transferred** in circuits to do **work**. The amount of energy transferred depends on the **current**, **time** and **potential difference**.

Calculating energy

The total energy transferred by a device depends on the current in it, the potential difference across it and how long it is switched on.

$$\text{Energy transferred (J)} = \text{current (A)} \times \text{potential difference (V)} \times \text{time (s)}$$

$$E = I \times V \times t$$

📇 **Maths skills** Cover up the quantity you want to find with your finger. The position of the other quantities tells you the formula.

$$V = E \div (I \times t)$$
$$I = E \div (V \times t)$$
$$t = E \div (V \times I)$$

Calculating power

Power is the energy transferred per second or the rate at which energy is transferred. It is measured in **watts**. For electrical devices, power depends on the current in the device and the potential difference across it, or the resistance of the device. It also depends on the total energy transferred and the time taken to transfer the energy.

📇 **Maths skills** The equation triangles for power can be used in the same way as for energy calculations.

There are three equations you need to know that can be used to calculate power:

1 electrical power (W) = current (A) × potential difference (V)
$$P = I \times V$$

LEARN IT! IT'S NOT ON THE EQUATIONS LIST

2 power (W) = energy transferred (J) ÷ time taken (s)
$$P = E \div t$$

LEARN IT! IT'S NOT ON THE EQUATIONS LIST

3 electrical power (W) = current squared (A²) × resistance (Ω)
$$P = I^2 \times R$$

LEARN IT! IT'S NOT ON THE EQUATIONS LIST

Worked example

(a) A current of 8 A flows for 4 minutes in a kettle that is connected to a potential difference of 230 V. Calculate how much energy is transferred. **(4 marks)**

$E = V \times I \times t$

$E = 230\,V \times 8\,A \times (4 \times 60)\,s = 441\,600\,J$

(b) A 2.2 kW hairdryer is used for 5 minutes. Calculate how much energy is transferred. **(4 marks)**

$E = P \times t$

$= 2200\,W \times (5 \times 60)\,s = 660\,000\,J$

Worked example

(a) Calculate the power of a microwave that transfers 30 000 J of energy in 35 s. **(4 marks)**

$P = E \div t$
$= 30\,000\,J \div 35\,s = 857\,W$

(b) Calculate the current that is taken by a device with a power rating of 3400 W when its resistance is 120 Ω. **(4 marks)**

$I = \sqrt{(P \div R)} = \sqrt{(3400\,W \div 120\,Ω)} = 5.3\,A$

Power can be measured in watts (W) or in joules per second (J/s). A power of 1 W means that 1 J of energy is being transferred each second.

Now try this

1 Calculate the power of an electric oven when 13 A flows through it when it is connected to the 230 V mains supply. **(3 marks)**

2 A current of 1.5 A flows for 2 minutes when a potential difference of 12 V is applied across the ends of a resistor. Calculate the amount of energy that is transferred. **(3 marks)**

A.c. and d.c. circuits

Circuits can be operated using **alternating current (a.c.)** or **direct current (d.c.)**.

Direct current

An **electric current** in a wire is a flow of electrons. The current supplied by **cells** and **batteries** is **direct current (d.c.)**. In a direct current the electrons all flow in the same direction.

cell

Electrons are pushed out of one end of the cell.

Electrons flow round to the other end of the cell.

There must be a complete circuit for the electrons to flow.

The oscilloscope trace for d.c. from a battery is a horizontal line. The potential difference can be read off the vertical scale.

The potential difference above has a constant value of 2.8 V.

Alternating current

Mains electricity supplied to homes and businesses is an **alternating current (a.c.)**. Alternating current is an electric current that changes direction regularly, and its potential difference is constantly changing.

For an a.c. supply, the movement of charge is constantly changing direction. The mains supply has an average working value of 230 V and a frequency of 50 Hz. This means that the electric current and voltage change direction 100 times every second.

D.c. and a.c. supply in the home

Both d.c. and a.c. can be used in the home. D.c. is supplied in the form of cells and batteries. A.c. is the mains supply. Both can be used by devices to transfer energy to motors and heating devices.

Different electrical appliances have different power ratings. The power rating tells you how much energy is transferred by the appliance each second.

Appliance	Power rating
kettle	2200 W
hairdryer	1500 W
microwave	850 W
electric oven	3000 W
electric shaver	15 W

Worked example

Compare the power rating of a hairdryer and an electric shaver, and the changes in stored energy when they are in use. **(4 marks)**

The hairdryer has a power rating of 1500 W, which means that it transfers 1500 J per second to stores of kinetic energy and thermal energy. The electric shaver has a power rating of one-hundredth of the hair dryer. It transfers only 15 J per second, mainly to a kinetic energy store.

Now try this

1 Give three examples of devices that use
   (a) d.c. **(3 marks)**
   (b) a.c. **(3 marks)**
2 Explain how a.c. and d.c. are
   (a) similar **(1 mark)**
   (b) different. **(2 marks)**
3 A 15 W electric shaver and a 3000 W electric oven are both used for the same amount of time. Compare the amount of energy transferred for the two appliances.
   (3 marks)

Mains electricity and the plug

Electrical energy enters UK homes as **mains electricity** at **230V a.c.** A mains plug has three wires, which have different roles in the operation of a.c. in the home.

The 13A plug

The earth (yellow and green) wire does not form part of the circuit but acts as a safety feature along with the fuse.

The neutral (blue) wire completes the circuit with the appliance. It is at a potential difference of 0V with respect to the earth wire.

The live, neutral and earth wires are made from copper, but covered in colour-coded insulating plastic so that the consumer is not exposed to a dangerous voltage.

The live (brown) wire carries the supply to the appliance. It is at a potential difference of 230V with respect to the neutral and earth wires.

The fuse is connected to the live wire and it contains a wire that will melt if the current gets too high. If the fuse blows, the device will be at 0V and not at 230V. A switch should also be connected in the live wire for the same reason.

Earthing and fuses

Earthing and fuses are safety features that are used to ensure that the user does not get electrocuted if a fault occurs.

Fuses

① The large current heats and melts the wire in the fuse, making a break in the circuit.

② The circuit is no longer complete, so there is no chance of electric shock or fire.

Earthing

① The live wire inside the appliance may come loose and touch a metal part of the device's casing.

② The earth wire is connected to the metal casing and a large current flows in through the live wire and out through the earth wire.

③ By having an earth wire connected to the metal casing, the user is not at risk if the live wire comes loose and touches anything metallic.

Worked example

(a) State the potential differences of the live, neutral and earth wires in a plug. **(3 marks)**

live: 230V; neutral and earth: both at 0V

(b) Name three safety features used by appliances. **(3 marks)**

earth wire, fuse and circuit breaker

Circuit breakers are also used as safety features in addition to fuses and earth wires. When circuit breakers detect that a current is too high, they use a magnetic field to open a switch and isolate the appliance, making it safe. They are easily reset by pressing a switch if they trip.

Now try this

1 State the colours of the
   (a) live wire **(1 mark)**
   (b) neutral wire **(1 mark)**
   (c) earth wire. **(1 mark)**

2 Give one advantage of a fuse and one advantage of a circuit breaker. **(2 marks)**

3 Explain how an earth wire and fuse protect the user when the live wire comes loose. **(4 marks)**

Extended response – Electricity and circuits

There will be one or more 6-mark questions on your exam paper. For these questions, you will need to think scientifically and structure your answer logically, showing how the points you make are related to each other. You can revise the topics for this question, which is about **electricity and circuits**, on pages 202–214.

on pages 202–214.

Worked example

Two identical bulbs can be connected to a 6 V cell in series or parallel as shown in the diagram.

Compare the brightness of the bulbs in the two circuits when the switches are closed.

Your answer should refer to the current, potential difference, energy stores and rates of energy transfer in both circuits.

(6 marks)

The brightness of the bulbs in the series circuit will be much less than the brightness of the bulbs in the parallel circuit.

The electrical energy that is transferred to light is directly proportional to the potential difference across each bulb and the size of the current flowing through each bulb. The brightness of the bulbs will be greatest when the energy transferred per second is greatest.

In the series circuit, the potential difference across each bulb will be 3 V, whereas in the parallel circuit the potential difference across each bulb will be 6 V. Also, the current flowing through each of the bulbs in the parallel circuit will be greater than the current flowing through the bulbs in the series circuit. Since the current and the potential difference in the parallel bulbs are greater, more energy will be transferred per second and the bulb will be brighter.

 The opening sentence simply states how the brightness of the lamps compares in each of the two circuits.

 The answer then states the relationship between electrical energy, current and potential difference before relating brightness to the energy transferred per second, or power, of the bulbs.

 The comparison of the bulbs' brightness is related to the relative sizes of any current, potential difference and energy transferred per second.

The rate at which energy is transferred from one form to another is called power. When dealing with electrical circuits, the power is calculated using the equation $P = IV$. You can read more about this on page 212.

You can read more about this on page 212.

Now try this

The UK mains electricity supply operates at 230 V a.c. Explain how safety features help to keep users safe. Your answer should refer to the structure and function of a plug. **(6 marks)**

Magnets and magnetic fields

Certain materials can be magnetised to become **permanent** or **temporary magnets**.

Magnets and magnetic fields

Like magnetic poles **repel**. **Unlike** magnetic poles **attract**.

The magnetic field is strongest at the poles. The field lines are shown to be closer together and more concentrated.

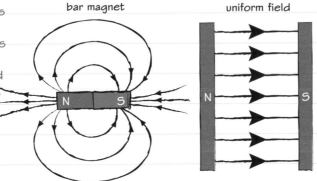

Magnetic field lines are always from N to S.

The field is constant. This is shown by parallel, equally spaced field lines.

Permanent and induced magnets

Magnetic materials include **cobalt, steel, iron, nickel** and magnadur.

A **permanent magnet** has poles which are N and S all of the time. They are made from steel or magnadur.

A **temporary magnet** can be magnetised by bringing a permanent magnet near to it. When the permanent magnet is removed, the temporary magnet loses its magnetism.

Uses of magnets

Permanent	Temporary
fridge magnets	electromagnets
compasses	circuit breakers
motors and generators	electric bells
loudspeakers	magnetic relays
door closers on fridges	

Plotting compasses

A plotting compass is used to plot the shape and direction of magnetic lines of force. You can do this by laying a bar magnet on a piece of paper. Put the plotting compass by one pole of the magnet. Draw a dot by the needle away from the magnet. Move the plotting compass so that the other point is by the dot you have just drawn. Continue doing this until you have mapped all the way around the magnet.

The Earth's magnetic field has the same pattern as that of a bar magnet and can be plotted using a plotting compass. The behaviour of compasses is evidence that the Earth has a magnetic field.

Worked example

What will the plotting compass needle look like when it is placed at point 1?   **(1 mark)**

☐ A: ⊙→
☑ B: ⊙↙
☐ C: ←⊙
☐ D: ⊙→

Explain how you can tell if a magnetic material is a permanent or a temporary magnet.   **(2 marks)**

A temporary magnetic material will always be attracted by a magnet, but a permanent magnet can be both attracted and repelled.

A magnadur magnet can be used to do this. Magnadur magnets are ceramic and have their poles on the larger flat faces.

Now try this

1 Draw the field lines for
   (a) a weak bar magnet   **(2 marks)**
   (b) a strong uniform field.   **(2 marks)**

2 Explain why unmagnetised iron is always attracted by a permanent magnet.   **(3 marks)**

3 Describe how a permanent and a temporary magnet are different from each other.   **(3 marks)**

Current and magnetism

An **electric current** will create a **magnetic field**. The **shape**, **direction** and **strength** of the field depend on a number of factors.

The magnetic field around a long straight conductor

The shape of the magnetic field around a long straight conductor can be thought of as a series of concentric circles.

Be careful! Do not confuse the direction of the current with electron flow. You need to use the direction of conventional current which is taken to be from + to –.

If you point the thumb of your right hand in the direction of the flow of conventional current, the direction that your fingers curl will be the direction of the magnetic field.

The strength of the magnetic field depends on:
- the size of the current in the wire: it is directly proportional to the current.
- the distance from the wire: it is inversely proportional to the distance from the wire.

The direction of the magnetic field depends on the direction of the electric current in the conductor.

You can use plotting compasses or iron filings to show the circular shape of the magnetic field around a current-carrying wire.

The solenoid

The magnetic field lines of the individual coils in a solenoid add up to give a very strong, uniform field along the centre of the solenoid. However, the field lines cancel to give a weaker field outside the solenoid.

Worked example

Explain how the strength of a magnetic field due to a current in a long straight wire changes when:
(a) the current increases   **(1 mark)**
It will increase.
(b) the distance increases.   **(1 mark)**
It will decrease.

📊 **Maths skills** **Directly proportional** means that as **one variable increases** the other **variable increases** at **the same rate**. If the current doubles, the magnetic field strength will also double.

📊 **Maths skills** **Inversely proportional** means that as **one variable increases** the other **decreases**. If the distance doubles, the field strength halves.

Now try this

1. Draw the magnetic field around a wire when the current is flowing downwards.   **(2 marks)**
2. The current flowing in a long straight wire and the distance from the wire are both doubled. Explain what effect this will have on the magnetic field strength.   **(3 marks)**
3. Suggest how the magnetic field strength inside a solenoid could be increased.   **(3 marks)**

Extended response – Magnetism and the motor effect

There will be one or more 6-mark questions on your exam paper. For these questions, you will need to think scientifically and structure your answer logically, showing how the points you make are related to each other. You can revise the topics for this question, which is about **magnetism** and the **motor effect**, on pages 216 and 217.

Worked example

A wire is arranged vertically as shown, with plotting compasses placed around it.

$I = 0$

Explain what happens once a current starts to flow in the wire.

Your answer should refer to what happens when the current, and the distance of the plotting compasses from the wire, are changed, and how the size of the magnetic field would change if measured with a meter. **(6 marks)**

At first, there is no current flowing in the wire, and the plotting compass needles all point in the same direction because they are aligned with the Earth's magnetic field.

When a current flows in a long straight wire, a circular magnetic field is produced around the wire and the compass needles will re-align to point in a circular direction. This will be clockwise if the current is in one direction and will be anticlockwise if the direction of the current is reversed.

The magnetic field will be stronger if the current is increased, and it will be stronger closer to the wire, and get smaller the further away from the wire you go.

Command word: Explain

When you are asked to **explain** something, it is not enough to just state or describe something. Your answer **must** contain some reasoning or justification of the points you make based on the appropriate physics. This needs to be communicated clearly using good spelling, punctuation and grammar.

The answer starts by stating how the compass needles are behaving before any current flows in the wire.

The answer then mentions that a magnetic effect is caused by the current, leading to a circular magnetic field around the wire.

The answer then mentions how changing the current and the distance affects the strength of the magnetic field.

Now try this

Magnetism can be used to attract a variety of materials of different masses. Explain how the strength of the magnetic field can be changed to make this possible. Your answer should refer to how the size of the magnetic field strength can be changed **with** and **without** the use of an **electric current**. **(6 marks)**

Transformers

Transformers can be used to **change the size** of an **alternating voltage** or **current**.
Electricity is transmitted across the UK by the National Grid.

Transformers

A transformer can be used to change the potential difference of an alternating electricity supply.

A transformer is made of two coils of insulated wire which are wound onto an iron core. There is no electrical connection between the two coils of wire.

Remember that the **primary coil** is the one connected to the electricity supply.

The National Grid

1 **Fossil fuels** or **nuclear fuel** are used to generate electrical energy.

2 A **step-up transformer** increases the voltage. For a fixed amount of electrical energy or power output, increasing the voltage means there will be a decrease in current. Electrical energy is transmitted at a high voltage and low current to reduce energy losses as heat in the wires. It also means thinner wires can be used, which reduces costs.

3 **Step-down transformers** decrease the voltages from the National Grid for safer use in our homes and industry. Reducing the voltage means there will be an increase in current.

Transformer efficiency

It is assumed that transformers are 100% efficient. They are connected by the equation:

$$V_p \times I_p = V_s \times I_s$$

| potential difference across primary coil (V) | × | current in primary coil (A) | = | potential difference across secondary coil (V) | × | current in secondary coil (A) |

Worked example

A transformer has a potential difference of 12 V a.c. across its primary coil and a current of 18 A flowing in the primary coil. The potential difference across the secondary coil is 144 V. Calculate the current flowing in the secondary coil.   **(4 marks)**

$$V_p \times I_p = V_s \times I_s$$
$$12V \times 18A = 144V \times I_s$$
$$I_s = 12V \times 18A \div 144V$$
$$= 1.5A$$

Now try this

1 Explain why electrical energy is transmitted at a high voltage and a low current on the National Grid.   **(3 marks)**

2 A transformer has a potential difference of 24 V across the primary coil. The potential difference across the secondary coil is 120 V and the current through it is 0.5 A. Calculate the current in the primary coil.   **(4 marks)**

Extended response – Electromagnetic induction

There will be one or more 6-mark questions on your exam paper. For these questions, you will need to think scientifically and structure your answer logically, showing how the points you make are related to each other. You can revise the topics for this question, which is about **the national grid**, on page 219.

Worked example

High voltage transmission lines

Consumers, for example homes, factories and shops

Power station   Step-up transformer   Step-down transformer

Electrical energy is transferred to consumers by the National Grid. Explain how electrical energy is transferred so that the process is as efficient as possible.

Your answer should refer to any changes in current or potential difference during the transmission of electricity across the UK in the National Grid.

This electrical power needs to be transmitted to consumers as efficiently as possible, which means that as little power as possible is wasted to the surroundings as thermal energy. Since the equation for electrical power is given by power = current × potential difference, the energy can be transmitted at a high current or at a high potential difference.

The potential difference is increased at the power station by step-up transformers. This means that the potential difference is increased and the current in the transmission lines is decreased so that energy lost by heating is minimised. The greater the current, the more energy is dissipated as thermal energy, so the current is kept low and the potential difference high.

Transformers are designed to be almost 100% efficient since they waste very little energy to the surroundings in the form of thermal energy. Step-down transformers are then used to decrease the potential difference to safe, manageable levels in homes. The current increases according to the power equation.

Command word: Explain

When you are asked to explain something, it is not enough to just state or describe something. Your answer must contain some reasoning or justification of the points you make based on the appropriate physics. This needs to be communicated clearly using good spelling, punctuation and grammar.

The answer starts by explaining the role of the National Grid and a quick explanation of the term efficiency. The equation for power is stated, as well as how electrical energy can be transmitted across the UK.

The role of a step-up transformer is explained, as is the principle of conservation of energy or power – there is a fixed amount of power to be transmitted, so if the potential difference increases, the current must decrease so that the amount of power remains constant throughout.

In addition to having an efficient process by having a low current, a mention is made that transformers are designed to be efficient as they waste very little energy when stepping up or stepping down potential differences.

Now try this

Transformers are used to step up and step down potential difference in the transmission of electricity across the UK. Explain how transformers work and why electricity is transmitted at a large voltage and a small current in the transmission lines of pylons.

Your answer should refer to an equation that relates power loss to electric current.

(6 marks)

Changes of state

Substances can change from one state of matter to another. The **change of state** depends on whether **energy is gained** or **lost** by the substance.

The three states of matter

solid   liquid   gas

In a solid the particles vibrate but they cannot move freely.

In a liquid the particles can move past each other and move around randomly.

In a gas the particles move around very fast and they move all the time. This is because they have a lot of **kinetic energy**.

Changing state

Changes of state are **physical** changes rather than chemical changes and they can be reversed.

The mass before the change is equal to the mass after the change. For example, when 500 kg of a solid melts it becomes 500 kg of a liquid.

When a body is heated or cooled, its temperature will change if its state of matter does not change. For example, if 750 ml of a liquid is heated, then the temperature will increase until it reaches its boiling point.

When a material changes state, it does so at a **constant** temperature. For example, when water boils, 1 kg of water at 100°C will turn to 1 kg of steam at 100°C. For more about this, see page 224.

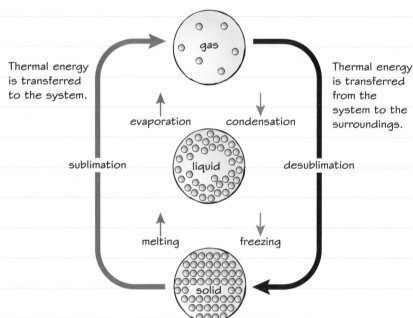

Thermal energy is transferred to the system.

Thermal energy is transferred from the system to the surroundings.

evaporation   condensation

sublimation   desublimation

melting   freezing

Worked example

Describe what happens when 2.0 kg of steam is allowed to cool against a glass plate, collected and then placed in a freezer. **(4 marks)**

2.0 kg of water will be produced when the steam turns to water at 100°C. It will then cool as a liquid from 100°C to room temperature. When placed in the freezer it will cool down from room temperature and turn to ice at 0°C before continuing to cool to around −18°C.

Now try this

1 Describe what happens when 1.5 kg of ice is left on a kitchen bench. **(3 marks)**

2 What effect does cooling a gas have on its pressure and volume? **(3 marks)**

3 Describe what happens when 200 kg of solid copper is heated to beyond its boiling point. **(5 marks)**

Density

The **density** of a material is a measure of the **amount of matter** that it contains **per unit volume**.

Density, mass and volume

Changing the amount of material will change **both** its mass and its volume. If the volume of a block of a particular material is doubled, its mass will also double.

The density of a material does not vary greatly for a given state of matter and relates to how closely packed the atoms or molecules are within the volume that it occupies.

The density of a material in the different states of matter varies greatly because of the arrangement of the particles in the state.

solid   liquid   gas

In a **solid**, the particles are closely packed together. The number of particles in a given volume is high.

In a **liquid**, the particles are usually less densely packed than in a solid. The number of particles in a given volume is less than for a solid. Solids are high density.

In a **gas**, the particles are spread out. The number of particles in a given volume is low. Gases are low density.

Calculating density

You can calculate density using the equation:

$$\text{density (kg/m}^3) = \frac{\text{mass (kg)}}{\text{volume (m}^3)}$$

$$\rho = \frac{m}{v}$$

LEARN IT! IT'S NOT ON THE EQUATIONS LIST

Changing the volume of a substance will change its mass, but its density will be constant.

Other units for density can also be used, such as g/cm^3. The density of copper is $8.96\,g/cm^3$. This means that every $1\,cm^3$ of copper metal has a mass of $8.96\,g$.

Worked example

(a) A body has a mass of 34 000 kg and a volume of 18 m³. Calculate its density. **(4 marks)**

density = mass ÷ volume
      = 34 000 kg ÷ 18 m³
      = 1900 kg/m³

(b) Calculate the mass of 0.2 m³ of this material. **(4 marks)**

mass = density × volume
    = 1900 kg/m³ × 0.2 m³ = 380 kg

🖩 Maths skills Using correct units

When performing calculations involving density, mass and volume check that:

☑ you are using the correct equation to find density, mass or volume

☑ the units are consistent.

When the mass is in kg and the volume is in m³ then the density will be in kg/m³. Sometimes you may be dealing with g and cm³, so check the units.

Worked example

A solid has a density of 3.6 g/cm³ and a mass of 320 g. Calculate its volume. **(4 marks)**

volume = mass ÷ density
     = 320 g ÷ 3.6 g/cm³ = 88.9 cm³

🖩 Maths skills Checking units

Since volume = mass ÷ density then the units here will be g ÷ g/cm³. This is the same as g × cm³/g, which means the grams cancel and we are left with cm³ – a unit of volume.

Now try this

1 Calculate the density of a material that has a mass of 862 g and a volume of 765 cm³. **(3 marks)**

2 The density of aluminium is 2700 kg/m³. Calculate the mass of a block of aluminium with a volume of 50 000 cm³. **(4 marks)**

Investigating density

 Practical skills You can measure the volume and mass of solids and liquids to determine their densities.

Core practical

Aim

To determine the densities of solids and liquids.

Apparatus

- measuring cylinder, displacement can, electronic balance, ruler, various solids and liquids

Method 1 (for a solid)

1 Measure the mass of the solid using an electronic balance and record its mass in your results table.

2 Determine the volume of the solid. This can be done by measuring its dimensions and using a formula, or by using a displacement can to see how much liquid it displaces. Record this value in your results table.

Method 2 (for a liquid)

1 Find the mass of the liquid by placing the measuring cylinder on the scales, and then zeroing the scales with no liquid present in the measuring cylinder. Add the liquid to the desired level.

2 Record the mass of the liquid in g from the balance and its volume in cm³ from the measuring cylinder.

Be careful to read the volume value correctly – at the bottom of the meniscus.

Results

Your results can be recorded in a table.

Material	Mass (g)	Volume (cm³)	Density (g/cm³)

Find the densities of the solid and liquid by using the equation density = mass ÷ volume.

Conclusion

The densities of a solid and a liquid can be determined by finding their respective masses and volumes. Dividing the mass by the volume gives you the density of the solid or liquid.

There is more information about the relationship between mass, volume and density on page 222.

Be careful to use solids and liquids that are safe to use in this investigation. Mercury (a liquid metal) was used in these investigations until it was found to be carcinogenic.

When taking volume readings, make sure that you read the scales with your eye at the same level as the meniscus. Otherwise a parallax error will arise and your values will be incorrect.

🖩 Maths skills **Converting between units**

Density can be given in g/cm³ or kg/m³.

Since 1 kg = 1000 g and 1 m³ = 1 000 000 cm³:
- to convert from g/cm³ to kg/m³ multiply by 1000
- to convert from kg/m³ to g/cm³ divide by 1000.

For example, water has a density of 1 g/cm³ or 1000 kg/m³.

Now try this

1 A measuring cylinder is placed on an electronic balance and its display is set to zero. The measuring cylinder is then filled with a liquid up to a volume of 256 cm³. The mass shown is 454 g. Calculate the density of the liquid. **(3 marks)**

2 Explain how misreading the mass and volume values may occur and how this can lead to a higher than normal density value. **(4 marks)**

Energy and changes of state

You can calculate how much energy you need to **change the temperature** and **state** of a substance.

Specific heat capacity

Specific heat capacity is the **thermal energy** that must be **transferred** to change the **temperature** of **1 kg** of a material **by 1 °C**. Different materials have different specific heat capacities. Water has a value of 4200 J/kg °C, which means that 1 kg of water needs 4200 J of thermal energy to be transferred to raise its temperature by 1 °C.

You can calculate the thermal energy required using the equation: $\Delta Q = m \times c \times \Delta\theta$

$$\underset{(J)}{\text{change in thermal energy}} = \underset{(kg)}{\text{mass}} \times \underset{(J/kg \,°C)}{\text{specific heat capacity}} \times \underset{(°C)}{\text{change in temperature}}$$

Specific latent heat

Specific latent heat is the **energy** that must be transferred to change **1 kg** of a material from one **state of matter to another**. There are usually two values for specific latent heat:

1 the **specific latent heat of fusion** when the change of state is between a solid and a liquid – during **melting** or **freezing**

2 the **specific latent heat of vaporisation** when the change of state is between a liquid and a gas – during **boiling** or **condensation**.

You can calculate the thermal energy required using the equation:

thermal energy for a change of state (J) = mass (kg) × specific latent heat (J/kg)

$$Q = m \times L$$

Specific latent heat should **not** be confused with specific heat capacity. Calculations involving **specific latent heat** involve changes of state and **never involve a change in temperature**, since **changes of state always occur** at a **constant temperature**.

Worked example

(a) A mass of 800 g has a specific heat capacity of 900 J/kg °C and is heated from 20 °C to 80 °C. Calculate how much thermal energy was supplied. **(3 marks)**

$\Delta Q = m \times c \times \Delta\theta$

$0.8 \times 900 \times (80 - 20) = 43\,200\,J$

(b) Calculate the energy required to convert 40 kg of ice at 0 °C to liquid water at 0 °C. The specific latent heat of fusion of water is 334 000 J/kg. **(3 marks)**

$Q = m \times L$

$Q = 40 \times 334\,000 = 13\,360\,000\,J$

Worked example

Ice at –40 °C is heated until it becomes steam at 110 °C. Sketch a graph to show the changes that take place during this process.

Now try this

1 Calculate the energy required to raise the temperature of 15 kg of water from 18 °C to 74 °C. **(3 marks)**

2 Calculate the amount of energy that needs to be supplied to convert 20 kg of ice at 0°C into 20 kg of water at 0°C. **(3 marks)**

Thermal properties of water

🧪 **Practical skills**   You can determine the specific heat capacity of water using an electric heater. You can also observe how water behaves when a sample of ice is melted.

Core practical

Aim

To determine the specific heat capacity of water.

Apparatus

- water, ice, thermometers, electric heater, power supply, insulation, beakers, electronic balance

Method

1. Set the apparatus up as shown in the diagram.

2. Measure the mass (m) of the water using an electronic balance.

3. Record the potential difference (V) of the power supply and the current (I) through the heater.

thermometer

to power supply

electric heater

4. Take temperature readings every 30 seconds for a time (t). Observe the state of water at each reading. Record the initial and final temperatures of the water and find the change in temperature (ΔT).

Results

Plot a graph of temperature against time. Calculate the specific heat capacity. The value c is found by substituting the results into the equation $c = (V \times I \times t) / (m \times \Delta T)$.

Conclusion

The specific heat capacity of water is the energy required to change 1 kg of water by a temperature of 1 °C. Its value is about 4200 J/kg °C.

There is more information about specific heat capacity on page 224, and more information about the energy transferred by a known current and potential difference on page 212.

Having insulation around the beaker will transfer less energy to the surroundings and give a more accurate value for the specific heat capacity of the water.

When recording the temperature readings, avoid parallax errors by reading the thermometer scale at eye level. Record the temperature values regularly, at equal intervals and ensure that the thermometer is in the middle of the liquid.

A graph of temperature against time for ice melting to water is shown here.

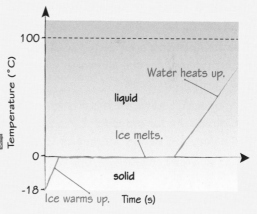

The word 'specific' here in this context is for 1 kg of mass. In other words, the values for specific heat capacity is for when 1 kg changes temperature by 1°C.

Now try this

1. Explain why insulating the beaker leads to a more accurate value for the specific heat capacity of water. **(3 marks)**

2. Describe when
   (a) heating water leads to a change in temperature **(2 marks)**
   (b) heating water does not lead to a change in temperature. **(2 marks)**

3. Draw the apparatus that would allow you to obtain the temperature–time graph of melting ice. **(3 marks)**

Pressure and temperature

The **pressure** of a **gas** can be explained in terms of the motion of its particles.

The pressure of a gas

Gas pressure depends on the motion of the particles in the gas. Gas particles strike the walls of a container at many different angles.

Pressure can be increased by:
- **increasing** the **temperature** of the gas
- **increasing** the **mass** of the gas
- **decreasing** the **volume** of the gas.

Pressure and temperature

The **pressure** of a **fixed mass** of **gas** at a **constant volume** depends on the **temperature** of the gas. When the temperature increases:

1. The gas molecules have a greater average kinetic energy.

2. The gas molecules move faster.

3. There are more collisions between the molecules and the walls of the container each second.

4. More force is exerted on the same area each second.

5. The pressure of the gas increases.

Absolute zero

As a gas is cooled the average speed of its particles falls and its volume gets smaller. At −273 °C the gas volume shrinks to zero. This temperature is called **absolute zero**. This is the zero temperature on the Kelvin scale. 0 K is equivalent to −273 °C.

The temperature of a gas is directly proportional to the average kinetic energy of the gas molecules.

Volume is directly proportional to temperature in Kelvin

To convert between the Kelvin and Celsius scales use the appropriate formula:
- Celsius → Kelvin **add** 273 to the Celsius temperature.
- Kelvin → Celsius **subtract** 273 from the Kelvin temperature.

Worked example

Explain gas pressure using kinetic theory.   **(3 marks)**

The particles (atoms or molecules) in a gas are continuously moving in a random way and colliding with the container walls. The force from these collisions produces pressure on the walls. On average the number and force of collisions is the same in all directions, so pressure is the same on all the walls of the container.

Worked example

Convert
(a) 150 °C to Kelvin   **(1 mark)**
150 + 273 = 423 K
(b) 150 K to degrees Celsius.   **(1 mark)**
150 − 273 = −123 °C

Now try this

1 (a) Convert 20 °C to its temperature on the Kelvin scale.   **(1 mark)**
   (b) Convert 300 K to its equivalent temperature on the Celsius scale.   **(1 mark)**
2 The temperature of a gas is doubled from 300 K to 600 K. Explain what happens to the average kinetic energy of the molecules in the gas when this happens.   **(3 marks)**
3 (a) State what happens to the average speed of gas particles as a gas is cooled.   **(1 mark)**
   (b) Explain the effect this has on the pressure of the gas in a rigid sealed container.   **(2 marks)**

Extended response – Density

There will be one or more 6-mark questions on your exam paper. For these questions, you will need to think scientifically and structure your answer logically, showing how the points you make are related to each other. You can revise the topics for this question, which is about the **particle model**, on pages 221–226.

Worked example

A team of investigators has been asked to determine whether rings being sold in a jeweller's shop are made from pure gold or whether they are fake.

Explain how the investigators could determine whether the rings were made from pure gold, which has a density of 19.3 g/cm³.

Your answer should refer to a suitable experimental method that will allow you to determine the density of the material and any equations you would need before use. **(6 marks)**

0.0000g

Density = mass ÷ volume; it is the mass per unit volume of a material. It is fixed for a substance in a given phase of matter.

> The answer starts with a brief explanation of what density is, as well as stating the equation.

To find the mass of a ring, we would put it on the electronic balance and get its mass in grams. To find the volume of the ring, we would lower it into a measuring cylinder of water and find the difference in the volume readings on the measuring cylinder scale. We do this by subtracting the volume reading before the ring has been submerged in the water from the volume reading after the ring has been submerged. This difference in volume is equal to the volume of the ring in cm³. Dividing the value for the mass of the ring in g by the volume of the ring in cm³ will get the value for the density of the ring in g/cm³.

> The method addresses how the mass and volume can be calculated. You could also refer to the use of a displacement can to determine the ring's volume.

If the value obtained for the density is very close to 19.3 g/cm³ then the ring *might be* made from gold. If the density is very different from the value of 19.3 g/cm³ then it is not pure gold.

> The final part of the answer explains how the density value obtained tells you whether the material is gold or not – notice how the answer states that the ring *might be* gold, since you cannot say for definite as other materials may have this density.

When you structure your answer, make sure that you address the question in an order that allows you to deal with each of the points being asked for. Do not just list equations and facts. Communicate to the examiner that you understand how to find the density of the rings and how it will allow you to determine if the rings are real or fake based on the known value for the density of gold.

Now try this

A gas contains many particles moving with random motion in a container of a fixed volume.

Explain how the pressure of a gas can be increased by changing temperature.

Your answer should refer to energy, forces and the motion of the particles in the gas. **(6 marks)**

Elastic and inelastic distortion

The distortion of a material may be described as being **elastic** or **inelastic** and **requires more than one force**.

Bending, stretching and compressing

compression

Bending requires two forces, one acting clockwise and one acting anticlockwise.

Stretching requires two forces of tension, acting away from each other.

Compression involves two equal forces acting towards one another.

Elastic distortion

Elastic distortion means that a material will return to its original shape when the deforming force is removed.

The stretched elastic bands return to their original shape after the distorting force is removed. They have undergone elastic distortion.

Inelastic distortion

Inelastic distortion means that a material will not return to its original shape when the deforming force is removed.

before   after

This spring has not returned to its original shape after being distorted, so it has undergone inelastic distortion.

Worked example

Describe what this graph shows for a spring that has been stretched. **(3 marks)**

Initially, the relationship between force and extension is linear, so the behaviour of the spring is elastic for smaller forces.

Point P is the elastic limit. For forces applied after this, the relationship is no longer linear and the spring will not return to its original shape – it will exhibit inelastic distortion.

Now try this

1 Explain the types of forces that cause
  (a) stretching   **(2 marks)**
  (b) compression.   **(2 marks)**

2 Give examples of materials that exhibit
  (a) elastic distortion   **(2 marks)**
  (b) inelastic distortion.   **(2 marks)**

3 Explain how you would know when a spring has been stretched beyond its elastic limit.   **(3 marks)**

Springs

Forces can lead to the **distortion** of **elastic** objects, resulting in **energy** being stored.

Elastic distortion

A force applied to a spring can make it undergo linear elastic distortion. The equation that describes this is:

force exerted on a spring (N) = spring constant (N/m) × extension (m)

$$F = k \times x$$

LEARN IT!
IT'S NOT ON THE EQUATIONS LIST

You can calculate the work done in stretching a spring using the equation:

energy transferred in stretching (J) = 0.5 × spring constant (N/m) × extension² (m²)

$$E = \tfrac{1}{2} \times k \times x^2$$

Force and linear extension

For elastic distortion, **extension** is **directly proportional** to the **force** exerted, **up to the elastic limit**.

The extension is the amount the spring stretches.

extension, x

Worked example

(a) Calculate the force needed to extend a spring of spring constant 20 N/m by 0.25 m.

(3 marks)

Force = spring constant × extension

= 20 N/m × 0.25 m = 5 N

(b) Calculate the total energy stored in the spring.

(4 marks)

energy stored = work done

$E = \tfrac{1}{2}k \times x^2$

$= \tfrac{1}{2} \times 20 \text{ N/m} \times (0.25 \text{ m})^2 = 0.625 \text{ J}$

When calculating the spring constant, work done or energy stored, ensure that force is in N and extension is in m.

Always use the extension. You may need to calculate this:

$$\text{extension} = \frac{\text{total stretched}}{\text{length}} - \text{original length}$$

Force–extension graph

The gradient tells you the value of the spring constant, k. This is only true when the spring is showing elastic behaviour, i.e. when the line is straight.

elastic limit

The area beneath a force-extension graph tells you the energy stored in the spring.

The area under the graph is the area of a

triangle $= \tfrac{1}{2} \times F \times x$

The force is given by the equation $F = k \times x$

Substituting this into the equation gives

$E = \tfrac{1}{2} \times k \times x \times x = \tfrac{1}{2}k \times x^2$

Now try this

1 (a) Calculate the force that is required to extend a spring of spring constant 30 N/m by 0.2 m. **(3 marks)**

(b) Calculate how much work is done on the spring under these conditions. **(3 marks)**

2 Describe how the value of the spring constant tells you how easy or difficult it is to cause a spring to extend. **(3 marks)**

3 Calculate how much elastic potential energy is stored in a spring of spring constant 45 N/m when it has an extension of 10 cm. **(4 marks)**

Forces and springs

🧪 **Practical skills** It is possible to determine the extension of a spring, and the work done, by applying different forces to the spring and then plotting a graph.

Core practical

Aim

To determine the extension and work done when applying forces to a spring.

Apparatus

- eye protection, spring, ruler, weights, retort stand, boss, clamp

Method

Arrange the apparatus as shown, with the ruler placed vertically alongside the spring and parallel to it. Add masses or weights and collect enough values to plot a graph of force against extension.

spring   ruler

weights

> Wear eye protection when taking readings. A stretched spring stores a lot of elastic energy and this could damage your eyes if released.

> When taking readings of the extension, read the values on the ruler at eye level to avoid parallax errors.

Weight and mass

Weight is a force, not a mass. A mass of 100 g is equivalent to a weight or force of 1 N.

Results

Taking readings for force and extension allows a force–extension graph to be plotted:

Extension (mm)

> Extension is equal to
>
> new length   _   original length
>   (m)   (m)
>
> Work done is equal to the energy stored in the spring.
>
> The gradient of a force–extension graph gives you the spring constant.
>
> The area beneath the line is the work done, or the energy stored as elastic potential energy, by the spring.

Conclusion

The gradient of the linear part of a force–extension graph gives you the value for the spring constant of the spring when it behaves elastically. The area beneath the graph equals the work done or the energy stored in the spring as elastic potential energy.

🧮 **Maths skills**   You will need to convert extension values from mm to m before you can calculate an energy value, and state the result in joules, J. Forces also need to be stated in N, so any mass values recorded need to be converted from g to N.

Now try this

1 Calculate the energy stored by a spring of spring constant 5 N/m when extended by 0.5 m. **(3 marks)**

2 Explain if and how the spring constant and the amount of energy stored can be calculated for springs that are being *compressed*. **(3 marks)**

Extended response – Forces and matter

There will be one or more 6-mark questions on your exam paper. For these questions, you will need to think scientifically and structure your answer logically, showing how the points you make are related to each other. You can revise the topics for this question, which is about **forces and matter**, on pages 228–230.

Worked example

A student performs an investigation to compare the behaviour of two different springs. The force–extension graph for these springs is shown on the right.
Compare the springs by using information from the graph. Your answer should refer to the spring constants of the springs, the energy they store and the elastic or inelastic nature of their behaviour. **(6 marks)**

The force–extension graph shows two springs that have both been extended with a maximum load of 29 N. Spring A produces the greater gradient, so it has a higher spring constant than spring B. This means that spring A requires a greater force to extend it by the same amount. Spring A has a spring constant of 500 N/m whereas spring B has a spring constant of 375 N/m.

Spring A behaves elastically throughout as the gradient is constant throughout the experiment because the extension is directly proportional to the force applied. Spring B behaves elastically up to a load force of about 25 N, at which point it starts to behave inelastically. This is shown by the reduction in gradient as the force leads to a greater and greater extension as the layers of atoms slide further apart. Upon removal of the load, spring A will return to its original shape but spring B will not – it will remain extended.

The energy stored by the springs is calculated by using the equation $E = \frac{1}{2} \times k \times x^2$. For the same extension, x, spring A will store a greater elastic potential energy due to its higher spring constant. For an extension of 4 cm, spring A will store 0.4 J whereas spring B will store only 0.3 J.

The answer starts with a quick explanation of what the graph shows. The gradient tells you the spring constant.
For spring A it is 25 N ÷ 0.05 m = 500 N/m and for spring B it is 22.5 ÷ 0.06 m or 375 N/m. Note that the extension has been converted to metres for the calculation: 5 cm = 0.05 m and 6 cm = 0.06 m.

After discussing the spring constant values, the answer then focuses on the elastic and inelastic nature of the springs, using values from the graph and giving an explanation as to what will happen to the springs.

Finally, the answer addresses the energy stored in each of the springs. Notice how the extension has to be converted into m to do the calculation.
4 cm = 0.04 m, so
for spring A, $E = \frac{1}{2} \times 500 \, \text{N/m} \times (0.04 \, \text{m})^2 = 0.4$ J
for spring B, $E = \frac{1}{2} \times 375 \, \text{N/m} \times (0.04 \, \text{m})^2 = 0.3$ J

Now try this

Describe the difference between elastic and inelastic distortion and explain how the spring constant of a spring and the elastic potential energy it stores can be determined when it is behaving elastically.
Your answer should refer to any graph, or equations, that may be useful. **(6 marks)**

Answers

Biology

1. Plant and animal cells

1 Muscle cells respire more (**1**); they need more ATP/energy (**1**); they carry out (aerobic) respiration/produce ATP. (**1**)

2 any four from: cell membrane (**1**); nucleus (**1**); ribosomes (**1**); mitochondria (**1**); cytoplasm (**1**)

3 some cells are not exposed to light (**1**); named example, e.g. roots/xylem, or explanation, e.g. light does not penetrate inside plant (**1**)

2. Different kinds of cell

1 Similarity – one from: has cell membrane/cytoplasm/DNA/ ribosomes (**1**)

Difference – one from: no nucleus/no nuclear membrane/no mitochondria/has plasmid/has cell wall (**1**)

2 It has a long thin root hair/protrusion (**1**), which increases the surface area for absorbing water/diffusion. (**1**)

3. Microscopes and magnification

(a) ×400 (**1**)

(b) 1.2/400 = 0.003 mm or 3 micrometres (**1**)

4. Dealing with numbers

1 cell 0.1 millimetres (0.1 mm); chloroplast 2 micrometres (2 μm); protein molecule 10 nanometres (10 nm) all three correct (**2**); two correct (**1**)

2 130 micrometres (**1**)

3 approx. 1 μm (**1**)

5. Using a light microscope

(a) Answer should include the following points (**4**):
- place the lowest power objective below the eyepiece
- place the slide on the microscope stage
- use the coarse focusing wheel to focus the image
- if needed, move a higher power objective into place and focus using the fine focusing wheel.

(b) C (**1**)

6. Drawing labelled diagrams

Drawing of one red blood cell and one white blood cell using all rules described:
- clean sharp pencil lines
- drawn from photo
- correct relative sizes
- labelled to show nucleus and cytoplasm in white blood cell (no labelling expected on red blood cell)
- labels surrounding drawing with no overlapping label lines
- appropriate title with magnification
  (**3 marks** for all points, **2 marks** for points 1–3 correct, **1 mark** for points 1–2 correct).

7. Enzymes

1 The part of the enzyme molecule where the substrate binds/ bonds/fits; (**1**) where the reaction takes place. (**1**)

2 This means that enzymes are always at their optimum temperature (**1**), so that reactions occur at the fastest rate. (**1**)

8. pH and enzyme activity

1 (a) rate of reaction = $\frac{1}{80}$ = 0.013/s (**1**)

   (b) It took the least time for the mixture to stop reacting with iodine (**1**), so the rate of reaction was at its fastest. (**1**)

2 The values of pH used are much closer together than in the first experiment (**1**), so the results should produce a more accurate value for the optimum pH. (**1**)

9. The importance of enzymes

1 The enzyme that digests lipids/lipase has a specific active site (**1**); only lipids will fit in/proteins will not fit in. (**1**)

2 ribosomes (**1**)

10. Getting in and out of cells

1 Osmosis is the diffusion of water/net movement of water molecules from a region of higher water concentration to a region of lower water concentration (**1**) across a partially permeable membrane. (**1**)

2 (a) Neither diffusion nor osmosis need energy. (**1**)

   (b) One from: Diffusion does not need energy but active transport does need energy; diffusion takes place down a concentration gradient; active transport takes place against a concentration gradient. (**1**)

3 water absorbed by osmosis (**1**); this is diffusion/passive/ does not require energy (**1**); mineral ions absorbed by active transport (**1**); requires energy from respiration/cannot happen when respiration is stopped (**1**)

11. Osmosis in potatoes

(a) **2 marks** for four or five correct; **1 mark** for two or three correct, OR for correct method (change in mass divided by original mass ×100%) but arithmetic error.

solution concentration (mol dm^{-3})	percentage change (%)
0.0	+22.0
0.2	+5.0
0.4	−8.0
0.6	−14.9
0.8	−24.1

(b) The solute concentration of the potato cells was between 0.2 and 0.4 mol dm^{-3} (**1**). This is because at that concentration there would be no osmosis/net movement of water into or out of the potato cells, and so no gain or loss in mass. (**1**)

12. Extended response – Key concepts

*Answer could include the following points, to **6 marks**:

Description of graph:

- As starch concentration increases the activity of the enzyme increases.
- Reference to values at key points on the graph, e.g. change in activity fastest between about 75 and 85 g dm^{-3}.
- Change in activity at different concentrations, as shown by steepness of curve.
- Change in activity is greatest where the graph line is steepest.
- Activity slows at higher starch concentration.
- Curve flattens after about 125 g dm^{-3}.

Explanation of graph:

- Starch is the substrate of amylase.
- At lower starch concentrations, there are many free active sites on enzyme molecules.
- At lower starch concentrations, adding more substrate means more substrate molecules can fit into free active sites and be broken down, so activity increases.
- At higher starch concentrations, most active sites of enzyme molecules are filled with substrate molecules.
- At higher starch concentrations, adding more substrate only increases activity slightly because substrate molecules must wait till an active site becomes free.

13. Mitosis

They will be identical to the parent cell **(1)**, with the same number of chromosomes. **(1)**

14. Cell growth and differentiation

1 cancer is uncontrolled cell division **(1)**; drugs stop cancer cells dividing **(1)**

2 a cell that is adapted to carry out a specific function **(1)**

3 It allows cells to become specialised **(1)** so they can carry out a function more effectively. **(1)**

15. Growth and percentile charts

1 one from: measure its change in height over time, measure its change in mass over time, measure the change in number and size of leaves over time (or similar) **(1)**. *The key point to mention is change over time.* If the measurements increase over time, then the plant is growing. **(1)**

2 A percentile chart compares the growth (or an aspect of growth e.g. length, body mass) of an individual **(1)** against the growth (of the same aspect) of other individuals of the same sex and age. **(1)**

3 The increase in size of a balloon is not a permanent increase in size **(1)**, while the increase in size of a child is a permanent increase in the number of cells in the child's body. **(1)**

16. Stem cells

1 an unspecialised cell **(1)** that divides to form specialised cells **(1)**

2 Cutting the top off the shoot removes the meristem **(1)**, so the growing and dividing region is removed. **(1)**

3 Embryos have to be destroyed when the stem cells are removed **(1)**; some people think it is wrong to do this because they believe embryos have a right to life. **(1)**

4 (a) one from: they are easier to extract / they can produce more different kinds of cell. **(1)**

   (b) Adult stem cells from the patient will be recognised **(1)** but embryonic stem cells will not and the body will reject them. **(1)**

17. Neurones

1 Sensory neurones carry impulses from receptors to the CNS/brain/spinal cord **(1)**. Motor neurones carry impulses from the CNS/brain/spinal cord to effectors/muscles/glands **(1)**. Relay neurones carry impulses from one part of the CNS to another. **(1)**

2 The long axon and dendron of the sensory neurone means the cell can collect impulses from receptor cells and carry them through the body to the central nervous system/spinal cord/brain **(1)**. The myelin sheath insulates the neurone from surrounding neurones and helps the electrical impulse to travel faster. **(1)**

18. Responding to stimuli

1 receptor in skin detects stimulus **(1)**; impulses pass along sensory neurone to spinal cord **(1)**; impulses pass to relay neurone **(1)**; impulses pass along motor neurone to muscle **(1)**

2 three from: impulse reaches the end of an axon/neurone **(1)**; neurotransmitter released **(1)**; diffuses across gap and fits into receptors **(1)**; causes impulse to start/be set up in next neurone **(1)**

19. Extended response – Cells and control

*Answer could include the following points, to **6 marks**:

- receptor cells in the eye detect a stimulus
- the stimulus is the bright light/increase in light intensity
- receptor cells pass impulses to a sensory neurone
- sensory neurone passes impulses to a relay neurone
- relay neurone is in the spinal cord/central nervous system
- relay neurone passes impulse to a motor neurone
- motor neurone passes impulse to the effector/muscle in the iris
- muscle contracts/makes pupil smaller
- synapses between neurones
- chemicals carry impulse across the synapse.

20. Meiosis

1 four cells produced **(1)**; haploid **(1)**; genetically different **(1)**

2 halves chromosome number so diploid number restored at fertilisation **(1)**; gametes genetically different so offspring show variation. **(1)**

3 haploid = one set of chromosomes **(1)**; diploid = two sets of chromosomes/chromosomes are in pairs **(1)**

4 B **(1)**

21. DNA

1 (a) a piece of DNA that codes for a protein **(1)**
   (b) the entire DNA of an organism **(1)**

2 GCTA **(1)**; because A pairs with T and C pairs with G. **(1)**

3 DNA forms a double helix structure **(1)**, which consists of two strands coiled together **(1)** and held together by the weak hydrogen bonds **(1)** that link the complementary base pairs of A and T or C and G. **(1)**

22. Genetic terms

1 A chromosome is a long strand of DNA **(1)**. A gene is a small section of a chromosome/DNA that gives the instructions for producing a particular characteristic **(1)**. An allele is an alternative form of a gene. **(1)**

2 (a) It is heterozygous **(1)** because it has one dominant and one recessive allele. **(1)**

   (b) Purple flowers **(1)**, because purple is dominant over white **(1)**. *Remember that phenotype is what it looks like, so writing down the alleles would give you no marks for this question.*

23. Monohybrid inheritance

genetic diagram or Punnett square showing this information (any appropriate letter used):

		parent genotype Bb	
	parent gametes	B	b
parent genotype bb	b	Bb brown	bb black
	b	Bb brown	bb black

(**1 mark** for setting out the parent genotypes and gametes correctly, **1 mark** for completing the offspring genotypes and phenotypes correctly)

The predicted outcome of phenotypes is 50% chance of brown and 50% chance of black (could also be presented as a ratio 1 : 1, or probability 1 in 2 for both colours). **(1)**

24. Family pedigrees

(a) heterozygous/Tt (other letters allowed) **(1)**

(b) genetic diagram or Punnett square showing offspring of Tt × tt **(1)**; 50% or 0.5 **(1)**

25. Sex determination

1 A **(1)**

2 chance is 50% **(1)**; diagram or Punnett square as shown on page 25 (**1 mark** for parent phenotype, **1 mark** for gametes, **1 mark** for possible outcomes)

3 There is always an X from the mother **(1)** because women are all XX and can only pass on an X chromosome. **(1)**

26. Variation and mutation

1 Identical twins have the same genes because they come from the same fertilised egg, so characteristics controlled by genes will be the same **(1)**. Any characteristics affected by the environment may be different between the twins because different things may happen to them as they grow up. **(1)**

2 Most body cells will not contain the new allele **(1)**. Most body cells do not divide so they will not produce new cells containing the new allele. **(1)**

27. The Human Genome Project

1 doctors can find out if their patients are at risk of certain diseases **(1)**; so the patients can make lifestyle changes/doctors can find out what form of a disease a patient has / patients can be given drugs to target that form of the disease. **(1)**

2 They have the same genes but different alleles **(1)**, therefore a different sequence of bases in their DNA. **(1)**

28. Extended response – Genetics

*Answer could include the following points, to **6 marks**:

- parents must be heterozygous/Rr
- because some offspring have smooth coat/rr
- (smooth-coated guinea pigs) inherit one allele from each parent
- parental gametes shown as R and r
- genotypes of offspring as 1 RR : 2 Rr : 1 rr
- phenotypes correctly identified as RR and Rr rough-coated, rr smooth-coated

29. Evolution

bacteria show variation in antibiotic resistance/some bacteria are more resistant to antibiotics than others **(1)**; when antibiotics used, non-resistant bacteria die/the more resistant bacteria survive **(1)**; these reproduce **(1)**; and pass on (the gene for) antibiotic resistance to their offspring **(1)**

30. Human evolution

1 two suitable features, such as: increase in brain size, increase in height, upright posture and ability to walk over long distances. **(2)**

2 two from: greater variety of tools/named examples **(1)**; made from fine flakes broken off larger stones **(1)**; more flint flaked off giving sharper edges **(1)**

31. Classification

1 The three domains are: Eubacteria **(1)**, Eukaryota (including plants, animals, fungi, protists) **(1)**, Archaea (mainly bacteria living in hot/salty conditions) **(1)**.

2 it showed that prokaryotes/bacteria need to be split into two groups **(1)**; some bacteria/archaea have genes that work more like eukaryotes **(1)**

32. Selective breeding

1 Advantage: get crop plants/animals with higher yield/more meat/disease resistance etc. **(1)**

Disadvantage: you breed closely related organisms so they show less genetic diversity/may show genetic defects **(1)**

OR

may inherit a good characteristic but also less desirable characteristics **(1)**

OR

many offspring do not inherit the desired characteristics **(1)**

2 three from: select parent sheep that have thick wool **(1)**; interbreed **(1)**; select the offspring with the thickest wool and interbreed **(1)**; repeat many generations **(1)**

3 little genetic variation in the population **(1)**; so if a new disease appears, it might spread very easily. **(1)**

33. Genetic engineering

1 transferring a gene from one organism to another/inserting new genes into an organism/modifying the genome of an organism **(1)**, so the desired characteristic is produced in the organism/so that the organism has a new characteristic **(1)**

2 advantage: greater crop yield (because weeds are killed) **(1)**

disadvantage: one from: gene for herbicide resistance may be transferred to weeds **(1)**; some people do not want to eat GM crops **(1)**

34. Extended response – Genetic modification

*Answer could include the following points, to **6 marks**:

Similarities:

- Both involve selecting a desirable characteristic.
- Both involve modifying the genome of the plant.
- Both involve human intervention / are not natural processes.
- Both cause changes that can be inherited.

Differences:

- Selective breeding takes several generations but genetic engineering takes one generation.
- Selective breeding takes longer than genetic engineering.
- Selective breeding involves genes found in the plant species but genetic engineering can use genes found in other species.

35. Health and disease

1 bacterium (1); virus (1); fungi (1); protist (1)

2 non-communicable because it is not caused by a pathogen (1); blood clots are not spread from one person to another (1)

36. Common infections

(a) HIV or Ebola

two suitable signs (2), e.g.

(HIV) no signs/symptoms for a long time; flu-like symptoms on first infection; many repeated infections as immune system stops working

OR

(Ebola) internal bleeding and fever; severe headache; muscle pain; vomiting; diarrhoea

(b) malaria

two suitable signs (2), e.g. fever; weakness

(c) *Chalara*

two suitable signs (2), e.g. leaf loss; bark lesions/damage; dieback of top of tree

37. How pathogens spread

The mosquito is a vector because it infects the human with the parasite/pathogen (1). Plasmodium/the protist is the pathogen because this infects the cells and causes the disease/symptoms. (1)

38. STIs

1 sexually transmitted infections (1); spread by contact with sexual fluids/not using a condom during sexual intercourse. (1)

2 The condom is a barrier between the man's skin and his partner's sexual fluids, (1) so pathogens that cause STIs cannot reach the man's skin or mucous membranes. (1)

39. Human defences

1 unbroken skin/mucus in breathing system (1); lysozyme in mucus/saliva/tears OR hydrochloric acid in stomach (1)

2 skin is broken/damaged (1); so bacteria/pathogens can enter the body (1)

40. The immune system

Answer could include the following points (3):

- The pathogen has an antigen on its surface (that is unique to it).
- A lymphocyte with an antibody that fits the antigen is activated.
- This lymphocyte divides repeatedly; and secretes antibodies that destroy the pathogen.

41. Immunisation

1 A vaccine contains a dead or harmless form of a pathogen or antigenic material that is used to immunise a person (1). Immunisation means giving a vaccine to cause an immune response in the body. (1)

2 two from: this gives the person another injection of antigens (1); increases the number of memory cells present (1); immune response greater/more antibodies made (1)

42. Treating infections

1 Antibiotics only kill bacteria/do not destroy viruses. (1)

2 bacteria die if they cannot make proteins (1); but the antibiotic does not affect human cells (1)

43. New medicines

1 Two from:
- B may be cheaper (1);

- A may have side-effects (1);
- patient may be allergic to A (1);
- A may not be suitable for pregnant women (1);
- A may not be compatible with other drugs the patient is taking (1)

2 The benefit of using animals as models is that the drugs can be tested for safety without harming humans (1). A problem with using animals as models for humans is that the drugs may not work in the same way in the animal as they would do in a human. (1) (*Other problems may be acceptable, e.g. many people are against the use of animals for testing.*)

44. Non-communicable diseases

(a) So we can compare the different groups (1), as different groups have different numbers of people in them. (1)

(b) (Yes) (no mark). Answer could include the following points (2):
- risk of cancer much higher in people with mutation;
- use of figures from graph to support answer;
- but only gives data for two kinds of cancer/may not be true for all cancers

45. Alcohol and smoking

(a) The more cigarettes smoked, the more likely a person is to die of coronary heart disease (1). The older a person is, the more likely they are to die of coronary heart disease. (1)

(b) (chemicals in cigarettes) make blood vessels too narrow (1); increasing blood pressure (1)

46. Malnutrition and obesity

1 (a) 0.97 (1)

(b) He is at risk because the ratio is above 0.95. (1)

2 She has a BMI of 31 (1) and is obese. (1)

47. Cardiovascular disease

three from: give up smoking (1); exercise more (1); lose weight (1); eat lower fat/lower salt diet (1)

48. Extended response – Health and disease

*Answer could include the following points, to **6 marks**:

Factors correctly related to a type of cancer, e.g.:
- UV radiation/sunbathing/sunbeds can cause skin cancer.
- Processed meat/named example linked to colon/bowel cancer.
- Smoking linked to lung cancer.
- Alcohol linked to mouth/pharynx/larynx/oesophageal cancer.
- Dietary fat linked to breast cancer.
- High salt linked to stomach cancer.

General statement that chemicals in food/cigarette smoke/pollution can cause cancer.

49. Photosynthesis

1 Energy is taken in (1). Energy in the form of light is transferred to energy in the form of chemical (potential) energy in sugars. (1)

2 Plants carry out photosynthesis, (1) which uses energy transferred by light (1) to produce glucose (1) which can be converted into other food substances and are a source of food for other organisms. (1)

50. Limiting factors

1 Something that limits the rate of photosynthesis (1) when it is at a low level. (1)

2 Photosynthesis produces oxygen **(1)**. The more rapidly oxygen is released, the faster the photosynthesis reactions must be happening. **(1)**

51. Light intensity

1 Carbon dioxide is taken in by plants when they photosynthesise **(1)**. Removing carbon dioxide from the solution will increase its pH **(1)**. The rate of change in pH will indicate the rate at which carbon dioxide is removed from the solution. **(1)**

2 Temperature also affects the rate of photosynthesis **(1)**. If temperature is not controlled, then it will change with distance and so affect the results. **(1)**

3 The tube will act as a control **(1)** as it should show no change in pH as there will be no photosynthesis in the tube. **(1)**

52. Specialised plant cells

1 mitochondria supply energy from respiration/ATP **(1)**; for active transport (of mineral ions) **(1)**

2 Answer could include the following points:
- **1 mark** for feature and **1 mark** for explanation, e.g.
- Pits in side walls; for sideways movement of water/mineral ions.
- No cell contents; so water flow not obstructed.
- No end walls; so water flow not obstructed.
- Thick walls made of lignin; so cell does not collapse/is strong.

53. Transpiration

1 Movement of water through a plant **(1)** from roots to leaves. **(1)**

2 any four from: water enters root hair cell by osmosis **(1)**; moves through plant via xylem **(1)**; evaporates from leaf as water vapour **(1)**; via stomata **(1)**; draws water out of leaf cells/xylem **(1)**

54. Translocation

1 phloem, xylem **(2)**

2 From the phloem **(1)**, because dissolved sugars are transported around the plant in phloem. **(1)**

3 downwards/from leaf to potato **(1)**; sucrose formed in leaves/in photosynthesis **(1)**; converted to starch in potatoes **(1)**

55. Water uptake in plants

(a) 10 mm/min **(1)**

(b) rate of evaporation is higher **(1)**; so water travels through the shoot faster/water uptake is faster **(1)**

(c) all conditions kept the same except temperature **(1)**; one example is, e.g. air movement/light intensity **(1)**

56. Extended response – Plant structures and functions

*Answer could include the following points, to **6 marks**:
Function similarities:
- both tissues are found in roots, shoots and leaves.

Function differences:
- xylem transports water and mineral ions
- phloem transports sucrose/amino acids
- xylem carries substances in one direction only/from roots to shoots
- phloem carries substances in both directions/from source to sink.

Structure similarities:
- both tissues have a tubular shape.

Structure differences:

- xylem consists of dead cells but phloem consists of living cells
- xylem has no end walls but phloem does/phloem has sieve plates
- xylem is strengthened with rings of lignin but phloem is not
- xylem has pits in its cell walls but phloem does not.

57. Hormones

1 two from: a substance produced by an endocrine gland **(1)**; travels in blood **(1)**; affects target organ/cells **(1)**

2 two from: Hormones are chemical; nerve impulses are electrical/ionic **(1)**. Hormones travel in blood to all parts of the body; nerve impulses travel directly to the site of action **(1)**. Nerve impulses usually only affect one organ; hormones may affect several organs **(1)**. Nerve impulses short-lived; hormones usually last longer. **(1)**

58. The menstrual cycle

1 If the egg is fertilised the uterus lining is maintained. **(1)**

2 advantage: implant longer lasting so don't need to remember a daily pill **(1)**

disadvantage: if the woman wants to have a baby, she has to get implant removed **(1)**

59. Blood glucose regulation

1 gland is pancreas **(1)**, target organ is liver **(1)**

2 A change in blood glucose causes mechanisms to act that bring about the opposite change **(1)**, so that blood glucose concentration is maintained within a small range. **(1)**

60. Diabetes

1 More insulin is needed if a big meal is taken rather than a small meal **(1)**. More insulin is needed if a meal contains a lot of sugar/carbohydrates **(1)**. Less insulin is needed if the person is exercising; because glucose used up in respiration. **(1)**

2 person still makes insulin/has enough insulin **(1)**; but liver and muscle/body cells resistant to it **(1)**

61. Extended response – Control and coordination

*Answer could include the following points, to **6 marks**:
- Blood glucose concentration rises after absorbing glucose from a digested meal.
- Blood glucose concentration falls as glucose is taken from blood by cells for respiration or storage.
- As blood glucose concentration rises, cells in pancreas respond by releasing the hormone insulin into the blood.
- Insulin causes cells to take up more glucose.
- Liver and muscle cells store extra glucose as glycogen.
- When blood glucose concentration falls too low, less insulin is released into the blood.
- Liver cells convert glycogen into glucose and release it into the blood.
- Blood glucose concentration is kept within limits, which is homeostasis.
- Control of blood glucose concentration shows negative feedback as a change in one direction causes a change in the opposite direction to happen.

62. Exchanging materials

1 lungs **(1)** *There are other possible answers, e.g. small intestine, kidney, but you will be expected to know about the lungs.*

2 can rely on diffusion because flatworm is very flat and thin **(1)**; large surface area to volume ratio **(1)**; every cell in the flatworm is close to the surface **(1)**

63. Alveoli

1 any one from: less oxygen/more carbon dioxide/more water **(1)**

2 reduced surface area **(1)**; less oxygen absorbed **(1)**

3 maintains a concentration gradient **(1)**; larger surface area for exchange **(1)**

64. Blood

1 oxygen in red blood cells **(1)**; glucose in plasma **(1)** *You must say which substance is carried by each part of the blood. In an exam, you would not get marks for just saying 'red blood cells and plasma'.*

2 flexible shape **(1)**; to engulf pathogens **(1)**

65. Blood vessels

1 (a) B **(1)**

(b) A **(1)**

2 Every body cell needs oxygen and glucose for respiration, and to get rid of waste products such as carbon dioxide **(1)**. If this does not happen quickly enough then the cell may be damaged **(1)**. Capillaries are the blood vessels that exchange substances with the body cells **(1)**. A short distance for diffusion between a body cell and a capillary helps to make diffusion rapid. **(1)**

66. The heart

1 They prevent the blood flowing the wrong way in the heart. **(1)**

2 The right ventricle pumps blood to the lungs, which are not far away **(1)**. The left ventricle pumps blood out around the rest of the body, including as far as the toes and fingers **(1)**. So the left ventricle needs to pump with greater force than the right ventricle. **(1)**

67. Aerobic respiration

1 The break down of glucose to release energy **(1)** using oxygen. **(1)**

2 two from: muscle contraction **(1)**; synthesising proteins **(1)**; maintaining body temperature **(1)**; producing fats **(1)**; producing glycogen **(1)**

68. Anaerobic respiration

1 It releases less oxygen per glucose molecule **(1)**. It does not release enough energy for rapid activity. **(1)**

2 glucose is not fully broken down **(1)**

69. Rate of respiration

(a) Rate of oxygen uptake (cm^3/min) = volume absorbed in 20 min ÷ 20 **(1)**

5 °C: 0.03 cm^3/min

10 °C: 0.05 cm^3/min

15 °C: 0.085 cm^3/min

20 °C: 0.12 cm^3/min **(1)**

(b) suitable scales **(1)**; axes labels with quantity and unit **(1)**; axes points plotted accurately **(1)**; line or curve of best fit drawn **(1)**

(c) As temperature increases, the rate of oxygen uptake of the organisms increases **(1)**, which means that their rate of respiration increases. **(1)**

70. Changes in heart rate

1 As exercise level increases/gets more intense **(1)** the heart rate increases **(1)**. OR As exercise level reduces/gets easier **(1)** the heart rate decreases **(1)**. *It is not enough to say 'heart rate increases'. You need to link how heart rate changes as exercise level changes to get both marks.*

2 4500/75 = 60 cm^3

(**2 marks** for correct answer; **1 mark** for correct method with arithmetic error)

3 Cardiac output is heart rate multiplied by stroke volume **(1)**. A trained athlete will have a similar cardiac output because their stroke volume is much larger. **(1)**

71. Extended response – Exchange

*Answer could include the following points, to **6 marks**:

- Arteries have thick walls to withstand high pressure.
- Arteries have muscle/elastic fibres which stretch then contract as blood passes.
- Arteries have muscle/elastic fibre to make blood flow smoothly.
- Veins have thin walls/thinner walls than arteries because blood pressure in them is lower.
- Veins have large space inside to let blood flow through easily.
- Veins have valves so blood flows one way/to stop blood flowing the wrong way.
- Capillaries are narrow/wide enough for one red blood cell.
- The walls of capillaries are one cell thick so diffusion happens quickly.

72. Ecosystems and abiotic factors

large surface area to volume ratio **(1)**; so loses heat rapidly **(1)**

73. Biotic factors

1 So that the plants do not compete **(1)** for an environmental factor such as light/water/nutrients. **(1)**

2 Predators of milk snakes may confuse them with the poisonous coral snakes **(1)** and avoid them because they know that coral snakes are poisonous. **(1)**

74. Parasitism and mutualism

1 A parasite is an organism that feeds on and causes harm to a host organism while living on or in the host. **(1)**

2 when two organisms both benefit from a close relationship **(1)**

3 The bacteria benefit from getting e.g. glucose or amino acids from the plant and protection from the environment **(1)**. The plant benefits from getting nitrogen compounds/nitrates from the bacteria, which it needs to make proteins for healthy growth. **(1)**

75. Fieldwork techniques

1 to estimate population number/size **(1)**

2 When you want to study the effect of abiotic and biotic factors on where organisms live **(1)** to link a change in distribution with a change in a physical factor. **(1)**

76. Organisms and their environment

(a) graph with axes as for graph shown in Core practical; with primrose data correctly substituted for cowslip data (**1 mark** for correct axes, **1 mark** for accurately plotted points joined by straight lines)

(b) Primroses are more common where there is some light **(1)**, but not where there is a lot of light in the open meadow. **(1)**

77. Human effects on ecosystems

(growth of surface plants) blocks light so plants die **(1)**; increase in bacteria uses up oxygen **(1)**; fish and other animals die **(1)**

78. Biodiversity

One mark for a suitable effect of hedges on the environment, e.g. provides food/shelter/nesting places **(1)**; one mark for sensible consequence of this effect, e.g. more species of animals supported/more food chains possible/different species can reproduce **(1)**

79. The carbon cycle

1 Decomposers release carbon back into the air as carbon dioxide from respiration. **(1)**

2 Respiration releases carbon from compounds in living organisms as carbon dioxide gas into the air. **(1)** Photosynthesis takes carbon dioxide gas from the air and converts it into carbon compounds in plants. **(1)** Combustion releases carbon from compounds in fossil fuels as carbon dioxide gas into the air. **(1)**

80. The water cycle

1 Answer could include the following points **(4)**:
- water evaporates;
- forms clouds;
- condenses into precipitation/rain;
- runs off land in rivers;
- is taken up by plants;
- filters through ground

2 Answer could include the following points **(3)**:
- less water available in rivers;
- less precipitation;
- less water in aquifers/drier soil;
- less flooding

81. The nitrogen cycle

1 clover roots contain nitrogen-fixing bacteria, which means fewer nitrates removed from soil **(1)**; adds nutrients to the soil when clover plants ploughed in **(1)**

2 The stubble contains proteins **(1)**. Decomposers break down these proteins and release the nitrogen compounds as ammonia into the soil **(1)**. This makes the ammonia available to nitrifying bacteria, which convert it to nitrates **(1)**. Plants that grow in this soil later will be able to take in the nitrates and use them to make proteins, which they need for healthy growth. **(1)**

82. Extended response – Ecosystems and material cycles

*Answer could include the following points, to **6 marks**:
Similarities:
- mutualism and parasitism involve two species
- they are examples of interdependence.

Differences:
- mutualism benefits both species but parasitism only benefits the parasite/does not benefit the host
- behaviour of the parasite can damage the host/cause it to die.

Examples of mutualism (at least one given):
- oxpecker and gazelle
- oxpecker gets food, gazelle gets rid of skin parasites
- cleaner fish and shark
- cleaner fish get food, shark gets rid of dead skin/parasites
- nitrogen-fixing bacteria and legume plant
- bacteria protected from the environment/get food from the plant, plant gets nitrogen compounds.

Examples of parasitism (at least one given):
- flea/headlouse feeds on the blood of other organisms
- tapeworm absorbs nutrients from food in the host's intestine
- mistletoe absorbs nutrients from host plant.

Chemistry

83. Formulae

1 A molecule consists of two bromine atoms **(1)** chemically joined together. **(1)**

2 $CuCO_3$ **(1)**
No marks if 3 is shown as superscript or element symbols do not start with capital letters.

3 two from, for **1 mark** each:
- It contains two oxygen atoms and two hydrogen atoms for every magnesium atom.
- It has three different elements/five atoms in total, chemically joined together.
- It contains one magnesium ion and two hydroxide ions.

84. Equations

1 (a) $2Mg + O_2 \rightarrow 2MgO$ **(1)**
  (b) $N_2 + 3H_2 \rightarrow 2NH_3$ **(1)**
  (c) $CH_4 + 2O_2 \rightarrow CO_2 + 2H_2O$ **(1)**

2 (a) copper oxide + nitric acid $\rightarrow$ copper nitrate + water **(1)**
  (b) $2Fe(s) + 3Cl_2(g) \rightarrow 2FeCl_3(s)$ (**1 mark** for balancing, **1 mark** for state symbols)

85. Hazards, risks and precautions

1 one from: to warn about the dangers; to let people know about precautions to take; for people who cannot read **(1)**

2 chlorine: Use a fume cupboard/open the windows **(1)**. hydrogen: Avoid naked flames. **(1)**

86. Atomic structure

1 central nucleus **(1)** containing protons and (usually) neutrons **(1)** surrounded by electrons **(1)** in shells **(1)**

2 Atoms contain equal numbers of protons and electrons **(1)**. Protons have a +1 charge and electrons have –1 charge (so charges cancel out). **(1)**

3 In the nucleus **(1)** because the nucleus contains protons and neutrons **(1)** which have a much higher mass/relative mass than electrons. **(1)**

87. Isotopes

1 the same number of protons in the nucleus **(1)** and this is unique/different from atoms of another element **(1)**

2 17 protons **(1)**, (35 – 17) = 18 neutrons **(1)**, 17 electrons **(1)**

88. Mendeleev's table

1 in order of increasing atomic mass **(1)**, taking into account the properties of the elements and their compounds **(1)**

2 one from: It had gaps/there were pair reversals/some groups contained metals and non-metals. **(1)**

89. The periodic table

1 groups **(1)**

2 in order of increasing atomic number **(1)** in rows/periods **(1)**; elements with similar properties in columns/groups **(1)**

90. Electronic configurations

1 diagram with three circles **(1)** with two electrons in the first circle, eight in the second and seven in the outermost circle **(1)**, e.g.

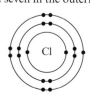

You can show electrons as dots or as crosses.

2 The number of occupied shells is the same as the period number **(1)**; the number of electrons in the outer shell is the same as the group number (except for the elements in group 0, which have full outer shells). **(1)**

91. Ions

1 (a) Li^+ **(1)**

(b) Mg^{2+} **(1)**

(c) S^{2-} **(1)**

(d) Br^- **(1)**

2 10 **(1)**

3 10 **(1)**

92. Formulae of ionic compounds

(a) CaS **(1)**

(b) $FeCl_2$ **(1)**

(c) NH_4OH **(1)**

(d) $(NH_4)_2CO_3$ **(1)**

(e) Na_2SO_4 **(1)**

93. Properties of ionic compounds

(a) Its ions are not free to move/are held in fixed positions (in the lattice). **(1)**

(b) Heat it **(1)** until it melts/becomes molten. **(1)**

Remember: aluminium oxide is insoluble, so you cannot dissolve it in water.

(c) Aluminium oxide has a high melting point **(1)** so a lot of energy is needed. **(1)**

94. Covalent bonds

1 (strong) bond formed when a pair of electrons is shared **(1)** between two atoms **(1)**

2 dot-and-cross diagram for oxygen, e.g.

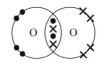

two overlapping circles with two dots and two crosses in the overlap **(1)**

two pairs of non-bonding electrons in each oxygen atom **(1)**

95. Simple molecular substances

1 There are weak intermolecular forces between ammonia molecules **(1)**, which are easily overcome/need little energy to break. **(1)**

2 The intermolecular forces between petrol molecules and water molecules are weaker **(1)** than those between petrol molecules **(1)** and between water molecules. **(1)**

96. Giant molecular substances

1 the following points for **1 mark** each to a maximum of **4 marks**:

similarities:

• only contain carbon atoms

• atoms covalently bonded to each other

• lattice structure.

differences:

• Diamond has four covalent bonds per atom *and* graphite has three.

• Diamond has no delocalised electrons *and* graphite does.

• Graphite has a layered structure (with weak intermolecular forces) *and* diamond does not.

2 It will not conduct electricity **(1)** because it has no delocalised electrons/all the outer electrons are involved in covalent bonding. **(1)**

97. Other large molecules

1 two from, for **1 mark** each: almost transparent/flexible/conducts electricity

2 Buckminsterfullerene is not a giant molecular substance **(1)**, weak intermolecular forces are overcome on heating **(1)**, but there are many strong covalent bonds to break in diamond. **(1)**

98. Metals

1 (a) Layers of positive ions/atoms **(1)** can slide over each other. **(1)**

(b) Delocalised electrons/free electrons/sea of electrons **(1)** can move through the structure. **(1)**

2 (It should conduct electricity) because it will have delocalised electrons. **(1)**

99. Limitations of models

One limitation of each model:

• Empirical formula does not show: actual number of atoms/how the atoms are arranged/three-dimensional shape of molecule/bonding and non-bonding electrons/sizes of atoms relative to their bonds **(1)**.

• Molecular formula does not show: how the atoms are bonded/three-dimensional shape of molecule/bonding and non-bonding electrons/sizes of atoms relative to their bonds **(1)**.

• Structural formula does not show: three-dimensional shape of molecule/bonding and non-bonding electrons/sizes of atoms relative to their bonds **(1)**.

• Drawn formula does not show: three-dimensional shape of molecule/bonding and non-bonding electrons/sizes of atoms relative to their bonds **(1)**.

• Ball-and-stick model does not show: element symbols/bonding and non-bonding electrons/sizes of atoms relative to their bonds **(1)**.

• Space-filling model does not show: element symbols/bonding and non-bonding electrons/some atoms in complex models **(1)**.

• Dot-and-cross diagram does not show: three-dimensional shape of molecule/sizes of atoms relative to their bonds. **(1)**

100. Relative formula mass

(a) 18 **(1)**

(b) 44 **(1)**

(c) 40 **(1)**

(d) 154 **(1)**

(e) 134.5 **(1)**

(f) 142 **(1)**

(g) 78 **(1)**

(h) 234 **(1)**

101. Empirical formulae

Mg: $\dfrac{0.36}{24} = 0.015$ and O: $\dfrac{0.24}{16} = 0.015$ **(1)**

Divide by 0.015

Mg: $\dfrac{0.015}{0.015} = 1$ and O: $\dfrac{0.015}{0.015} = 1$ **(1)**

Empirical formula is MgO **(1)**

102. Conservation of mass

1. M_r of $CH_4 = 12 + (4 \times 1) = 16$ **(1)**

   M_r of $O_2 = (2 \times 16) = 32$ **(1)**

   10 g of CH_4 reacts with $\left(2 \times \dfrac{32}{16}\right) \times 10$ g of O_2 **(1)**

   $= 40$ g **(1)**

2. $2K + Cl_2 \rightarrow 2KCl$ **(1)**

   A_r of $K = 39$ and M_r of $KCl = 39 + 35.5 = 74.5$ **(1)**

   20 g of KCl is produced from $\left(\dfrac{39}{74.5}\right) \times 20$ g of K **(1)**

   $= 10.5$ g or 10.47 g **(1)**

103. Concentration of solution

1. (a) $\dfrac{0.40}{0.50} = 0.80$ g dm^{-3} **(1)**

   (b) 100 cm$^3 = \dfrac{100}{1000} = 0.100$ dm^3 **(1)**

   $\dfrac{1.25}{0.100} = 12.5$ g dm^{-3} **(1)**

2. 150 cm$^3 = \dfrac{150}{1000} = 0.150$ dm^3 **(1)**

   $mass = concentration \times volume$

   $mass = 40 \times 0.150 = 6.0$ g **(1)**

104. Extended response – Types of substance

*Answer could include the following points, to **6 marks**:

- Mercury contains positively charged mercury ions.
- It is not in a regular lattice.
- There is a sea of delocalised electrons.
- The electrons are free to move and carry charge.
- Paraffin oil molecules are attracted to each other by weak intermolecular forces.
- The molecules are free to move.
- The molecules are uncharged so paraffin oil does not conduct electricity.

105. States of matter

change of state: sublimation **(1)**

Forces of attraction (between particles) are overcome (as energy is transferred to the particles) **(1)**. Arrangement changes from regular to random **(1)**. Arrangement changes from close together to far apart **(1)**. Particles no longer just vibrate about fixed positions but can move quickly in all directions. **(1)**

106. Pure substances and mixtures

1. A pure substance contains only one element or compound **(1)**, but mineral water will be a mixture **(1)** of water and other substances. **(1)**

2. 18-carat gold must be a mixture **(1)** because pure substances have a sharp melting point/mixtures melt over a range of temperatures. **(1)**

107. Distillation

(a) to cool the vapour **(1)**; to turn it from the gas state to the liquid state **(1)**

(b) (different) boiling points **(1)**

(c) hottest at the bottom and coldest at the top/gets cooler towards the top **(1)**

108. Filtration and crystallisation

Answer could include the following points **(4)**:

- Add water to dissolve the copper chloride.
- Filter to remove the glass and dust (as a residue).
- Heat the filtrate to produce copper chloride crystals (by crystallisation).
- Pat the copper chloride crystals dry with filter paper/put them in a warm oven.

109. Paper chromatography

1. A 0.2 **(1)** E 0.9 **(1)**

2. The substance forms stronger attractive forces with the solvent/mobile phase **(1)** than with the paper/stationary phase. **(1)**

110. Investigating inks

Answer could include the following points (**1 mark** each to a maximum of **2 marks**):

- Clamp the boiling tube.
- Use a blue flame with the air hole half open.
- Do not heat to dryness.
- Put the test tube in a beaker of cold water/iced water.

111. Drinking water

1. safe to drink **(1)**

2. Sedimentation removes **large** insoluble particles **(1)**; filtration removes **small** insoluble particles **(1)**; chlorination kills microbes/sterilises the water. **(1)**

112. Extended response – Separating mixtures

*Answer could include the following points, to **6 marks**:

- Add water to the mixture.
- Stir the mixture.
- Sodium carbonate should dissolve but calcium carbonate should not.
- This is because their solubility is different/calcium carbonate is (almost) insoluble.
- Filter the mixture.
- Calcium carbonate stays behind as a residue.
- Wash the residue in the filter paper (to remove any sodium carbonate).
- Leave washed residue in a warm place to dry.
- Filtrate is sodium carbonate solution.
- Heat to evaporate (most of) the water.
- Leave solution to cool/crystallise sodium carbonate.
- Filter/decant to separate crystals.
- Leave crystals in a warm place to dry.

113. Acids and alkalis

1. Sodium chloride solution is neutral but hydrogen chloride solution is acidic **(1)**. Sodium chloride does not release hydrogen ions when it dissolves but hydrogen chloride does **(1)**. Hydrogen ions make the solution acidic. **(1)**

2. The indicator turns pink **(1)** because the solution is alkaline, containing hydroxide ions. **(1)**

3. **1 mark** for each correct row:

	Acidic solution	Alkaline solution
Red litmus	(stays) red	(turns) blue
Blue litmus	(turns) red	(stays) blue

114. Bases and alkalis

1. An alkali is a soluble base **(1)** but most bases are insoluble (so are not alkalis). **(1)**

2. NaCl – sodium chloride **(1)**; $Cu(NO_3)_2$ – copper nitrate **(1)**; $MgCl_2$ – magnesium chloride **(1)**; $Al_2(SO_4)_3$ – aluminium sulfate **(1)**; $CaCl_2$ – calcium chloride **(1)**

115. Neutralisation

(a) two steps for precise measurements for **1 mark** each, to give a total of **2 marks**, e.g.
- Use a measuring cylinder with a capacity similar to the volume being used/use a (volumetric) pipette.
- Use a balance of 2 decimal places (±0.01 g).
- Use a pH meter.
- Calibrate the pH meter.

(b) Add a spot of liquid to the universal indicator paper **(1)**. Match the colour to the pH colour chart **(1)**. Work carefully, e.g. dip a glass rod into the reaction mixture/put the indicator paper on a white tile/wait 30 s for colour to develop. **(1)**

(c) The pH will be 0–6 at the start **(1)** because the solution contains excess $H^+(aq)$ ions **(1)**. The pH will be 7 at some point **(1)** because the acid will be neutralised by the base/alkali **(1)**. The pH will be 8–14 at the end **(1)** because the solution contains excess $OH^-(aq)$ ions. **(1)**

116. Salts from insoluble bases

(a) during the reaction: bubbling **(1)**; the white solid disappearing **(1)**

when calcium carbonate in excess: a white solid mixed with the liquid/cloudy mixture **(1)**

(b) **1 mark** for each of the following points, to **6 marks** maximum:
- Put some dilute nitric acid into a beaker/suitable container.
- Add calcium carbonate.
- Add until bubbling stops/excess solid is seen.
- Filter (to remove excess solid).
- Heat the filtrate.
- This will remove some of the water.
- Leave to cool.
- Decant/pour away/filter to remove the excess liquid.
- Leave crystals in a warm place/dry with paper.

117. Salts from soluble bases

(a) burette **(1)**
(b) pipette **(1)**

118. Making insoluble salts

(a) calcium carbonate **(1)**
(b) no precipitate **(1)**
(c) lead sulfate **(1)**

119. Extended response – Making salts

*Answer could include the following points, to **6 marks**:
- suitable solutions: lead(II) nitrate and sodium chloride/potassium chloride/ammonium chloride
- Lead compounds are toxic.
- Wear eye protection.
- Wear gloves.
- Mix the two solutions.
- Filter the mixture.
- Lead(II) chloride stays behind as a residue.
- Wash the residue in the filter paper.
- Use water/distilled water.
- This works because lead(II) chloride is insoluble.
- Leave washed residue in a warm place to dry.

120. Electrolysis

(a) potassium at the cathode/negative electrode **(1)**; iodine at the anode/positive electrode **(1)**

(b) aluminium at the cathode/negative electrode **(1)**; oxygen at the anode/positive electrode **(1)**

121. Electrolysing solutions

(a) H^+ from water and acid **(1)**; OH^- from water **(1)**; SO_4^{2-} from acid **(1)**

(b) hydrogen at the cathode/negative electrode **(1)**; oxygen at the anode/positive electrode **(1)**

122. Investigating electrolysis

(a) Ethanol evaporates more quickly/has a lower boiling point than water. **(1)**

(b) **1 mark** for each of the following points, to **2 marks** maximum:
- Some copper did not stick to the cathode/fell off during the experiment.
- Some copper fell off the cathode during washing/drying/weighing.
- Some metal fell off the anode during the experiment.
- The anode was not pure copper/contained other metals.

123. Extended response – Electrolysis

*Answer could include the following points, to **6 marks**:
dissolving in molten potassium chloride:
- Ions are not free to move in solid lithium chloride.
- Ions must be free to move for electrolysis to happen.
- Ions will be free to move in liquid/molten potassium chloride.
cathode process:
- Lithium ions are attracted to the cathode.
- Lithium ions gain electrons and become lithium atoms.
anode process:
- Chloride ions are attracted to the anode.
- Chloride ions lose electrons and become chlorine atoms.
- Covalent bond forms between two chlorine atoms.
- There is a shared pair of electrons.
- Pairs of chlorine atoms form chlorine molecules.

124. The reactivity series

(a) magnesium/calcium **(1)**
(b) iron **(1)** and zinc **(1)**

125. Metal displacement reactions

magnesium, zinc, iron, copper **(1)** This is in order of decreasing change in temperature. **(1)**

126. Explaining metal reactivity

Aluminium is more reactive than iron **(1)** because it can displace iron from iron(III) oxide **(1)**. This is because it has a greater tendency to lose electrons/form cations. **(1)**

127. Metal ores

1 Copper is more resistant to corrosion **(1)** because it is lower in the reactivity series. **(1)**

2 Iron(III) oxide is reduced because it loses oxygen **(1)**; carbon is oxidised because it gains oxygen. **(1)**

3 Platinum is low in the reactivity series/below gold/very unreactive **(1)**, so it does not combine with other elements. **(1)**

128. Iron and aluminium

1 Tin is less reactive than carbon/carbon is more reactive than tin **(1)**. Calcium is more reactive than carbon/carbon is less reactive than calcium **(1)**. So carbon can reduce tin oxide to tin, but not calcium oxide to calcium. **(1)**

2 Electrolysis uses electricity (1). This is expensive/more expensive than using carbon. (1)

129. Recycling metals

1 two from, for **1 mark** each: less waste rock produced/less carbon dioxide (or named pollutant) produced/less waste sent to landfill

2 Less energy is needed to melt aluminium than to melt steel (1). More energy is needed to extract aluminium by electrolysis than is needed to extract iron in the blast furnace. (1)

3 Recycling uses metals already extracted from ores (1), so no ore/less ore must be mined to produce new metal. (1)

130. Life-cycle assessments

1 The four main stages in a life-cycle assessment are: obtaining raw materials, manufacture, use, disposal. (1)

2 Another reason for carrying out a life-cycle assessment is to identify a stage that could be improved on. (1)

131. Extended response – Reactivity of metals

*Answer could include the following points, to **6 marks**:
expected order of reactivity:

- magnesium > zinc > copper

basic method:

- Add one of the solutions to three test tubes/other suitable container, e.g. spotting tile.
- Add a metal powder to each test tube.
- Observe a change in the solution and/or the metal powder, e.g. a colour change or temperature increase.
- Repeat with each of the other two solutions in turn.

expected results:

- An orange–brown coating of metal is obtained when magnesium or zinc is added to copper sulfate.
- The temperature increases when magnesium or zinc is added to copper sulfate.
- The blue colour of the solution fades when magnesium or zinc is added to copper sulfate.
- There is a black coating of metal when magnesium is added to zinc sulfate solution.
- There is no observed change with other combinations of metal and solution.

explanation:

- Magnesium and zinc are more reactive than copper/can displace copper from its compounds.
- Magnesium and zinc have a greater tendency than copper to lose electrons/better reducing agents.
- $Mg + CuSO_4 \rightarrow MgSO_4 + Cu$
- $Zn + CuSO_4 \rightarrow ZnSO_4 + Cu$
- Magnesium is more reactive than zinc/can displace zinc from its compounds.
- Magnesium has a greater tendency than zinc to lose electrons/ is a better reducing agent.
- $Mg + ZnSO_4 \rightarrow MgSO_4 + Zn$
- Copper is less reactive than magnesium and zinc/cannot displace magnesium and zinc from their compounds.
- Zinc is less reactive than magnesium/cannot displace magnesium from its compounds.

132. The Haber process

(a) The symbol means that the reaction is reversible. (1)

(b) Add the substance to be tested to anhydrous copper sulfate (1). If the copper sulfate turns blue, water is present. (1)

133. The alkali metals

(a) $2Cs + 2H_2O \rightarrow 2CsOH + H_2$
(**1 mark** for correct symbols and formulae; **1 mark** for correct balancing)

(b) two from, for **1 mark** each:
- violent/very violent reaction/explosion
- sparks/flames
- hydrogen/bubbles produced
- metal disappearing

(c) two from, for **1 mark** each:
- good conductors of heat/electricity
- shiny when freshly cut
- soft
- low melting points

134. The halogens

(a) The elements get darker going down the group. (1)

(b) melting point in the range 250 °C to 350 °C (1), justification, e.g. extrapolated melting points from chlorine to iodine (1)
Accepted estimate for melting point is 302 °C.

135. Reactions of halogens

1 Hydrogen fluoride (1); it dissolves (1) to form an acidic solution. (1)

2 Chlorine atoms are smaller than bromine atoms (1); so they gain electrons more easily. (1)

136. Halogen displacement reactions

1 bromine + potassium iodide → potassium bromide + iodine (1)

2 Chlorine is more reactive than bromine (1); so it can displace bromine from potassium bromide (1); bromine solution is orange. (1)

3 Astatine will not react with potassium iodide solution because:
- reactivity decreases down group 7 (1)
- astatine is less reactive than iodine. (1)

137. The noble gases

1 The densities of helium and neon are less than the density of air (1) but the densities of argon and krypton are greater than the density of air. (1)

2 It is inert/non-flammable (1). It is denser than air so it sinks and excludes air. (1)

3 Its outer shell is full (1), so it does not lose/gain/share electrons. (1)

138. Extended response – Groups

*Answer could include the following points, to **6 marks**:
experiment:

- Put potassium chloride solution in three test tubes.
- Add a few drops of halogen solution to each one.
- Observe any changes.
- Record in a suitable table.
- Repeat with potassium bromide and potassium iodide.

precautions:

- Wear eye protection because solutions are irritants.
- Avoid contact with skin because solutions are irritants.
- Avoid breathing in vapours/keep lab well ventilated because vapours are toxic/harmful.

expected results:

- No changes with potassium chloride.

- Potassium bromide turns darker when chlorine solution is added.
- Potassium iodide turns darker when chlorine solution is added.
- Potassium iodide turns darker when bromine solution is added.

using the results:
- Chlorine can displace bromine and iodine.
- Bromine can displace iodine.
- Iodide cannot displace chlorine or bromine.
- Order of reactivity, most reactive to least reactive: chlorine, bromine, iodine.

139. Rates of reaction

(a) The rate of reaction increases **(1)**, the surface area:volume ratio of the marble increases **(1)** and so the frequency of collisions increases. **(1)**

(b) The rate of reaction decreases **(1)**, the acid particles become less crowded/there are fewer reactant particles in the same volume **(1)** and so the frequency of collisions decreases. **(1)**

140. Investigating rates

three from, for **1 mark** each:
- same volume of sodium thiosulfate solution
- same concentration of sodium thiosulfate solution
- same amount of cloudiness (measured using the disappearing cross)
- same volume of diluted acid.

These factors also affect the rate of reaction/measured rate of reaction. **(1)**

141. Skills – Rates of reaction

(a) 0 s to 45 s: $\frac{43}{45}$ **(1)** = 0.96 cm³/s **(1)**

45 s to 90 s: $\frac{50-43}{45}$ **(1)** = 0.16 cm³/s **(1)**

(b) Measure and record the mass of manganese dioxide at the start **(1)**. (Afterwards) filter **(1)**, dry **(1)**, measure and record the mass of manganese dioxide again. **(1)**

142. Heat energy changes

1 mark for each correct column (**0 marks** if two ticks in a column)

	Breaking bonds	Making bonds	Temperature of reaction mixture	
			Increases	Decreases
Exothermic process		✓	✓	
Endothermic process	✓			✓

143. Reaction profiles

1 Activation energy is the minimum energy **(1)** needed to start a reaction/to break the bonds in the reactant particles. **(1)**

2 (a) correct axes and shape of graph **(1)**; reactants and products identified **(1)**; activation energy identified **(1)**; energy change identified **(1)**

(b) correct axes and shape of graph **(1)**; reactants and products identified **(1)**; activation energy identified **(1)**; energy change identified **(1)**

144. Crude oil

1 (a) A hydrocarbon is a compound of carbon and hydrogen **(1)** only. **(1)**

(b) covalent bond **(1)**

2 Crude oil takes millions of years to form/is made extremely slowly **(1)** or is no longer being made. **(1)**

3 chains **(1)**; rings **(1)**

4 (a) (petroleum) gases/petrol/kerosene/diesel oil/fuel oil **(1)**
not bitumen

(b) polymers/named polymer, e.g. poly(ethene) **(1)**

145. Fractional distillation

1 It is difficult to ignite/not very flammable **(1)**; it has a high viscosity/is very viscous/does not flow easily. **(1)**

2 Oil is evaporated **(1)** and passed into a column, which is hot at the bottom and cool at the top **(1)**. Hydrocarbons (rise), cool and condense at different heights. **(1)**

146. Alkanes

1 three from, for **1 mark** each:
- same general formula
- molecular formulae of neighbouring members differ by CH_2
- gradual variation in physical properties
- similar chemical properties.

2 $C_{21}H_{44}$ **(1)**

3 −40 °C (answer in range −35 °C to −45 °C) **(1)**

147. Incomplete combustion

1 There is a poor supply of air/oxygen **(1)**, so carbon in the fuel is only partially oxidised to carbon monoxide **(1)** or released as carbon particles/soot. **(1)**

2 It is odourless **(1)** and colourless. **(1)**

3 Soot shows that incomplete combustion is happening **(1)**. Carbon monoxide might be forming but soot does not prove this/carbon monoxide is likely to be forming as well (which could be confirmed using a carbon monoxide detector). **(1)**

148. Acid rain

1 two from, for **1 mark** each:
- weathering of buildings/statues
- damage to trees
- harm to living things in river/lakes/soil

2 (a) Hydrocarbon fuels contain impurities of sulfur compounds **(1)**. The sulfur is oxidised to sulfur dioxide when the fuel is used. **(1)**

(b) Nitrogen and oxygen from the air **(1)** react together in the high temperatures inside an engine. **(1)**

149. Choosing fuels

1 Petrol contains hydrocarbons **(1)**. The carbon in these molecules is oxidised to carbon dioxide **(1)**. Hydrogen does not contain carbon/consists only of hydrogen. **(1)**

2 (a) Crude oil and natural gas are non-renewable **(1)**. They are being used faster than they are formed. **(1)**

(b) Carbon dioxide may be produced during the manufacture/transport of the fuel **(1)**. For example, fossil fuels are used (in power stations) to generate electricity/to react with steam to make hydrogen. **(1)**

150. Cracking

(a) C_2H_4 **(1)**

(b) This hydrocarbon can be used to make polymers. **(1)**

151. Extended response – Fuels

*Answer could include the following points, to **6 marks**:

similarities of hydrogen and diesel oil:

- Both produce water when burnt.
- Both transfer energy to the surroundings when burnt.

differences between hydrogen and diesel oil:

- Hydrogen can be produced by the electrolysis of water.
- If water is the raw material, hydrogen could be a renewable fuel (diesel oil is a non-renewable fuel).
- The electricity needed could be generated using renewable resources (sun, wind, tidal, biomass).
- Carbon dioxide is released when diesel oil is burnt but not when hydrogen is burnt.
- Hydrogen is a gas at room temperature and pressure, but diesel oil is a liquid.
- Hydrogen is more difficult to store/may need to be stored under pressure/low temperatures.
- There are fewer hydrogen filling stations than diesel oil filling stations.
- Hydrogen is usually produced from natural gas/coal but diesel oil comes from crude oil.
- Diesel oil produces carbon particles/soot in use.
- Diesel oil produces sulfur dioxide (unless sulfur impurities are removed from fuel before use) but hydrogen does not.
- Hydrogen can be used in fuel cells but diesel oil cannot.

152. The early atmosphere

1 (a) Carbon dioxide dissolved in the oceans. **(1)**

(b) Plants produced oxygen **(1)** by photosynthesis. **(1)**

2 Scientists cannot be certain about the Earth's early atmosphere because no measurements were made then/no humans were on Earth then. **(1)**

153. Greenhouse effect

1 (a) carbon dioxide **(1)**, methane **(1)**

(b) carbon dioxide from burning fossil fuels **(1)**, methane from cattle/livestock/rice paddy fields **(1)**

2 Greenhouse gases absorb heat radiated from the Earth **(1)**. The gases then release the heat (into the atmosphere). **(1)**

3 Fossil fuels give off carbon dioxide during combustion **(1)**. Increased consumption releases more carbon dioxide **(1)**, which is a greenhouse gas **(1)**, so the greenhouse effect increases. **(1)**

154. Extended response – Atmospheric science

*Answer could include the following points, to **6 marks**:

processes that remove carbon dioxide:

- photosynthesis by plants/algae
- making oxygen and glucose/carbohydrates/starch
- carbon dioxide dissolving in seawater

processes that release carbon dioxide:

- combustion of fossil fuels

- combustion of biomass/plants/trees
- respiration
- volcanic eruptions

observed increase:

- rate of release greater than rate of removal
- increasing use of fossil fuels
- deforestation means less photosynthesis
- limit to the rate at which carbon dioxide can dissolve in the oceans

Physics

155. Key concepts

1 (a) 3 **(1)**

(b) 4 **(1)**

(c) 5 **(1)**

2 (a) $12 \times 60 \times 60$ **(1)** $= 43\,200\,s$ **(1)**

(b) $= 17.8\,m/s$ **(1)**

3 $58.3\,MW = 58\,300\,000\,W$ **(1)** $= 5.83 \times 10^7\,W$ **(1)**

4 1.0 **(1)** $\times 10^{-10}\,m$ **(1)**

156. Scalars and vectors

1 (a) A quantity that has a size or a magnitude only. **(1)**

(b) A quantity that has a size or magnitude and a direction. **(1)**

2 (a) **C (1)**

(b) **D (1)**

3 (a) $4\,m/s$ **(1)**

(b) $-4\,m/s$ **(1)**

157. Speed, distance and time

1 speed $= 120\,m \div 8\,s$ **(1)**, speed $= 15$ **(1)** m/s **(1)**

2 Distance $=$ average speed $\times$ time **(1)**, $= 9\,m/s \times 30\,m = 270$ **(1)** m **(1)**

3 gradient of zero at origin **(1)**, increasing gradient of graph shown **(1)**, distance and time shown as correct y- and x-axes, respectively **(1)**

158. Equations of motion

1 $a = (8\,m/s - 2\,m/s) \div 5\,s$ **(1)** $= 6\,m/s \div 5\,s = 1.2$ **(1)** m/s^2 **(1)**

2 Acceleration $=$ change in velocity $\div$ time taken **(1)** $= (6\,m/s - 18\,m/s) \div 4\,s = -3$ **(1)** m/s^2 **(1)**

3 Final velocity^2 – initial velocity^2 = 2 × acceleration × distance **(1)**

Final velocity^2 – $(5\,m/s)^2 = 2 \times 2.0\,m/s^2 \times 180\,m$ **(1)**

Final velocity$^2 = 720 + 25 = 745$ **(1)**

Final velocity $= \sqrt{745} = 27.3\,m/s$ **(1)**

159. Velocity/time graphs

1 (a) Gradient of a velocity/time graph gives acceleration. **(1)**

(b) Area beneath a velocity/time graph gives distance travelled. **(1)**

2 Distance on y-axis, time on x-axis **(1)**, 200 m shown as covered after 8 s **(1)**, 300 m shown as total distance after 33 s **(1)**, axes units given as m on y-axis and s on x-axis. **(1)**

3 (a) Velocity in m/s plotted on y-axis, time in s plotted on x-axis **(1)**, diagonal line from origin to 10 m/s after 4 s drawn **(1)**, horizontal line at 10 m/s for the next 8 s drawn **(1)**, axes units given as m/s on y-axis and s on x-axis. **(1)**

(b) Distance is area beneath the graph. Area for first 10 s = ½ × 10 × 4 = 20 m **(1)**, area for the next 8 s is 10 m/s × 8 s = 80 m **(1)**, total distance run = 80 m + 20 m = 100 m. **(1)**

160. Determining speed

1 time taken **(1)** for the object to travel over a known distance **(1)**

2 Light gates do not introduce a human reaction time or human error **(1)** which would increase the actual time value and they can measure to a higher degree of accuracy and to a smaller fraction of a second. **(1)**

3 The trolley will accelerate **(1)** due to the component of its weight acting down the slope **(1)** and this means that the speed increases with time/distance travelled. **(1)**

161. Newton's first law

1 balanced or equal and opposite **(1)** OR no forces acting **(1)**

2 The forces acting on the moving body are in different/opposite directions **(1)** of different sizes **(1)**, or a diagram drawn to show this. These forces could be antiparallel or even at an angle, such as at 90° to the initial movement. A change in direction will occur if the forces oppose the original motion or act in a way to change the direction.

3 diagrams showing:

(a) two forces of 100 N **(1)** acting in directly opposite directions **(1)**

(b) two forces of 100 N **(1)** acting in directly opposite directions **(1)**

(c) two forces of 100 N **(1)** both acting to the left **(1)**

162. Newton's second law

1 $F = 1.2\,kg \times 8\,m/s^2$ **(1)** $= 9.6$ **(1)** N **(1)**

2 Force = mass × acceleration, so mass = force ÷ acceleration **(1)** $= 24\,N \div 2\,m/s^2$ **(1)** $= 12\,kg$ **(1)**

3 Force = mass × acceleration, so acceleration = force ÷ mass **(1)** $= 6000\,N \div 1200\,kg$ **(1)**, $= 5\,m/s^2$ **(1)**

163. Weight and mass

1 (a) weight $= 50\,kg \times 10\,N/kg$ **(1)** $= 500\,N$ **(1)**

(b) weight $= 50\,kg \times 26\,N/kg$ **(1)** $= 1300\,N$ **(1)**

2 Weight = mass × g, so mass = weight ÷ g **(1)**, mass $= 480\,N \div 10\,N/kg$ **(1)** $= 48\,kg$ **(1)**

3 $g = W \div m$ **(1)** $= 54\,N \div 18\,kg$ **(1)** $= 3\,N/kg$ **(1)**

164. Force and acceleration

1 More accurate/repeat readings **(1)** can be taken with little or no human error **(1)** and calculations can be performed quickly by the data logger to provide speeds and accelerations, etc. **(1)**

2 more accurate mass **(1)**, more accurate slope/gradient **(1)**, reduce friction, more readings for mass **(1)**, repeat readings to determine the precision **(1)**

3 constant mass throughout/other variables controlled **(1)**, change slope by 10° at a time **(1)**, same starting point along slope **(1)**, record enough values for change in velocity and change in times between two light gates **(1)**, repeat readings to determine the precision **(1)**

165. Newton's third law

1 The forces pairs acting on a body have the same size **(1)**, act in opposite directions **(1)** and act on different bodies. **(1)**

2 A force from the ball acts on the gloves **(1)**, an equal and opposite force **(1)** acts from the gloves on the ball. **(1)**

166. Human reaction time

1 (a) Human reaction time is the time between a stimulus occurring and a response. **(1)**

(b) three from: tiredness **(1)**, alcohol **(1)**, drugs **(1)**, distractions **(1)**, age **(1)**

2 Reaction time $= \sqrt{2 \times distance \div g}$ **(1)** $= \sqrt{2 \times 0.24\,m \div 10\,m/s^2}$ **(1)** $= 0.22\,s$ **(1)**

167. Stopping distances

1 (a) two from, **1 mark** each: speed, tiredness, alcohol, drugs, distractions, reaction time

(b) two from, **1 mark** each: speed, icy or wet roads, worn tyres or brakes, mass of car, any reference to friction being less than normal

2 less friction/force between tyres and road **(1)** so increased braking distance **(1)**, so a greater stopping distance **(1)**

168. Extended response – Motion and forces

*Answer could include the following points, to **6 marks**:

- reaction times and thinking distance – as reaction time increases so does thinking distance. Reaction time is the time between seeing the hazard and applying a force to the brakes.

- speed of car – affecting thinking and braking distance. More speed means a greater distance is covered when thinking and braking compared with a lower speed.

- alcohol, drugs or tiredness – affecting reaction times and thinking distance. Both will increase if drivers are under the influence of these since they will be less alert.

- condition of tyres – bald tyres means greater braking distance as there will be less grip.

- condition of road (icy or wet) resulting in less grip.

- mass of car/number of passengers increases braking distance at a given speed due to greater inertial mass/constant force needed over a longer time to stop.

169. Energy stores and transfers

1 Energy store diagram should include the chemical energy, kinetic energy and gravitational potential energy stores and the thermal energy store shown as the wasted form. At each part of the journey of the car uphill, the total of these four stores should be constant. The diagram should show

chemical store → (mechanical → kinetic store
(decreases)   energy transfer)   (increases)

+ gravitational potential store + thermal store
(increases)   (increases)   **(4)**

2 The kinetic energy store of the car increases **(1)**. The force transfers energy to this store **(1)**. Some of the energy is transferred to the environment by friction with the air and tyres with the road **(1)** and stored as thermal energy. **(1)**

170. Efficient heat transfer

1 efficiency $= (14\,J \div 20\,J) \times 100\%$ **(1)** $= 70\%$ **(1)**

2 Increase the thickness of the wall **(1)** and use a material with a lower thermal conductivity. **(1)**

171. Energy resources

1 (a) Diagram should show gpe → kinetic → electrical → (thermal energy as wasted). **(3)**

(b) Diagram should show chemical → heat or ... chemical → electrical or ... chemical → kinetic. **(3)**

2 biofuels advantages: reliable, can be replaced, can be readily grown and converted to fuels for use in cars, can be stored, renewable, cheap **(any 1 for 1 mark)**; biofuels disadvantages: gives off CO_2/greenhouse gases when burned, not renewable if not regrown **(any 1 for 1 mark)**; solar advantages: renewable, almost infinite energy supply, no cost for the solar energy **(any 1 for 1 mark)**; solar disadvantages: solar cells are expensive to make and buy, unreliable (when not sunny or at night), difficult to store the energy in electrical form, production of cells in manufacturing will pollute **(any 1 for 1 mark)**

172. Patterns of energy use

1   two from: threats to food supplies for those who need them **(1)**, global warming and floods due to using fossil fuels **(1)**, running out of non-renewable resources **(1)**

2   Wood has been readily available **(1)** for thousands of years **(1)** and has not had to be discovered, mined or have any extra technology developed (e.g. nuclear reactors/power stations) in order for it to be used to produce thermal energy. **(1)**

173. Potential and kinetic energy

1   $\Delta GPE = m \times g \times \Delta h = 5\,kg \times 10\,N/kg \times 18\,m$ **(1)** $= 900$ **(1)** J **(1)**

2   Kinetic energy $= \frac{1}{2} \times mass \times velocity^2 = \frac{1}{2} \times 60\,kg \times (5\,m/s)^2$ **(1)** $= 750$ **(1)** J **(1)**

3   $30\,km/h = 30\,000\,m \div 3600\,s = 8.3\,m/s$ **(1)**, $KE = \frac{1}{2} \times 80\,kg \times (8.3\,m/s)^2$ **(1)** $= 2778$ **(1)** J **(1)**

174. Extended response – Conservation of energy

*Answer could include the following points (for **6 marks**, two advantages and two disadvantages with good supporting explanation should be supplied):

*   advantages of wind – renewable, no fuel needed, no carbon dioxide gas emissions
*   disadvantages – unsightly, unreliable
*   advantages of coal – efficient, reliable
*   disadvantages – non-renewable, carbon dioxide and sulfur dioxide gas emissions

175. Waves

1   (a)   amplitude **(1)**   wavelength **(1)**   for correct shape **(1)**

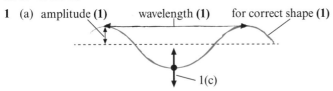

1(c)

(b)   ← or → **(1)** (c) arrow shown above **(1)**

2   A particle moves backwards and forwards about a fixed position **(1)** and parallel to the direction of energy transfer. **(1)**

3   2.2 mm **(1)** *Any answer between 2.1 and 2.4 is acceptable.*

176. Wave equations

1   (a)   Wave speed = frequency × wavelength = 100 Hz × 3.3 m **(1)** = 330 **(1)** m/s **(1)**

(b)   Wavelength = wave speed ÷ frequency = 330 m/s ÷ 1650 Hz **(1)** = 0.2 **(1)** m **(1)**

2   1 minute = 60 seconds **(1)**; $x = 25\,m/s \times 60\,s$ **(1)** = 1500 **(1)** m **(1)**

177. Measuring wave velocity

1   Wave speed = distance ÷ time = 30 m ÷ 5 s **(1)** = 6 **(1)** m/s **(1)**

2   wave speed = frequency × wavelength = 4 Hz × 0.08 m **(1)** = 0.32 **(1)** m/s **(1)**

3   Make a sound that is a large, known distance away from a wall **(1)**. Find the time between the generation of the sound and the detection of the reflected sound/echo accurately **(1)**. Use the equation total distance travelled ÷ total time **(1)** to find the speed. Use equipment that has high accuracy for measuring distance and time. **(1)**

178. Waves and boundaries

Light ray may change direction **(1)** and bend away from normal **(1)** as it moves from glass to air if angle of incidence is not along the normal. There will be no change in direction if the light ray moves into air from glass along the normal. **(1)**

179. Waves in fluids

1   Wave speed = distance travelled ÷ time taken **(1)**; wave speed = frequency × wavelength **(1)**

2   As wave speed = frequency × wavelength **(1)**, wavelength increases and frequency stays the same **(1)** so the wave velocity will increase. **(1)**

180. Extended response – Waves

*Answer could include the following points, to **6 marks**:

*   Water wave or sound wave generated.
*   Object placed on water wave or in the region of the sound waves.
*   Object does not move in direction of wave when wave is generated
*   but will move up or down on the water wave,
*   backwards and forwards in the sound wave.
*   Suitable equipment suggested.

181. Electromagnetic spectrum

1   (a)   radio waves **(1)**

(b)   gamma-rays **(1)**

2   Wave speed = frequency × wavelength = 3000 m × 100 000 Hz **(1)** = 300 000 000 **(1)** m/s **(1)**

3   Wave speed = frequency × wavelength, so frequency = wave velocity ÷ wavelength **(1)** = 300 000 000 m/s ÷ 0.05 m **(1)** = 6 × 10^9 **(1)** Hz **(1)**

182. Investigating refraction

1   its direction **(1)**

2   angles of refraction are less than their corresponding angles of incidence **(1)**; angles of refraction are greater than the corresponding angles of refraction for those in the glass block. **(1)**

183. Dangers and uses

1   They can cause damage to the skin such as sunburn **(1)**, skin cancer **(1)** as well as damage to the eyes. **(1)**

2   X-rays are useful to doctors as they allow them to detect broken bones **(1)** but can damage cells **(1)**, which could cause them to mutate/lead to cancer. **(1)**

3   Gamma-rays can pass through the body and be detected by, e.g., a gamma camera, allowing a doctor to see if cancer is present **(1)**. Gamma-rays may cause cancer, but this is a risk worth taking if there is a possibility that the patient has a malignant cancer which may lead to death if not detected. **(1)**

184. Changes and radiation

1   Electron energy levels or shells **(1)** and in the nucleus. **(1)**

2   (a)   Electrons move to higher energy levels **(1)** with the difference in energy between the levels equal to the energy of the electromagnetic radiation. **(1)**

(b)   An electron falls down from a higher to a lower energy level **(1)** with a photon emitted having with energy equal to the energy difference between the two levels. **(1)**

185. Extended response – Light and the electromagnetic spectrum

*Answer could include the following points, to **6 marks**:

*   radio waves: including broadcasting, communications and satellite transmissions
*   microwaves: including cooking, communications and satellite transmissions

- infrared: including cooking, thermal imaging, short-range communications, optical fibres, television remote controls and security systems
- visible light: including vision, photography and illumination
- ultraviolet: including security marking, fluorescent lamps, detecting forged bank notes and disinfecting water
- X-rays: including observing the internal structure of objects, airport security scanners and medical X-rays
- gamma-rays: including sterilising food and medical equipment, and the detection of cancer and its treatment

186. Structure of the atom

(a) Diameter of atom ÷ diameter of nucleus = $10^{-10} \div 10^{-15}$ **(1)** = 10^5 or 100 000 times **(1)**

(b) Diameter of molecule/diameter of nucleus = $10^{-9} \div 10^{-15}$ **(1)** = 10^6 or 1 000 000 times **(1)**

187. Atoms and isotopes

1 Atoms A and B are isotopes **(1)** as they both contain the same number of protons. **(1)**

2 $^{11}_{5}B$ **(1)**

188. Atoms, electrons and ions

1 (a) nucleus **(1)**

(b) nucleus **(1)**

(c) in orbits or shells around the nucleus **(1)**

2 Atoms of an element contain the same number of protons as electrons **(1)** and have a neutral charge overall **(1)**, whereas ions of an element have the same number of protons but can gain electrons so that they have a negative charge (more electrons than protons) **(1)** or lose electrons so that they have a positive charge (more protons than electrons). **(1)**

3 (a) A charge of +2 **(1)** as two negative electrons of charge –1 each have been lost **(1)**.

(b) A charge of –1 **(1)** as it has gained an electron of charge –1. **(1)**

189. Ionising radiation

1 Alpha particles/radiation **(1)**

2 You cannot predict **(1)** when a nucleus will decay by emitting radiation. **(1)**

190. Background radiation

1 D **(1)**

2 Low level radiation **(1)** that is present all around us **(1)** and comes from natural and man-made sources. **(1)**

3 (a) The sector for radon would be much smaller. **(1)**

(b) The sector for radon would be bigger. **(1)**

191. Measuring radioactivity

1 dosimeter/film badge **(1)**, Geiger–Müller tube **(1)**

2 Lead sheet stops alpha and beta radiation but some gamma will penetrate it **(1)**; gamma is dangerous to the body from an external source **(1)** so the worker knows that they have been exposed to it and needs to seek help. **(1)**

192. Models of the atom

1 Plum pudding model with negative plums in a positive 'dough' **(1)**. Rutherford atom model with a small positive nucleus compared to overall atomic diameter **(1)**. Bohr model with electrons orbiting a positive nucleus in definite, discrete energy levels. **(1)**

2 Positive alpha particles were fired at nucleus **(1)**. Most went through undeflected **(1)**, so most of the atom must be empty space **(1)**. A very few alpha particles were repelled back, so the nucleus must have been small and positive. **(1)**

3 Evidence **(1)** is collected from experiments **(1)** and if this shows that the new model is better than a previous model it will be accepted as a better model by scientists. **(1)**

193. Beta decay

1 (a) A neutron turns into a proton **(1)** and an electron is emitted **(1)**. (b) A proton turns into a neutron **(1)** and a positron is emitted. **(1)**

2 A beta particle is an electron that is emitted from an unstable nucleus **(1)** and an electron in a stable atom is found in shells orbiting the nucleus. **(1)**

3 $^{66}_{28}Ni$ **(1)** $\rightarrow ^{66}_{29}Cu$ **(1)** $+ ^{0}_{-1}\beta$ **(1)**, beta minus decay **(1)**

194. Radioactive decay

1 (a) $^{10}_{6}C \rightarrow ^{10}_{5}B + ^{0}_{1}\beta$ **(1)**, beta plus decay **(1)**

(b) $^{232}_{90}Th \rightarrow ^{228}_{88}Ra + ^{4}_{2}He$ **(1)**, alpha decay **(1)**

2 (a) Mass number = 92 + 146 = 238 **(1)**, atomic number is the number of protons = 92 **(1)**.

(b) An alpha particle has a mass of 4 and an atomic number of 2 **(1)** so losing two alpha particles means the mass number decreases by 8 and the atomic number by 4 **(1)**, a beta particle being emitted causes the mass number to stay the same and the atomic number to go up by 1 **(1)**, so the final mass number will be 230 and the atomic number will be 89. **(1)**

195. Half-life

1 (a) it will halve **(1)** to a value of 2000 Bq **(1)**

(b) it will halve from the 2 day rate of 2000 Bq **(1)** to 1000 Bq **(1)**

(c) it will quarter from the 4 day rate of 1000 Bq **(1)** to 250 Bq **(1)**

2 120 Bq to 30 Bq is one quarter of the activity or two half-lives in 4 hours **(1)**, so one half-life is half of four hours = 2 hours. **(1)**

3 After 15 minutes: $\frac{1}{2}$; after 30 minutes: $\frac{1}{4}$ **(1)**; after 45 minutes: $\frac{1}{8}$ **(1)**; after 60 minutes: $\frac{1}{16}$. **(1)**

196. Dangers of radiation

1 two from: can cause cells to become ionised, which leads to chemical reactions taking place in cells **(1)** causing them to die **(1)** or mutate **(1)**, which can lead to cancer **(1)**

2 Ionising radiation knocks electrons from shells **(1)** making them more reactive and allowing change to DNA to occur **(1)**, whereas non-ionising radiation cannot do this as there is not enough energy to knock electrons from shells. **(1)**

3 minimise the time they are exposed to the radiation **(1)**; wear protective clothing (e.g. lead apron) **(1)**; increase the distance from the radioactive source to the person **(1)**

197. Contamination and irradiation

1 (a) Irradiation is the exposure of the body to ionising radiation **(1)** from a source that is outside the body. **(1)**

(b) Contamination is exposure to ionising radiation from a source that is taken into the body **(1)**, by eating, breathing in, drinking, injection or via contact with ionising radiation on the surface of the skin. **(1)**

2 Alpha particles are highly ionising due to their charge and mass **(1)** and will cause damage inside the body as they have a short range **(1)** and will come into contact with cells. Outside the body they are unlikely to reach the body as they have a range of only 5 cm in air and so cannot easily reach the body to cause any ionisation in cells. **(1)**

3 Some sources of background radiation do not come into contact with the body such as cosmic rays from the Sun and medical X-rays **(1)**, but other sources such as radon gas and radioisotopes in food are taken into the body. **(1)**

198. Extended response – Radioactivity

*Answer could include the following points, to **6 marks**:

- Mention of plum pudding model with electrons inside a positive dough.
- Mention of Rutherford model with small, positive nucleus which is concentrated in a tiny space around which electrons orbit.
- Mention of Bohr model with electrons in defined energy shells.
- Mention of experimental methods for refining models (e.g. a description of how Rutherford's alpha particle experiment was conducted).
- Mention of evidence collected from experiments to show new, better models.
- Mention that evidence from experiments shows a better understanding and that this new knowledge replaces older knowledge since the new model is better.
- Mention that experiments need to be conducted to provide evidence based on calculations or theories that have been developed. Only when the experiment provides evidence for a new, better model is it accepted by the scientific community.

199. Work, energy and power

1 work = $F \times d$ = 350 N × 30 m **(1)** = 10 500 **(1)** J **(1)**
2 energy = $P \times t$ = 1800 W × 8 × 60 s **(1)** = 864 000 **(1)** J **(1)**
3 power = $E \div t$ = 3600 W ÷ 60 s **(1)** = 60 **(1)** W **(1)**

200. Extended response – Energy and forces

*Answer could include the following points, to **6 marks**:

- Refer to power as the rate of energy transfer (or similar).
- Refer to gain in gravitational potential energy as $mg\Delta h$ where Δh is the change in height that masses are lifted.
- Δh is a control variable.
- Time measurement is needed.
- Refer to the change in gravitational potential energy for both weightlifters over a period of time.
- Compare their power values using the equation: power = energy/time or $P = mg\Delta h/t$.
- Refer to the greater distance lifted per unit time as showing the most powerful weightlifter.
- Refer to keeping it a fair test – e.g. same masses for both weightlifters.

201. Interacting forces

1 Gravity is always an attractive force, whereas magnetism and the electrostatic force can be attractive or repulsive. **(1)**
2 Friction and drag always work to oppose motion/slow down a moving object. **(1)**
3 Contact forces are two from: drag **(1)**, normal **(1)** and upthrust **(1)**. Non-contact force is the force of gravity acting on the ship. **(1)**

202. Circuit symbols

1 filament lamp **(1)**; motor **(1)**; LED **(1)**
2 ammeters in series **(1)**; voltmeters in parallel **(1)**
3 circuit to contain a cell **(1)**; lamp **(1)**; LDR **(1)**

203. Series and parallel circuits

1 Series: current same at all points **(1)**, potential differences across components add to give potential difference across cell **(1)**. Parallel: current splits at a junction **(1)**, potential difference across each branch is same as potential difference across cell. **(1)**
2 Current will stop flowing in series if one bulb breaks **(1)**, so parallel arrangement so that other lights stay on **(1)** if one or more bulbs break. **(1)**
3 More bulbs in parallel means a higher current **(1)** is drawn from the cell, so finite amount of stored chemical energy **(1)** decreases **(1)** more rapidly. **(1)**
4 $A_1 = A_2 = 1$ A **(1)** $V_1 = V_2 = 3$ V **(1)**

204. Current and charge

1 charge: coulomb **(1)**; current: ampere **(1)**
2 $Q = I \times t$ = 0.25 A × (60 × 60) s **(1)** = 900 **(1)** C **(1)**
3 Charge = current × time, 3000 C = 0.25 A × time **(1)**, time = 3000 C ÷ 0.25 A **(1)** = 12 000 **(1)** s **(1)**

205. Energy and charge

1 $E = Q \times V$ = 24 C × 6 V **(1)** = 144 **(1)** J **(1)**
2 $V = E \div Q$ **(1)**, so since unit of energy is J and charge is C **(1)**, we get 1 V = 1 J/C **(1)**
3 Energy = charge × potential difference, 400 J = 50 C × V **(1)**, so V = 400 J ÷ 50 C **(1)**, = 8 **(1)** V **(1)**

206. Ohm's law

1 $V = I \times R$ = 3.2 A × 18 Ω **(1)** = 57.6 **(1)** V **(1)**
2 $R = V \div I$ = 28 V ÷ 0.4 A **(1)** = 70 **(1)** Ω **(1)**

207. Resistors

$I = V \div R$ = 12 V ÷ 120 Ω **(1)** = 0.1 **(1)** A **(1)**

208. I–V graphs

(a) graph of S-shaped curve through origin of I against V for filament lamp **(1)**; labelled axes **(1)**
(b) As the current goes up, the temperature goes up **(1)** and as the temperature goes up the resistance goes up **(1)** and the gradient goes down. **(1)**

209. Electrical circuits

1 Current will flow through the components **(1)** in either arrangement, with the shape of the I–V graph being determined by the structure **(1)** of the component and whether it obeys Ohm's law or not **(1)**, not on how it is arranged in a circuit, since heat will still be dissipated in each circuit. **(1)**
2 As the p.d. increases across the filament lamp, the current through the filament lamp also increases **(1)** and as current increases, the energy is dissipated as heat increases leading to more vibrations of the metal ions in the filament **(1)**, which increases the resistance of the lamp **(1)** so the current increases by less and less per unit increase in p.d. **(1)** leading to a graph of decreasing gradient as the p.d. gets bigger and bigger. **(1)**

210. The LDR and the thermistor

1 (a) temperature **(1)**
  (b) light intensity **(1)**
2 Provide an example of a circuit where temperature **(1)** and light intensity **(1)** vary their resistances **(1)** to turn on an output device. **(1)** *The marks can only be awarded if the operation of the circuit is described in terms of changing light levels and temperature. An example would be for a circuit that turns a light/heater on or off in a greenhouse, for example.*

211. Current heating effect

1 three devices, e.g. oven, iron, heater, hair dryer, toaster, grill **(1 mark each)**

2 Large current **(1)**, transfers much thermal energy **(1)** which may lead to a fire. **(1)**

3 The potential difference causes a current to flow **(1)**, the current causes the metal atoms to vibrate **(1)** the vibrations of the atoms cause thermal energy **(1)** to be dissipated. **(1)**

212. Energy and power

1 Power = current × potential difference = 13 A × 230 V **(1)** = 2990 **(1)** W **(1)**

2 Energy transferred = current × potential difference × time **(1)** = 1.5 A × 12 V × 120 s **(1)** = 2160 **(1)** J **(1)**

213. A.c. and d.c. circuits

1 (a) three devices, e.g. remote controls, torches, mobile phones, calculators, watches **(1 mark each)**

(b) three mains-operated devices, e.g. electric oven, microwave oven, fridge, freezer, tumble dryer, hairdryer, TV **(1 mark each)**

2 (a) They both transfer energy **(1)**

(b) Potential difference in a.c. alternates **(1)** but in d.c. it is constant. **(1)**

3 Energy transferred = power × time **(1)**. The power rating of the electric oven is 200 times bigger than that of the electric shaver **(1)**. So the energy transferred (in the same amount of time) will be 200 times bigger for the oven than the shaver. **(1)**

214. Mains electricity and the plug

1 (a) brown **(1)**

(b) blue **(1)**

(c) yellow and green **(1)**

2 advantage of fuse: cheaper **(1)**; advantage of circuit breaker – one from: more sensitive to current **(1)**, does not need to be replaced (reset by pressing a switch) **(1)**, more reliable **(1)**, responds faster **(1)**

3 Live wire touches metal case **(1)**, earth wire forms circuit with live wire and pulls a large current through the fuse **(1)**, large current melts fuse and isolates appliance **(1)**, device now at 0 V and no longer dangerous to user. **(1)**

215. Extended response – Electricity and circuits

*Answer could include the following points, to **6 marks**:

- Fuse will melt if the current entering an appliance is too big.
- Earth wire pulls a large current through a fuse and melts the fuse wire if the live wire comes into contact with the metal casing.
- Mention that fuse/earth wire are safety devices.
- Mention fuse is connected to live wire so that device will be at 0 V when the fuse blows.
- Fuse/earth wire isolate the appliance so that device case cannot become live and so protects the user from the electrocution/fires occurring due to overheating.
- The fuse rating should be close to, but above, the current taken by the appliance so as to avoid any risk of the device overheating/catching fire due to the current becoming too high and producing too much thermal energy.

216. Magnets and magnetic fields

1 (a) similar to the diagram for the bar magnet **(1)** but with fewer field lines **(1)**

(b) similar to the diagram for the uniform field **(1)** but with more field lines **(1)**

2 The permanent magnet always induces **(1)** the opposite pole **(1)** next to its pole causing it to attract. **(1)**

3 A permanent magnet has N and S poles all of the time **(1)**, a temporary magnet is a magnetic material that does not have magnetic poles **(1)** but can be magnetised/attracted when placed near a permanent magnet. **(1)**

217. Current and magnetism

1 similar to diagram on page 217 **(1)**, but with the arrows in the opposite direction **(1)**

2 Current doubles so field doubles **(1)**, distance doubles so field halves **(1)**, so overall there is no change. **(1)**

3 Increase the size of the current flowing **(1)**, increase the number of turns of wire per metre on the coil **(1)**, insert a magnetic material as the core. **(1)**

218. Extended response – Magnetism and the motor effect

*Answer could include the following points, to **6 marks**:

- The closer a magnet is to an object, the stronger the magnetic field that it will experience, so the greater the mass it can attract.
- A greater electric current will cause the strength of the magnetic field around an electromagnet to be greater.
- More turns on the coil or a coiled wire instead of a straight wire increases the strength of the magnetic field from the electromagnetic field, so a greater mass can be picked up or attracted.
- Using a soft iron core will increase the strength of the magnetic field around a solenoid/electromagnet so more mass can be attracted.
- Mention that certain materials where magnetism can be induced will be attracted, whereas others will not – iron, cobalt, nickel, steel will be, but others will not be.
- Mention that certain materials that are themselves permanent magnets will be attracted based on their magnetic field strengths, even when no current flows through an electromagnet.

219. Transformers

1 The amount of electrical energy dissipated and wasted to the surroundings as heat in the National Grid is related to the size of the current **(1)**, so with a small current, energy transferred by heating is reduced **(1)** which increases the efficiency of the system. **(1)**

2 $V_p \times I_p = V_s \times I_s$, 24 V × I_p = 120 V × 0.5 A **(1)**, I_p = 120 V × 0.5 A ÷ 24 V **(1)** = 2.5 **(1)** A **(1)**

220. Extended response – Electromagnetic induction

*Answer could include the following points, to **6 marks**:

- Transformer has primary and secondary coil and works with a.c. input.
- The current is stepped down when the voltage is stepped up to conserve power and not violate the principle of conservation of energy.
- Voltage is stepped up by transformers when it leaves the power station for transmission across the UK on wires.
- Voltage is stepped down to safer levels when electricity is supplied to homes, hospitals and factories.
- Lower current means thinner wires means less expensive to buy means lower cost to the consumer.

221. Changes of state

1 Thermal energy is transferred from the warmer room to the ice **(1)** and causes the ice to melt **(1)** and become 1.5 kg of liquid water. **(1)**

2 As the gas cools, the particles slow down and occupy a smaller volume **(1)** and make fewer collisions with the container they are in **(1)** so the pressure decreases too. **(1)**

3 Thermal energy is supplied to the copper metal, bonds are broken and it turns from a solid to a liquid at a constant temperature **(1)** once it reaches its melting point **(1)**. Further heating of the liquid copper causes its temperature **(1)** to rise until it reaches its boiling point, at which point it turns from a liquid to a gas at a constant temperature **(1)**. If the gaseous copper atoms continue to be heated then the temperature of the gas will increase. **(1)**

222. Density

1 density = mass ÷ volume = 862 g ÷ 765 cm³ **(1)** = 1.1 **(1)** g/cm³ **(1)**

2 50 000 cm³ = 5000 ÷ 1 000 000 m³ = 0.05 m³ **(1)**, mass = density × volume = 0.05 m³ × 2700 kg/m³ **(1)** = 135 **(1)** kg **(1)**

223. Investigating density

1 density = mass ÷ volume = 454 g ÷ 256 cm³ **(1)** = 1.77 **(1)** g/cm³ **(1)**

2 Mass reading can be misread by human error / parallax error / systematic error **(1)**; volume can be misread by parallax error or reading the top of the meniscus for water **(1)**; a value that is too high for the mass **(1)** or too low for the volume will lead to a value that is too high for the density. **(1)**

224. Energy and changes of state

1 ΔQ = 15 kg × 4200 J/kg°C × (74 °C – 18 °C) **(1)** = 3 528 000 **(1)** J **(1)**

2 Energy supplied = specific latent heat of melting of water × mass of water, = 334 000 J/kg × 20 kg **(1)**, = 6 680 000 **(1)** J **(1)**

225. Thermal properties of water

1 Less thermal energy is lost to the surroundings **(1)** and more is used to heat the water **(1)** so the value obtained is closer to the true value required to cause a temperature change of 1 °C for that mass of liquid **(1)**; alternatively, state that losing more to the surroundings **(1)** requires more energy than necessary to be supplied for unit temperature change **(1)** of unit mass. **(1)**

2 (a) When water is heated in liquid form/the same state of matter **(1)** such as when water is being heated in a pan or being boiled in a kettle. **(1)**

   (b) When water is changing state **(1)** e.g. when it is melting or boiling. **(1)**

3 Diagram should show ice in a funnel over a beaker, with an electric heater **(1)** and a thermometer (which should be away from the heater) **(1)** and a stopwatch. **(1)**

226. Pressure and temperature

1 (a) 20 + 273 = 293 K **(1)**

   (b) 300 – 273 = 27 °C **(1)**

2 The kinetic energy of a gas is directly proportional to the temperature **(1)** of the gas in kelvin **(1)** so doubling the temperature doubles the average kinetic energy of the molecules in the gas. **(1)**

3 (a) The average speed is slower. **(1)**

   (b) The pressure is reduced **(1)** because there are fewer collisions/the particles do not hit the walls as hard. **(1)**

227. Extended response – Density

*Answer could include the following points, to **6 marks**:

- Pressure is caused by moving particles colliding with the sides of a container.
- Motion of the particles is random.
- Pressure is force per unit area.

- Increasing the temperature of a gas at constant volume means that the particles have greater kinetic energy and speed and so collide more frequently with the area, so greater pressure.
- The internal energy of a gas is entirely kinetic.
- When work is done on the gas the kinetic energy/speed of the particles increases.
- Faster moving particles collide with the walls/area more frequently, leading to an increase in pressure.

228. Elastic and inelastic distortion

1 (a) two equal forces **(1)** of tension acting in opposite directions **(1)**

   (b) two equal forces **(1)** acting towards one another **(1)**

2 (a) two suitable examples, e.g. springs **(1)**, elastic bands **(1)**, rubber **(1)**, skin **(1)**

   (b) two suitable examples, e.g. springs beyond elastic limit **(1)**, putty **(1)**, Plasticine **(1)**, bread dough **(1)**, wet chewing gum **(1)**

3 It will not return to its original shape **(1)** when the force is removed **(1)** and will be longer than it was originally/extended. **(1)**

229. Springs

1 (a) Force = spring constant × extension = 30 N/m × 0.2 m **(1)** = 6 **(1)** N **(1)**

   (b) Work done = energy stored = $\frac{1}{2}$ × spring constant × extension² = $\frac{1}{2}$ × 30 N/m × (0.2 m)² **(1)** = 0.6 **(1)** J **(1)**

2 The greater the value of the spring constant **(1)**, the greater the force is needed **(1)** to extend the spring by the same amount/by 1 m. **(1)**

3 10 cm = 0.1 m **(1)**, energy stored = $\frac{1}{2}$ × spring constant × extension² = $\frac{1}{2}$ × 45 N/m × (0.1 m)² **(1)** = 0.225 **(1)** J **(1)**

230. Forces and springs

1 energy stored = $\frac{1}{2} kx^2$ = $\frac{1}{2}$ × 5 N/m × (0.5 m)² **(1)** = 0.625 **(1)** J **(1)**

2 Yes; a force has been applied to *decrease* the length of the spring which still means that elastic potential energy is stored in the spring/work has been done on the spring when it is being compressed **(1)**.

The spring constant can be calculated from the gradient of a force/compression graph or a force/extension graph **(1)**.

The energy stored in the spring can be found from the area beneath a force/compression or force/extension graph. **(1)**

231. Extended response – Forces and matter

*Answer could include the following points, to **6 marks**:

- Distortion is when a force causes a body to extend or change shape.
- The extension is directly proportional to the load/force applied for elastic distortion.
- The body/spring/material will return to its original shape when the force/load is removed.
- Inelastic distortion is when the body is extended beyond its elastic limit.
- The body will then not return to its original shape but will remain permanently extended.
- The spring constant for a spring is found from the gradient of the force–extension graph provided that the linear region only is used.
- The spring constant may be found from $k = F \div x$.
- Energy stored is found from $E = \frac{1}{2} kx^2$ or from the area beneath the line.

The Periodic Table of the Elements

Key

| relative atomic mass |
| **atomic symbol** |
| name |
| atomic (proton) number |

Example: 1 / **H** / hydrogen / 1

1	2	3	4	5	6	7	0
							4 **He** helium 2
7 **Li** lithium 3	9 **Be** beryllium 4	11 **B** boron 5	12 **C** carbon 6	14 **N** nitrogen 7	16 **O** oxygen 8	19 **F** fluorine 9	20 **Ne** neon 10
23 **Na** sodium 11	24 **Mg** magnesium 12	27 **Al** aluminium 13	28 **Si** silicon 14	31 **P** phosphorus 15	32 **S** sulfur 16	35.5 **Cl** chlorine 17	40 **Ar** argon 18
39 **K** potassium 19	40 **Ca** calcium 20	45 **Sc** scandium 21	48 **Ti** titanium 22	51 **V** vanadium 23	52 **Cr** chromium 24	55 **Mn** manganese 25	(see transition metals below)
85 **Rb** rubidium 37	88 **Sr** strontium 38	89 **Y** yttrium 39	91 **Zr** zirconium 40	93 **Nb** niobium 41	96 **Mo** molybdenum 42	[98] **Tc** technetium 43	
133 **Cs** caesium 55	137 **Ba** barium 56	139 **La*** lanthanum 57	178 **Hf** hafnium 72	181 **Ta** tantalum 73	184 **W** tungsten 74	186 **Re** rhenium 75	
[223] **Fr** francium 87	[226] **Ra** radium 88	[227] **Ac*** actinium 89	[261] **Rf** rutherfordium 104	[262] **Db** dubnium 105	[266] **Sg** seaborgium 106	[264] **Bh** bohrium 107	

Transition and following groups (continued):

Fe	Co	Ni	Cu	Zn	Ga	Ge	As	Se	Br	Kr
56 **Fe** iron 26	59 **Co** cobalt 27	59 **Ni** nickel 28	63.5 **Cu** copper 29	65 **Zn** zinc 30	70 **Ga** gallium 31	73 **Ge** germanium 32	75 **As** arsenic 33	79 **Se** selenium 34	80 **Br** bromine 35	84 **Kr** krypton 36
101 **Ru** ruthenium 44	103 **Rh** rhodium 45	106 **Pd** palladium 46	108 **Ag** silver 47	112 **Cd** cadmium 48	115 **In** indium 49	119 **Sn** tin 50	122 **Sb** antimony 51	128 **Te** tellurium 52	127 **I** iodine 53	131 **Xe** xenon 54
190 **Os** osmium 76	192 **Ir** iridium 77	195 **Pt** platinum 78	197 **Au** gold 79	201 **Hg** mercury 80	204 **Tl** thallium 81	207 **Pb** lead 82	209 **Bi** bismuth 83	[209] **Po** polonium 84	[210] **At** astatine 85	[222] **Rn** radon 86
[277] **Hs** hassium 108	[268] **Mt** meitnerium 109	[271] **Ds** darmstadtium 110	[272] **Rg** roentgenium 111							

Elements with atomic numbers 112–116 have been reported but not fully authenticated.

*The lanthanoids (atomic numbers 58–71) and the actinoids (atomic numbers 90–103) have been omitted.

The relative atomic masses of copper and chlorine have not been rounded to the nearest whole number.

Combined Science Equations List

In your exam, you will be provided with the following list of equations. Make sure you are clear which equations will be given to you in the exam. You will need to learn the equations that aren't on the equations list.

(final velocity)^2 – (initial velocity)^2 = 2 × acceleration × distance $v^2 - u^2 = 2 \times a \times x$
energy transferred = current × potential difference × time $E = I \times V \times t$
For transformers with 100% efficiency, potential difference across primary coil × current in primary coil = potential difference across secondary coil × current in secondary coil $V_p \times I_p = V_s \times I_s$
change in thermal energy = mass × specific heat capacity × change in temperature $\Delta Q = m \times c \times \Delta\theta$
thermal energy for a change of state = mass × specific latent heat $Q = m \times L$
energy transferred in stretching = 0.5 × spring constant × (extension)^2 $E = \frac{1}{2} \times k \times x^2$